It Takes an Ecosystem: Understanding the People, Places, and Possibilities of Learning and Development Across Settings

A Volume in:
Current Issues in Out-of-School Time

Series Editor:
Helen Janc Malone

Current Issues in Out-of-School Time

Series Editor:
Helen Janc Malone

Books in This Series:

Measure, Use, Improve!
Data Use in Out-of-School Time (2021)
Christina A. Russell & Corey Newhouse

At Our Best:
Building Youth-Adult Partnerships in Out-of-School Time Settings (2020)
Gretchen Brion-Meisels, Jessica Tseming Fei, & Deepa Sriya Vasudevan

Changemakers!
Practitioners Advance Equity and Access in Out-of-School Time Programs (2019)
Sara Hill & Femi Vance

Social and Emotional Learning in Out-Of-School Time:
Foundations and Futures (2018)
Elizabeth Devaney & Deborah A. Moroney

The Growing Out-of-School Time Field:
Past, Present, and Future (2017)
Helen Janc Malone & Tara Donahue

Book Series Board

It Takes an Ecosystem: Understanding the People, Places, and Possibilities of Learning and Development Across Settings

Thomas Akiva
Kimberly H. Robinson

INFORMATION AGE PUBLISHING, INC.
Charlotte, NC • www.infoagepub.com

Library of Congress Cataloging-In-Publication Data

The CIP data for this book can be found on the Library of Congress website (loc.gov).

Paperback: 978-1-64802-667-6
Hardcover: 978-1-64802-668-3
E-Book: 978-1-64802-669-0

Printed in the United States of America

CONTENTS

SECTION I

AN ECOSYSTEM OF YOUTH-SERVING FIELDS

SECTION IV

PLACES: CASE STUDIES OF LEARNING AND DEVELOPMENT ECOSYSTEMS

SECTION V

LOOKING AHEAD

DEDICATION

We dedicate this volume to those who rose up to support children, youth, and families during the dual pandemics of 2020–2021: racism and COVID-19.

FOREWORD

Karen Pittman

What a feat! *It Takes an Ecosystem: Understanding the People, Places, and Possibilities of Learning and Development Across Settings* is the *sixth* volume to be published in the *six* years since Dr. Helen Janc Malone became the series editor of the Current Issues in Out-of-School Time book series. This is the sixth time that out-of-school time (OST) researchers and field leaders have come together to chronicle the progress being made to position OST as a critical vehicle for young people's development and to reflect on next steps needed to advance research, measurement, policy, and practice improvement strategies.

This is the third time I have had the honor of contributing to one of the volumes. In the first volume, *The Growing Out-of-School Time Field: Past, Present and Future*, I wrote the concluding chapter in which I argued that the future of the OST field hinges on our ability to be valued for what and how we support young people's development, not for where and when we run programs (Pittman, 2017).

I contributed two chapters in the second volume, *Social and Emotional Learning in Out-of-School Time: Foundations and Futures*. I co-authored a chapter on describing and measuring adult instructional practice with my colleagues at the Forum for Youth Investment's David P. Weikart Center for Youth Program Quality (Bednar et al., 2018). I also took a second stab at presaging the future, this time in a closing commentary in which my calls for a field-wide pivot were even

It Takes an Ecosystem: Understanding the People, Places, and
Possibilities of Learning and Development Across Settings, pages xiii–xvii.
Copyright © 2022 by Information Age Publishing
All rights of reproduction in any form reserved.

more forceful (Pittman, 2018). My stint as a Commissioner on the National Commission on Social, Emotional, & Academic Development made me both pleased and concerned (National Commission on Social, Emotional, & Academic Development, 2019). Pleased that the things I associated most closely with the youth development approach and the OST field—commitments to social and emotional skill-building, community-level program coordination, and a focus on assessing against shared standards to improve learning settings—were being acknowledged and adopted by K–12 educators. Concerned that, not only were we not getting credit for good work done, we were also not seen as essential to the important new work needed.

In the closing chapter for this volume (Pittman, 2018) I argued that to be successful going forward, we have to clearly (but humbly) claim expertise; actively acknowledge the expertise and value that other organizations, systems and fields that have been on the youth development journey with us but don't lead with the OST label; and, again, consider adopting a new descriptor that better reflects our roles and contributions.

The National Commission ended in early 2019, but my vocal arguments that the science of learning and development does not just push our thinking about how learning happens, but also about where and when learning happens, earned me a governing partner seat on the Science of Learning and Development (SoLD) Alliance (SoLD Alliance, n.d.). The SoLD Alliance, like the National Commission on Social, Emotional, and Academic Development, however, was primarily focused on transforming the education system. This is why, in November 2019, the Forum for Youth Investment team (Karen Pittman, Merita Irby, and Kimberly Robinson) partnered with the University of Pittsburgh School of Education (Thomas Akiva and Kevin Crowley) to bring K–12 and OST researchers, practitioners, funders, and policy advocates together to explore opportunities to use the convergent science findings about how, when, where and with whom learning happens to aggressively "soften the walls" between K–12 and OST system improvement efforts. This seminal convening was, in retrospect, the soft launch of the Readiness Projects, a three-year, foundation-supported effort to capitalize on the momentum built (without dedicated funding) since the SEAD Commission co-led by the Forum, the National Urban League and the American Institutes for Research (key allies with us in both the SEAD and SoLD initiatives).

This volume is one of the earliest, most direct, and most ambitious projects enabled, in a small way, by the Readiness Projects. Drs. Akiva and Robinson were co-planners of the November 2019 meeting. Many of the chapter authors were participants at the meeting or have subsequently joined the Readiness Projects as co-strategists (Readiness Projects, 2020a). And, most importantly, the focus of this volume—the learning ecosystem—is Readiness Projects' raison d'etre. Our goal: To change the odds for youth by using science-informed strategies to upend inequity and accelerate progress *together* by creating equitable, learning, and development ecosystems.

So, it is not surprising that, after a three-year hiatus, I not only volunteered to write the Foreword, but to co-author a chapter and contribute to the conclusion. Never, in my 50-year career as a youth worker, youth development researcher, youth development advocate, and national organization leader have I felt closer to success. I do not make this claim lightly. Almost 20 years ago, youth development advocates were giddy with the National Research Council's release of *Community Programs to Promote Youth Development* (NRC, 2002), a powerful, research-based call for the creation of community-level infrastructures to coordinate assets-based programming for adolescents. Formally acknowledging my mantra ("problem-free is not fully prepared; Pittman, 1992), the Council advocated for the youth development approach not as a substitute for prevention programs, but as a critical complement:

> An exclusive focus on problems… narrows the vision that society should have for all of its young people. Many who study adolescent development and work with young people have increasingly come to believe that being *problem-free is not fully prepared*. Beyond eliminating problems, one needs skills, knowledge, and a variety of other personal and social assets to function well during adolescence and adulthood. Thus, a broader, more holistic view of helping youth to realize their full potential is gaining wider credence in the world of policy and practice.
>
> …Public and private organizations are now engaged in a wide array of activities that fall within this framework. Such programs include mentoring, school-based community service programs and other volunteer activities, school-to-work transition programs, parenting skills, arts and recreation activities, among others. All are part of a new direction in public policy that places children and adolescents once again at the center of neighborhood and community life, where they can engage with caring adults inside and outside their families, develop a sense of security and personal identity, and learn rules of behavior, expectations, values, morals, and skills needed to move into healthy and productive adulthood. (NRC, 2002, pp. 2–3, italics added)

This report issued in more than a decade of accelerated work with child welfare, juvenile justice, youth employment, adolescent health systems, and prevention leaders who took the call to rethink success measures, retrain staff, and recalibrate their program goals and policies to better acknowledge youth assets and potential, broaden adult responsibilities and supports and shift system accountability. Consider, for example, the Administration for Children and Families formal goal expansion from child protection to child well-being (Center for the Study of Social Policy, 2013). Merita Irby and I co-founded the Forum for Youth Investment in 1998 to spearhead this movement. Then, like now, our work was sparked by reports from two commissions—the W.T. Grant Foundations Commission on Work, Family and Citizenship's report, *The Forgotten Half* (1988), and the Carnegie Task Force on the Education of Young Adolescents' report, *Turning Points* (Carnegie Corporation of New York, 1989). Our reflection on the progress sparked by these commissions, however, was bittersweet (Pittman, 1998). In our chapter "Unfinished Business: Further Reflections on a Decade of Promoting Youth Development" (Pittman et al., 2001) we called for a cohesive strategy for preparing young people for young adulthood that presaged the ecosystem approach elaborated in this volume. This call to action is the introductory chapter to *Trends in Youth Development: Visions, Realities, and Challenges* (Benson & Pittman, 2001), which included chapters from the leading reform thinkers in the allied youth fields (e.g.,, youth employment, juvenile justice, child welfare, primary community supports). Notably absent from this volume is a chapter on K–12 education reforms. The youth development approach was accepted as a needed expansion to traditional problem-prevention and remediation approaches. *It was not, however, seen as relevant for K–12 school reform.*

This is why I am so excited about this volume and, about the larger opportunities we have to advance its major themes. We can, and must, as OST practitioners, administrators, researchers, funders, and advocates use not only the power of the science but the disruptions of the times to not just build our OST systems back better, but to also be relentless in our commitment to do this in a way that propels us, schools and other community organizations and public systems committed to learning and development to build forward together (Readiness Projects, 2020b). This commitment is not just about creating city-wide youth master plans or transactional programmatic partnership agreements. It is not just about the need to personalize learner experiences. It is about a fundamental shift from siloed systems-focused to dynamic ecosystem-focused thinking. It is about, in the end, recognizing that the power to change the odds for young people in this country lies with the adults—"the keystone species" in the learning ecosystem—who, working with youth and young adults can assess, expose and, with resources, improve the learning and development ecosystems in their communities.

REFERENCES

Bednar, K., Pittman, K., Bertoletti, J., Borah, P., Peck, S., & Smith, C. (2018). Describing and measuring adult instructional practice in OST settings for middle and high school youth. In E. Devaney & D. Moroney (Eds.), *Social and emotional learning in out-of-school time: Foundations and futures.* Information Age Publishing.

Benson, P., & Pittman, K. (2001). Moving the youth development message: Turning a vague idea into a moral imperative. In P. Benson & K. Pittman (Eds.), *Trends in youth development: Visions, realities, and challenges.* Springer Science + Business Media New York.

Carnegie Corporation of New York. (1989). *Turning points: Preparing American youth for the 21st century.* https://www.carnegie.org/publications/turning-points-preparing-american-youth-for-the-21st-century/

Center for the Study of Social Policy. (2013). *Raising the bar: Child welfare's shift toward well-being.* https://childwelfaresparc.files.wordpress.com/2013/07/raising-the-bar-child-welfares-shift-toward-well-being-7-22.pdf

National Commission on Social, Emotional, & Academic Development. (2019). *From a nation at risk to a nation at hope.* Aspen Institute.

National Research Council and Institute of Medicine. (2002). *Community programs to pro- mote youth development.* National Academies Press. The National Academy of Sci- ences Report Brief: Community Programs to Promote Youth Development (PDF) summarizes the study findings.

Pittman, K. (1992). *Youth today: Let's make youth work a field.* Forum for Youth Invest- ment. http://forumforyouthinvestment.org/content/youth-today-lets-make-

Pittman, K. (1998). *Reflections on a decade of promoting youth development.* American Youth Policy Forum.

Pittman, K. (2017). Securing the future: Pivoting OST from where and when to what and how. In H. J. Malone & T. Donahue (Eds.), *The growing out-of-school time field.* Information Age Publishing.

Pittman, K. (2018). Conclusion. In E. Devaney & D. Moroney (Eds.), *Social and emotional learning in out-of-school time: Foundations and futures.* Information Age Publish- ing.

Pittman, K., Irby, M., & Ferber, T. (2001). Unfinished business: Further reflections on a decade of promoting youth development. In P. Benson & K. Pittman (Eds.), *Trends in youth development: Visions, realities, and challenges.* Springer Science + Busi- ness Media New York.

Readiness Projects. (2020a). *Who we are.* Forum for Youth Investment. https://forumfyi. org/the-readiness-projects/who-we-are/

Readiness Projects. (2020b). *Build forward together.* Forum for Youth Investment. https:// forumfyi.org/wp-content/uploads/2020/11/Build-Forward-Together-one-pager.pdf

Science of Learning and Development Alliance. (n.d.). *Who we are.* https://www.soldalli- ance.org/who-we-are

William T. Grant Foundation Commission on Work, Family, and Citizenship. (1988). *The forgotten half: Non-college youth in America : An interim report on the school-to- work transition.* William T. Grant Foundation.

SECTION I

AN ECOSYSTEM OF YOUTH-SERVING FIELDS

CHAPTER 1

INTRODUCTION

A New Way Forward

Kimberly H. Robinson and Thomas Akiva

The idea for this book started as a series of conversations between colleagues from the Forum for Youth Investment and the University of Pittsburgh School of Education. Over a weekend in Pittsburgh in the fall of 2018, we discussed how research evidence clearly supports the notions that relationships and context shape learning and development across settings and that current educational systems are not equipped to address this. We talked about how current approaches in out-of-school time (OST)—like the decades-old attempt to professionalize the youth development workforce—are not making the progress needed. We discussed how *we need a paradigm shift across the youth fields.* These conversations ultimately led to the development of the four themes that guide this volume: 1) the value of an ecosystem framework for moving youth fields forward, 2) the need to better make use of the science of learning and development, 3) the aspirational idea of the allied youth fields, and 4) the critical importance of centering equity and justice. And they led to a series of ambitious initiatives called the Readiness Projects—of which this volume is one—aimed at changing the odds for youth by using science-informed strategies to upend inequities and accelerate progress (Readiness Projects, 2020; Chapter 16 by Irby et al. in this volume).

It Takes an Ecosystem: Understanding the People, Places, and
Possibilities of Learning and Development Across Settings, pages 3–11.
Copyright © 2022 by Information Age Publishing

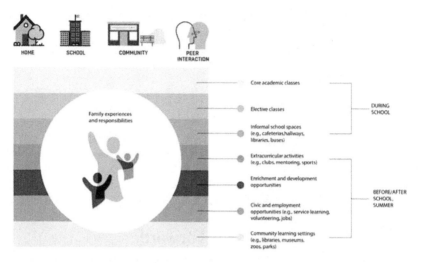

FIGURE 1.1.   Where and When Learning Happens: Expanding Our Understanding of all the Places and Times Young People Grow and Learn. Originally published in *From a Nation at Risk to a Nation at Hope* (January 2019) from The Aspen Institute National Commission on Social, Emotional, and Academic Development and licensed under CC BY 4.0.

This conversation was before the COVID-19 pandemic created ecosystem disturbances larger than any in our lifetimes. It was before the murders of George Floyd, Breonna Taylor, and many others that sparked millions to join in protests against police violence—and more broadly, to protest the pandemic of racism that continues to ravage our country. It was before these dual pandemics made even more clear that the inequities built into our education and health systems have a devastating effect on too many young people. But the dual pandemics only make the aim of this book even more critical, urgent, and salient. Now is the time to reframe our education and development systems to more equitably serve young people.

When we proposed this book, our aim was to create a canvas for moving the OST field forward—toward the paradigm shift that is so needed. And we're very pleased that this is what this has become: a collection of thoughtful chapters about moving this field forward by expanding the field, focusing on equity, and building on new research and ideas. Back in 2018, we realized there was tremendous synergy in using scientific understanding of how and where learning happens to spark connections between out-of-school time, libraries, museums, maker spaces, and other educational settings in communities and in schools. Leveraging the "when and where learning happens" graphic (Figure 1.1) from the National Commission for Social, Emotional, and Academic Development (SEAD, 2019), we not only saw connections in wide ranging areas of youth development and education, but we posited that better connecting these themes could strengthen systems that are designed to support young people—but too often fail to meet that aspiration.

THE THEMES OF THIS BOOK

Four themes guide this book, and each theme is about *reframing* the ways we have approached OST, education, and development. The importance of frames should not be underestimated. How we frame a topic affects what is emphasized, what is explained, and what is left out. It shapes how the public sees a topic and the frames we use ultimately affect funding, policy, and lives (Frameworks Institute, 2020).

Far too often the frames we use in research or as advocates seem obvious to us but are obtuse or even counterproductive when used with others, especially when other frames are triggered (Lakoff, 2004). For example, if you ask a random person about childhood learning, they are likely to evoke the dominant frame that the primary settings for children and youth are schools. In this frame (also referred to as a logic), OST programs are supplements to the goals of school (Akiva et al., 2020). The school-centered frame is so ingrained that it's often not even noticed, and people assume that the current educational landscape is unchangeable, even inevitable. This, of course, is not the case at all; indeed, the idea of school as the primary place for childhood education and socialization is only a few hundred years old, and though the school-centered frame is salient today, it's not the only way to consider education and development.

Similarly, even the term Out-of-School Time (OST) invokes the frame of school in the name of a sector that is intended to be complementary to, but not dependent on schools. For this reason, some OST systems prefer to use the term Expanded Learning to shift the focus from school to learning (see Chapter 15 by Davis in this volume). Others use the terms "community-based youth work" or "community-based educational spaces" (Baldridge, 2018) in order to decenter schools in our frames of when, where, and how learning happens.

We need alternative frames to gain prominence—frames that include the many important contexts for learning and development, including family, workplaces, and a wide variety of community-based settings that offer opportunities for learning and development. This includes settings such as libraries, parks, youth programs, and art studios. What if we recognized that compulsory education does not mean all children learn all things in schools? What if we strove to better understand and invest in the various parts of children and youth's learning and development ecosystems in such a way that more of the people, places, and possibilities for learning were more deliberately and effectively utilized to create healthier and more equitable learning experiences for all youth?

To this end, we asked chapter authors to reflect on four themes—which are frames—that we think can be woven together in order to truly change the odds for young people. We will describe briefly what we mean by each of these themes, and then provide an overview of how they are woven together throughout this book.

First, as noted in the title of this volume, we root this book in the frame of **learning and development ecosystems.** Building on the work of Hecht and

Crowley (2019) and Akiva et al. (2020), our ecosystem approach borrows from biological ecosystem management, bringing new insights to the youth fields. Chapter 2 expands on this framework. It includes several important concepts, including the insight that *ecosystems have no center*—and therefore, need to be managed as complex systems. Our framework also borrows from biological ecology the idea of keystone species as driver of the health of an ecosystem that impacts many other species across the system. We consider adult leaders to be the *keystone species* in learning and development ecosystems, and this highlights the idea that supporting a healthy ecosystem necessitates investing in the adults who support young people across the allied youth fields.

A learning and development ecosystem framework marks a significant departure from our current educational system, which we consider to be dramatically school-centric and designed and built to perpetuate inequality. The disruptions to current systems due to COVID-19 offer an opportunity to reimagine new ways to support learning and development that may look different, but be dramatically more effective—particularly for the most vulnerable young people.

Second, **the science of learning and development** (SoLD Alliance, n.d.) builds from multiple scientific fields to bring a new clarity and consensus to key ideas, including the potential in every child, the developmental importance of relationships with peers and adults, and the past failures of the educational system to serve equitably. The SoLD Alliance—a partnership led by leaders and visionaries in education and youth development—aims to increase the accessibility of the science of learning and development in order to transform U.S. educational systems. The findings summarized in SoLD Alliance publications will not come as a shock to practitioners in the allied youth fields—on the contrary, many scientific findings about how young people grow, learn, and thrive, reinforce the powerful practices in place in youth programs across settings.

The third theme you'll find in these pages is the vision for the **allied youth fields,** an aspirational term that suggests increased connection, alignment, and complementarity across the multiple societal systems in which adults engage with young people. This includes community organizations such as OST, afterschool, summer, and employment pathway programs. It includes the education sector—including P–12 schools, post-secondary colleges and universities, and career certification systems. It includes child welfare, juvenile justice, and police. And it includes social services and other services like mental health, housing, and transportation. If you consider all of the adults across fields that engage and support young people, it is an enormous and powerful group! We hope that by elevating the idea of the allied youth fields, this volume helps spark connections and help the fields move toward a more cohesive and stronger presence.

Finally, we asked authors to shape their chapters through a lens of equity and justice, to prioritize issues of equity and inequity, antiracism and racism, access, and inclusion. We suggest that the existing, narrow views of and infrastructures for learning sustain inequity. Making equity and justice central is a framing that is necessary (but not sufficient) for moving toward a more just educational system. The learning ecosystems for allied youth fields approach may provide new routes forward for moving toward more just and equitable opportunities for learning and development for young people.

These four themes provide the rationale and context for this volume. We aim to make the case that SoLD sets the stage for a renewed push to shape societal systems to better and more equitably serve children and youth—by providing the argument that relationships (particularly adult-youth relationships) shape learning and development and that our school-centered frame is inadequate and unresponsive to science. The allied youth fields approach (also called thriving youth fields in some circles) aims to address the workforce issues; i.e., that relational work is undervalued, often invisible, and that people across fields do not see their natural affinities. We suggest that the "youth worker" professionalism frame that the field has been pushing for two decades is too limiting. The allied frame attempts to bring more folks into the tent and recognize that adult-youth interaction and relationships are at the core of many more jobs and careers than we usually consider. Finally, a learning ecosystems framework, borrowing from biological ecosystem management, may provide a conceptual and practical glue to advance the allied youth fields on multiple levels.

In addition, this book was written in the midst of the COVID-19 pandemic and the new momentum of the Black Lives Matter movement. As awful as the COVID-19 pandemic is and has been, it does present potential opportunities for reshaping learning and development systems (see Pittman et al., 2020). Organizing this effort during the COVID-19 pandemic and the beginning of a national reckoning about racial injustice sets these people, places, and possibilities in a particular historical moment—but it also suggests the need to commit to more radically centering racial equity and social justice in the design of systems, programs, and experiences of young people. Such prioritization is necessary in order to meet the demands of this moment in a way that carves a path toward genuine transformation.

ORGANIZATION OF THE BOOK

This book is organized into five sections that expand on the title of this book. The first, An Ecosystem of Youth Serving Fields, describes what we mean by the idea that "it takes an ecosystem," and provides the foundational definitions and key concepts that ground the rest of the book, including descriptions of the book's four primary themes. The second, The People and Practices that Support Healthy Learning and Development Ecosystems, expands on the people part of the subtitle, exploring the key people who play a part in shaping ecosystems, including families, youth workers, and leaders, as well as the relational practices that these people use to strengthen learning and development. The third section expands on the notion of possibilities. In Possibilities: Tools and Structures for Shaping Learning and Development Ecosystems, the chapters focus on specific strategies, tools, and structures that can support thriving learning and development ecosystems. The fourth section, Places: Case Studies of Learning and Development Ecosystems, provides illustrations of ecosystem approaches to working with young people. In each chapter, the authors describe broadening the ways that OST systems support learning and development through an ecosystems lens and offer insights on the kinds of cross-sectoral collaborations that are possible—and indeed, are underway—in work across the country. The final section, Looking Ahead, offers reflections on the opportunities described in this book and the commitments and actions that it will take to make the transformations we know are necessary and we believe are possible.

An Ecosystem of Youth Serving Fields. In the second chapter of this introductory section, Thomas Akiva, Marijke Hecht, and Dale Blyth explore the ecosystem framework that forms the foundation of the volume—describing ecosystems as encompassing the people, places, and possibilities for learning and development. They apply insights from biological ecosystems to learning and development ecosystems to envision a broader conceptualization of learning and development, and the collaboration and coordination necessary to support learning in all the places where it happens. Next, in Chapter 3, field leaders Karen Pittman, Jill Young, David Osher, Rob Jagers, Hal Smith, Merita Irby, and Poonam Borah share insights from the science of learning and development that elevate the importance of broadening understandings of how learning happens. They caution that assumptions about "typical development" often result in narrow approaches to education across settings and describe how better application of the science would better meet the diverse needs of learners across settings. Finally, Chapter 4 by Roderick Carey, Camila Polanco, and Horatio Blackman sets the book in context of the intersecting public health crises of COVID-19 and police violence on Black and Brown[1] bodies. The authors consider what mattering means for the allied youth fields, as we seek to create learning settings and ecosystems that truly support all children to thrive.

The People and Practices that Support Healthy Learning and Development Ecosystems. The chapters in Section II describe specific people who play critical roles in shaping ecosystems and the practices that they use to support learning and development. The section begins with Lori Delale-O'Connor's Chapter 5 on the critical role of families in promoting, facilitating, and managing life-wide learning for young people. As we consider ways to strengthen alliance

---

[1] Throughout this volume, we capitalize Black and Brown, consistent with APA and AP styles; we do not capitalize white. Scholars and journalists have made arguments both for and against capitalization. Some argue that white, like Black, should be capitalized so that white is not subtly equated with "normal" and whiteness is not made invisible (e.g., Ewing, 2020). Others argue against capitalizing white as an explicit way to decenter whiteness and delegitimize white supremacist hate groups (e.g., Bauder, 2020). The latter argument, emphasizing decentering whiteness, was recommended by several authors of color in this volume, especially the authors of Chapter 8. Their usage has been adopted throughout the volume.

across youth serving fields and build ecosystems that support learning and development, families must be considered critical to this effort. In Chapter 6, Junlei Li and Dana Winters emphasize the extraordinary importance of interaction and relationships in learning and development ecosystems. They describe research and practice that offer insights into what is possible when relationships are prioritized in child and youth contexts. Next, in Chapter 7, Sharon Colvin and Annie White describe youth workers as the *keystone species* in learning and development ecosystems, discussing the ways that professional identities vary across youth serving fields, and opportunities to strengthen learning and development ecosystems by strengthening the alliances across and the health of youth workers. Finally, this section concludes with Chapter 8 by Fatima Brunson, DaVonna Graham, Tanja Burkhard, and Valerie Kinloch in which they consider the important role of leaders in organizing for equity. They argue that efforts to center equity and justice require new forms of leadership that go beyond traditional approaches.

Possibilities: Tools and Structures for Shaping Learning and Development Ecosystems. The three chapters that comprise Section III of the book focus on structural elements that support alliance across the youth fields, as well as opportunities and challenges of allying the youth-serving fields to support thriving for all young people. The structural elements that support alliance across the youth fields include systems that support continuous improvement as a way to build alignment and coordinate practices that support equitable learning ecosystems, intermediary organizations that support coordination at the local level, and policy coordination and alignment. First, in Chapter 9, Alicia Wilson-Ahlstrom and David J. Martineau draw on their decades of experience with the Youth Program Quality Intervention (YPQI; www.forumfyi.org/weikartcenter) as a tool for continuous quality improvement to discuss building continuous improvement systems centered on equity and justice. Next, in Chapter 10, Jessica Donner and Priscilla Little discuss the role of intermediaries in nurturing diverse ecosystems. Drawing on examples from OST intermediaries across the country and insights gathered by Every Hour Counts (everyhourcounts.org), the authors highlight how intermediaries can create the conditions for positive change. Finally, in Chapter 11, Michelle J. Boyd-Brown, Jill Young, and Deborah Moroney discuss the important role that policy and advocacy play in creating the conditions for equitable learning to occur. They describe how policy alignment and coordination across agencies at the federal, state, and local levels could better set the stage for youth serving fields to collaborate in their efforts to support learning and development.

Places: Case Studies of Learning and Development Ecosystems. Section IV focuses on communities that are putting these ideas into practice, with case studies that illustrate efforts around the country to create and strengthen learning and development ecosystems. This section also highlights the potential of OST organizations to lead the way in this effort by partnering with other youth serving sectors in order to strengthen the people, places, and possibilities for learning. Each chapter provides illustrative examples of efforts currently underway that point toward a healthier and more allied ecosystem. Some chapters focus on strengthening connections between OST and other community-based organizations, others focus on connections between OST and other sectors—like school or health. In Chapter 12 by Mac Howison, Esohe Osai, and Thomas Akiva, the authors discuss the role of philanthropy, along with research and evaluation, in learning and development ecosystem management, using a case study of a partnership to support the creative learning ecosystem in Pittsburgh. Similarly, in Chapter 13, Linda W. Braun and Lance Simpson discuss connections between OST programs, libraries, and arts and culture organizations in the context of connected learning, with illustrations from programs in urban, suburban, and rural areas across the country. Next, Candace Brazier Thurman and Saskia K. Traill, in Chapter 14, describe the work that ExpandED (www.expandedschools.org) has done in New York City to forge partnerships between OST programs and the public school system, highlighting a range of innovations that support learning and development in school and out of school. Finally, in Chapter 15, Jeff Davis from the California Afterschool Network (www.afterschoolnetwork.org) closes this section with a description of the ongoing work across the state of California to create ecosystems that support whole child and whole family health and well-being, with OST programs as critical partners who are setting the vision and supporting breaking down silos across disparate systems.

Looking Ahead. In the final section of the book, Chapter 16, Merita Irby, Karen Pittman, Hal Smith, and Deborah Moroney, the co-leaders of the Readiness Projects (2020), offer strategies for putting the ideas illustrated in this volume into action, including how to shape ecosystems to strengthen the allied youth fields. They conclude with a call to action about what it takes to leverage the opportunities described in this volume and in the current moment to change the odds so that all young people are ready for college, work, and life.

CONCLUSION

This book represents work in progress, aiming to move ideas to impact. Although some of these ideas are not new, we think that the time is now ripe to put these ideas into action for a new way forward. The COVID-19 pandemic and ongoing reckonings for racial justice have made these topics described here both more urgent—and more possible. Even as we finalize this volume, these ideas are being sharpened for greater impact. We hope that you will be able to see yourself in this conversation and find opportunities to use this book to bring these ideas to life in the ecosystems where you live, work, and play.

REFERENCES

Akiva, T., Delale-O'Connor, L., & Pittman, K. J. (2020). The promise of building equitable ecosystems for learning. *Urban Education.* https://doi.org/10.1177/0042085920926230

Baldridge, B. (2018). On educational advocacy and cultural work: Situating community-based youth work[ers] in broader educational discourse. *Teachers College Record, 120*(2), 1–28.

Bauder, D. (2020, July 20). *AP says it will capitalize Black but not white.* Associated Press. https://www.ap.org/ap-in-the-news/2020/ap-says-it-will-capitalize-black-but-not-white

Ewing, E. L. (2020, July 2). *I'm a Black scholar who studies race. Here's why I capitalize 'White.'* Medium. https://zora.medium.com/im-a-black-scholar-who-studies-race-here-s-why-i-capitalize-white-f94883aa2dd3

Frameworks Institute. (2020). Five questions about framing. *Frameworks Library.* https://www.frameworksinstitute.org/article/five-questions-about-framing/

Hecht, M., & Crowley, K. (2020). Unpacking the learning ecosystems framework: Lessons from the adaptive management of biological ecosystems. *Journal of the Learning Sciences, 2*(29). https://doi.org/10.1080/10508406.2019.1693381

Lakoff, G. (2004). *Don't think of an elephant! Know your values and frame the debate.* Chelsea Green Publishing Company.

National Commission on Social, Emotional, & Academic Development. (2019). *From a nation at risk to a nation at hope.* Aspen Institute. http://nationathope.org/wp-content/uploads/2018_aspen_final-report_full_webversion.pdf

Pittman, K., Moroney, D., Osher, D., Smith, H., & Irby, M. (2020, June 26). Summer. Learning. Loss. Leadership. *The Readiness Projects Blog.* https://medium.com/changing-the-odds/featured-summer-learning-loss-leadership-661e077c3445.

Readiness Projects. (2020). *Who we are.* Forum for Youth Investment. https://forumfyi.org/the-readiness-projects/who-we-are/

Science of Learning and Development Alliance. (n.d.). *Who we are.* https://www.soldalliance.org/who-we-are

CHAPTER 2

USING A LEARNING AND DEVELOPMENT ECOSYSTEM FRAMEWORK TO ADVANCE THE YOUTH FIELDS

Thomas Akiva, Marijke Hecht, and Dale A. Blyth

When Katherine reflected on what led to her work as an informal climate change educator, she couldn't point to just one thing that influenced her learning and development. She was a participant in a research project that aimed to understand how adults develop a lifelong connection with nature (see Hecht et al., 2019). During an hour-long life history interview, Katherine, a 38-year-old Black woman, described how a multitude of experiences had supported her interest in science and the environment. She recalled influential experiences as a Girl Scout, her interactions with adult leaders in Girl Scouts, the impact of having two parents who were K–12 educators, her fond memories of animals in her 7th grade science classroom, and her leadership in high school afterschool clubs like the Science Olympiad and an Earth Club. The major educational spaces of home, school, and out-of-school programs all provided opportunities for her to develop her interest in science and the environment, ultimately leading her to undergraduate and PhD degrees in STEM and a career in the sciences.

It Takes an Ecosystem: Understanding the People, Places, and
Possibilities of Learning and Development Across Settings, pages 13–36.
Copyright © 2022 by Information Age Publishing
All rights of reproduction in any form reserved.

During the interview, Katherine shared that she thought it was the volume and combination of experiences that had had such a big impact on her. When asked to reflect on the impacts of each of these experiences on their own she remarked, "It's really, really hard to separate. I mean all of these things I think are influences." Katherine's sense that her experiences were inseparable is a reminder of the complexity of how humans learn and develop. People learn and develop through a "constructive web" that can "support or undermine learning" (Cantor et al., 2019, p. 316.). This constructive web of learning arises from what Blyth (2006) described as the basic developmental building blocks—the interactions between and among all the *people*, *places*, and *possibilities* youth experience and accumulate over time. Or, put another way, learning is life-long (across the lifespan), life-wide (across all settings), and life-deep (includes beliefs, values, ideologies, orientations to life; Banks et al., 2007).

This chapter explores the idea of learning and development (L&D) ecosystems in ways that reorient commonly used ecological approaches. Rather than center individuals and how various forces come to shape an individual's development, we present an approach that centers the ecosystem as a whole and the various systems within it. We consider how a L&D ecosystem can be intentionally designed and managed to foster ample opportunities for learning and development. To do this, we borrow principles and concepts from biological ecosystems management, which are shown in Table 2.1, and apply these concepts to learning and development. We use the word ecosystem, over ecology or community, to emphasize the whole system and the complexity of the interactions with people, places, and possibilities associated with different sectors and systems of learning and development, such as those Katherine described. In line with this volume, we focus primarily on out-of-school programs and activities, but recognize that vibrant L&D ecosystems include myriad influences both across the allied youth fields (e.g., learning at the library, learning at school, learning through sports programs) and in other sectors (e.g., learning at the doctor's office).

In summary, we define L&D ecosystems as collections of people, places, and possibilities that constitute an environment full of learning and development opportunities—opportunities that particular youth will or will not actually experience within the ecosystem. The mere presence of opportunities and positive elements in an ecosystem do not mean that all in the ecosystem can or do experience them equally or equitably. There are undoubtedly other girls and boys who grew up in the same broad ecosystem as Katherine but whose actual experiences lined up very differently in part because of their own interests and the sequence of people, places, and possibilities they experienced (i.e., the opportunities they actually took part in growing up). As we discuss later in the chapter, the overall L&D ecosystem is *complex*, and has multiple levels (e.g., city, neighborhood, within a youth program) and operates for varied purposes and with various sub-ecosystems (e.g., youth arts ecosystem, STEM learning ecosystem). The overall *health* of an ecosystem and its subsystems helps shape whether the supports and

TABLE 2.1. Ecosystem Principles and Concepts

Principles	Concepts
The Systems Principle Ecosystems have no one center. In nature, an ecosystem has no center; rather it is a collection of elements that interact in complex ways. It is important, therefore, to focus efforts on the system as a whole. This principle encourages us to consider how an L&D ecosystem as a whole is operating verses how it influences the development of one individual.	**Adaptive management**—Intentional, regular and ongoing monitoring and flexible maintenance of disrupted stressed areas using evidence-based approaches to better manage resources and their interactions—e.g., lakes, rivers, forests and farmland or in the L&D ecosystem, the opportunities created by and supports provided to the people places and possibilities in the ecosystem.
The Complexity Principle Ecosystems are complex. The many elements of an ecosystem are always moving and changing so an ecosystem is dynamic (ever-changing) and complex (not just complicated).	**Disturbance**—Powerful and sometimes dramatic force(s) that may both cause damage and open up possibilities for regrowth (e.g., fire or flooding in a forest ecosystem; a change in leadership in an L&D ecosystem, the COVID 19 pandemic in the L&D ecosystem)
The Health Principle Ecosystems may be generally healthy or unhealthy. A healthy ecosystem would be defined as one with effective and positive interactions between learning ecosystem elements, particularly the people, places, and possibilities that create opportunities for learning and development.	**Indicator and keystone species**—*Indicator species* are animals, plants, or insects that are most sensitive to unhealthy conditions, such as pollution, and the strength of their presence or absence is a good indicator of the health of an ecosystem. In an L&D ecosystem, children and youth, or particular subgroups of them may be the indicator group. *Keystone species* are those that are key to supporting the health of many other species in the ecosystem. They are change agents that influence the dynamics within the ecosystem. They are used deliberately as a management tool (e.g., wolves in Yellowstone National Park). In an L&D ecosystem, adults who work with young people are likely the keystone group.

opportunities for learning and development within them are accessible, equitable, and positive (healthy) or inaccessible, negative and toxic (unhealthy). Examining the health of an ecosystem and intentionally managing it allow us to focus on factors that keep it healthy or make it unhealthy for some—particularly for traditionally marginalized youth.

In Katherine's case, we can see her experiences within a healthy L&D ecosystem—one where the people (parents, adult leaders), places (schools, camp, park), and possibilities (science Olympiad, Girl Scouts) she experienced contributed positively to her learning and development in ways that led to desirable outcomes. Multiple people supported her learning in a rich variety of interconnected places that provided ample possibilities for learning and development. But we know that many children do not have access to nor are they supported in weaving such a constructive web of experiences. In this chapter, a primary purpose in exploring the L&D ecosystems framework is to better understand and address equitable and inequitable learning ecosystems in the United States. Our goal is to enhance the ways we think about the components and interactions of the L&D ecosystems and the ways youth experience them in order to more intentionally and strategically support their healthy design and management so that all children and youth benefit. We begin with consideration of the ecological framework most commonly used in education and developmental science, then present and connect the ecosystem ideas from Table 2.1 as tools for the final discussion about designing healthier and more equitable L&D ecosystems.

SHIFTING FROM AN ECOLOGICAL PERSPECTIVE TO AN L&D ECOSYSTEM APPROACH

An ecological perspective helps highlight that learning happens not just in school or during childhood, but in a variety of settings and across the course of our lives (Bevan, 2016; Falk & Dierking, 2018; Knutson et al., 2011). Understanding and positioning learning as life-long and life-wide (Banks et al., 2007) helps reveal the interconnections and complexity of learning both academically and social-emotionally. One way to make sense of Katherine's experience within a learning ecosystem would be to conceptualize each learning space—home, school, various other settings– as surrounding and supporting Katherine, as the learner, in the center of the system as depicted in Bronfenbrenner's Ecological Systems Theory in Figure 2.1 (Bronfenbrenner & Morris, 2007). Bronfenbrenner's work helped expand views of child development to assert that development happens in context (Christensen, 2016; Lerner, 2005) and inform the ways we think about context differently.

The ecological model describes five systems, arranged by the directness of the influence they have on a child, from proximal (i.e., close to the child) to distal (farther away). In the typical model, the developing person is in the center and surrounded by *microsystems*—such as school, peer group, family, and OST programs—in which the young person spends time and experiences directly. The *mesosystem* includes interactions between microsystems; for example, relationships between schoolteachers and parents or between school and OST staff. The *exosystem* includes things like neighborhood, parents workplaces, and the media. Even more distal is the *macrosystem* which includes cultural, political, and economic forces that affect a child's world. In these models, learning and development happen over time (the *chronosystem*) and influences are bidirectional, with the child shaping them as well as being shaped by them, Of course, a child has much more influence on the proximal systems than the distal systems. It's important to remember that although systems may be distal in terms of influence, they can be felt quite directly and immediately—for example, racism, which exists at multiple system levels including macro, but clearly affects the everyday experiences of youth—particularly youth of color.

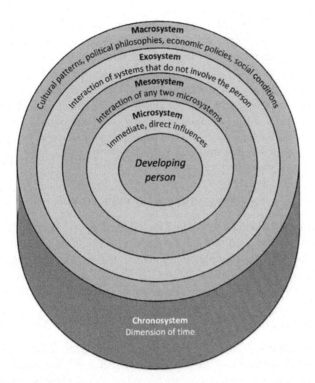

FIGURE 2.1.   Ecological Systems Theory. Based on the bioecological model presented in Bronfenbrenner and Morris (2006).

We think of this as an *individualized developmental ecosystem* because the purpose of the model is to understand individual development, as indicated by the placement of the child at the center. Bronfenbrenner's model has been iterated on countless times and adjusted to various contexts, and usually with the learner or child at the center (e.g., STEM Ecosystems model in Krishnamurthi, 2014). The model helps us see that learning is not a simple universal process. Rather, the model argues that learning and development are more complicated and require working outwards from the individual to ever more distal influences.

In contrast, we propose a *community L&D ecosystem*. We suggest that it is necessary and helpful to shift our gaze from the individual learner in order to more fully consider the context—i.e., the microsystem, mesosystem, and exosystem in Bronfenbrenner's model. We suggest this for three reasons: (a) development always occurs in specific contexts and over time (Murry et al., 2015; Osher et al., 2018); (b) those contexts include a variety of people, places, and possibilities (Blyth, 2006) that create learning opportunities, and (c) we seek to support, in systematic ways, the development of "constructive webs" (Cantor et al., 2019) to support learning and development equitably for all youth. Much of the inequity in learning and development come not from individual differences that an individual or even people around an individual can control but rather from systematic, institutionalized aspects of the community's overall ecosystem—and the need to manage and be intentional about it. To explore this idea, we draw on biological ecosystem management as a guidepost for L&D ecosystem design principles. We believe that intentional, active, and successful management of L&D ecosystems would benefit from shifting the focus of ecological thinking toward a more holistic ecosystem focus supported by a few principles and concepts used in biological ecosystem management (Hecht & Crowley, 2020), as noted in Table 2.1 and presented in the next section.

THREE PRINCIPLES OF ECOSYSTEMS

In this section, we elaborate on the nature of learning and development ecosystems. Specifically, we elaborate on the three principles shown in Table 2.1: The Systems Principle, The Complexity Principle, and the Health Principle. These provide a conceptual grounding, then in the next section we draw on additional ideas from biological ecosystem management to apply to L&D ecosystems.

The Systems Principle

Perhaps the most striking departure from the individualized developmental ecosystem frame, is what we call The Systems Principle. This emerges from the observation that in biology, *ecosystems have no center*. Rather, an ecosystem is a collection of elements with different purposes that interact in various ways. For example, consider the ecosystem depicted in Figure 2.2. It contains living elements such as trees, shrubs, small woodland creatures, birds, worms, insects, and bacteria. It contains important nonliving components, too, like soil and rotting logs. Plants transform sunlight into nutrients which cycle through the forest. Water plays a similar important role spreading energy through the system. The ecosystem is all of these and other parts and their dynamic interaction. And a critical feature of using an ecosystem approach is that it looks at the whole and the roles different parts play rather than raising one part as at the center.

It is important to note that the word "center" has two meanings in this context—(a) the middle point (noun) or to place in the middle (verb) and (b) or to prioritize (verb). To say that ecosystems have no center (middle point) is not at all to say that we shouldn't center (prioritize) the needs of individual children and youth in daily educational practice—we should absolutely prioritize the needs of children and youth during interpersonal interactions. In fact, learner-centered approaches often engage adults to be advisors or coaches whose role is to help the youth seek out and connect with learning and development opportunities in the community. Doing this well requires being aware both of the individual youth's interests and passions *and* what is available in the community; that is, the set of people, places, and opportunities that a youth may access.

FIGURE 2.2.   Example of Biological Ecosystem. Original image by Mario Quinn Lyles.

But a focus on "child at the center," which may be a valuable approach at the interpersonal level, may have unintended consequences if the level of L&D ecosystem design and management is ignored. Neither individual children nor youth, nor their families or guardians can create the full set of opportunities needed in a healthy ecosystem. These systems need support from the broader community (exosystem level) as well as the macrosystem level. When we focus too much on individual children or youth, it is a small step to then hold them responsible for dysfunctional ecosystems. If we want to take a systemic approach to educational improvements, we need to move beyond both a narrow, school-focused view of the L&D ecosystem and an emphasis on how individual children and youth gain opportunities and experiences. Instead, we need to learn how to design supportive system infrastructures (Akiva et al., 2020; Penuel et al., 2014) to ensure healthy ecosystems that operate to support all youth more equitably.

Figure 2.3 shows how a *community L&D ecosystem* contains many opportunities and supports provided by people, places, and possibilities. It includes OST child and youth organizations (including but not limited to schools and academic-focused organizations). These people, places, and possibilities are connected or not connected in various ways (and not just to individual youth). Although people, places, and possibilities often cluster together (e.g., an adult leader at a youth program offers learning activities), sometimes they're disconnected (e.g., a place that might not have an adult leader, such as playground equipment at a park). It is from this community of elements that individual young people build/experience their individual developmental ecosystems (i.e., the Bronfenbrenner child-centered orientation).

Surrounding people, places, and possibilities are the networks and professional learning communities of staff that do or do not exist in the ecosystem. These networks (which occur at the mesosystem level in Bronfenbrenner's framework) are critical for establishing congruence and connections across microsystems (where the people, places, and possibilities for learning and development are). This ring also includes others in ecosystem management roles including support organizations such as afterschool intermediaries (see Chapter 10 by Little and Donner in this volume), school-based intermediaries, funders (See Chapter 12 by Howison, Osai, and Akiva in this volume), and others (e.g., workforce development organizations that include youth employment funding and programs). Outside this ring are the organizations and systems not directly connected to child and youth organizations—like the vibrancy of the arts or the nature of the business and scientific communities emphasis on learning and development or workforce development.

A community's mesosystem can help to structure and connect elements and resources in the ecosystem. So, for example, in a community L&D ecosystem with a large number of OST program leaders (people) and programs (places and possibilities), the greater the probability that an individual youth will experience such programs and learn about other programs. Further, if support organizations provide strong and accessible professional development or quality improvement infrastructure (see Chapter 9 by Wilson-Ahlstrom and Martineau in this volume), this may increase the chances an individual youth experiences a high-quality program opportunity. Similarly, a strong mesosystem that connects parents and guardians as well as OST program leaders to what is available in the L&D ecosystem (e.g., a strong program finder system), the more likely parents can find and utilize these opportunities in supporting the L&D of their youth.

The Complexity Principle

Part of the reason that the individualized developmental ecological model is inadequate for designing and adaptively managing healthy L&D ecosystems is because this model suggests an ecosystem that is complicated rather than complex. According to Westley et al. (2007) phenomena occur at the simple, complicated, and complex levels. Baking a cake is a relatively simple process where use of a

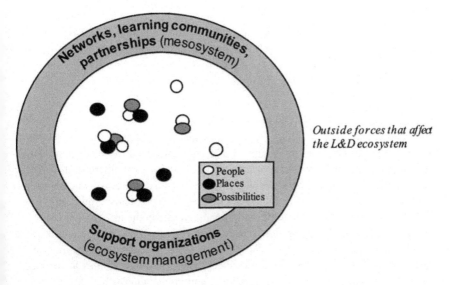

FIGURE 2.3. Model of a Community L&D Ecosystem

recipe will generally provide consistent results. A problem like landing a man on the moon, is more complicated, but can be planned and accomplished because the laws that apply are known and consistent. Complicated problems can be solved by careful planning and by using replicable solutions. Complex problems, however, like the learning and development of children and youth, are dynamic, changing, and in need of constant adjustments.

The design of healthy L&D ecosystems is a complex problem (Jacobson et al., 2019; Lemke & Sabelli, 2008; Mason, 2008). Dismissing this complexity and proceeding as if ecosystems are only complicated leads to recipes that do not work or complicated plans that fail because the nature of the problem is changing dynamically. These approaches will not help us to adequately address inequitable L&D ecosystem systems, which are a combination of complex, dynamic forces operating at many levels and that need to be addressed more holistically.

Another aspect of complexity involves the size or level of ecosystems. In this chapter, we describe L&D ecosystems as a single ecosystem for a given geographical region such as a city. However, in reality, ecosystems occur at multiple levels. For example, your body is an ecosystem, with various microbes that interact in community with your cells, organs, and tissue (Mullard, 2008). A family, classroom, library, and youth program, are all ecosystems with their own dynamics and characteristics. Within a region, there are likely multiple L&D ecosystems, which we refer to as sub-ecosystems; for example, a sub-ecosystem around STEM learning, an educational technology sub-ecosystem, and a youth arts & music sub-ecosystem. These ecosystems and sub-ecosystems also interact with systems outside of learning and development. For example, a youth arts sub-ecosystem overlaps in important ways with the city community focuses on arts and culture. For example, a visual artist may spend her days in the adult art world and her afternoon working as a teaching artist at a community-based youth arts program. All this to say, ecosystems are complex.

The Health Principle

Through ecological thinking, we can consider the health of the system—and as an ecosystem can only be healthy if it is equitable, focusing on system health is focusing on equity. L&D ecosystems exist in both healthy and unhealthy states. The complex interactions between elements will occur regardless of whether or not we choose to engage in active management of these ecosystems. However, we believe that we must take a proactive and intentional role in the management of these ecosystems toward equity and justice. A rich and healthy L&D ecosystem like that which Katherine was a part of doesn't happen for everyone—and should not only happen by having a family that can connect them. The opportunities for connecting with constructive places, caring people and challenging possibilities need to be available and accessible to all youth and families. Unhealthy factors may occur at any number of points in an L&D ecosystem—home, school, out-of-school programs, peers—and impact critical L&D factors such as learner motivation.

A healthy ecosystem, therefore, would not be defined by the experiences of and impacts on an individual child, but would instead be defined as equitable, effective, and positive interactions between L&D ecosystem elements, particularly the people, places, and possibilities that create opportunities for learning and development. Used in this way, we come to recognize that our communities are full of both healthy and unhealthy connections or barriers that affect children, youth, and adults in varied ways. Some ecosystems, like the one Katherine experienced, are healthy—with the people, places, and possibilities fitting together over time. For far too many others, the people they experience may be more uncaring than caring, the places they experience more toxic than constructive, and the possibilities for learning less accessible and less designed for scaffolded learning. The health of a community's L&D ecosystems is not their impact on a given individual but their collective impact on all its children and youth.

As with biological ecosystems, L&D ecosystems thrive when various elements—both small and large—work in harmony with one another. For many individuals to thrive in an equitable way, the system must function well. When there is a great deal of discordance between elements in an ecosystem (e.g., when the multiple settings youth experience are not constructive and safe or lack connections to caring people and accessible challenging possibilities), the ecosystem will not optimally support the learning and development for many of the individuals within it. For example, when a community has dramatic differences in the safety and availability of parks or has what might be considered opportunity deserts where few people, places, and possibilities for learning development occur, or where schools will not allow access for out of school time programs, the L&D ecosystem is less healthy. It is likely the case that ecosystem health might be increased when elements of the ecosystem—people, places, possibilities—work with awareness towards ecosystem goals, particularly the learning and development of all children and youth.

THREE ECOSYSTEM CONCEPTS

In this section, we draw on three concepts used with biological ecosystems and apply them to L&D ecosystem work: adaptive management, disturbances, and indicator/keystone species.

Adaptive Management

Adaptive management is the design and shaping of L&D ecosystems with the recognition that intentionality with constant monitoring and adjustments will need to be made as reality changes. This definition really contains two main ideas: the shift to the ecosystem as the area of focus and the need to be adaptive and responsive to changing conditions within and across the ecosystem. Ecosystem management for us focuses on the youth programs (microsystems) and networks (mesosystems) in a community. Importantly, ecosystem management already occurs in OST ecosystems, notably through the mesosystem work of both intermediary organizations (see Chapter 10 in this volume) and the deployment of quality improvement systems, which are ecosystem focused efforts to improve the health of microsystems (see Chapter 9 in this volume). The growing awareness and emphasis on program quality, continuous improvement, as well as many professional development efforts increasingly draw upon lessons from improvement science and implementation science on how best to implement and sustain changes over time in a system or organization (see Fixsen et al., 2015 for an overview).

The adaptive aspect of ecosystem management is especially important, given the complex and dynamic nature of ecosystems, discussed above in the Complexity Principle. Ecosystem leaders, including practitioners, researchers, and advocates, must become comfortable with and responsive to the dynamic, interactive, and changing nature of ecosystems. Adaptive management also benefits from partnership and coordination. Every day, parks and schools, businesses and nonformal learning programs—and the staff that make them possible in a community—are changing. And with those changes come changes in the existence, nature, quality, and accessibility of the people, places and possibilities that shape learning and development. Authentic collaborative work, where the strengths and needs of all partners are utilized, is essential for adaptive management to be effective.

Disturbances

In biological ecosystems, disturbances are considered natural and even necessary for change and growth (e.g., forest fires are needed to sustain a healthy forest; Ricklefs & Miller, 2000). Disturbances can be expected to occur, even if sometimes unpredictably, and will often help transform the ecosystem—destroying some parts to let other parts take their place. In a biological ecosystem that is dependent on fire, like Western U.S. forests, the disturbance of a fire helps open seeds on fire-dependent tree species. But there can be too much damage from fire if we suppress fire for too long. Similarly, in an L&D ecosystem, disturbances can cause a rapid shift in how learning and development happens. For example, the COVID-19 pandemic is a massive disturbance that has caused a rapid shift to remote learning and virtual settings and how to maintain and build relationships in these contexts. Such disturbances require radical rethinking and lead to potential for major changes in leadership, policy shifts, and funding that may be needed to establish the growth and development of new L&D ecosystems. Theoretically, if they can be embraced and managed well, they may have less of a negative impact on the ecosystem overall and more of a positive transformative effect.

Just as in the history of formal education, the histories of youth fields are in part stories of ecosystem disturbances; that is, discrete events or movements that lead to pronounced system change (Turner, 2010). For example, the origins of youth programs are usually attributed to the twin disturbances of the decline in young people working due to child labor laws and the rise in schooling stimulated by compulsory schooling laws (Halpern, 2003). The school day was not as long as the workday, which led to a need for something to fill that afternoon gap. These great disturbances in L&D ecosystems created a "supervision gap" and led to the creation of boys' clubs and youth programs, which emerged at the end of the 1800s (Mahoney et al., 2009, p. 2.). The goals of such youth programs varied widely over their early history but included keeping children off the streets, instilling religious faiths, character development, play, and the "Americanization" of immigrants (Halpern, 2003). Similarly, the idea of youth programs as supplemental to schools' goals of academic success, so prevalent today, essentially emerged in the 1990s and solidified after the emergence and growth of 21st Century Community Learning Centers (Halpern, 2005). This pressure to utilize out-of-school time settings in the service of school goals was another important disturbance in America's L&D ecosystems. This disturbance may be felt in varied ways by youth programs; for example, most now offer homework help, which may be valuable for children and caregivers and may also push out other content that might normally occur during that time. Other parts of the allied youth fields have had their own paths of disturbance and development.

Finally, not all disturbances affect all people or places equally. This can be seen in both the forest fire example above and the current pandemic's differential toll on people of color, those with fewer resources, and those in specific industries. It can also be seen in the historical context of the creation of the OST field, as many early programs were segregated by race and tended to be shaped around deficit views for Black youth (Baldridge, 2019). How we choose to respond and adaptively manage such effects makes a great deal of difference for the health of the ecosystem. This includes disturbances that differentially affect particular people, such as institutional racism and the impact of seeing people of color killed by authorities.

Indicator and Keystone Species

Whereas Katherine's thriving is an example of the impact of a healthy L&D ecosystem on an individual's developmental ecology, an ecosystem framework requires us to ask about how all children and youth were doing and what factors in the ecosystem could be managed to improve the odds for all children and youth. It is looking at all children and youth—what ecosystem models would call the ***indicator species***—that we seek to manage the environments and opportunities they experience. This calls to mind the Maasai greeting, "And how are the children?." This traditional greeting among the Maasai illustrates the indicator species concept: "if the children are good, life is good" (Allen, 2018, p. 1). For example, when we look at graduation rates by schools or states we are looking at how the indicator species—namely all children in that school or state—are doing and what we can do to improve their performance. Instead of looking at how one individual does we need to look at the success rate of the species as a whole.

We also need to attend to those elements of the system that have the greatest potential to positively influence many other elements of the systems. Restoration ecologists call these influential species ***keystone species***. A common example of a keystone species are the wolves that were reintroduced to Yellowstone National Park. By creating conditions for the wolves to thrive, conditions for many other flora and fauna, some of which could be used as indicator species, also improved. As indicated in the design challenges below, we propose that the youth fields' workforce—teachers, librarians, youth and afterschool workers, coaches, and camp counselors, to name just a few—are the keystone species for a healthy L&D ecosystem that supports children and youth (See Chapter 6 by Colvin & White in this volume). It is these people who design, manage, and implement the opportunities that matter for learning and development. They are the caring people youth connect to, they work in the places youth are, and they are the ones who design and implement the processes that create possibilities for youth. They are central to both creating the opportunities and connecting youth to them so they become developmental experiences that accumulate over time. When we invest in these critical adults (such as through offering professional development, structures for professional learning communities, and higher wages), they enrich the people, places, and possibilities that occur in the environment both within and between ecosystem elements. Such an enriched ecosystem of opportunities and the experiences youth have as a result lead to higher levels of learning and development.

Additional Concepts From Biological Ecosystem Management

The three ideas presented in this chapter provide a start to applying ecosystem management to learning and development; however, our list is not meant to be comprehensive. For example, the concept of *energy* and the transfer of energy is fundamental to understanding biological ecosystems. In L&D ecosystems, energy might be represented in various ways, including funding (as described in Chapter 12 in this volume). Another potentially useful concept is *ecotones*, which are boundary-crossing regions, such as the area between the forests and the rivers or between the mountains and the plains. In L&D ecosystems the ecotones involve spaces like between home and school or between school and OST programs. Like the spaces they bridge, ecotones often have their own form and functions (Hecht & Crowley, 2020, pp. 274–275). With the potentially rich area of different systems, organizations, places (real and virtual), and people providing learning and development opportunities to youth, the boundary areas between these may be facilitators or barriers to connected learning.

HOW MIGHT WE DESIGN A HEALTHIER LEARNING AND DEVELOPMENT ECOSYSTEM?

As we write this chapter, the world is going through a massive disturbance that is profoundly reshaping L&D ecosystems: the COVID-19 pandemic. This pandemic has in a matter of months radically changed the nature of schooling and the places, people and possibilities where learning and development are expected to occur. As Pittman (2020) noted, essentially all learning during the pandemic is out-of-school time learning. Given the nature and impact of this disturbance, as well as the rapid rise in awareness and demand for action around long-standing racial injustice and inequities, what better time to reframe how we think about the complex and shifting L&D ecosystems that youth actually experience? How can we seek to redesign these systems and their interconnections so that we more intentionally and strategically support and connect the variety of people, places, and possibilities that shape young people's learning and development?

Given what we know from the science of learning and development and using an ecosystems framework, how might we employ adaptive management to redesign and shape a successful and equitable L&D ecosystem—especially if we aren't limited to current educational structures? Such a healthy ecosystem could better address urgent issues affecting learning and development. Specifically, we argue that a healthy L&D ecosystem would better support three things: (a) equitable opportunities and ways for accessing them, (b) fuller use of the multiple contexts for learning, and (c) increased support for the critical adults who create these opportunities and staff these contexts—the "keystone species" whose talents and well-being are integral to helping the ecosystem thrive.

To design and shape a healthy ecosystem, we must consider the multiple settings in which learning and development occur and the various adults that work in these fields. Blyth and LaCroix-Dalluhn (2011) outlined three broad approaches to learning that clarify important distinctions young person experience: *Formal*, structured learning approaches tend to focus on academic achievement and have compulsory attendance and assessment (e.g., school); *nonformal* approaches are structured and intentional, but have voluntary attendance and support mastery (e.g., youth programs); and *informal* approaches that are designed to facilitate learning on one's own or with others in a given situation or setting (e.g., car trips, museums, zoos). The authors argue that settings using a predominately formal approach tend to focus on content to be learned; nonformal approaches and settings prioritize youth and their learning interests; and informal settings highlight resources available in natural and designed environments. It is important to note that any setting can and often does use more than one of these approaches. A healthy ecosystem does not divide and restrict settings to use one or another approach but values that learning and development happens with each. The opportunities for learning that these approaches generate can be planned and intentional or spontaneous. As these various approaches to learning create opportunities for learning, how they are experienced, processed and reflected on by the young person is critical. The point here is not that one approach is better than another, but rather, that a healthy L&D ecosystem would feature a diversity and balance of learning approaches and settings and that these would be equitably available to and accessed by youth as well as supported by adults who are helpful. Some young people who do not thrive in compulsory, content-based learning, for example, might excel at voluntary, interest-based learning. Positive experiences in one setting might then affect or enhance learning in another; that is, getting excited about learning in different ways and places can often help young people find new energy and motivation to learn in traditional settings. In a healthy ecosystem all children and youth could find, access, experience, and process the variety of learning opportunities that they need to advance their learning journeys.

A Healthy L&D Ecosystem Must be Equitable

A common way of thinking about educational inequality is to consider disparities in per capita school spending across more versus less financially rich communities (Kozol, 1991; Putnam, 2015).This is an important perspective, associated with devastating data that reflects how forces outside of schools affect the resources and qualities of learning environments within schools, but it is only part of the picture. Inequities in nonformal and informal learning opportunities are as, or even more, prevalent. For example, many informal and nonformal opportunities offered are fee based (e.g., dance lessons, piano, many museums and zoos), so access is linked to household income (Duncan & Murnane, 2011). Other opportunities are offered free but may not appeal to diverse youth or their families due to their locations, activities reputations or non-representative staff. This is often especially true for racial, ethic, immigrant, and other cultural groups that are marginalized intentionally and unintentionally by the dominant white culture. Formal learning settings (schools) have universal access but inequities in both the opportunities they offer and how the people, places and possibilities are actually experienced. Nonformal learning settings are less universally accessible and tend to suffer from both inequitable access as well as inequitable allocation of resources (McNamara et al., 2020). Informal learning also too often depends upon the web of resources a young person has access to rather than being driven by their curiosity and thirst for learning—factors that would be primary drivers of accessing learning opportunities in a more robust and equitable L&D ecosystem. In short, far too much of the current L&D ecosystem is dependent on family, neighborhood and community resources even though a healthy L&D environment collectively benefits the wider society. In the United States, location matters and far too many of a young person's learning opportunities are heavily influenced by their zip code, race, and family income.

In order to create healthy L&D ecosystems that are defined by equity, we need to identify and monitor barriers and facilitators of access to nonformal and informal, choice-based learning, including factors such as transportation, program cost, and professional learning for adult leaders. However, equitable nonformal learning opportunities don't just mean making sure all programs are free or affordable. Exclusion can still happen even when programs are free of cost as young people must also feel welcome and a sense they belong if they are to engage in a program (Dawson, 2014). Similarly, interest is not just something young people have or don't have—it is nurtured and depends heavily on prior experiences – experiences that are encouraged or discouraged by the people, places, and possibilities youth encounter. Designing for equity does not simply mean providing wide access to whatever young people are interested in as if interest is only a predisposition; it also involves nurturing interest development through exploration as well as development of mastery over time and space (Hidi et al., 2004).

Ecosystem design for equity also requires an expansion of what "counts" as legitimate learning, beyond standardized tests or other indicators of academic achievement (for more complete discussion, please see Chapter 3 by Pittman et al. in this volume). If, for example, pursuit of deep, interest-based learning (e.g., in youth activism tactics or robotics competitions) did not always take a back seat to school-sanctioned topics, nonformal learning settings might have a more prominent place in L&D ecosystems and the overall health of the ecosystem would likely increase (and thereby also the learning of the children and youth in them). Similarly, ecosystem design would include social and emotional learning as a key goal, as many have argued (e.g., the Commission on Social, Emotional and Academic Development [nationathope.org]; the Science of Learning and Development Alliance [www.soldalliance.org]).

Using an adaptive management approach, a healthy ecosystem would monitor where learning and development is happening across and within settings and use that data to allocate resources and provide adaptive management strategies to ensure effectiveness. Schools letting go of their control of the "canon" of what counts may seem revolutionary, but it's really the only thing that makes sense in the face of the rate at which knowledge is increasing (e.g., Fuller, 1981) and the ways access to information continues to rapidly change. Youth's collective interests, access, and experiences might then be used as indicators of L&D ecosystem equity and overall health. This could, for example, mean disaggregating data by geography and system level factors rather than primarily by individual student characteristics. Additionally, allied youth workers—as the keystone species—must be more heavily invested in and supported.

A HEALTHY L&D ECOSYSTEM FOCUSES SUPPORT ON THE ADULTS WHO SUPPORT YOUNG PEOPLE— THE "KEYSTONE SPECIES"

For a healthy L&D ecosystem to support equitable learning across contexts and topics, we must invest in the people that make that happen. People are the driving energy that create places and people implement the possibilities that exist in places. In the U.S. and most of the world, ample societal investments do not even occur for teachers, who make less than the average person with a college degree (Allegretto & Mishel, 2019). Adult leaders in nonformal learning settings across the youth fields, however, are particularly undervalued and underpaid (Gannett & Starr, 2016). Lack of pay and societal status likely keeps many from entering or staying in the youth fields and negatively affects those who choose nonformal youth work as a career. This is not just a matter of fairness; it is also supported by the Science of Learning and Development initiative (discussed in several chapters in this volume including Chapters 1 and 3). A chief finding of this multi-disciplinary scholarship is that adult-youth relationships are critically important for learning and development and that these relationships occur across multiple settings in young people's lives (Osher et al., 2018). Although adult-youth relationships can support healthy development, they can also undermine it, and this can happen in relatively evident ways such as abuse or neglect and much more subtle or unintentional ways such as reinforcing a deficit mindset—suggesting that we need greater intentionality in preparation of adults around what makes for strong developmentally-supportive relationships (See Chapter 6 by Li and Winters in this volume).

In a healthy L&D ecosystem, people who lead activities and work with young people would be well-paid, well-prepared, and highly valued members of society. In other words, in order for them to act as learning and development professionals, they would be treated as professionals. This is akin to the idea of focusing restoration and management efforts on keystone species. Educators are a keystone species in a L&D ecosystem. When they are healthy, the system is healthier overall. In a healthy L&D ecosystem, this would be the case for teachers as well as other adults who engage with young people.

The need for raising the societal status of the youth worker field has been acknowledged and noted for decades (e.g., Fusco, 2012; Pozzoboni & Kirshner, 2016; VanderVen, 1991). We have seen movements for standards, credentialing, and expertise-based training. The addition that an ecosystem framework provides is the expansion of the youth fields and the potential strengths that a larger set of allied fields may bring. This brings the nuance that although professional training for adult leaders in a healthy L&D ecosystem would have great diversity in terms of content knowledge (e.g., from library science to fine arts to programming), we would have similarity in terms of training for developmental relationships (Akiva et al., 2020). An adaptive management approach would involve ongoing work with members of the allied youth field to understand and monitor their financial and psychological wellbeing—along with real time adjustments that would support greater health for them. As keystone species, it is their health that is able to provide the support and structure for vibrant learning experiences for youth.

A HEALTHY L&D ECOSYSTEM CAPITALIZES ON THE MULTIPLE WAYS THAT YOUNG PEOPLE LEARN AND DEVELOP

Willingham (2009) reminds us that children are "more alike than different" in how they learn (p. 147). This suggests that we need a systems approach to designing L&D ecosystems. There is no simple recipe. Rather, a rich diversity of types of people and places as well as possibilities—instructional pedagogies, guided discovery, mentorship, apprenticeship, interest-based pursuits, etc.—are important for learning and development.

Although L&D ecosystems currently include a wide variety of nonformal learning settings—many large U.S. cities have a variety of nonformal art, STEM, activism, and myriad other youth clubs and programs—access to these opportunities is limited for many young people (McNamara et al., 2020). The over-focusing on school for all primary learning creates a situation in which the dominant approach is a particular, language-based way of learning (reading, writing, taking tests). Our current ecosystem features inadequate focus on the whole child and over-emphasis on some contexts (schools) and outcomes (particularly academic achievement)—which leads to the marginalization of non-school, non-academic youth programs and the many adults who are not teachers in formal settings. This overemphasis on schooling may even backfire on the goals of schooling as suggested by the research on the summer learning gap (e.g., Alexander et al., 2007). That is, research finds that the achievement gap widens in the summer along lines of socioeconomic level (whereas this is generally not the case during the school year), suggesting that the attainment of school goals is likely heavily shaped by non-school factors.

In a L&D ecosystem framework, we could consider a region as a meaningful unit to focus on, monitor, and work toward balance in the diversity of learning approaches and settings available to young people. A healthy L&D ecosystem offers a variety of formal, nonformal, and informal approaches and contexts for learning and these opportunities are not concentrated on only a small number of young people. One measure of this might be the overall number of opportunities available in the communities as well as the number of such opportunities per youth in the community—something we are currently unable to reasonably estimate, though it may be a powerful indicator of the health of a L&D ecosystem.

An ecosystem approach also leads to a recognition of the diversity of settings and expanding who is understood to be part of the L&D youth fields. We would attend to whether school structures and personnel support (or undermine) an easy flow into nonformal learning opportunities offered at the school and in the community. We might intentionally design pathways for learning over time—which moved both within and between formal and nonformal programs and organizations. For example, a young person interested in visual arts might move back and forth between school and community-based art programs as, over time, they grow in interest and skill (Akiva et al., 2016). Making such pathways intentional requires attention to interactions between programs, and to ecotones; the spaces that offer transition between settings. For example, the school grounds—where a child spends time after school before visiting a nearby community program—can be a critical place for connecting different types of learning and development. All of this requires an adaptive management approach to be most effective. In other words, any interventions in the L&D ecosystem should be monitored and adjusted over time.

In a biological ecosystem, it is important to distinguish the different parts and how they contribute to the whole. A central idea of complexity theory is that the whole is greater than the sum of its parts. Returning to the idea of a forest ecosystem, a forest has many separate elements that include physical features, such as soil and rocks, and biological elements, such as soil microbes, understory plants, large trees, and the animals that use the forest for habitat. The forest ecosystem is the interactions and relations between all of these separate elements or sectors. In coming together, they have formed something new. Similarly, in an L&D ecosystem framework, we distinguish between different parts or sectors of the ecosystem and their unique styles and contributions to learning. For example, youth arts programs—that focus on both art and education—are a known sector. Within that sector, different programs have different aims. For example, some might focus on "arts exposure" activities like bringing a 3rd grade classroom to the opera, and others might focus on longer-term expertise building for a smaller, interested set of participants (for more on this example, see Akiva et al., 2019).

WHAT MIGHT A HEALTHIER L&D SYSTEM LOOK LIKE?

A few examples exist of L&D ecosystem approaches that begin to address the challenges described in this section. One example of adaptive management may be seen in Iceland's approach to problems of teen alcohol use (Sigfúsdóttir et al., 2008). In this case the country explored and implemented multiple ways to positively engage and connect young people in healthy opportunities and were able to reduce teenage drinking significantly. Multiple sectors including school, youth programs, and social services, worked together across many years to make this happen. Another example is how Finland dramatically improved its educational outcomes by investing in making teaching a highly respected and valued profession that attracted the best and the brightest (Sahlberg, 2011), supporting educators as keystone species. As these examples reflect countries that are much smaller than most U.S. states, a lesson may be that such efforts should be adapted to local efforts. However, it is also possible that the establishment of a youth policy in the U.S. could vastly improve L&D ecosystems across the country.

In the U.S., we have examples of L&D ecosystem approaches that originate in the out-of-school time sector. For example, the AfterZone model for middle school age youth in Providence, Rhode Island, features a "city as campus" design (see www.mypasa.org). Young people and families do not sign up for individual programs, but join the AfterZone and then have access to a large and diverse set of nonformal opportunities (with centrally provided transportation). The system monitors youth interests and seeks to build opportunities for youth to use. Furthermore, over time this effort helped establish stronger coordination with the schools and even lead to a major effort to rethink summer school and summer programming by having teachers and youth workers working together to both design and implement new efforts.

Another example is Remake Learning, a formal-informal network organization in Pittsburgh, Pennsylvania, which focuses on celebrating formal/informal educators and building professional learning communities, particularly in areas of equity and education technology (Gatz, under review). For examples of similar initiatives in other cities see Chapter 10 in this volume by Little and Donner).

Efforts to design healthier L&D ecosystems would use data on the keystone species—adults in the youth fields—with the understanding that the health of keystones is integrally connected to the health of the ecosystem. This might include data about professional characteristics such as pay, benefits, job satisfaction, as well as data on what adult leaders do, how they do it, and the professional development opportunities available to support them. Efforts to design healthier L&D ecosystems would also involve data on the indicator species—children and youth—that might include the percentage of youth in different nonformal and informal settings, the level of engagement they experience, the number of opportunities available per youth in the area, and the perception of supportive learning climates at school, as well as the nature and number of adults in their lives. To some extent, the developmental asset surveys developed and used by Search Institute provides an early iteration of what such measurement of both internal and external assets exist among youth in a community (Roehlkepartain & Blyth, 2020; Scales et al, 2000). Similarly, the MDI (Middle Childhood Index) is used in places in Canada and elsewhere to capture youths' perceptions of their community in ways that get communicated to the community, not just the schools (Guhn, et al., 2012 and see http://earlylearning.ubc.ca/maps/mdi/nh/ for sample reports). Such community level reports could also be designed to investigate subgroup similarities and differences as a way to identify equity concerns that require actions (one of the benefits of No Child Left Behind policies, which also had other less fortunate impacts). In some cases, efforts by schools to rethink the connections to community do occur; for example, in community schools (See communityschools.futureforlearning.org). Similarly, in Tacoma, Washington, community and school efforts to use a whole child approach have helped reshape school and afterschool connections (see https://www.edutopia.org/video/connecting-school-and-afterschool-shared-practices).

These types of strategies—from measuring the L&D of the children and youth differently, to measures of the health of the ecosystem itself, to measures of the preparedness and capacity of the adults in the ecosystem—would lead to greatly expanded approaches to learning as well as content areas—in particular an expansion of what "counts" for learning, the expansion of nonformal enrichment across the youth fields, and potentially a system that could much better respond to the giant corpus of findings around learning motivation (Cantor et al., 2019). Such strategies would spread content and investments across the ecosystem (e.g., make it normative for environmental education to occur at local parks with expert, nonschool personnel), rather than overly concentrate them in schools. This would result in a school system that was much less cut off from the rest of society and an ecosystem that tapped more resources and was more responsive to the diverse needs of learners.

REFERENCES

Akiva, T., Delale-O'Connor, L., & Pittman, K. J. (2020). The promise of building equitable ecosystems for learning. *Urban Education.* https://doi.org/10.1177/0042085920926230

Akiva, T., Hecht, M., & Osai, E. (2019). *Creative learning in Pittsburgh.* University of Pittsburgh School of Education.

Akiva, T., Kehoe, S. S., & Schunn, C. D. C. D. (2016). Are we ready for citywide learning? Examining the nature of within- and between-program pathways in a community-wide learning initiative. *Journal of Community Psychology, 45*(3), 413–425. https://doi.org/10.1002/jcop.21856

Alexander, K. L., Entwisle, D. R., & Olson, L. S. (2007). Lasting consequences of the summer learning gap. *American Sociological Review, 72,* 167–180.

Allegretto, S., & Mishel, L. (2019, April 24). *The teacher weekly wage penalty hit 21.4 percent in 2018, a record high: Trends in the teacher wage and compensation penalties through 2018.* Economic Policy Institute, Center on Wage & Employment Dynamics.

Allen, T. (2018). Detroit's children should be part of city's resurgence, too. *Detroit Free Press.* https://www.freep.com/story/opinion/contributors/2018/03/04/detroit-children-poverty-education/390506002/

Baldridge, B. J. (2019). *Reclaiming community: Race and the uncertain future of youth work.* Stanford University Press.

Banks, J. A., Au, K. H, Ball, A. F., Bell, P., Gordon, E. W., Gutiérrez, K. D., Heath, S. B., Lee, C. D., Lee, Y., Mahiri, J., Nasir, N. S., Valdés, G., & Zhou, M. (2007). *Learning in and out of school in diverse environments.*

Bevan, B. (2016). STEM learning ecologies: Relevant, responsive, and connected. http://csl.nsta.org/2016/03/stem-learning-ecologies/

Blyth, D. A. (2006). Toward a new paradigm for youth development. *New Directions for Youth Development, 112*, 25–43.

Blyth, D. A., & LaCroix-Dalluhn, L. (2011). Expanded learning time and opportunities: Key principles, driving perspectives, and major challenges. *New Directions for Youth Development, 131*, 15–27.

Bronfenbrenner, U., & Morris, P. A. (2007). The bioecological model of human development. In W. Damon & R. M. Lerner (Eds.), Handbook of child psychology, Vol. 1: Theoretical models of human development (6th ed., pp. 793–828). New York: John Wiley.

Cantor, P., Osher, D., Berg, J., Steyer, L., & Rose, T. (2019). Malleability, plasticity, and individuality: How children learn and develop in context. *Applied Developmental Science, 23*(4), 307–337. https://doi.org/10.1080/10888691.2017.1398649

Christensen, J. (2016). A critical reflection of Brofenbrenner's development ecology mmodel. *Problems of Education in the 21st Century, 69*, 1979. https://doi.org/10.13140/RG.2.1.2959.7681

Dawson, E. (2014). Equity in informal science education: developing an access and equity framework for science museums and science centres. *Studies in Science Education, 50*(2), 209–247. https://doi.org/10.1080/03057267.2014.957558

Duncan, G. J., & Murnane, R. J. (2011). Introduction: The American dream, then and now. In *Whither opportunity? Rising inequality, schools, and children's life chances* (pp. 3–23). Russell Sage Foundation.

Dunlap, K. (1929). Is compulsory education justified? *The American Mercury*, 211–214. https://www.unz.com/print/AmMercury-1929feb-00211/

Falk, J. H., & Dierking, L. D. (2018). Viewing science learning through an ecosystem lens: A story in two parts. In D. Corrigan, C. Buntting, A. Jones, & J. Loughran (Eds.), *Navigating the changing landscape of formal and informal science learning opportunities* (pp. 9–29). Springer International Publishing.

Fixsen, D., Blase, K., Metz, A., & Van Dyke, M. (2015). Implementation Science. In J. D. Wright (Ed.), *International encyclopedia of the social and behavioral sciences* (2nd Ed., pp. 695–702). Elsevier.

Fuller, B. (1981). *Critical path.* St. Martins Press.

Fusco, D. (2012). *Advancing youth work: Current trends, critical questions. Advancing youth work: Current trends, critical questions.* https://doi.org/10.4324/9780203829769

Gannett, E., & Starr, E. (2016). Credentialing for youth work: Expanding our thinking. In *The changing landscape of youth work: Theory and practice for an evolving field* (pp. 31–50). Information Age Publishing.

Gatz., E. (under review). *Walking this path: The role of professional networks for formal and informal educators.*

Guhn, M., Schonert-Reichl, K. A., Gadermann, A. M., Marriott, D., Pedrini, L., Hymel, L., & Hertzman, C. (2012). Well-being in middle childhood: An assets-based population-level research-to-action project. *Child Indicators Research Child, 5*, 393–418. DOI 10.1007/s12187-012-9136-8

Halpern, R. (2003). *Making play work: The promise of after-school programs for low income children.* Teacher's College Press.

Halpern, R. (2005). Instrumental relationships: A potential relational model for inner-city youth programs. *Journal of Community Psychology, 33*(1), 11–20. https://doi.org/10.1002/jcop.20032

Hecht, M., & Crowley, K. (2020). Unpacking the learning ecosystems framework: Lessons from the adaptive management of biological ecosystems. *Journal of the Learning Sciences, 2*(29). https://doi.org/10.1080/10508406.2019.1693381

Hecht, M., Knutson, K., & Crowley, K. (2019). Becoming a naturalist: Interest development across the learning ecology. *Science Education, 103*(3), 691–713. https://doi.org/10.1002/sce.21503

Hiki, S., Renninger, K. A., & Krapp, A. (2004). Interest, a motivational variable that combines affective and cognitive functioning. In D. Y. Dai & R. J. Sternberg (Eds.), *Motivation, emotion, and cognition: Integrative perspectives on intellectual functioning and development* (pp. 89–115). Routledge.

Jacobson, M. J., Levin, J. A., & Kapur, M. (2019). Education as a complex system: Conceptual and methodological implications. *Educational Researcher, 48*(2). https://doi.org/10.3102/0013189X19826958

Janak, E. (2019). *A brief history of schooling in the United States: From pre-colonial times to the present.* Springer Nature Switzerland AG. https://doi.org/10.1080/004676 0x.2020.1715491

Knutson, K., Crowley, K., Russell, J. L., & Steiner, M. A. (2011). Approaching art education as an ecology: Exploring the role of museums. *Studies in Art Education: A Journal of Issues and Research in Art Education, 52*(4), 310–322. http://search.ebscohost.com/login.aspx?direct=true&AuthType=ip,uid&db=eric&AN=EJ96033 4&scope=site

Kozol, J. (1991). *Savage inequalities: Children in America's schools.* Crown Publishing Group.

Krishnamurthi, A. (2014). *STEM learning across settings: Cultivating learning ecosystems.* http://www.afterschoolalliance.org/afterschoolsnack/ASnack.cfm?idBlog=42F434BF-215A-A6B3-02FE5A2917CC75A9

Lemke, J. L., & Sabelli, N. H. (2008). Complex systems and educational change: Towards a new research agenda. *Educational Philosophy and Theory, 40*(1), 118–129. https://doi.org/10.1111/j.1469-5812.2007.00401.x

Lerner, R. M. (2005). Foreward: Urie Bronfenbrenner: Career contributions of the consummate developmental scientist. In U. Bronfenbrenner (Ed.), *Making human beings human: Bioecological perspectives on human development* (pp. ix–xxvi). Sage Publications.

Mahoney, J. L., Parente, M. E., & Zigler, E. F. (2009). Afterschool programs in America: Origins, growth, popularity, and politics. *Journal of Youth Development, 4*(3), 23–42. https://doi.org/10.5195/jyd.2009.250

Mason, M. (2008). What is complexity theory and what are its implications for educational change? *Educational Philosophy and Theory, 40*(1), 35–49. https://doi.org/10.1111/j.1469-5812.2007.00413.x

McNamara, A. R., Akiva, T., & Delale-O'Connor, L. (2020). Opportunity gaps in out-of-school learning: How structural and process features of programs relate to race and socioeconomic status. *Applied Developmental Science, 24*(4), 17. https://doi.org/10.1080/10888691.2018.1513794

Mullard, A. (2008). The inside story: Human microbiome. *Science, 453*, 578–580. https://doi.org/10.1108/sr.2000.08720caa.001

Murry, V. M., Hill, N. E., Witherspoon, D., Berkel, C., & Bartz, D. (2015). Children in diverse social contexts. In *Handbook of child psychology and developmental science, ecological settings and processes* (7th Ed., pp. 416–454). John Wiley & Sons, Inc.

National Research Council. (2015). *Identifying and supporting productive STEM programs in out-of-school settings. Identifying and supporting productive STEM programs in out-of-school settings*. Board on Science Education, Division of Behavioral and Social Sciences and Education. The National Academies Press. https://doi.org/10.17226/21740

Osher, D., Cantor, P., Berg, J., Steyer, L., & Rose, T. (2018). Drivers of human development: How relationships and context shape learning and development. *Applied Developmental Science, 24*(1), 6–36. https://doi.org/10.1080/10888691.2017.1398650

Penuel, W. R., Lee, T. R., & Bevan, B. (2014). *Research synthesis: Designing and building infrastructures to support equitable STEM learning across settings. Research + Practice Collaboratory Research Synthesis.*.

Pittman, K. (2020). *What happens when out-of-school time is all the time?* https://forumfyi.org/blog/what-happens-when-out-of-school-time-is-all-the-time/?_sft_post_tag=karen-pittman

Pozzoboni, K., & Kirshner, B. (2016). *The changing landscape of youth work: Theory and practice for an evolving field.* Information Age Publishing.

Putnam, R. D. (2015). *Our kids: The American dream in crisis.* Simon & Schuster.

Rabkin, N., Reynolds, M., Hedberg, E., & Shelby, J. (2011). *Teaching artists and the future of education. Teaching Artist Journal.* https://doi.org/10.1080/15411796.2012.630633

Ricklefs, R. E., & Miller, G. L. (2000). *Ecology* (4th ed.). W.H. Freeman and Company.

Sahlberg, P. (2011). *Finnish lessons: What can the world learn from educational change in Finland?* Teachers College Press.

Sigfúsdóttir, I. D., Thorlindsson, T., Kristjánsson, Á. L., Roe, K. M., & Allegrante, J. P. (2008). Substance use prevention for adolescents: The Icelandic Model. *Health Promotion International, 24*(1), 16–25. https://doi.org/10.1093/heapro/dan038

Turner, M. G. (2010). Disturbance and landscape dynamics in a changing world. *Ecology, 91*(10), 2833–2849.

VanderVen, K. (1991). How is child and youth care work unique—and different—from other fields? *Journal of Child and Youth Care, 5*(1), 15–19.

Westley, F., Zimmerman, B., & Patton, M. Q. (2007). *Getting to maybe: How the world is changed.* Penguin, Random House.

Willingham, D. T. (2009). *Why don't students like school? A cognitive scientist answers questions about how the mind works and what it means for your classroom.* John Wiley & Sons Inc.

CHAPTER 3

WHY NARROW DEFINITIONS OF HOW, WHERE, AND WHEN LEARNING HAPPENS UNDERMINE EQUITY

How OST Leaders Can Help

Karen Pittman, Jill Young, David Osher,
Rob Jagers, Hal Smith, Merita Irby, and Poonam Borah

There may be conceptual reasons for distinguishing between "cognitive" and "non-cognitive" factors, but this distinction has no functional meaning. Cognition, emotion, affect, and behavior are reflexive, mutually reinforcing, and inextricably associated with one another as a part of development and learning. Adults will make little headway if they target only one component or subcomponent in isolation.... Ensuring all young people have access to a multitude of rich developmental experiences is imperative to their success (Nagaoka et al., 2015, p. 7).

INTRODUCTION

Narrow, compartmentalized definitions of learning—definitions that prioritize certain functions and experiences and ignore others, as the quote from our Univer-

It Takes an Ecosystem: Understanding the People, Places, and
Possibilities of Learning and Development Across Settings, pages 37–66.
Copyright © 2022 by Information Age Publishing

sity of Chicago Consortium on School Research colleagues explain, can severely limit adults' effectiveness as educators, mentors, or life coaches.

Equally important, narrow definitions of learning contribute to the persistent under-education and under-valuation of marginalized groups. There is overwhelming agreement that didactic linear teaching, tight age and ability groupings, content versus concept mastery, and standardized outcome measures that undergird U.S. education dampen overall levels of engagement in and effectiveness of youth and adults in our public schools. Volumes of studies show that these outdated approaches are less well suited for—but nonetheless used more with—marginalized student groups (Cantor et al., 2021). This extreme mismatch of approaches has tipped the scales in favor of white, affluent, non-immigrant, abled students so much and for so long that, until recently, persistent "achievement gaps" were interpreted as capacity and motivation gaps, not "opportunity gaps" (e.g., McClellan et al., 2018). Unless rigorously challenged, these narrow definitions of how learning happens will continue to undermine well-meaning attempts to upend inequity. They will dampen appetites to describe, assess, and increase the "multitude of rich developmental experiences" imperative to the success of young people currently experiencing a multitude of inequities (Nagaoka et al., 2015, p. 7).

This is a unique moment in history, even before the COVID-19 pandemic. The preponderance of science findings on how learning happens has escalated efforts in school and out-of-school time (OST) systems to elevate the need to invest not only in social and emotional skill development of young people, but also in the development and empowerment of the adults who, with youth, co-create environments that accelerate the learning and development of each and every student. This includes developing and empowering the administrators who manage the resources and requirements that support or constrain the enterprise (Akiva et al., 2020; Hecht & Crowley, 2019; National Commission on Social, Emotional, and Academic Development [NCSEAD], 2019; Osher et al., 2019).

We, the authors, believe that OST leaders have a critical role to play in changing the national and local narratives about how, where, when, with whom, and *for* whom learning happens (Moroney et al., 2020; NCSEAD, 2018; Osher et al., 2020). Doing so, however, requires more than a recommitment to increasing the quality and quantity of available programming. It requires a dual commitment: We must: 1) champion the need for schools and OST providers—and, more broadly, for the systems and decision makers that support them—to commit to operating as parts of dynamic learning and development ecosystems, and 2) aggressively demonstrate the value of this admittedly complex approach. (Note: We use the OST acronym in this chapter to refer to leaders, organizations, and programs that operate as a part of a loose, nonformal learning and development delivery system that operates primarily, but not exclusively in the hours that complement the school day.)

The opportunity for OST systems and settings to be viewed as key partners in education transformation rather than just as complementary services providers has become increasingly ripe over the past several years. For example, the National Commission on Social, Emotional, and Academic Development began with a charge to help transform PreK–12 education and inform the education ecosystem, but through that process intentionally engaged the youth development community. The visual frames and recommendations produced reflect their original PreK–12 charge—they were developed for the education system, not the full learning and development ecosystem. However, in some ways this clear education system focus makes them even more important and inspiring. The carefully crafted frames and recommendations demonstrate the shifts in language and perspectives that can happen when youth development leaders are fully engaged in the process. The speed with which they have been not only adopted but adapted signals the growing momentum to support key shifts in framing how, when, where, and with whom learning happens.

In this chapter, we explore the value of leveraging four "moving trains"– broad efforts that are gaining momentum, led primarily by education reformers and transformers, that validate the broad tenets of positive youth development that undergird OST:

- Link academic competence to broader definitions of how, where, when, with whom, and why learning happens.
- Link learning and development advances more specifically to equitable ecosystem goals.
- Advance social and emotional learning as critical to the development of competence, identity, and agency.
- Establish universal practice principles that support optimal learning, development, and thriving in all learning settings.
- Prioritize adolescence as a critical time for innovation, involvement, and investments.

Each of these efforts is positioned by their champions as a way to challenge both schools and OST providers to recognize and upend inequities. Each emphasizes the importance of the practitioners—the adults charged with working with and for young people in the places where learning and development are expected to happen.

We end with specific recommendations on what OST leaders—practitioners, administrators, champions—can do to advance more inclusive definitions of learning and of learning and development ecosystems that speak to a broader end goal: equitable expectations and opportunities for youth thriving.

LINKING ACADEMIC COMPETENCE TO BROADER DEFINITIONS OF HOW, WHERE, AND WHEN LEARNING HAPPENS

Students, families, communities, and educators are demanding a more balanced approach to our vision of learning: One that recognizes learning is always social, emotional, and academic, and these strands cannot be teased apart (NCSEAD, 2018, para 1).

The National Commission for Social, Emotional, and Academic Development [The Commission/NCSEAD] was disbanded in early 2019, but its legacy continues. The Commission's dogged push to make the research and practice findings synthesized by its councils of experts accessible and available to practitioners and families led to the development of robust communications efforts that are now being expanded to showcase the role of OST staff, settings, and systems. The original *How Learning Happens* series of videos developed by Edutopia have been viewed by tens of millions of practitioners. The first set of short videos predominantly featured classroom teachers and schools. Thanks to persistent requests from OST leaders, the series was recently expanded to include another set of videos that explicitly show the practice principles in operation in OST settings staffed by non-classroom teachers. The combined series now features nearly three dozen videos narrated by Dr. Pamela Cantor, Dr Linda Darling-Hammond, and Karen Pittman, coded by topic (e.g., social and emotional learning, environmental education, after-school learning, mental health, student wellness, professional development, family engagement, classroom management, arts integration; Edutopia, 2020).

The six main recommendations in *From A Nation at Risk to A Nation at Hope* are written for K–12 educators (NCSEAD, 2019). They are consistent with the Commission's K–12 focus. They also reflect the calls from the authors[1] and others to use more inclusive language to signal the need to acknowledge and support the efforts of all adults in all learning settings to ensure the success of all learners:

1. Set a clear vision that broadens the definition of student success to prioritize the whole child.
2. Transform learning settings so they are safe and supportive for all young people.
3. Change instruction to teach students' social, emotional, and cognitive skills; embed these skills in academics and schoolwide practices.
4. Build adult expertise in child development.
5. Align resources and leverage partners in the community to address the whole child.

---

[1] Three of the chapter authors (Pittman, Osher, and Smith) were formally involved in the full two years of NCSEAD deliberations and supported by our organizational colleagues.

6.   Forge closer connections between research and practice by shifting the paradigm for how research gets done.

The Commission's theory of action describing the practice base for how learning happens is a visual demonstration of this commitment. It shifts the framing from learning content to learning context and, concomitantly, shifts the burden of success from students and families to adults. It explicitly suggests that student outcomes are the result of student experiences in and outside of classrooms, and that those experiences, in turn, are shaped by the quality of the learning environment, starting with strong relationships. The implications of these shifts in directionality and language are not fully realized in the Commission's more detailed recommendations and examples. That said, the specific language from the report (NCSEAD, 2019) is worth noting:

*   **Learning Settings.** Learning and development are influenced by the familial, community, and societal contexts in which students grow. Learning systems that support young people's comprehensive growth often focus on three essential elements (safe and relationship-based learning environments; teaching and practicing, social, emotional, and cognitive skills; and embedding social, emotional, and cognitive skills into academic learning).
*   **Student Experience.** These settings lead to learning experiences where young people are more likely to be engaged and grasp academic content (sense of belonging and connection to community; engagement, ownership, and purpose; rigorous academic content and learning experiences).
*   **Student Outcomes.** The evidence shows that students who experience these learning settings are more likely to achieve success both now and, in the future, (academic success and educational attainment, civic and community engagement, work and career success, life well-being; NCSEAD, 2019).

In the final year of the Commission, these intentional shifts were reinforced by the creation of an ad hoc Youth Development Working Group led by Karen Pittman and staffed by the Forum for Youth Investment. Ms. Pittman was also co-chair of the Outreach and Engagement Committee responsible for creating a partner engagement strategy. This provided a structured way for youth development organizations to organize their feedback and, more importantly, co-author, *Building Partnerships to Support Where, When and How Learning Happens* (NCSEAD, 2018), the last formal issue brief published by the Commission, which informed the final report.

Formal opportunities to grow the seeds planted by the Commission into K–12 system support for the kind of community-level learning and development ecosystems long-promoted by the Forum, envisioned by the Working Group, and described by Akiva, Hecht and Blyth (Chapter 2 in this volume) were severely limited by the fact that there was no orchestrated pushout strategy for the recommendations. The

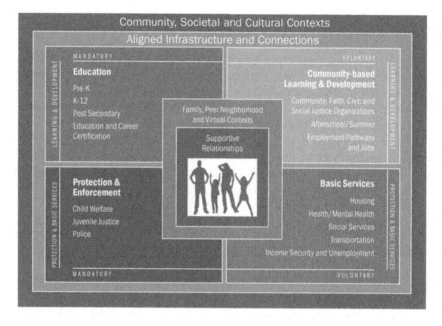

FIGURE 3.1. Ecosystems for Youth Belonging, Opportunity, and Success. Reprinted from The Readiness Projects by the Readiness Projects, 2020a. Copyright 2020 by the Forum for Youth Investment.

Commission members general receptivity to the suggestions of the Working Group reinforced the need to not only call for stronger partnerships between schools and community organizations, but to also continue to also help K–12 leaders understand and appreciate the intentional differences between the two complementary systems that support these important learning and development settings.

Thanks to continued support from the Wallace and S.D. Bechtel Jr. Foundation, the Forum, the National Urban League, and the American Institutes for Research were able to continue to craft and staff these important cross-system discussions as a goal of The Readiness Projects. The Readiness Projects supports youth thriving by upending inequities, embracing science-informed strategies, and accelerating progress of existing initiatives. As part of this effort, we introduced a series of visuals. The first sorts the systems and organizations that young people come in contact with along two dimensions: participation (voluntary vs. mandatory) and focus (learning and development vs. basic services and protections; Readiness Projects, 2020a; Figure 3.1). We had three goals for this framing:

1. Visually name and connect the broader set of systems and organizations that support learning and development ecosystem (the top two quadrants).

2. Intentionally call out the fact that there are multiple "systems" that support families and youth by providing voluntary, interest- or culture-driven learning and development opportunities.

3. Remind ourselves that young people and families that rely on public services to meet their basic needs and/or have found themselves forcibly involved with child welfare, juvenile justice, or law enforcement systems are frequently ill-served by and sometimes formally disconnected from learning and development systems—formal and voluntary.

The second visual zooms in on the community quadrant, further delineating those community-based programs in the "learning and development" space (Figure 3.2). While all these programs are primarily focused on learning and development (the top row) a number include broader goals as well (e.g., prevention, re-engagement, social justice, etc.). Many are also seen as focusing primarily on children and youth (left column) while others (on the right) are for the more gen-

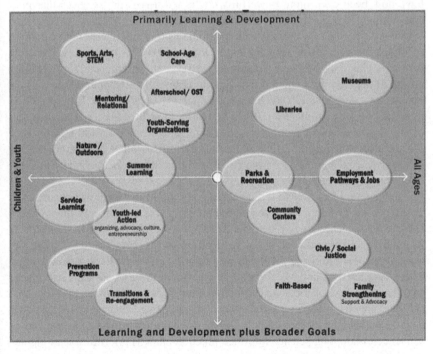

FIGURE 3.2. Community Programs Across Dimensions of Focus and Age. Reprinted from *The Places and Spaces for "Community" Learning and Development*, part of the Equitable Ecosystems for Youth and Young Adults Idea Exploration Series, 2021. Copyright 2021 by the Forum for Youth Investment. Source: SoLD Alliance, 2020b

eral public and/or for children, youth, AND their families. Not fully captured in these quadrants are those community-based nonprofits that are intentional bridges into the other learning quadrant, providing staff and staff training making school recess and playtime an opportunity for intentional building of social and emotional skills; coordinating support services; bringing trained mentors, tutors, and success coaches into the building to work with staff and students; coordinating interest-driven, hands-on learning opportunities on and off-campus that complement classroom instruction.

LINKING LEARNING AND DEVELOPMENT ADVANCES MORE SPECIFICALLY TO EQUITABLE ECOSYSTEM GOALS

"Learning happens everywhere." "Learning takes place twenty-four hours a day and seven days a week." Statements like these have always had a place in positive youth development literature. They are, in many ways, the field's raison d'etre. Youth development researchers and practitioners have long embraced the ideas of life-long and life-wide learning (e.g., Banks et al., 2007), reinforcing ideas that have now been even more powerfully confirmed across the sciences that push conventional ideas not only about where and when learning happens, but also how learning happens and what the goals and domains of learning are (Figure 3.3).

Thanks to decades of work by organizations like the Collaborative for Academic, Social, and Emotional Learning (CASEL), the intentional, high visibility efforts of the Commission, and the ongoing efforts of collaboratives such as the Science of Learning and Development (SoLD) Alliance and the Building Equitable Learning Environments (BELE) Network, these broader conceptualizations of learning and development are at the center of education reform efforts. They are not just in the preambles. Tight summaries of the science of learning and development are being used to drive policy and practice implications into the core of education reform proposals.

The general ideas behind these neuroscience informed findings are consistent positive youth development research and practice. To date, however, the most visible summaries and policy recommendations using these findings have been produced by foundation funded initiatives focused on K–12 reform (e.g., NCSEAD, SoLD Alliance) or broader public system reform (e.g., National Academy of Sciences, Engineering, and Medicine). The Readiness Projects co-leads saw a need to create a review of the science findings that 1) defined and focused on youth thriving, not on a particular system-linked outcome (e.g., educational attainment), 2) positioned equity at the center of the equation, rather than as an assumed consequence of adopting science informed practices, and 3) prioritized learning and development as a transformative process rather than a series of mastery hurdles.

Figure 3.4 shows six actions that all system leaders—including those in OST and youth development—need to make to ensure that they are optimizing their interactions with youth to support thriving, rather than specific content mastery or behavior changes as the end goal. These actions are derived from the Readi-

The science of learning and development offers a series of integrated findings regarding how children learn and develop and what we can and must do to help all young people thrive. These findings are greatly significant for the education of all children, and they are particularly drivers of equity in that they dispel false myths and biases that have long held us back and illuminate approaches to have the greatest positive impact on young people who are most marginalized and least served by our current systems. Together, these findings call for a transformation in our education and other family- and youth-serving systems. For example:

- *The science affirms* that every young person has incredible **potential**—billions of neurological pathways to success – including both the ability to master an array of critical knowledge and skills *and* numerous areas of specific talent and interest in which they can excel. Further, the science proves that every young person's brain is highly **malleable** and resilient throughout their lives—particularly in early childhood and adolescence, but also at every point in between. …
- *The science establishes* that **context**—the **environments, experiences, cultures, and (particularly) relationships** that young people experience – is far and away the most significant variable that determines each person's trajectory in learning and life. … Adversity, both individual and collective, can have profound effects on children and youth. But we can and must design learning environments and create conditions and supports that build strong relationships, overcome the effects of adversity, and maximize each child's developmental range to help each and every young person thrive, including in response to current crises.
- *The science shows* that each young person is **unique and individual** based on their singular lived experience and genetic expression. While each young person learns and develops on a **continuum**, building on what came before, the brain is a complex web, and the learning journey is jagged and nonlinear – more like moving up a climbing wall than a ladder. There is no such thing as an average or "normal" learner. Every child learns differently, and all learning is variable. …
- *The science shows* that learning and development are deeply **integrated** in terms of social, emotional, cognitive, and academic development. These are not separate or in conflict but rather are mutually reinforcing. It is this kind of integrated learning that builds new, increasingly complex neural connections in the brain and demands that education be both a learning and development enterprise by design. The science explains how people learn by continuously **making meaning** – connecting new information and experiences to their prior knowledge, cultures, and contexts. This is how new, deeper understandings and ideas are born, particularly in adolescence, when young people's identities are ripening.

Source: SoLD Alliance (2020b)

FIGURE 3.3.   Integrated Findings from Science of Learning and Development. Quoted with permission from *Federal Education Policy Recommendations from the SoLD Alliance,* Science of Learning and Development Alliance. (2020).

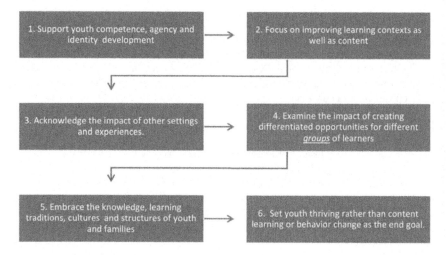

FIGURE 3.4.   Six Actions Towards Creating Equitable Opportunities for Thriving Youth

ness Projects foundational research synthesis paper, *Thriving, Robust Equity, and Transformative Learning & Development: A More Powerful Conceptualization of the Contributors to Youth Success* (Osher et al., 2020). They have been used in presentations on the Readiness Projects "formula for youth success" (Pittman, 2021). Pittman selected these actions for three reasons. Each has *implications for equity* (because of the disproportionate impact the status quo has on marginalized groups), *implications for OST leaders* (because they speak to existing capacities and acknowledged commitments), and *general relevance for advancing ecosystem thinking* (because they are not only relevant but in use in multiple systems).[2]

Support Youth Competence, Agency, and Identity Development

Knowledge, skill, and competency development are an important part learning and development. But, as noted, an overemphasis on cognitive skills and academic content ignores that learning is holistic and integrated across several dimensions, including social, emotional, cognitive, spiritual, aesthetic, kinesthetic, and expressive. All these dimensions must be considered for youth to make meaning out information and experiences. When the system, rather than the young person or the community, defines the topics, selects the content, and prescribes the application opportunities, a young person's motivation for knowledge and skill

---

[2] Each proposed action, although not with these explicit headings, is documented in recent paper that several of the authors contributed to (e.g., Osher et al., 2020). Citations of some additional sources are included as well.

acquisition can become more external than internal. Knowledge and competency development should be in service to young people's quest for agency and identity—the other key contributors to youth success. Prioritization of competency development, in the absence of a clear commitment to the development of agency and identity, is particularly detrimental to young people of color who, because of more frequent exposure to non-supportive contexts and adults, have to work harder to achieve these assets (Ginwright, 2016; Nagaoka, et al., 2015).

Focus on Improving Learning Contexts as Well as Content

Traditional approaches to improving learning often stress the importance of learning content. But access to high-quality learning content is not enough; the learning environment itself must be high-quality and address the young people as whole learners. The science of learning and development outlines five essential practice components for whole child design that characterize high-quality learning environments for young people (Darling-Hammond et al., 2019). These essential practice components include: 1) positive developmental relationships; 2) environments filled with safety and belonging; 3) rich learning experiences; 4) development of knowledge, skills, habits, and mindsets; and 5) integrated support systems (discussed in more detail later in this chapter).

These five practice components are context non-negotiables, and they are consistent with the characteristics of developmental contexts summarized by the National Research Council and Institute of Medicine (2002) and the practice standards for youth development programs that have been codified into the Youth Program Quality Pyramid widely used by afterschool and youth development programs (Smith et al., 2012).

Acknowledge the Impact of Other Settings, Experiences,
Opportunities, and Adversities

Standard approaches to learning are often narrow, and frequently focused on academic content, extrinsic motivation, and remediation. Humans learn and develop in all settings, with all adults, across their life span—not just (or even primarily) in schools, with teachers, or in their school age years. Young people may interact with many people throughout any given day—family, teachers, coaches, afterschool professionals, childcare staff, support staff, volunteers, and more. Learning is both individual and social; young people learn alone but also with peers. Each experience a young person has offers the potential for learning and development—including those that happen in nonformal learning settings (Cantor et al., 2021).

Informal learning settings, including OST, sports teams, religious youth groups and others provide young people with opportunities for social exploration, personal discovery, and experimentation that are not always possible in the formal classroom setting (Cantor et al., 2021). Young people's experiences, opportunities, and adversities in other settings impact how they learn in school. Those experiences influence a young person's thoughts, feelings, behaviors, and attainments in any learning setting (Cantor et al., 2021). Inequitable opportunities based on race, ethnicity, gender, religion, community, access, etc., impact a young person's ability to learn, develop, and thrive (Cantor et al, 2021). Inequitable experiences also impact a young person's feelings and beliefs about themselves as a learner and community member.

Examine the Impact of Creating Differentiated Learning Opportunities for Different Groups of Learners

When learning is seen as linear and potential is considered fixed, young people are often grouped in ways that limit growth and engagement. The current PreK–12 model often selects, sorts, and segregates young people into specified groups (e.g., students with disabilities, English language learners, gifted and talented learners, students with behavioral challenges) and adjusts learning approaches and the rigor, breadth, and pacing of learning content even when these students are in the same building. Although adults may have good intentions behind sorting young people into groups, such as leveling the playing field or making youth feel included, these specified groupings, at best, are designed to expedite the use of specific resources (e.g., specialized teachers and equipment) to advance a narrow set of outcomes, usually academic. But this sorting and segregation of young people can also perpetuate institutionalized racism, classism, and segregation (Cantor et al., 2021). Additionally, sorting or grouping young people is not the same as attending to the individual learner.

Embrace the Knowledge, Learning Traditions, Cultures, and Structures of Youth and Families

Traditional approaches to learning do not leverage the cultural resources of communities, ecological resources of environments, and the funds of knowledge that youth develop through self-directed, peer-directed, and family and community facilitated opportunities to learn. Young people are situated in families and communities with histories that shape learning and development. Learning environments should be culturally responsive and attend to intersectionality and to intersectional identities of young people, their families, and communities.

Set Youth Thriving Rather than Learning as the End Goal

Limited definitions of learning do not address or under address two other factors that are interrelated with learning—thriving and robust equity. Thriving, robust equity, and learning and development should be linked in thinking and practice. When we provide equitable opportunities for transformative learning and development, young people can thrive and succeed. Research on teen brains, such as the studies led by Mary Helen Immordino-Yang (2020) explain why. Transformative learning and development approaches rationalize skill-building and knowledge acquisition not for credentialing, but for meaning making. The goal is to help learners equip themselves, individually and collectively, with the skills and knowledge they need to analyze their contexts, build their identities, and develop a strong sense of individual and collective agency. When young people from communities marginalized because of race, color, income, citizenship, or ability are encouraged to reflect on information and ideas that are relevant to their lives, they not only become more engaged, but their brains also become more active, creating more complex neural networks. Setting thriving, rather than academic learning, as the end goal creates space and pressure to develop alternative indicator systems for progress and mastery that acknowledge the dimensions of thriving, and focus on longitudinal outcomes, rather than one moment in time (Cantor et al., 2021).

ADVANCING SOCIAL AND EMOTIONAL LEARNING AS CRITICAL TO THE DEVELOPMENT OF COMPETENCE, IDENTITY, AND AGENCY

One of the most successful efforts to expand narrow definitions of learning that has clear relevance for OST is the social and emotional learning (SEL) movement. In a recently updated definition, CASEL defines social emotional learning as follows:

> Social emotional learning (SEL) is an integral part of education and human development. SEL is the process through which all young people and adults acquire and apply the knowledge, skills, and attitudes to develop healthy identities, manage emotions and achieve personal and collective goals, feel and show empathy for others, establish and maintain supportive relationships, and make responsible and caring decisions (CASEL, 2020).

CASEL was established in 1994 to advance the notion that more holistic, strengths-based approaches to schooling could benefit students of *all* backgrounds. CASEL was also intended to bring some coherence to overlapping subfields such as prevention science, character education, school-based mental health, health education, and positive youth development.

Much of the current impetus for the social emotional learning movement was spawned by several meta-analyses that helped to synthesize the available research and establish an evidence base that has been pivotal to CASEL's field building efforts (e.g., Durlak et al., 2011; Taylor et al., 2017). These analyses revealed that, across hundreds of experimental studies, well-implemented, classroom based SEL programs significantly reduced problem behaviors and attitudes and increased social, emotional, and academic competence development among participating children and youth. The positive impact of these programs on standardized test scores and other academic outcomes was essential to the uptake and expansion of commitments to social emotional learning in states and districts across the country. CASEL is currently a field leader in advancing social emotional learning research, practice, and policy (Tyton Partners, 2020) and is generally credited with its increasing prominence in PreK–12 education.[3]

The positioning of social, emotional, and cognitive development as a driver of human learning and development has been greatly facilitated by recent efforts such as the NCSEAD and SoLD Alliance. As with CASEL, these efforts have PreK–12 system leaders as their primary audience. The broadened discourse about how learning happens, and more specifically, how it relates to SEL, have sparked calls for greater explanation of 1) how and how well SEL approaches are used in OST programming, 2) whether SEL approaches (especially those used in K–12) are working equally well for all learners, especially Black and Brown learners, and 3) how SEL contributes to broader goals related to youth success (e.g., identity, agency, broader competencies). Note that in the sections that follow we use the acronym SEL to be consistent with most of the studies and reports being referenced. Frequently, these studies are referring to the use of specific SEL frames, competency definitions, or curricula.

SEL and OST

In the OST field, CASEL is known for the meta-analysis of afterschool programs (Durlak et al., 2010). Durlak and colleagues (2010) examined afterschool programs that focus on enhancing the personal and social skills of children and youth. The researchers found that, compared to control groups, participants made significant gains in their self-perceptions and bonding to school, positive social behaviors, school grades and academic achievement, as well as reductions in problem behaviors (Durlak et al., 2010). The researchers then identified four recommended practices indicative of effective skill training that moderate several outcomes: successful program activities that enhance personal and social skills should be sequenced, active, focused, and explicit. These results from the meta-analysis helped the OST field better understand the critical connection between the quality of program and practice and skill or outcome development. The results also helped the OST field embrace SEL as an intentional practice (Moroney & Young, 2019).

---

[3] CASEL has developed and offered technical assistance and coaching models and a range of tools (e.g., a framework, theories of action for states, districts and schools) and resources (e.g., district and school guides, program guide and assessment guide) to support high-quality implementation of systemic SEL. Our theory of action advises districts and schools to 1) engage local stakeholders (educators, families, and students) in a visioning and planning process, 2) support adult SEL, 3) select and implement an appropriate student SEL program/approach and 4) employ continuous improvement throughout this process. We advocate for systemic SEL (Mahoney et al., 2020) which implies coordination among leaders and units (e.g., SEL, teaching and learning, research, and evaluation) at each level (state, district, and school) as well as alignment and synchrony across these levels. CASEL has established and maintained state and district collaboratives as learning communities to determine the utility of these tools and resources.

In 2014, the Susan Crown Exchange, a national foundation, and the Forum for Youth Investment's David P. Weikart Center for Youth Program Quality set out to determine how OST programs throughout the country could be more intentional about providing social and emotional skill development through the SEL Challenge. The SEL Challenge was designed to identify promising practices for building skills in six areas: emotion management, empathy, teamwork, initiative, responsibility, and problem solving. The SEL Challenge elevated promising practices to "standards" that met three criteria: they 1) appeared across exemplary programs, 2) were described as important by practitioners, and 3) were supported in the evidence base. The SEL Challenge produced 32 standards for practice and 58 practice indicators in the six SEL domains. Each standard consists of both adult practices (e.g., modelling appropriate use of emotion) as well as program structures that adults put into place (e.g., recruitment policy) to create youth experiences that leads to the development of resilience, identity, and a sense of agency.

The results of the SEL Challenge revealed that regardless of whether young people were building boats or writing a musical, with the right adult practices that promote quality learning environments, young people develop social and emotional skills, and these practices can be replicated at any program. Statistically significant skill growth was observed in all six SEL domains, with the group of students who started with the weakest skills (bottom third) experiencing the greatest skill growth (Smith et al., 2016). These findings validate the efficacy of the embedded practices versus explicit curricula approaches to SEL skill building that stands out as one of the primary differences between the professional development commitments made by OST and school systems. Moving forward, this difference will hopefully be less of an obstacle to system-level school-OST partnerships as school districts are seeing the adoption of system-wide curricula as only a starting point for widespread implementation.

The SEL Challenge served as a launchpad for conversations and actions that helped OST programs focus on SEL, assess their performance, and improve over multiple program cycles. The hope is that OST systems already working on creating quality learning environments will incorporate these standards of SEL practices into their definition of high-quality services and use their existing quality improvement systems to build SEL capacity.

SEL and Equity

In recent years, calls for greater attention to issues of equity have become more pronounced. These calls have been given greater resonance in the context of the dual crises of a pandemic and state violence which lay bare persistent health, economic, and social inequities that disproportionately affect Black people. Documentation of concerns, however, predates the dual pandemics (Educational Trust, 2020).

As the field of SEL has grown, concerned scholars, caregivers, community stakeholders, and policymakers have appropriately raised questions about how to ensure that SEL is communicated and implemented with the intended asset-based frame that affirms the strengths, values, cultures, and lived experiences of students from diverse backgrounds (e.g., Hoffman, 2009). Miscommunication or poor implementation will lead / has already begun to lead to a misperception of SEL as a way to "fix" the behaviors or attitudes of poor or Black/Brown children or as a means to offer even greater social and economic advantages to those in well-resourced schools and communities.

The roots of many of the concerns about the appropriateness of many current SEL programs for students of color can be traced to the fact that most of the more prominent SEL programs do not explicitly address the development of identity, agency and belonging (Jagers, 2016; Jagers et al., 2018). Additionally, most frameworks for the development of social and emotional competence do not address matters that relate to addressing privilege, bias, and cultural competence (Berg et al., 2017; Berg et al., 2019). The SEL field is built largely on accumulated evidence from randomized control trials of classroom-based programs which reinforce narrow definitions of learning. Additionally, schools and youth development programs have a long tradition of acculturating young people, and SEL has been part of this tradition.

This summary of the field's origins speaks directly to educational equity advocates' concerns. Without explicit commitments to the transformation, personalization, empowerment, and cultural affirmation of poor students and students of color, SEL programs, especially those implemented in schools, can be promoted as a way to help school districts claim technical learning victories (e.g., reduce discipline problems and report attendance, achievement, and attainment gains) while doing little to promote the competence, identity, and agency development of marginalized students.

It is noteworthy that CASEL directly addresses these concerns in the second part of their revised definition:

> SEL advances educational equity and excellence through authentic school-family-community partnerships to establish learning environments and experiences that feature trusting and collaborative relationships, rigorous and meaningful curriculum and instruction, and ongoing evaluation. SEL can help address various forms of inequity and empower young people and adults to co-create thriving schools and contribute to safe, healthy, and just communities (CASEL, 2020).

In order for SEL to adequately serve those from underserved communities—and promote the optimal developmental outcomes for all children, youth, and adults—it must cultivate in them the portable knowledge, attitudes, and skills required for critically examining and taking collaborative action to address root causes of inequities. This goal—SEL as a springboard to agency, critical analysis, and action—is not just a stretch for schools. There is a subset of youth serving organizations that explicitly focus on youth governance, organizing, action, leadership, and youth service. These organizations, however, are not always explicitly included in local OST networks and these activities are not always prioritized by more traditional OST providers, even those who work with adolescents.

SEL, Identity and Agency

CASEL has introduced the concept of *transformative SEL* to better articulate the potential of SEL to mitigate the educational, social, and economic inequities that derive from the legacy of racialized cultural oppression in the U.S. and globally. Transformative SEL represents an as-yet underutilized approach that SEL researchers and practitioners can use if they seek to effectively address issues such as power, privilege, prejudice, discrimination, social justice, empowerment, and self-determination. This conceptualization of transformative SEL addresses CASEL's five key social and emotional competencies with an equity lens. It operationalizes identity, agency, belonging, and engagement as "transformative expressions" of the five competencies (self-awareness, self-management, social awareness, relationship skills, and responsible decision-making; Jagers et al., 2018). The five social and emotional competencies represent large categories or conceptual buckets for organizing a range of intra- and interpersonal knowledge, skills, and abilities (Weissberg et al., 2015). CASEL views these competencies as interrelated, synergistic, and integral to the growth and development of justice-oriented, global citizens.[4]

This broader, bolder goal—skill building for critical analysis and collaborative action—is an updated and strengthened version of goals implied in the definition of positive youth development (PYD) used by the Interagency Working Group on Youth Programs, a collaboration of 21 federal departments and agencies that support youth:

> PYD is an intentional, prosocial approach that engages youth within their communities, schools, organizations, peer groups, and families in a manner that is productive and constructive; recognizes, utilizes, and enhances young people's strengths; and promotes positive outcomes for young people by providing opportunities, fostering positive relationships, and furnishing the support needed to build on their leadership strengths (Youth.gov, n.d.).

ESTABLISHING UNIVERSAL PRACTICE PRINCIPLES THAT SUPPORT LEARNING, DEVELOPMENT AND THRIVING IN ALL SYSTEMS AND SETTINGS

As noted, the centrality of the role of adults, especially those with defined roles related to supporting roles related to learning and development, is evident in sev-

---

[4] Since the CASEL framework for systemic SEL includes engaged citizenship as a long-term developmental outcome, they found it useful to construe SEL as part of a civic socialization process. CASEL researchers considered citizenship typologies (Banks, 2017; Westheimer & Kahne, 2004) and proposed three forms of SEL: personally responsible, participatory, or transformative SEL.

eral major reports and research summaries produced in the past two years (Cantor et al., 2019; Darling-Hammond et al., 2019; NCSEAD, 2019; Osher et al., 2019).

Of particular note is the push, led by several members of the SoLD Alliance, to use convergent science findings about how learning happens to link traditional calls for professional development, autonomy, and greater resource supports for educators to research-based, practice-affirmed definitions of what optimal learning settings look like. The "blue wheel," as it is affectionately known, draws directly from the Darling-Hammond et al. (2019) article on the practical implications of the science of learning and development. It has been used extensively with PreK–12 and youth development audiences and vetted formally by two advisory groups brought together to create design principles for K–12 and youth development practitioners (Figure 3.5).

Taken alone, none of the five foundational practice components is new or unique to either K–12 education or OST systems. OST and youth development practitioners and organizations have always emphasized relationships, safety, and belonging. They have always worked to create learning experiences that match youth interests and help them build skills and habits, and worked to affirm, if not meet, youth and family needs for services. Schools have prioritized the provision of rich learning experiences that result in knowledge acquisition and skill mastery, have worked to create safe, supportive school climates and

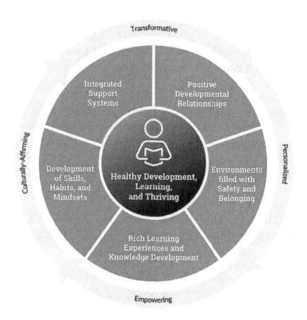

FIGURE 3.5.   Guiding Principles for Equitable Whole-Child Design.
Reprinted from *Guiding Principles of Whole Child Design* by SoLD Alliance. Copyright 2021 by SoLD Alliance.

ensure that extra supports, such as academic, behavioral, and basic services, are available for young people who need them, and, as noted, become increasingly committed to SEL.

What is new and compelling about this visual presentation is the idea that foundational practice components *are non-negotiable*. Because all aspects of learning and development are highly integrated and linked to the broader goal of thriving, ignoring one of these components leads to almost certain reductions in the effectiveness of other efforts.

The "blue wheel" is a visual affirmation of the University Chicago Consortium quote used at the beginning of the chapter. Not only does it communicate why *"adults will make little headway if they target only one particular component or subcomponent in isolation"* (Nagaoka et al., 2015, p. 7). It also explains why communities need to ensure that *"young people have access to a multitude of rich developmental experiences is imperative to their success"* (Nagaoka et al., 2015, p. 7). Adults in any setting who are charged with co-creating learning experiences need to attend to each of the foundational practice components to make sure they are not doing harm and to strive to provide basic levels of support. However, no setting, or even clustering of settings, will likely be able to prioritize all the elements equally.

- Some will lead with rich instructional experiences and knowledge, habit and skill mastery (e.g., performing arts or STEM programs), others with relationships and belonging (e.g., mentor programs, advisories, social and cultural clubs), others with integrated services (e.g., prevention, reconnection and recovery programs).
- Some will recruit by age, some by interest, some by geography, and some by identity. Some will have youth assigned. Some will recruit staff and volunteers from the communities or cultures represented by their participants, while others will rely heavily on adults who bring specific content or service expertise but have different demographic backgrounds.
- Some will be housed within larger organizations and systems that support these "blue wheel" foundational practice components by having administrative policies and practices in place that emphasize and create space and resources for adults to create personalized, empowering, transformational and cultural-affirming experiences for young people (the criteria in the outer ring of the wheel). Some will be housed within organizations and systems bound by accountability requirements that run counter to these goals. Staff who want to adopt these goals may not only have to finance their own professional development but decide to implement these practices at their own risk.

The integrated science findings from the SoLD Alliance affirm the significance of context—the environments, experiences, cultures, and relationships that young people experience—and affirms that while every young person is unique and individual, every young person has incredible potential that can be revealed and achieved in supportive contexts. These concepts can be very roughly applied to structured settings where youth and adults come together to co-create learning experiences.

Each setting is individual and unique, the result of combining the histories and characteristics of the adults with those of the young people, tempered by the constraints, opportunities, expectations, resources, structures, and histories of the place, organization or system that houses it. Although the risks and supports associated with doing so vary, the adults in each setting have the potential to optimize learning and development by using the blue wheel components as guideposts against which to assess risks and leverage combined assets of the adults, the youth, and the setting/system.

The need for greater emphasis on the adults and the settings within schools was affirmed by CASEL in a recent report that shed light on the various ways in which some of their collaborating districts were addressing issues of equity in their own contexts (Schlund et al., 2020). CASEL also engaged in a landscape scan to discern how best to have the intersecting issues of equity, adult SEL, and the integration of academic social and emotional learning reflected in all aspects of its work (Jagers et al., 2018). This allowed CASEL to place greater emphasis on the role of adults in the construction of relationships and experiences that foster the desired academic, social, and emotional development of children and youth. Several collaborative projects have been undertaken to develop, test, and refine theoretical and practical assumptions with students, families, and educators in diverse school communities.

REPOSITIONING ADOLESCENCE AS A CRITICAL TIME FOR INNOVATION, INVOLVEMENT, AND INVESTMENTS

Adolescence—beginning with the onset of puberty and ending in the mid-20s—is a critical period of development during which key areas of the brain develop and mature. These changes in brain structure, function, and connectivity mark adolescence as a period of opportunity to discover new vistas, to form relationships with peers and adults, and to explore one's developing identity. It is also a period of resilience that can ameliorate childhood setbacks and set the stage for a thriving trajectory over the life course. Because adolescents comprise nearly one-fourth of the entire U.S. population, the nation needs policies and practices that will better leverage these developmental opportunities to harness the promise of adolescence—rather than focusing myopically on containing its risks (National Academies of Sciences, Engineering, and Medicine, 2019, p. 1).

Media coverage of adolescents since the abrupt school closings in 2020 demonstrate the importance of the NASEM recommendation. Early coverage played into the "adolescents as risk takers" theme, profiling stories about teens and young adults who continued to gather selfishly in defiance of social distancing recommendations. Concomitantly, early stories on the impact of school closings and the shift to virtual learning focused on elementary school students who have more obvious needs for supervision and learning support. Readiness Projects staff were some of the first to call out this coverage gap (Readiness Projects, 2020b).

As time passed, however, coverage of the extent of the disruptions to adolescents' opportunities to maintain relationships and routines, adjust to virtual learning, complete school requirements, and activate transitions to college increased (Prothero, 2020a; Rich & Saias, 2020), as did articles on mental health tolls associated with sustained disconnection (Prothero, 2020b; Rothstein, 2020).

Equally important were articles covering the hard choices older teens and young adults are having to make because of responsibilities to help support their families (Jacobsen, 2021) and the leadership roles they are taking on as they work to make meaning out of the incredible circumstances of the times (Prothero, 2020c).

MOVING FORWARD: TWO WAYS TO USE 2020 DISRUPTIONS TO ELEVATE NONFORMAL PROGRAMMING AS CRITICAL PART OF THE LEARNING AND DEVELOPMENT ECOSYSTEM

Disruption creates opportunity. COVID-19 and racial reckonings have pulled back the curtain on inequity and inefficiency, to reveal to all what has been known by many for a long time: The PreK–12 education system was not working as well as it should or as collaboratively as it could to support families with children, especially with the fewest means to adjust. 2020 disruptions also created an opportunity for community-based OST providers of nonformal learning and development activities (including afterschool and summer programs, libraries and recreation departments, and neighborhood and family support centers) to step in to not only become hot spots for virtual learning, but to demonstrate their value as relationship-based, community-oriented, interest-driven partners that are often very closely connected to young people and their families.

These efforts were noticed and documented. These efforts to go above and beyond to maintain relationships and provide supports and enrichment opportunities to youth and families were deeply appreciated given the resource challenges faced by this system that does not have the same job and resource securities as public schools. The big question, however, is whether these heroic efforts will lead to lasting change. We believe that they can, but only if the field steps forward quickly to address two challenges.

OST Challenge #1: Use 2020 Disruptions to Build Back Better

COVID-19 and racial reckonings have pulled back the curtain on inequity and inefficiency, to reveal to all what has been known by many for a long time: The PreK–12 education system was not working as well as it should or as collaboratively as it could to support families with children, especially with the fewest means to adjust.

There are clear reasons why OST programs were better suited to respond flexibly during the pandemic (Afterschool Alliance, 2020; Moroney & Newman, 2020; Pittman, 2020) and are being called into service by school and city leaders. OST programs, sheerly by nature of the fact that they are voluntary, not mandatory, can provide inclusive spaces that are safe and supportive, allow young people to create meaningful, mutually respectful relationships with each other and with adults, explore their interests, and engage in experiences that foster learning and development (Hall et al., 2003; Moroney & Young, 2019). OST programs, by design:

- **Provide Diverse, Interest-Driven Opportunities** for young people to develop and practice their skills. What those specific skills are varies, depending on the program model, content area, or organizational priorities. For example, in an arts program, young people may learn how to paint on canvas or direct a music video, while young people in a STEM program learn how to write code or design video games.
- **Help Young People Not Only Develop Skills but Transfer Them to Other Settings, Such as School, Home, or Work.** OST practitioners also often recognize that young people are whole people and meeting the whole young person's needs requires partnerships with schools and other community resources. Young people bring with them both the positive and negative experiences not only to the school day but to other settings as well. OST programs can provide a refuge to young people who have negative experiences at school, home, or in other settings by providing them with a place to belong and explore their interests and develop new skills.
- **Support Belonging and Community in Inclusive, Emotionally Safe Environments.** OST programs, because of their size and relative autonomy, can be intentionally designed to reflect the culture, context, and communities where they are situated and the intersectional identities and interests of youth who are involved (Moroney & Young, 2019).
- **Engage Families.** Family engagement, at some level, is a prerequisite for program participation because most OST programs are voluntary. The size, informality, and nature of OST programs (located in the community, staffed, or managed by familiar community organizations) also makes them less intimidating than schools for many families.

Clearly, more can be done to help OST practitioners and administrators improve the quality of OST programs and ensure their relevance and appropriateness. OST programs have been hit hard by the pandemic; a third of program providers reported their organization experienced furloughs or suspended work; 31% experienced reduced hours, and 18% experienced layoffs (Afterschool Alliance, 2020). Building back basic capacities is a challenge. As noted, however, disruption does create opportunity. OST funders in particular should protect their investments in rebuilding capacity by ensuring that practitioners and programs—especially those being rehired and reopened—receive the training, support, resources, and overall organizational time needed to:

- **Provide More Intentional Opportunities for Young People to Learn Portable and Adaptable Social, Emotional, and Cognitive Competencies** to address life's continually evolving demands, multiple social contexts, and to work with other to address the individual and collective problem that their communities and the world face including the causes and impacts of prejudice, privilege, and inequity. Documented approaches with tested staff trainings, supports, and practice examples include not only SEL, but character education, prosocial education, emotional intelligence, 21st Century Learning, life skills, and positive youth development (Berg et al., 2017; Elias et al., 2019; Kidron & Osher, 2012; Osher et al., 2016; Smith et al., 2016).

- **Understand and Safely Solicit Information on What Young People are Experiencing and Learning Across Multiple Settings,** so that they are better able to help them overcome obstacles and leverage potentially unrecognized opportunities to learn, develop, and thrive. OST practitioners, because of the breadth and flexibility of the relationships they can build with youth and families, have opportunities to build on young people's strengths while addressing their needs. The challenge for OST practitioners is often how to set safe boundaries: how to ally with a young person who is facing adversity, while also trying to improve that situation with the young person within the limits of what they (as staff) and the program (as a part of an organization) can do safely.

- **Work With Families and Communities to Co-Construct Programs That Reflect Cultures and Funds of Knowledge.** This requires OST practitioners to actively engage families not only in their children's participation in the program, but in their children's learning opportunities (Rosenberg et al., 2017). For example, OST practitioners may provide opportunities for families to attend program sessions and participate in their young person's learning, solicit feedback from families at multiple points during the program, or share information with families about their young people's learning (Rosenberg et al., 2017).

- **Create Identity-Affirming Environments.** Organizations and OST systems need to invest in professional development trainings and tools to build and assess OST practitioners' social and emotional competencies to ensure programs are reflective of culture, contextually rich, and have developmental intentionality or fit (Moroney & Young, 2019). Organizations need to do more to recruit and retain OST practitioners who are committed to thriving and robust equity, and who reflect the communities and cultures, and have experience supporting the interests and needs of young people in the programs (Moroney & Young, 2019).

- **Co-Create Authentic Opportunities for Youth to Practice Leadership and Agency and Co-Create Knowledge.** Most OST programs, unless they are specifically designed to work with older adolescents, see steady declines in participation in the teen years. Creating opportunities for youth to authentically exercise their voice and choice on issues that are of deep importance to them in their programs, in their schools, and in their communities requires staff who to have different skills and approaches (Moroney & Young, 2019). This is especially true when adults are working to co-create spaces for young people from marginalized communities to become active participants in the change processes. This requires more than acknowledgment of injustices. Staff need to be prepared to support a critical examination of the oppressive forces and the knowledge-power-privilege nexus that systematically works against marginalized communities, especially for our Brown, Black, and Indigenous young people. Empowering youth with critical cognitive skills to decolonize their minds—recognize that nothing is inherently wrong with them—so that they can challenge existing socio-political and historical structures that control them, means empowering youth to take actions that may make some staff, administrators, and funders uncomfortable.

OST CHALLENGE #2: BUILD FORWARD TOGETHER: CHAMPION SUPPORT FOR ADULTS ACROSS THE LEARNING & DEVELOPMENT ECOSYSTEMS AS A WAY TO UPEND INEQUITY

There is broad agreement that the 20th century model of schools is outdated and damaging, especially to marginalized populations that do not "fit the mold" and, equally important, that this model was not designed for equity. The factory-based model of schools combined with a standard-based model of assessment, categorizes young people as products of varying quality and tracks them accordingly. The system was not designed to maximize potential, but to maintain status quo, leading to the reproduction, reinforcement, and extension of existing oppressive structures such as racism and classism. Leading with this fact accelerates calls for wholesale education system transformation, not just innovative school reforms:

> The establishment of American schools meant the devaluing of the forms of education [indigenous and racially marginalized people] were experiencing in their own communities, tribes, from their elders and passed down from their ancestors. ... Liberatory education must therefore begin with schools giving up their power and returning the control of education back to the communities who have been disenfranchised (Vossoughi & Tintiangco-Cubales, 2020, p. 1).

There is broad recognition that high-quality OST programs feature many of the elements highlighted by the science of learning and development, such as supportive relationships that foster motivation and competence, opportunities for social and emotional learning, cultural competence and responsiveness, equity, connections to family and community, and identity-safe environments (Moroney & Young, 2019). Strategies to braid public and private funding to scale and sustain affordable OST programs have contributed to the growth of local and state OST networks and systems.

Researchers and advocates, however, highlight the need to increase quantity *and* quality. Low income, Black and Brown youth not only have less access to OST programs, they are also more likely to be enrolled in OST programs that, because of an emphasis on addressing academic deficits, mirror rather than mitigate their school systems' priorities and approaches. Arguments such as those shared in the Vossoughi and Tintiangco-Cubales quote above, flag the need for OST programs to be much more intentionally aware of the broader "community learning ecosystem" of which they are a part.

Akiva, Hecht, and Blyth (Chapter 2 in this volume) argue that a healthy L&D ecosystem should support three things: 1) equitable opportunities and supports, 2) multiple contexts for learning, and 3) adult leaders. They call these diverse group of adult leaders the "keystone species" that helps the ecosystem thrive." We could not agree more. The youth fields workforce (e.g., teachers, youth and afterschool workers, librarians, camp staff)—not only works directly with youth to co-create and enrich the environments *within* the microsystem elements (e.g., schools, camps, youth organizations, employment programs, faith-based organizations). In a healthy ecosystem, however, these adults are also supported within the mesosystem—spaces outside of their individual organizations where intentional connections can be made that increase access (by addressing issues such as transportation, referrals, costs) to different learning experiences and increase the quality of experiences and consistency of expectations across contexts (through supports such as professional development, information sharing agreements).

"All learners, all adults, all settings" has become the mantra of Readiness Projects challenge to PreK–12 OST/community partners to use 2021 and 2022 to Build Forward Together (Readiness Projects, 2020c). We explicitly use the "all" language to highlight communities can only upend inequity by intentionally assessing whether *each* type of learner, adult, setting, learning approach has the resources and respect needed to succeed. The opportunity to challenge schools to assess the extent to which they are truly addressing "all" created a way to breathe new life with greater into the core "positive youth development" that have undergirded calls for "allied youth fields" for decades. SEL, SEAD, SoLD, COVID-19, and the call for explicit anti-racist commitments create concrete opportunities to push schools and, in so doing, promote a broad, new, powerful public idea that promotes educational equity as achievable through a commitment to:

- **All Systems.** There are real, concrete opportunities to get the education system to actively see itself as a part of a broader community ecosystem that includes other public systems as well as the array of "invisible" community partners.
- **All Adults.** There are real, concrete opportunities to call for sustained and more substantial investments in adults who see themselves as contributors to youth success and who, therefore, need training, supports, resources to optimize the relationships they have with youth and the experiences they

co-create. This includes, and must prioritize, but not be limited to staff in nonformal and informal learning settings

- **All Settings.** There are real, concrete opportunities to use the science findings to push beyond big descriptors that describe systems and organizations– school, youth program—to describe the settings within them (classrooms, gyms, playgrounds, cafeterias) where gathering happens with some regularity, some resources, and usually some adult supervision.
- **All Learners.** There are real, concrete opportunities to put a spotlight on adolescents as a group that is increasingly distinct from "enrolled secondary students"—who are, and need to be, engaged with multiple systems beyond PreK–12 in order to thrive and succeed.
- **All Learning Approaches.** There are real, concrete opportunities to emphasize the importance of "nonformal and informal" learning experiences for overall development of competencies and agency and identity.

Pittman and Irby (2020) have used the "blue wheel" (introduced above) to bring adults into view more visibly as learning setting optimizers. Our goal: to signal that the role of adults is not simply to implement good practice (e.g., an evidence-based curriculum) but is to execute good judgement. Doing so requires understanding that the dynamic interactions between the adults and the young people within the specific context of the learning setting are dependent upon the characteristics of the adults (professional, demographic, personal), the characteristics of the young people (demographics, accomplishments, experiences), the characteristics of the setting (resources, requirements, structure, expectations). Transparency is especially important to adolescents. A healthy learning and development ecosystem is one in which there are adults in all of the places where young people spend their time who are willing and able to name these characteristics, discuss their importance, and work with adolescents to assess challenges and optimize experiences in ways that benefit all participants.

Building back better will be a tall order for OST programs. There is an opportunity, however, to set the bar even higher. We, the authors, believe that OST leaders, even as they struggle to regain capacity, need to focus not just on building back better, but on *building forward together* (Readiness Projects, 2020d): 1) with each other (not as separate brands), 2) with other public and non-profit organizations and associations in the community that have broad learning and development goals but don't consider themselves, or are not always included as OST, and 3) with PreK–12 schools and other local education entities (e.g. community colleges, training programs).

Because of how they do their jobs, OST leaders have a more intuitive sense and, usually, a more empirical view of where and how the people, places, and possibilities they offer young people fit into the larger learning and development ecosystem. This understanding has led to competition between organizations and brands. It has led to calls to "go it alone"—to invest first in standing up OST as the "nonformal" learning and development ecosystem that is better equipped to meet young people's broader social and emotional needs. These are reasonable and valid impulses. A healthy learning and development ecosystem requires both and strategies.

CONCLUSION

OST programs and practitioners are not stifled by as many constraints as PreK–12 system leaders. Opportunity and intent do not guarantee success. And they do not automatically address inequities.

With full acknowledgement of the work that needs to be done within ranks, OST leaders can play a critical role in efforts to use recent science findings and syntheses (about learning, ecosystems, equity) to upend inequity and accelerate progress throughout the ecosystem, by documenting and advocating for the roles of nonformal and informal educators; elevating the roles of families and caregivers; and insisting on cultural responsibleness and resonance.

We believe that OST national and local leaders are not only best equipped to carry these messages but have the most to gain from galvanizing around a clear call for investments across the full spectrum of systems, settings, adults, learners, and approaches that support learning and development.

REFERENCES

Afterschool Alliance. (2020). *Afterschool Alliance COVID-19 tracking program provider survey.* http://www.afterschoolalliance.org/documents/Afterschool-COVID-19-Wave-1-Wave-2-Provider-Comparison-Toplines.pdf

Akiva, T., Delale-O'Connor, L., & Pittman, K. (2020). The promise of building equitable ecosystems for learning. *Urban Education Online First,* 1–27. doi.org/10.1177/0042085920926230

Banks, J., Au, K., Ball, A. F., Bell, P., Gordon, E., Gutierrez, K., Brice-Heath, S., Lee, C. D., Mahiri, J., Nasir, N., Valdes, G., & Zhou, M. (2007). *Learning in and out of school in diverse environments: Life-long, life-wide, life-deep.* The LIFE Center (University of Washington, Stanford University and SRI) & the Center for Multicultural Education.

Berg, J., Osher, D., Same, M., Nolan, E., Benson, D., & Jacobs, N. (2017). *Identifying, defining, and measuring social and emotional competencies.* American Institutes for Research.

Berg, J., Nolan, E., Yoder, N., Osher, D., & Mart, A. (2019). *Social-emotional competencies in context: Using social-emotional learning frameworks to build educators' understanding.* American Institute for Research.

Cantor, P., Lerner, R., Pittman, K., Chase, P., & Gomperts, N. (2021). *Whole-child development, learning, and thriving: A dynamic systems approach* (Elements in Child Development). Cambridge University Press.

Cantor, P., Osher, D., Berg, J., Steyer, L., & Rose, T. (2019). Malleability, plasticity, and individuality: How children learn and develop in context. *Applied Developmental Science, 23*(4), 307–337. https://doi.org/10.1080/10888691.2017.1398649

CASEL. (2020). *What is SEL?* https://casel.org/what-is-sel/

Darling-Hammond, L., Flook, L., Cook-Harvey, C., Barron, B., & Osher, D. (2019). Implications for educational practice of the science of learning and development. *Applied Developmental Science, 24*(2), 97–140. https://doi.org/10.1080/10888691.2018.1537791

Durlak, J. A., Weissberg, R. P., Dymnicki, A. B., Taylor, R. D., & Schellinger, K. B. (2011). The impact of enhancing students' social and emotional learning: A meta-analysis of school-based universal interventions. *Child Development, 82*, 405–432.

Durlak, J. A., Weissberg, R. P., & Pachan, M. (2010). A meta-analysis of after-school programs that seek to promote personal and social skills in children and adolescents. *American Journal of Community Psychology, 45*(3–4), 294–309.

Educational Trust. (2020). *Social, emotional, and academic development through an equity lens.* https://edtrust.org/social-emotional-and-academic-development-through-an-equity-lens/

Edutopia. (2020). *How learning happens.* https://www.edutopia.org/how-learning-happens

Elias, M. J., Brackett, M. A., Miller, R., Jones, S., Kahn, J., Mahoney, J. L., Weissberg, R. P., & Chung, S. Y. (2019). Developing social and emotional skills and attitudes and ecological assets. In D. Osher, M. J. Mayer, R. J. Jagers, K. Kendziora, & L. Wood (Eds.), *Keeping students safe and helping them thrive: A collaborative handbook on school safety, mental health, and wellness* (pp. 185–209). Praeger/ABC-CLIO.

Ginwright, S. (2016). *Hope and healing in urban education.* Taylor & Francis.

Hall, G., Yohalem, N., Toleman, J., & Wilson, A. (2003). *How afterschool programs can most effectively promote positive youth development as a support to academic achievement: A report commissioned by the Boston After-School for All Partner.* National Institute on Out-of-School Time.

Hecht, M., & Crowley, K. (2019). Unpacking the learning ecosystems framework: Lessons from the adaptive management of biological ecosystems. *Journal of the Learning Sciences, 29*(2), 264–284. doi.org/10.1080/10508406.2019.1693381

Hoffman, D. (2009). Reflecting on social emotional learning: A critical perspective on trends in the United States. *Review of Educational Research 79*(2), 533–556.

Immordino-Yang , M. H. (2020). Building meaning builds teens' brains. *Learning and the Brain, 77*(8), 36–43.

Irby, M., Little, P., & Pittman, K. (2021). *The places and spaces for "community learning and development.* Forum for Youth Investment.

Jacobsen, L. (2021). *I had no other option: Teens balance zoom classes and fast-food jobs—Sometimes at the same time—To support struggling families.* 74 Million. https://www.the74million.org/article/i-had-no-other-option-teens-balance-zoom-classes-and-fast-food-jobs-sometimes-at-the-same-time-to-support-struggling-families/

Jagers, R. J. (2016). Framing social and emotional learning among African American youth: Toward an integrity-based approach. *Human Development, 59*, 1–3.

Jagers, R., Rivas-Drake, D., & Borowski, D. (2018). *Equity & social and emotional learning: A cultural analysis.* CASEL. https://casel.org/wp-content/uploads/2020/04/equity-and-SEL-.pdf

Kidron, Y., & Osher, D. (2012). The history and direction of research about prosocial education. In P. M. Brown, A. Higgins-D'Alessandro, & M. Corrigan (Eds.), *Handbook of prosocial education* (pp. 51–70). Rowman & Littlefield.

McClellan, C., McKnight, C., Isselhardt, E., & Jeffries, J. (2018). *Rebuilding the ladder of educational opportunity.* National Network of State Teachers of the Year.

Moroney, D., Singer, J., Little, P., & Young, J. (2020). *Putting the science into practice: Community programs*. American Institutes for Research.

Moroney, D., & Young, J. (2019). *The science of learning and development in afterschool settings and systems*. American Institutes for Research.

Nagaoka, J., Farrington, C. A., Ehrlich, S. B., & Heath, R. D. (2015). *Foundations for young adult success: A developmental framework. concept paper for research and practice*. University of Chicago Consortium on Chicago School Research.

National Academies of Sciences, Engineering, and Medicine. (2019). *The promise of adolescence: Realizing opportunity for all youth*. The National Academies Press. https://doi.org/10.17226/25388

National Commission on Social, Emotional, and Academic Development. (2018). *Building partnerships in support of where, when, & how Learning happens*. Aspen Institute.

National Commission on Social, Emotional, and Academic Development. (2019). *From a nation at risk to a nation at hope*. Aspen Institute.

National Research Council and Institute of Medicine. (2002). *Community programs to promote youth development*. National Academies Press. The National Academy of Sciences Report Brief: Community Programs to Promote Youth Development (PDF) summarizes the study findings.

Osher, D., Cantor, P., Berg, J., Steyer, L., & Rose, T. (2019). Drivers of human development: How relationships and context shape learning and development. *Applied Developmental Science, 24*(1), 6–36. https://doi.org/10.1080/10888691.2017.1398650

Osher, D., Pittman, K., Young, J., Smith, H., Moroney, D., & Irby, M. (2020). *Thriving, robust equity, and transformative learning & development: A more powerful conceptualization of the contributors to youth success*. Forum for Youth Investment.

Osher, D., Yael, K., Brackett, M., Dymnicki, A., Jones, S., & Weissberg, R. P. (2016). Advancing the science and practice of social and emotional learning: Looking back and moving forward. *Review of Research in Education, 40*(1), 644–681.

Pittman, K. (2020). *What happens when out-of-school time is all the time*. Forum for Youth Investment. https://forumfyi.org/blog/what-happens-when-out-of-school-time-is-all-the-time/

Pittman, K. (2021). *Transformative learning, robust equity, youth thriving: A science-informed formula for youth success* (Keynote power point presentation deck). The Readiness Projects.

Prothero, A. (2020a). Is online learning worse than being in school? Majority of teens say yes. *Education Week*. https://www.edweek.org/leadership/is-online-learning-worse-than-being-in-school-majority-of-teens-say-yes/2020/09

Prothero, A. (2020b). Teens are growing depressed and disconnected from school, survey finds. *Education Week*. https://www.edweek.org/leadership/teens-are-growing-depressed-and-disconnected-from-school-student-survey-finds/2020/06

Prothero, A. (2020c). It's all we can talk about: High schoolers react to protests over police violence. *Education Week*. https://www.edweek.org/leadership/its-all-we-can-talk-about-high-schoolers-react-to-protests-over-police-violence/2020/06

Readiness Projects. (2020a). *The readiness projects*. Forum for Youth Investment. https://forumfyi.org/wp-content/uploads/2020/04/ReadinessProjects_About_April2020.pdf

Readiness Projects. (2020b). *Hearing and acting—Increasing the visibility of marginalized adolescents*. Forum for Youth Investment. https://medium.com/changing-the-odds/hearing-and-acting-increasing-the-visibility-of-marginalized-adolescents-ed-6ba69e38f9

Readiness Projects. (2020c). *Empowering essential adults: All adults, all settings.* Forum for Youth Investment. https://medium.com/changing-the-odds/empowering-essential-adults-all-adults-all-settings-3f6d0e0a2879

Readiness Projects. (2020d). *Build forward together.* Forum for Youth Investment. https://forumfyi.org/wp-content/uploads/2020/11/Build-Forward-Together-one-pager.pdf

Rich, E., & Saias, B. (2020). A year interrupted: 2020 high school seniors face COVID-19 and an uncertain future. *Education Week.* https://www.edweek.org/a-year-interrupted-2020-high-school-seniors-face-covid-19-and-an-uncertain-future/12/20

Rosenberg, H., Wilkes, S., & Harris, E. (2017). *Bringing families into out-of-school time learning.* Harvard University.

Rothstein, A. (2020). *COVID-19 and trauma: Mental health struggles among Black teens.* Children's Minnesota. https://www.childrensmn.org/2020/07/16/covid-19-trauma-mental-health-struggles-among-black-teens/

Schlund, J., Jagers, R., & Schlinger, M. (2020). *Emerging insights: Advancing social and emotional learning (SEL) as a lever for equity and excellence.* CASEL. https://casel.org/wp-content/uploads/2020/08/CASEL-Equity-Insights-Report.pdf

Science of Learning and Development Alliance. (2020). *Federal education policy recommendations from the SoLD alliance.* https://www.soldalliance.org/post/federal-education-policy-recommendations-from-the-sold-alliance

Smith, C., Akiva, T., Sugar, S. A., Lo, Y. J., Frank, K. A., Peck, S. C., Cortina, K. S., & Devaney, T. (2012). *Continuous quality improvement in afterschool settings: Impact findings from the Youth Program Quality Intervention study.* Forum for Youth Investment.

Smith, C., McGovern, G., Peck, S. C., Larson, R., Hillaker, B., & Roy, L. (2016). Preparing youth to thrive: Methodology and findings from the social and emotional learning challenge. In *Forum for youth investment.* Forum for Youth Investment.

Taylor, R. D., Oberle, E., Durlak, J. A., & Weissberg, R. P. (2017). Promoting positive youth development through school-based social and emotional learning interventions: A meta-analysis of follow-up effects. *Child Development, 88*(4), 1156–1171.

Tyton Partners. (2020). *Time for class: COVID-19 edition.* https://tytonpartners.com/wp-content/uploads/2020/10/10.05.2020.Time-for-Class-COVID-19-Part-2-Planning-for-Fall-Like-No-Other-V2.pdf

Vossoughi, S., & Tintiangco-Cubales, A. (2020). Radically transforming the world: Re-purposing education & designing for collective learning & well-being. *Equitable Learning & Development Project, Framework for Liberatory Education: First Installment.* University of Chicago Consortium on School Research, CASEL, and the National Equity Project.

Weissberg, R. P., Durlak, J. A., Domitrovich, C. E., & Gullotta, T. P. (2015). Social and emotional learning: Past, present, and future. In J. A. Durlak, C. E. Domitrovich, R. P. Weissberg, & T. P. Gullotta (Eds.), *Handbook of social and emotional learning: Research and practice* (pp. 3–19). Guilford Press.

Youth.gov. (n.d.). Positive youth development. https://youth.gov/youth-topics/positive-youth-development

CHAPTER 4

MATTERING IN ALLIED YOUTH FIELDS

Summoning the Call of Black Lives Matter to Radically Affirm Youth Through Programming

Roderick L. Carey, Camila Polanco, and Horatio Blackman

Few rallying cries have rung out louder and more effectively for social transformation than *Black Lives Matter*. The irrefutable power and popularity of "those three words" (Lebron, 2017) has catapulted the Black Lives Matter movement to the forefront of global-wide discussions and action for overturning racist social policies that keep Black life at the margins. Black Lives Matter, with its demonstrations, its discourse, and the feelings it elicits, serves as a powerful interjection into the status quo, which thrives on the fundamental, state-sponsored devaluing of Black life everywhere.

Black Lives Matter movement projects emerged as community responses to extra-legal, unwarranted violence primarily against Black youth, which was captured typically on bystanders' cellphone videos and dispersed via social media outlets. Yet, the radical significance, importance, or *mattering* this movement affirms for Black life is more than a response to rampant extrajudicial killings of unarmed Black people. Black Lives Matter counters systemic racism appearing

It Takes an Ecosystem: Understanding the People, Places, and
Possibilities of Learning and Development Across Settings, pages 67–86.

in social policies and practices by inserting and asserting the mattering of Black life against anti-Black structures that rely on Black peoples' demise (Camp & Heatherton, 2016). For instance, the recent COVID-19 pandemic, which disproportionately impacted the Black community, brought into sharper relief the devastating health vulnerability experienced by low-income communities of color. COVID-19 exacerbated and exposed the perilous realities of economically stratified Black life at the margins—the same realities that Black Lives Matter had been calling our attention to for years. For those within the allied youth fields (see Chapter 1 of this volume by Robinson & Akiva) Black Lives Matter, especially in the wake of COVID-19, forces us to reckon with and clarify our interventionist stance for children and families (see Watson et al., 2020), whose experiences with anti-Black inequities, prove to them—prove to us all—that their lives do not matter. Thus, we call upon those within the allied youth fields to build on the present energy to reorient their programming to ensure Black youth feel that their present and future lives matter.

Yet, what exactly is Black Lives Matter? How do the tragedies of COVID-19 and extrajudicial anti-Black violence—referenced as "dual pandemics"—shape the experiences of already marginalized youth? What lessons does Black Lives Matter offer for our work with youth in ways that are responsive to the Science of Learning and Development (SoLD; see Darling-Hammond et al., 2020)? And, how can those within the allied youth fields center mattering in programming to radically affirm the lives of racially and ethnically marginalized community members across the learning ecosystem (e.g., formal educational domains, community organizations, and through health and social service providing)? In this chapter, we take up these questions and pose insights based in what we have started to glean during our school-based youth program called *The Black Boy Mattering Project*. In sum, we believe that by centering the concept of "mattering" within allied youth field programming, the systems in which adults engage with young people can address racialized trauma, re-establish trust across the learning ecosystems, and as a result, better guide the healthy development of racially and ethnically marginalized youth.

BLACK LIVES MATTER: WHAT IS IT, AND WHAT IS IT TELLING US?

Founded on July 13, 2013, #BlackLivesMatter began as a social media organizing tool by Black activists, Alicia Garza, Patrisse Khan-Cullors, and Opal Tometi, after the acquittal of George Zimmerman in the murder of unarmed, Black 16-year-old Travon Martin in February 2012. It shifted from the hashtag to the Black Lives Matter movement, gaining its momentum due to acute responses to the deaths of those like Eric Garner (July 17, 2014), John Crawford III (August 5, 2014), Michael Brown (August 9, 2014), Tamir Rice (November 23, 2014), Freddie Carlos Gray Jr. (April 19, 2015), and Alton Sterling (July 5, 2016). It arguably reached its first peak after the police shooting death of Michael Brown, where Black Lives Matter "migrated from the virtual world of social media to the real politics of the street" (Ransby, 2018, p. 6) during the fiery Ferguson, Missouri uprising during the late summer of 2014. Since then, "Black Lives Matter" as a banner or slogan, and eventually as an organization (Black Lives Matter Global Network) has prompted street demonstrations and advocacy for social programs, policies, and discourses that affirm the value and significance of Black people across the globe (Bunyasi & Smith, 2019; Garza, 2016; Hill et al., 2020; Lebron, 2017; Ransby, 2018; Ray, 2020).

As Black Lives Matter developed a widespread following between 2013–2016, its calls for policy reforms and systematic overhauls garnered more attention and gradually wider acceptance. Dozens of grass-roots level groups, including the Black Lives Matter Global Network organized under the Movement for Black Lives (M4BL), a coalition of organizations and individuals who engage in bold direct activism and craft policy documents to steer momentum to specific causes (Ransby, 2018; Ray, 2020). Yet, after the shooting death of Ahmaud Arbery (February 23, 2020) at the hands of white residents, and the police inflicted killings of Breonna Taylor (March 13, 2020) and George Floyd (May 25, 2020), individuals organized under the slogan of Black Lives Matter during a recharged, second wave of unprecedented popularity. Millions across the U.S. took to the streets exclaiming *Black Lives Matter!* while demanding systemic changes including a fiscal divestment from police departments, the closure of prisons and immigrant detention centers, the end to the war on drugs, LGBTQIA+ and human rights, and the end to voter suppression practices. According to data gathered by Civis Analytics and reported in the *New York Times*, between 15 and 26 million people reported protesting in some form in June of 2020 (Buchanan et al., 2020). Teens and young adults, in particular, used social media to participate in Black Lives Matter responses. The Pew Research Center revealed that eight in ten Black social media users between the ages of 18 and 49 used #BlackLivesMatter when they posted pictures and videos, shared information about protests, rallies, and events, and voiced their personal experiences with and responses to racism and discrimination (Auxier, 2020). Given collective energy such as this, some have argued that Black Lives Matter is the largest movement in U.S. history (Buchanan et al., 2020).

THE "DUAL PANDEMICS" AND
UNHEALTHY LEARNING ECOSYSTEMS

Calls from Black Lives Matter and the Movement for Black Lives have advanced our understandings of how Black dehumanization is upheld in systems, policies, and institutions (Ray, 2020). Paramount among these issues are the pervasive health and wellness injustices that plague Black life across the lifespan. As a second wave of momentum for Black Lives Matter emerged, it did so almost simultaneously with the outbreak of COVID-19, a pandemic that, due to pervasive health and social inequities, disproportionately impacted ethnically, racially, and economically marginalized youth and adults. The same deadly inequities Black

Lives Matter drew our attention to were undeniably brought front and center on the global stage.

The COVID-19 pandemic wrought terror on Black youth and families due in part to its role in amplifying the preexisting barriers individuals face in accessing equitable health services. However, in developing a way forward, understanding COVID-19's disproportional impact on the physical and mental health of Black individuals only gets us so far. Black youth must now navigate what many are calling the effects of the "dual pandemics": COVID-19 and racial violence (see Endo, 2021; Shelton, 2021). And, allied youth workers must understand the impacts of both phenomena to formulate responsive and radically affirming programming.

The research literature is replete with recent studies that document how those within the allied youth fields support young people in navigating and dismantling the academic, social, and health-related systemic barriers that prevent their development (Akiva et al., 2017; Baldridge, 2019; Bloemraad & Terriquez, 2016; Carey et al., 2020; Cedeño et al., 2020; Christens, 2019; Clay & Turner, 2021; Seider et al., 2020). However, those positioned to support youth across overlapping systems must continue their efforts mindful of the immediate and lingering impacts of the dual pandemics. To better ground the developmental and educational implications of SoLD (see Darling-Hammond et al., 2020), we must expand what we know about the role these dual pandemics play in the social, geographic, and cultural adaptive systems that underscore Black youths' development.

Black youth survived the threat of COVID-19 amidst constant visual and sonic reminders of their subjugation, which were reflected in racially motivated extrajudicial killings shared widely on social media and on television. As such, Black youth have been made intensely aware of the systemic racism that both passively and directly affects their lives. Black youth internalize the message these systems (e.g., healthcare, urban housing, criminal justice systems, etc.) so clearly convey: Black lives do not matter. Delineating the inner workings of these systems affords us the opportunity to understand how stakeholders can better relate to youth across systems, a key component of the SoLD framework (Darling-Hammond et al., 2020). Moreover, doing so can bolster the relational potential of youth programs and provide stakeholders with a means to strengthen youths' "inferred significance" (see Rosenberg & McCullough, 1981), or their perceived mattering. Before discussing "mattering" further, and the implications this concept has for allied youth fields, we explore some of the challenges Black young lives and their families faced prior to and during the "dual pandemics."

COVID-19, BLACK TRAUMA, AND MISTRUST

Prior to COVID-19, Black youth and their families were already marginalized due to anti-Black systemic racism, state-sanctioned violence, and other disparate life outcome determinants. Many Black youth face psychological distress and trauma due to cumulative experiences with ecological threats and stressors from microaggressions, discrimination, and/or living within racially segregated communities (Alvarez, 2020; Assari et al., 2018; Dutil, 2019; Smith et al., 2019). Black communities often mistrust certain public entities due to disjointed and unjust systems of social, educational, and health services (Scharff et al., 2010). The mistrust of health systems among members of low-income Black communities is due in part to a history of inhumane treatment of and experimentation on Black bodies (e.g., the Tuskegee Syphilis Study, the forced sterilization of Black women in the 20th century). Contemporary outcomes like disparate infant mortality rates among Black families (Hauck et al., 2011; U.S. Dept. of Health and Human Services, 2008) and racial discrimination in treatment (Williams & Rucker, 2000) reveal the impacts of racial bias that persist in health and human services. These outcomes also offer evidence for why Black families are justified in their mistrust of health institutions.

COVID-19 compounded the trauma experienced by Black youth and their families. It magnified the impact of living with and among those with preexisting health issues (e.g., diabetes, obesity, hypertension, asthma), systemic healthcare inequalities, lack of access to healthy food options (see Karpyn et al., 2020), and the availability of clean air and water (Millett et al., 2020). In addition to facing constant threats of viral contraction, Black families also encountered severe COVID-19-related economic and socio-emotional impacts. Already economically vulnerable Black families worried of job and income loss (Hill et al., 2020). Since Black and Brown people are overrepresented as grocery store and restaurant workers, maintenance staff, and as public transit employees, telework and other socially distanced work solutions were privileges denied to many working class families of color (Ray & Rojas, 2020). In addition, many Black and Brown families were additionally taxed with emotional exhaustion due to tending to the sick or grieving the death of friends, fictive kin, or direct relatives (Moore et al., 2020).

We also know that even the components of learning ecosystems meant to support Black youth have perpetuated or caused trauma in their lives. For example, Black youth are less likely than youth from other racial groups to believe that legal entities will treat them fairly and more likely to harbor cynicism and mistrust for police and criminal justice systems (Hitchens et al., 2018; Payne et al., 2017). This historic, deeply ingrained, and increasing mistrust implies a need to revisit the relational boundaries between Black youth and the systems and adults that are tasked with fostering their development. Schools are especially salient among these systems.

Schooling Interruptions, Homework Gaps, and Black Learners

After the World Health Organization declared COVID-19 an official pandemic on March 11th, 2020, principals, district leaders, and eventually state governors temporarily closed school buildings. By the middle of April of 2020, *Education Week* estimated that schools attended by 50.8 million U.S. public school students were recommended or ordered to remain closed for the remainder of the year.

With school buildings shuttered, educators quickly shifted classroom learning to virtual formats. As a result, students relied on digital technologies to continue their school engagement, a feat that placed students at risk for academic failure if they were without computers or broadband internet service to stream lesson content or download assignments (see Ferdig et al., 2020).

Prior to the pandemic, Black family households were less likely than those from other racial groups to have internet access (Future Ready Schools, 2020). Specifically, 31% of Black and Latinx families did not have high-speed internet in their home—twice the rate of white families (Future Ready Schools, 2020). This lack of connectivity contributed to already weakened school-family networks and families' inability to support their children's online learning, a phenomenon known as the "homework gap" (Auxier & Anderson, 2020; Clausen et al., 2020). Compounding this issue, nearly 20% of Black and Latinx households did not have a computer (e.g., desktop, laptop, or tablet) in their home, compared to 8% of white households (Future Ready Schools, 2020). With limited access to internet connectivity and needed devices, Black and Brown children were more likely to be disconnected, literally, from their school-based learning. As evidence of their resilience in the face of adversity, Black youth in some of the most economically stratified communities, such as those in rural areas, resorted to mailing completed homework assignments via the United States Postal Service (Bacher-Hicks et al., 2020). Outcomes such as these reveal how the dual pandemics exacerbated educational disparities that pre-existed in many marginalized communities of color.

School building closures had more than just academic-related implications for already marginalized students. Some schools, like those who adopted elements of a Full-Service Community School model, provided vulnerable students and families physical and mental health and wellness supports, meals, transportation, and other social safety nets (McKinney de Royston & Madkins, 2019). When these types of schools shuttered, particularly those within urban settings, many already vulnerable Black and Brown families were left without crucial social services. Youth also missed out on extracurricular activities that spur artistry, creativity, athleticism, and a host of other factors that underscore their physical and emotional development (see Heath et al., 2018). Students lost access to community-based arts and music programs that bolster youths' creative expression and development (see Ngo et al., 2017). Secondary-level students also lost opportunities to partake in rituals like school dances, proms, and traditional graduation ceremonies that for many families of color is an almost sacred culminating celebration of collective educational resilience and achievement (see Jett, 2019).

The second of the dual pandemics—racial violence—was made more palpable for Black students, who were now awash in even more imagery that signaled the peril facing them and their communities. With schools and other programs shuttered, Black students were left to maneuver with little help, the visceral imagery caused by waves of racial violence, the responses of Black Lives Matter, and even the counter-protests for causes such as "Blue Lives Matter." In order to understand the challenges many Black youth faced due to shifting from in-person classroom to online virtual formats, it is key to also consider other features of their schooling experiences prior to the pandemic.

Some scholars have labeled U.S. public schooling as a project that reifies schools as sites of Black suffering (Dumas, 2014; Pabon, 2017). Due to implicit bias, stereotypes, and latent anti-Black sentiments operating unchecked in the minds of educators, Black children often face disproportional disciplining (Annamma et al., 2019; DeMatthews et al., 2017; Irby, 2014; Milner et al., 2018; Milner, 2020) and racial microaggressions that contribute to unequal academic outcomes (Allen et al., 2013), feelings of non-belonging (Brooms, 2019), and perceived non-mattering (Carey, 2019, 2020a). Moreover, educators reinforce the message that Black lives do not matter when they fail to be empathetic to the challenges facing minoritized students (Huerta et al., 2020; Warren, 2018) or ignore heightened racialized trauma, like that caused by the death and ensuing protests for those like Ahmaud Arbery, Breonna Taylor, George Floyd, Daniel Prude, Adam Toledo, and Daunte Wright. Teachers may further exacerbate these issues by directly engaging in anti-Black practices by policing Black students' bodies, hairstyles, voices, and demeanors (Carey, 2019; Nyachae & Ohito, 2019; Woodson, 2020). Without interrupting and resisting such practices, those working across the allied youth fields will fail to provide an affirming environment in which Black youth can thrive.

Scholars have called for the recruitment of more Black and Brown teachers to protect and buffer schoolchildren of color from the systemic harm and trauma hegemonic schooling contexts cause them and their families (Bristol & Goings, 2019; Carey, 2020b; McKinney de Royston et al., 2020; Powell & Coles, 2020; Wallace, 2020). However, the often fragile relationships between Black youth and their teachers (see Voight et al., 2015) may have been further diminished by the separation caused by COVID-19. Moreover, due to site closures at out-of-school time programs, youth experienced significant relational strain with adult workers across youth fields. As such, COVID-19 posed a challenge to asset-based educators and youth workers; they were tasked with ensuring that Black students perceived they mattered virtually within a heightened racialized context that signaled otherwise.

BUT, WHAT IS MATTERING?

The social-psychological construct of mattering, first introduced by researchers Rosenberg and McCullough (1981), describes the extent to which an individual perceives that their presence and involvement plays a fundamental role in others' lives and to their larger society. Elliott et al. (2004), extended this notion of mattering in terms of interpersonal relationships, suggesting that feelings of mattering were a product of being noticed, important, and relied upon by others. Researchers within both developmental and educational research have noted the positive relationship between youths' perceived mattering, their mental health, and academic outcomes (e.g., Dixon et al., 2009; Elliott et al., 2011; Flett, 2018; Lemon & Watson, 2011; Marshall & Tilton-Weaver, 2019; Rayle & Myers, 2004; Tucker et al., 2010).

Rosenberg and McCullough (1981) and Elliott et al. (2004) asserted that mattering is important in shaping an individual's self-concept. This is especially pertinent for youth during adolescence, when their self-concepts become more elaborate due to increased cognitive abilities, more complex peer relationships, and a deeper awareness of the challenges framing their worlds and places within it (Crone & Fuligni, 2020). Mattering can also be influential in improving one's sense of belonging, which incorporates feelings of acceptance, relatedness, and mutual respect from others (Baumeister et al., 2000; Brooms, 2019; Gray et al., 2018).

Partly as a response to the movement and discourses of Black Lives Matter, Carey (2019, 2020a) deployed social-psychological definitions of mattering to theorize on the racialized experiences Black boys and young men face with being (de)valued and rendered (in)significant within schools and society. Carey (2019) did so mindful of their experiences being marginalized by others who wield a fearful contempt of their bodies. Carey also considered their experiences being just selectively loved for certain talents or facets that can be capitalized on. Three types of mattering emerged from Carey's theoretical investigation of the social and school lives of Black boys—*marginal, partial,* and *comprehensive* mattering. Although originally considered in the school context, these three formulations hold promise for understanding how all Black youth of various genders can perceive their mattering across learning and development ecosystems.

Marginal mattering implies a systemic disregard or a fearful awareness harbored by the general public. Ongoing incidents such as clashes with law enforcement officers can also convey to Black and Brown communities that they marginally matter. Moreover, when youth marginally matter, they are deemed only valuable or significant at the peripheries. This form of mattering emerges from a historical lineage of structural racism that has disproportionately pushed Black and Brown communities to the "margins" and worked to frame them in the minds of actors as social problems that need to be "fixed" or "silenced." When youth feel like they marginally matter, they may mistrust those positioned to serve them across various systems (e.g., healthcare systems, social services, law enforcement, and even educators) due to prior experiences being disregarded, misunderstood, or stereotyped. The racial health disparities amplified during the COVID-19 pandemic revealed how Black and Brown communities marginally matter.

Partial mattering implies how Black youth are valued, yet only for their skills, talents, and specific contributions that can be capitalized on. For Black boys, this usually means that social actors selectively value their athletic, artistic, and heroic attributes instead of their full humanity (Carey, 2019, 2020a). When Black youth partially matter within the domain of allied youth fields, their value is attached to their ability to master things that are countable, fundable, or their prowess at mastering feats that uplift the individual instead of the community. Youth programs that are geared toward improving test scores on standardized assessments or work to reorient the respectability of Black youth to master hegemonic norms (see Dumas & Nelson, 2016; Nyachae & Ohito, 2019) do little more than compel Black youth to matter within society and to themselves in fragmented, otherwise partial ways (Carey, 2020a).

Comprehensive mattering, which is mainly aspirational, works to envision how Black youth can matter fully or robustly to individuals and society broadly. When youth matter comprehensively, they count not because of what they can or cannot do, but simply because they exist. Comprehensive mattering is a radical approach to working with youth. It focuses on building the types of relational parameters between youth and adult workers that seeks a transcendent vision and version for self-hoods denied or unimagined in society (Carey, 2019, 2020a). It resists prior formulations that have rendered youth of color as damned, demeaned, and stereotyped as requiring of fixing. Rather, when allied youth workers make children feel they comprehensively matter they engage in activities aimed at liberatory, emancipatory endeavors geared toward freeing the self of binds society has kept us all within. Comprehensive mattering compels youth to not only matter as high-performing students, but as long-term learners, who are inspired to live out the fullness of their self-hoods, and who work to matter to their community.

APPLIED MATTERING: THE BLACK BOY MATTERING PROJECT

With insights from prior research, mattering can inform the course of action for promoting resilient, responsive, anti-racist, and healthy learning ecosystems. For example, our present research partnership explores the salience of mattering in the lives of Black boys and young men across the ecosystem. *The Black Boy Mattering Project*, a qualitative, school-based research project conducted with 17 high school Black boys, empirically connected the construct of mattering to societal and interpersonal domains using Carey's (2019, 2020a) concepts of marginal, partial, and comprehensive mattering.

In our project we conducted interviews, focus groups, and engaged in creative endeavors aimed at understanding both how Black boys indicate their perceived mattering and how they imagine the ways their educators and other stakeholders can create contexts where Black boys matter comprehensively. In this project, we provided a space for the boys to reflect on how their experiences across the various contexts that make up their ecosystem—their families, communities, peers, the media, and educators—signify how they matter and are valued as Black boys and young men. We also provided them with experiential learning opportunities, such as a field trip to an art museum's exhibit of African American photographic beauty. This trip offered the boys an opportunity to discover the ways art can be used to reimagine how Black lives could be rendered more robustly through art and as such, comprehensively matter.

Our data from the project reveals that interpersonal relationships and perceptions drawn from societal messaging impacted boys' perceived mattering, and thus their self-concepts. While the boys shared ample experiences with marginal mattering and perceived that they only mattered partially for athletics and entertainment in society, and sometimes to teachers and peers in schools, there were positive encounters that made them infer their mattering. Family members relied on the boys to tend to younger siblings; coaches instilled the boys' importance on the playing field by providing them opportunities to lead; and teachers augmented the boys' perceived mattering when they checked on their home lives and valued their minds as much as their athletic prowess. Findings such as these reveal the power of mattering for shaping adolescents' self-concepts. But, what promises does centering mattering hold for allied youth fields, generally?

COMPREHENSIVE MATTERING ACROSS ALLIED YOUTH FIELDS

The energy for Black Lives Matter along with the social-psychological mattering we describe offers those working across the allied youth fields a useful re-framing for how to engage with children and adolescents. Mattering reflects the centrality of relationships for fostering youth development, which is a key component of the SoLD framework (Darling-Hammond et al., 2020, Li & Winters, Chapter 6 of this volume). Moreover, by centering mattering, stakeholders have the potential to create radically affirming contexts spurred on by re-imagined relational contexts for youth often scripted into marginality or only partial social significance. We pose five concluding considerations for those within the allied youth fields to center mattering in ways responsive to the "dual pandemics": create trauma-informed programming, provide healing centered engagement, build on family-based assets, resist respectability and individual-centric interventions, and bolster youths' critical consciousness to help them radically matter within their community.

Trauma-Informed Programming

Mindful of the "dual pandemics," which have illuminated the racial disparities that exist in healthcare and justice (i.e., COVID-19 and Black Lives Matter protests), those who work with youth of color need to acknowledge how race and culture have an effect on trauma and our understanding of trauma (Alvarez, 2020). Although many schools have begun to focus on trauma-informed and culturally relevant and responsive practices (Gay, 2018; Ladson-Billings, 1995, 2014), there appears to be less energy for continuing or building on these practices in out-of-school time (OST) settings. In their work with Puerto Rican youth whose families were displaced after Hurricane Maria, Monte Verde et al. (2019) set forth applicable trauma-informed and culturally-responsive recommendations for youth workers.

First, when working with marginalized youth, it is necessary to conduct *risk and reality assessments* with youth, families, and/or community stakeholders.

Such assessments determine what resources are needed, and the sustainability and feasibility of strategies devised to target their needs. Additionally, it is also important for youth workers to reflect on their experiences, biases, and beliefs, especially if they do not identify with the same cultural and racial backgrounds as the youth with whom they work. In doing so, they identify culturally appropriate ways that they can relate to youth and build meaningful, trusting relationships. Further, a few of the trauma-informed practices applied by Monte Verde et al. (2019) mainly consisted of understanding how youth process their trauma: what led to the youth's trauma, and listening to the voices of youth to figure out how they coped with their trauma and how it affected them. Family and community engagement is also key in successful trauma-informed work. As noted in the Black Boy Mattering Project, youths' relationships with family and others in and outside of school was important to their perceived mattering. Therefore, along with engaging in culturally-responsive reflections and trauma-informed practices, efforts must be made to strengthen family and community engagement.

Healing Centered Engagement

We also draw attention to healing centered engagement (HCE; Ginwright, 2018) as a means to augment marginalized youth's perceived mattering and healthy development. Practitioners and policymakers focusing on youth development have built on the concepts that guide trauma-informed care, arguing that such approaches, while effective in many circumstances may leave room for the adoption of "deficit based, rather than asset driven strategies to support young people who have been harmed" (Ginwright, 2018, p. 2). One central principal of healing centered engagement—that trauma is a community-wide problem, and not contained within one individual—mirrors the learning ecosystems framework (see Hecht & Crowley, 2020) and offers considerable promise for ensuring that youth perceive their mattering across multiple contexts. In their review of interventions in response to community violence, Sinha and Rosenberg (2013) showed all children in high-violence neighborhoods exhibited behavioral and psychological markers of trauma, including symptoms indicative of posttraumatic stress disorder (PTSD) and depression. As such, when we shift our understandings of trauma from an individual manifestation to a community-based problem, we widen possibilities for determining how to support youth in healing not only themselves, but also their communities. In doing so, we show youth how much they matter for formulating solutions to community issues.

HCE takes an asset-based, culturally relevant, community-centered approach to healing. This approach works not to simply resolve issues that arise from traumatic experiences. Rather HCE extends that effort to "sustain well-being" (Ginwright, 2018, p. 4) through elevating and supporting the healthy expressions and activities of the harmed youth. During Ginwright's (2018) work, one student stated that "I am more than what happened to me, I'm not just my trauma" (p. 2). This quote illustrated HCEs focus on asset-based approaches that sustain individuals beyond resolving symptoms of trauma. This approach also recognizes and seeks to address the well-being of the adults who address youth trauma. Trauma affects a whole community and HCE attends to this problem, both at an individual level and through community action (e.g., protests, school walkouts, social media campaigns) to address trauma and build resilient communities. By fostering youths' healing, workers simultaneously ensure that youth infer their significance and their mattering to themselves, their peers, and their communities.

Building on Family-Based Assets

Sites that serve youth within out-of-school settings may view their role as supplementing what children and adolescents miss from their homes or families, more broadly. And programs that serve youth from this more charitable lens may view their role as needed to make up for material resource gaps caused by social forces, such as systematic racism and social disparities like health inequities, housing instability, and unemployment. However, communities of color, in particular, have communal and family-based strengths that should not be overlooked in building out programs (see Carey, 2016 for a school-based example). Since it is a relational phenomenon, centering youth mattering in the allied youth fields would urge stakeholders to draw upon and build on family-based assets, and the strengths, wisdom, and know-how youth gain from their families. In this way, for Black youth to know they matter, they must believe their families matter to their youth workers (Carey, 2019).

Resist Respectability and Individual-Centric Interventions

Allied youth workers have the potential to inspire youth to find new ways to matter to and within their communities. Instead, however, some youth programming workers (e.g., librarians, after-school program leaders, summer camp counselors) seek to re-orient the respectability of groups like Black youth, by urging them to shift their stylings, behaviors, and sensibilities toward the white, middle-class (see Baldridge, 2019). In this way, Black youth are taught to see themselves as their own problem, their only barrier to success (Carey, 2019; Dumas & Nelson, 2016; Nyachae & Ohito, 2019). However, program practices like these foster inner-turmoil within youth of color; young people begin to view themselves, their cultural features, and their attributes as problems to overcome. They are taught to focus on improving the self by adhering to white, middle-class modes of upward social mobility. In doing so Black youth are distracted from the anti-Black policies and practices that script them and their communities as unacceptable. Moreover, these sorts of programs let the systems that frame the challenges facing them and their communities off the hook for posing the actual barriers that cause their peril.

Programs that emphasize these sorts of individual-centric, respectability doctrines urge the individual to distance themselves from their family and their community. If one makes it, it proves they all can, which minimizes the role systematic racism plays in stymying opportunities and also "proves" the effectiveness (and fundability) of a particular program intervention. Yet, programs that emphasize the comprehensive mattering of youth of color can help them work to see themselves beyond white gazes and can awaken them to see themselves as embodied proofs of resiliency and their communities as rich in cultural assets.

Mattering in the Community Through Critical Consciousness Building

Allied youth workers can stimulate the perceived mattering of youth by ensuring they view themselves as a significant stakeholder in the success of their community. As such, allied youth workers can augment youths' perceived mattering by providing them the resources and encouragement to change their community. Instead of focusing youth programing toward a more charitable angle (e.g., volunteering), adult workers can inspire youths' political empowerment (Christens, 2019) or critical consciousness development (Carey et al., 2020; Diemer et al., 2016; Freire, 1985; Watts et al., 2011) by supporting youth in "reading their worlds" (Freire, 1985, p. 19) to transform the world through social action. For instance, COVID-19 offers both a challenge and a practical opportunity for allied youth workers to help ensure that youth of color know that their communities matter. COVID-19 revealed what happens when pervasive systemic barriers to adequate health care operate unchecked. While there are many things that individuals and families can do to ensure healthier lifestyles, deeply rooted systemic barriers were more culpable in contributing to Black and Brown contraction rates and the resulting death tolls. However, workers can reframe the devastation caused by COVID-19 by harnessing its impact to stimulate the critical consciousness and activist potential of youth.

One promising approach to augmenting youth's critical consciousness is through youth-led social change programs, also known as youth-organizing. Such programs foster youths' critical consciousness by not only teaching youth about the challenges their communities face, but rather supporting them in developing and enacting solutions (Akiva et al., 2017; Carey et al., 2020). As a result, youth-led social change programs can support youth in seeing themselves as significant to not only determining but also solving the challenges facing their communities.

CONCLUSION

The second wave of the Black Lives Matter movement drew significant attention to multiple systems keeping Black life at the margins. As such, this movement revealed the need for a multi-site, multifaceted, ecosystem-based approach to supporting Black youth development. Exposure to protests in the name of Black lives and graphic depictions of state-sanctioned violence represent disturbances in the learning ecosystem of Black youth. A healthy learning ecosystem would be contingent on adults formulating trusting relationships with Black youth, to support them as they wrestle with creating positive self-concepts while resisting societal messaging that indicates that Black lives do not matter. As we work to formulate a way forward in the wake of COVID-19 and anti-Black policies and practices, allied youth workers and those across the learning ecosystem are positioned to instill or revise efforts to make Black young lives matter. Importantly, mattering must be emphasized across interconnected systems that serve young lives and not be siloed off. Doing so will ensure that, regardless of where Black youth are located geographically, the systems working around them and with them signal their everlasting value, their importance, their mattering.

REFERENCES

Akiva, T., Carey, R. L., Cross, A. B., Delale-O'Connor, L., & Brown, M. R. (2017). Reasons youth engage in activism programs: Social justice or sanctuary? *Journal of Applied Developmental Psychology*, *53*, 20–30. https://doi.org/10.1016/j.appdev.2017.08.005

Allen, A., Scott, L. M,, & Lewis, C. W. (2013). Racial microaggressions and African American and Hispanic students in urban schools: A call for culturally affirming education. *Interdisciplinary Journal of Teaching and Learning*, *3*(2), 117–129.

Alvarez, A. (2020). Seeing race in the research on youth trauma and education: A critical review. *Review of Educational Research*, *90*(5), 583–626. https://doi.org/10.3102/0034654320938131

Annamma, S. A., Anyon, Y., Joseph, N. M., Farrar, J., Greer, E., Downing, B., & Simmons, J. (2019). Black girls and school discipline: The complexities of being overrepresented and understudied. *Urban Education*, *54*(2), 211–242. https://doi.org/10.1177/0042085916646610

Assari, S., Gibbons, F. X., & Simons, R. L. (2018). Perceived discrimination among black youth: An 18-year longitudinal study. *Behavioral Sciences, 8*(5), 44–55. https://doi.org/10.3390/bs8050044

Auxier, B. (2020, December 14). *Social media continue to be important political outlets for Black Americans.* Fact Tank: Pew Research Center. https://www.pewresearch.org/fact-tank/2020/12/11/social-media-continue-to-be-important-political-outlets-for-black-americans/

Auxier, B., & Anderson, M. (2020, March 16). *As schools close due to the coronavirus, some U.S. students face a digital 'homework gap.'* Fact Tank: Pew Research Center. https://www.pewresearch.org/fact-tank/2020/03/16/as-schools-close-due-to-the-coronavirus-some-u-s-students-face-a-digital-homework-gap/

Bacher-Hicks, A., Goodman, J., & Mulhern, C. (2020). Inequality in household adaptation to schooling shocks: COVID-induced online learning engagement in real time. *Journal of Public Economics, 193.* https://doi.org/10.1016/j.jpubeco.2020.104345

Baldridge, B. J. (2019). *Reclaiming community: Race and the uncertain future of youth work.* Stanford University Press.

Baumeister, R. F., Dale, K. L., & Muraven, M. (2000). Volition and belongingness: Social movements, volition, self-esteem, and the need to belong. In S. Stryker, T. J. Owens, & R. W. White (Eds.), *Self, identity, and social movements* (pp. 239–251). University of Minnesota Press.

Bloemraad, I., & Terriquez, V. (2016). Cultures of engagement: The organizational foundations of advancing health in immigrant and low-income communities of color. *Social Science & Medicine, 165*, 214–222. https://doi.org/10.1016/j.socscimed.2016.02.003

Bristol, T. J., & Goings, R. B. (2019). Exploring the boundary-heightening experiences of Black male teachers: Lessons for teacher education programs. *Journal of Teacher Education, 70*(1), 51–64. https://doi.org/10.1177/0022487118789367

Brooms, D. R. (2019). "I was just trying to make it": Examining urban Black males' sense of belonging, schooling experiences, and academic success. *Urban Education, 54*(6), 804–830. https://doi.org/10.1177/0042085916648743

Buchanan, L., Bui, Q., & Patel, J. K. (2020, July 3). Black Lives Matter may be the largest movement in U.S. history. *The New York Times.* https://www.nytimes.com/interactive/2020/07/03/us/george-floyd-protests-crowd -size.html

Bunyasi, T. L., & Smith, C. W. (2019). *Stay woke: A people's guide to making all Black lives matter.* New York University Press.

Camp, J. T., & Heatherton, C. (Eds.). (2016). *Policing the planet: Why the policing crisis led to Black Lives Matter.* Verso Books.

Carey, R. L. (2016). "Keep that in mind... You're gonna go to college": Family influence on the college going processes of Black and Latino high school boys. *The Urban Review, 48*(5), 718–742. https://doi.org/10.1007/s11256-016-0375-8

Carey, R. L. (2019). Imagining the comprehensive mattering of Black boys and young men in society and schools: Toward a new approach. *Harvard Educational Review, 89*(3), 370–396. https://doi.org/10.17763/1943-5045-89.3.370

Carey, R. L. (2020a). Making Black boys and young men matter: Radical relationships, future oriented imaginaries and other evolving insights for educational research and practice. *International Journal of Qualitative Studies in Education, 33*(7), 729–744. https://doi.org/10.1080/09518398.2020.1753255

Carey, R. L. (2020b). Missing misters: Uncovering the pedagogies and positionalities of male teachers of color in the school lives of Black and Latino adolescent boys. *Race Ethnicity and Education, 23*(3), 392–413. https://doi.org/10.1080/13613324.2019.1663991

Carey, R. L., Akiva, T., Abdellatif, H., & Daughtry, K. A. (2020). 'And school won't teach me that!' Urban youth activism programs as transformative sites for critical adolescent learning. *Journal of Youth Studies.* https://doi.org/10.1080/13676261.2020.1784400

Cedeño, D., Bergeson, C., Forenza, B., Reid, R. J., Garcia-Reid, P., & Lardier, D. T. (2020). Social exclusion among urban ethnic minority youth in the northeast united states: A reflective view on community supportive structures. *Community Psychology in Global Perspective, 6*(2), 38–55. https://doi.org/10.1285/i24212113v6i2-1p38

Christens, B. D. (2019). *Community power and empowerment.* Oxford University Press.

Clausen, J. M., Bunte, B., & Robertson, E. T. (2020). Professional development to improve communication and reduce the homework gap in grades 7–12 during COVID-19 transition to remote learning. *Journal of Technology and Teacher Education, 28*(2), 443–451. https://www.learntechlib.org/primary/p/216289/

Clay, K. L., & Turner III, D. C. (2021). "Maybe you should try it this way instead": Youth activism amid managerialist subterfuge. *American Educational Research Journal, 58*(2), 386–419. https://doi.org/10.3102/0002831221993476

Crone, E. A., & Fuligni, A. J. (2020). Self and others in adolescence. *Annual Review of Psychology, 71,* 447–469. https://doi.org/10.1146/annurev-psych-010419-050937

Darling-Hammond, L., Flook, L., Cook-Harvey, C., Barron, B., & Osher, D. (2020). Implications for educational practice of the science of learning and development. *Applied Developmental Science, 24*(2), 97–140. https://doi.org/10.1080/10888691.2018.1537791

DeMatthews, D. E., Carey, R. L., Olivarez, A., & Moussavi Saeedi, K. (2017). Guilty as charged? Principals' perspectives on disciplinary practices and the racial discipline gap. *Educational Administration Quarterly, 53*(4), 519–555. https://doi.org/10.1177/0013161X17714844

Diemer, M. A., Rapa, L. J., Voight, A. M., & McWhirter, E. H. (2016). Critical consciousness: A developmental approach to addressing marginalization and oppression. *Child Development Perspectives, 10*(4), 216–221. https://doi.org/10.1111/cdep.12193

Dixon, A. L., Scheidegger, C., & McWhirter, J. J. (2009). The adolescent mattering experience: Gender variations in perceived mattering, anxiety, and depression. *Journal of Counseling & Development, 87*(3), 302–310. https://doi.org/10.1002/j.1556-6678.2009.tb00111.x

Dumas, M. J. (2014). 'Losing an arm': Schooling as a site of Black suffering. *Race Ethnicity and Education, 17*(1), 1–29. https://doi.org/10.1080/13613324.2013.850412

Dumas, M. J., & Nelson, J. D. (2016). (Re) Imagining Black boyhood: Toward a critical framework for educational research. *Harvard Educational Review, 86*(1), 27–47. https://doi.org/10.17763/0017-8055.86.1.27

Dutil, S. (2019). Adolescent traumatic and disenfranchised grief: Adapting an evidence-based intervention for Black and Latinx youths in schools. *Children & Schools, 41*(3), 179–187. https://doi.org/10.1093/cs/cdz009

Elliott, G., Kao, S., & Grant, A. M. (2004). Mattering: Empirical validation of a social-psychological concept. *Self and Identity, 3*(4), 339–354. https://doi.org/10.1080/13576500444000119

Elliott, G. C., Cunningham, S. M., Colangelo, M., & Gelles, R. J. (2011). Perceived mattering to the family and physical violence within the family by adolescents. *Journal of Family Issues, 32*(8), 1007–1029. https://doi.org/10.1177/0192513X11398932

Endo, R. (2021). On holding various truths to (not) be self-evident: Leading during the dual pandemics of 2020 as a Racialized Body. *Cultural Studies ↔ Critical Methodologies, 21*(1), 116–121. https://doi.org/10.1177%2F1532708620960171

Ferdig, R. E., Baumgartner, E., Hartshorne, R., Kaplan-Rakowski, R., & Mouza, C. (2020). *Teaching, technology, and teacher education during the COVID-19 pandemic: Stories from the field.* Association for the Advancement of Computing in Education (AACE). https://www.learntechlib.org/p/216903/

Flett, G. (2018). *The psychology of mattering: Understanding the human need to be significant.* Academic Press.

Freire, P. (1985). *The politics of education: Culture, power, and liberation.* Greenwood Publishing Group.

Future Ready Schools. (2020, August 6). Students of color caught in the homework gap. https://futureready.org/wp-content/uploads/2020/08/HomeworkGap_FINAL8.06.2020.pdf

Garza, A. (2016). A herstory of the #BlackLivesMatter Movement. In J. Hobson (Ed.), *Are all the women still white? Rethinking race, expanding feminisms* (pp. 23–28). State University of New York Press.

Gay, G. (2018). *Culturally responsive teaching: Theory, research, and practice.* Teachers College Press.

Ginwright, S. (2018). The future of healing: Shifting from trauma informed care to healing centered engagement. *Occasional Paper, 25*, 1–7. http://kinshipcarersvictoria. org/wp-content/uploads/2018/08/OP-Ginwright-S-2018-Future-of-healing-care.pdf

Gray, D. L., Hope, E. C., & Matthews, J. S. (2018). Black and belonging at school: A case for interpersonal, instructional, and institutional opportunity structures. *Educational Psychologist, 53*(2), 97–113. https://doi.org/10.1080/00461520.2017.1421466

Hauck, F. R., Tanabe, K. O., & Moon, R. Y. (2011). Racial and ethnic disparities in infant mortality. *Seminars in Perinatology, 35*(4), 209–220. https://doi.org/10.1053/j.semperi.2011.02.018

Heath, R. D., Anderson, C., Turner, A. C., & Payne, C. M. (2018). Extracurricular activities and disadvantaged youth: A complicated—but promising—story. *Urban Education*, 1–35. Advanced online publication. https://doi.org/10.1177/0042085918805797

Hecht, M., & Crowley, K. (2020). Unpacking the learning ecosystems framework: Lessons from the adaptive management of biological ecosystems. *Journal of the Learning Sciences, 29*(2), 264–284. https://doi.org/10.1080/10508406.2019.1693381

Hill, M. L., Taylor, K., & Barat, F. (2020). *We still here: Pandemic, policing, protest, and possibility.* Haymarket Books.

Hitchens, B. K., Carr, P. J., & Clampet-Lundquist, S. (2018). The context for legal cynicism: Urban young women's experiences with policing in low-income, high-crime neighborhoods. *Race and Justice, 8*(1), 27–50. https://doi.org/10.1177/2153368717724506

Huerta, A. H., Howard, T. C., & Haro, B. N. (2020). Supporting Black and Latino boys in school: A call to action. *Phi Delta Kappan, 102*(1), 29–33. https://doi. org/10.1177/0031721720956846

Irby, D. J. (2014). Trouble at school: Understanding school discipline systems as nets of social control. *Equity & Excellence in Education, 47*(4), 513–530. https://doi.org/1 0.1080/10665684.2014.958963

Jett, C. C. (2019). "I have the highest GPA, but I can't be the valedictorian?": Two Black males' exclusionary valedictory experiences. *Race Ethnicity and Education*. https:// doi.org/10.1080/13613324.2019.1599341

Karpyn, A., Young, C. R., Collier, Z., & Glanz, K. (2020). Correlates of healthy eating in urban food desert communities. *International Journal of Environmental Research and Public Health, 17*(17), 1–13. https://doi.org/10.3390/ijerph17176305

Ladson-Billings, G. (1995). Toward a Theory of Culturally Relevant Pedagogy. *American Educational Research Journal, 32*(3), 465–491. https://doi. org/10.3102/00028312032003465

Ladson-Billings, G. (2014). Culturally relevant pedagogy 2.0: Aka the remix. *Harvard Educational Review, 84*(1), 74–84. https://doi.org/10.17763/haer.84. 1.p2rj131485484751

Lebron, C. J. (2017). *The making of Black Lives Matter: A brief history of an idea.* Oxford University Press.

Lemon, J. C., & Watson, J. C. (2011). Early identification of potential high school dropouts: An investigation of the relationship among at-risk status, wellness, perceived stress, and mattering. *Journal of At-Risk Issues, 16*(2), 17–23. https://eric. ed.gov/?id=EJ960073

Marshall, S. K., & Tilton-Weaver, L. (2019). Adolescents' perceived mattering to parents and friends: Testing cross-lagged associations with psychosocial well-being. *International Journal of Behavioral Development, 43*(6), 541–552. https://doi. org/10.1177/0165025419844019

McKinney de Royston, M., & Madkins, T. C. (2019). A question of necessity or of equity? Full- service community schools and the (mis) education of Black youth. *Journal of Education for Students Placed at Risk, 24*(3), 244–271. https://doi.org/10.1080/108 24669.2019.1615920

McKinney de Royston, M., Madkins, T. C., Givens, J. R., & Nasir, N. S. (2020). "I'm a teacher, I'm gonna always protect you": Understanding Black educators' protection of Black children. *American Educational Research Journal, 58*(1), 68–106. https:// doi.org/10.3102/0002831220921119

Millett, G. A., Jones, A. T., Benkeser, D., Baral, S., Mercer, L., Beyrer, C., Honermann, B., Lankiewicz, E., Mena, L., Crowley, J. S., Sherwood, J., & Sullivan, P. S. (2020). Assessing differential impacts of COVID-19 on Black communities. *Annals of Epidemiology, 47,* 37–44. https://doi.org/10.1016/j.annepidem.2020.05.003

Milner IV, H. R. (2020). Fifteenth annual AERA Brown Lecture in education research: Disrupting punitive practices and policies: Rac(e)ing back to teaching, teacher preparation, and Brown. *Educational Researcher, 49*(3), 147–160. https://doi. org/10.3102/0013189X20907396

Milner IV, H. R., Cunningham, H. B., Delale-O'Connor, L., & Kestenberg, E. G. (2018). *"These kids are out of control": Why we must reimagine classroom management for equity.* Corwin Press.

Monte Verde, P., Watkins, M., Enriquez, D., Nater, S., & Harris, J. C. (2019). Community youth development service-learning: Trauma-informed and culturally responsive. *Journal of Youth Development, 14*(2), 1–16. http://dx.doi.org/10.2139/ssrn.3459805

Moore, S. E., Jones-Eversley, S. D., Tolliver, W. F., Wilson, B. L., & Jones, C. A. (2020). Six feet apart or six feet under: The impact of COVID-19 on the Black community. *Death Studies.* https://doi.org/10.1080/07481187.2020.1785053

Ngo, B., Lewis, C., & Maloney Leaf, B. (2017). Fostering sociopolitical consciousness with minoritized youth: Insights from community-based arts programs. *Review of Research in Education, 41*(1), 358–380. https://doi.org/10.3102/0091732X17690122

Nyachae, T. M., & Ohito, E. O. (2019). No disrespect: A womanist critique of respectability discourses in extracurricular programming for Black girls. *Urban Education.* https://doi.org/10.1177/0042085919893733

Pabon, A. J. M. (2017). In hindsight and now again: Black male teachers' recollections on the suffering of Black male youth in US public schools. *Race Ethnicity and Education, 20*(6), 766–780. https://doi.org/10.1080/13613324.2016.1195359

Payne, Y. A., Hitchens, B. K., & Chambers, D. L. (2017). "Why I can't stand out in front of my house?": Street-identified Black youth and young adult's negative encounters with police. *Sociological Forum, 32*(4), 874–895. https://doi.org/10.1111/ socf.12380

Powell, T., & Coles, J. A. (2020). 'We still here': Black mothers' personal narratives of sense making and resisting antiblackness and the suspensions of their Black children. *Race Ethnicity and Education, 24*(1), 76–95. https://doi.org/10.1080/136133 24.2020.1718076

Ransby, B. (2018). *Making all Black lives matter: Reimagining freedom in the twenty-first century.* University of California Press.

Ray, R. (2020). Setting the record straight on the Movement for Black Lives. *Ethnic and Racial Studies, 43*(8), 1393–1401. https://doi.org/10.1080/01419870.2020.1718727

Ray, R., & Rojas, F. (2020, April 16). *Inequality during the coronavirus pandemic. Contexts: Sociology for the public.* https://contexts.org/blog/inequality-during-the-coronavirus- pandemic/

Rayle, A., & Myers, J. (2004). Counseling adolescents toward wellness: The roles of ethnic identity, acculturation, and mattering. *Professional School Counseling, 8*(1), 81–90. http://www.jstor.org/stable/42732418

Rosenberg, M., & McCullough, B. C. (1981). Mattering: Inferred significance and mental health among adolescents. *Research in Community & Mental Health, 2,* 163–182.

Scharff, D. P., Mathews, K. J., Jackson, P., Hoffsuemmer, J., Martin, E., & Edwards, D. (2010). More than Tuskegee: Understanding mistrust about research participation. *Journal of Health Care for the Poor and Underserved, 21*(3), 879–897. https://doi.org/10.1353/hpu.0.0323

Seider, S., Kelly, L., Clark, S., Jennett, P., El-Amin, A., Graves, D., Soutter, M., Malhotra, S., & Cabral, M. (2020). Fostering the sociopolitical development of African American and Latinx adolescents to analyze and challenge racial and economic inequality. *Youth & Society, 52*(5), 756–794. https://doi.org/10.1177/0044118X18767783

Shelton, S. A. (2021). Entangled time hops: Doomsday clocks, pandemics, and qualitative research's responsibility. *Qualitative Inquiry, 27*(7), 824–828. https://doi.org/10.1177/1077800420960188

Sinha, J. W., & Rosenberg, L. B. (2013). A critical review of trauma interventions and religion among youth exposed to community violence. *Journal of Social Service Research, 39*(4), 436–454. https://doi.org/10.1080/01488376.2012.730907

Smith, S. M., Sun, R., & Gordon, M. S. (2019). Racial discrimination and psychological distress among African American adolescents: Investigating the social support deterioration model. *Journal of Child and Family Studies, 28*(6), 1613–1622. https://doi.org/10.1007/s10826-019-01397-6

Tucker, C., Dixon, A., & Griddine, K. (2010). Academically successful African American male urban high school students' experiences of mattering to others at school. *Professional School Counseling, 14*(2), 135–145. https://doi.org/10.1177/2156759X1001400202

U.S. Dept. of Health and Human Services, Health Resources and Services Administration, Maternal and Child Health Bureau. (2008). *Evidence of trends, risk factors, and intervention strategies: a report from the healthy start national evaluation 2006: racial and ethnic disparities in infant mortality.* http://lib.ncfh.org/pdfs/2k9/8392.pdf

Voight, A., Hanson, T., O'Malley, M., & Adekanye, L. (2015). The racial school climate gap: Within-school disparities in students' experiences of safety, support, and connectedness. *American Journal of Community Psychology, 56*(3–4), 252–267. https://doi.org/10.1007/s10464-015-9751-x

Wallace, D. (2020). The diversity trap? Critical explorations of Black male teachers' negotiations of leadership and learning in London state schools. *Race Ethnicity and Education, 23*(3), 345–366. https://doi.org/10.1080/13613324.2019.1663977

Warren, C. A. (2018). Empathy, teacher dispositions, and preparation for culturally responsive pedagogy. *Journal of Teacher Education, 69*(2), 169–183. https://doi.org/10.1177/0022487117712487

Watson, M. F., Turner, W. L., & Hines, P. M. (2020). Black Lives Matter: We are in the same storm but we are not in the same boat. *Family Process, 59*(4), 1362–1373. https://doi.org/10.1111/famp.12613

Watts, R. J., Diemer, M. A., & Voight, A. M. (2011). Critical consciousness: Current status and future directions. *New Directions for Child and Adolescent Development, 2011*(134), 43–57. https://doi.org/10.1002/cd.310

Williams, D. R., & Rucker, T. D. (2000). Understanding and addressing racial disparities in health care. *Health Care Financing Review, 21*(4), 75–90. https://www.ncbi.nlm.nih.gov/pmc/articles/PMC4194634/

Woodson, A. N. (2020). Don't let me be misunderstood: Psychological safety, Black girls' speech, and Black feminist perspectives on directness. *Journal of Educational Psychology, 112*(3), 567–578. https://doi.org/10.1037/edu0000458

SECTION II

THE PEOPLE AND PRACTICES THAT SUPPORT
HEALTHY LEARNING AND DEVELOPMENT
ECOSYSTEMS

CHAPTER 5

FOSTERING, FACILITATING, AND CONNECTING

Families are a Critical Part of Young People's Learning and Development Ecosystems

Lori Delale-O'Connor

Young people's learning experiences are influenced and enhanced by the presence of caring and trusted adults (Milner, 2015; Milner et al., 2015), among and often at the head of which are familial[1] adults (such as parents and other primary caregivers) who play a significant role in children's learning and development life-wide (Castro et al., 2015; Harris & Goodall, 2008). Child-adult relationships are critical for healthy development across all cognitive, emotional, physical, and social domains (Osher et al., 2020). Developmentally, parental engagement in children's learning is linked to academic success across both age levels and ethnic and racial groups (Hill & Tyson, 2009; Wilder, 2014). When we consider "out-of-school" time for young people, much of it is spent with or conceptualized and coordinated by familial caregivers. Families are an invaluable part of learning and

---

[1] Throughout this chapter I use the words caregivers, family, and familial adults interchangeably to denote the caregiving roles that may be occupied by parents (biological and adoptive), grandparents, aunts, uncles, cousins, older siblings, or fictive kin in supporting young people. When studies focus specifically on "parents," I use that language as a reflection of the study cited.

It Takes an Ecosystem: Understanding the People, Places, and
Possibilities of Learning and Development Across Settings, pages 89–107.
Copyright © 2022 by Information Age Publishing

89

development (L&D) ecosystems that must be understood and included to support young people's experiences, outcomes, and life success. Relationships and interconnectedness with families are important for both schools and out-of-school time (OST) programs and learning opportunities.

During the COVID-19 pandemic, families have taken on a variety of different roles connected to both in school and out of school learning. Homes—which have long been sites of learning, even if they are not necessarily always acknowledged as such (Carter, 2020)—have become spaces where both schooling and OST programming occur, and as a result have made visible the importance of families. This shift has served to further highlight the inequities in the role of families in L&D ecosystems and the need for families to have additional supports. Similarly, racial inequities and state-sanctioned racial violence, which have always been present in the United States (U.S.), have recently become more visible, thus prompting greater focus on the race-based education and activities that Black, Indigenous, Latinx, Asian, and other racially minoritized families undertake to support their children in understanding and combatting racial oppression. The current moment offers both greater impetus and need to acknowledge and understand the role of families in L& D ecosystems. Although such relationships are often viewed as a positive part of learning, many families are disparaged, ignored, or marginalized when their practices and engagement with learning does not align with white[2], middle-class ways of supporting teaching and learning (Baqendano-López et al., 2013; Kim, 2009). It is important to recognize the varied ways that Black, Indigenous, Latinx, Asian, and other racially minoritized families, families living in economic poverty, and those whose native language does not align with the dominant language support their young people's learning experiences, as well as the barriers and gaps they face in pursuing learning experiences (Barton et al., 2004; Kim, 2009; Lopez & Caspe, 2014). For instance, white, middle-class parents may feel welcomed and have the resources (such as disposable income, childcare, and flexible work schedules) that allow them to attend in-school meetings and classroom events, as well as pay for structured lessons or learning opportunities. Black, Indigenous, Latinx, Asian, and other racially minoritized families, particularly those with fewer economic resources may not feel welcomed in schools, may be less aware of or able to access the expectations of outside structured learning opportunities, and may be engaged in more family-centric experiences.

In this chapter, I forward current understandings of families as both sources and coordinators of learning across L&D ecosystems. I follow this with an over-

---

[2] Throughout this chapter I capitalize Black but not white. This is a deliberate practice drawing from scholarship that recognizes capitalizing Black not only as denoting a racial category, but as a way to acknowledge that slavery forcibly stripped Black people of their national and ethnic ties in a way that was not done to white people (see the Columbia Journalism Review https://www.cjr.org/analysis/capital-b-black-styleguide.php for greater depth on these points). In addition, capitalizing Black but not white acts as a way to decenter whiteness, and in the case of this chapter the practices of white families, as the norm or default identity.

view of the differences in the ways that families are conceptualized as supporting and facilitating learning, with a particular focus on the barriers marginalized and minoritized families face in supporting and accessing learning for their young people. Finally, I conclude with some suggestions and opportunities for both in-school and OST educators to recognize and support the engagement of families in young people's L&D ecosystems.

FAMILIES AS SITES, EXTENSIONS, AND FACILITATORS OF LEARNING

Families are young people's first L&D ecosystems and themselves constitute natural learning environments (Dunst et al., 2000; LaRosa, 2013). Learning itself is a contextual process that encompasses both biological and social development (Osher et al., 2020). Learning in family and with familial caregivers encompasses formal, nonformal, and informal learning contexts (Akiva et al., Chapter 2 of this volume; Blyth & LaCroix-Dalluhn, 2011); may be deliberate or by chance; and spans and connects content areas, such as Science Technology Engineering and Math (STEM) and literacy (Dunst et al., 2000; Morris et al., 2019; Napoli & Purpura, 2018). Children learn and develop in informal settings through their participation in general activities with their families—such as daily practices in the home, shopping, and participation in community spaces and community life (Rogoff et al., 2016). They may also engage in formal settings through deliberate "pre-schooling," school-based learning, and they may interact in informal out-of-school learning spaces and programming with the support of their families. These settings, and the learning and development that children experience in each connect and impact each other (Osher et al., 2020). In this section, I offer insight into the ways that families are considered vis-à-vis young people's learning—broadly, as connected to formal learning settings and in relation to nonformal OST sites and programs. The goal of this overview is not simply to provide a general understanding of the impacts of these various framings of the role of family in learning, but also to demonstrate the necessity of problematizing what are often reduced to transactional connections—that is engaging families simply as those who bring young people to learning programs or events or as passive attendees of meetings and final showcases— in favor of seeing these contexts as connected (Osher et al., 2020) and positioning families through the lens of their "funds of knowledge" (González et al., 2006) and the associated opportunities this framing offers for young people.

"Pre"- Schooling and Families

One of the earliest connections that caregivers have to broader L&D ecosystems is the informal at-home learning that both precedes children's entry into formalized instructional activities and continues concurrently throughout their experiences with outside learning. This learning is often discussed and theorized through its connection to formal schooling outcomes and school-related engagement practices; that is, whether and how it prepares students for and acts as a complementary pre-cursor to formalized schooling (Bassok et al., 2016). Much of the research on learning at home with family is centered on the activities and developmental value of the space (e.g., including materials such as books, activities such as reading or social interaction) that will ultimately support preparation for school. This "pre"-schooling takes the form of language and vocabulary development (Tamis-LeMonda & Rodriguez, 2008)—which sometimes includes differences in "home language" and bilingualism (Mancilla-Martinez & Lesaux, 2011)—early numeration and math skills (Elliott & Bachman, 2018; Missall et al., 2015), and socialization for what is deemed "socially appropriate" or pro-social engagement.

A large body of work connects the informal learning experiences that children have at home to their outcomes in school. For instance, research points to the positive outcomes in educational testing and grade promotion that occur for children in language and print-rich environments with parents who read to and talk with them regularly (Sénéchal & LeFevre, 2002). Similarly, studies in early math skills, such as numeracy, patterns, and spatial recognition have found that both formal (e.g., work sheets and structured exercises) and informal math practices (e.g., exposure and noticing patterns in everyday experiences) are associated with better academic scores. Often these associations are framed through the backgrounds of caregivers—primarily parents—including their education and income levels, such that families with parents who have higher levels of income and/or education are more likely to raise young people who are better prepared for and have more positive outcomes in formal educational environments (Votruba-Drzal, 2003; Yeung et al., 2002). As will be discussed in more detail below, this association is also connected to the alignment that occurs across learning environments experienced most often by white, middle, and upper socioeconomic status (SES) families.

Another associated body of work looks at the value of formal preschool—rather than being at home with familial caregivers— for the achievement of "school readiness." For instance, children who attend formalized learning settings prior to kindergarten are found more likely to be better prepared for the schooling environment—not surprisingly because many components across these settings align (Bassock et al., 2019). Recent trends indicate that overall levels of attendance in formal, but non-compulsory programs have increased in recent decades, with Black and white families more likely to be in attendance, as compared to their Hispanic/Latinx counterparts, and families with parents who have higher levels of education more likely to be enrolled compared to families with parents who have lower levels of education (Child Trends Databank, 2019). This scholarship positions schooling as the critical site of learning, even before "school" is compulsory. However, this and other research also points to the importance of access to high quality early childcare and learning environments beyond children's immediate learning. For instance, high quality early childcare is positioned as a way to reme-diate later outcome gaps, as well as to allow children's caregivers to participate in the workforce.

Schooling and Families

Strongly connected to the family "pre"- schooling discussed above are the ways that families are regarding as connected or disconnected to formalized K–12 edu-cation spaces. Caregiver connections to schools have been explored in a variety of domains, including the association of parental engagement with child's school outcomes (Castro et al., 2015; Jeynes, 2007; Wilder, 2014), the positive outcomes for schools when families participate in desired/requested ways (Barnyak & Mc-Nelly, 2009; Dauber & Epstein, 1989; Lawson, 2003), and relationship challeng-es between educators and families, both connected to resources (Cutler, 2000; Lawson, 2003; Milner, 2015; Addi-Raccah & Ariv-Elyashiv, 2008; Lareau, 2003; Lareau & Muñoz, 2012; Lareau et al., 2018), and to the misalignment of educa-tors and school settings with families (Baquedano-López et al., 2013). Across literatures, relationships between schools and families vary; however, much is centered on the formal learning outcomes and the needs of the school, and fami-lies are often evaluated based on their ability to show up at certain events or participate in school sanctioned participation, rather than learning that may occur in other domains outside of school, including both formal OST learning spaces, broader community sites, and within the home. This connection changes across children's development and schools' expectations, with families engaged more directly when children are younger and offering more autonomy and less direct, hands-on engagement as they grow into adolescence (Reinke et al., 2019; Smith et al., 2019).

OST as Nonformal Family Learning

As noted above, families and the at-home learning that precede and run ad-jacent to schooling are not theorized in the same way vis-á-vis OST as they are with schools, although these experiences are happening concurrently. This likely occurs, in part, because for younger children, nonformal learning settings such as museums, libraries, science centers, and zoos may serve as complements or extensions to home learning and support the parents of younger children in learn-ing extension, as well as interest and skill development. Families' participation can further stimulate youth participation in these spaces (Simpkins et al., 2005).

Research on OST offers insights into the ways that caregiver interactions with spaces and exhibits extend and connect learning across space and time (Ellenbo-gen, 2002). This work offers strong examples of what is possible for capturing understandings of ecosystem operation. It is harder to make some of these con-nections in-homes, although digital learning opportunities and the movement of programs, exhibits, etc. to homes due to COVID-19 have increased the visibility of this approach. Further, where it is connected to OST, family engagement with learning is typically centered on information, connection, and selection (discussed more below). Black, Indigenous, Latinx, Asian, and other Families of Color and others who are minoritized due to language or SES are often the focus of engagement and outreach by these spaces, including a push for opportunities to access and connections to other community spaces to extend the value/serving-ness of the resources outside of their sites.

Funds of Knowledge and Familial Learning across Contexts

One of the shortcomings of formal "pre"-schooling or "schooling" is the lack of acknowledgement of the ways white, middle-class norms and values underlie and are themselves reinforced in these spaces. For instance, a strong example comes from the controversial "word gap" research, wherein there have been observations of variations in the verbal interactions that children experience based on race and income. Children from white, middle class families have been purported to hear the most words and experience greater school success as connected with their broader exposure. However, subsequent research has recognized the rich verbal interactions occurring in racially minoritized families and discussed the ways this "gap" and associated disparities may be more connected to the alignment between the home interactions and school interactions for white, middle class children, rather than a deficit of Black, Indigenous and other Families of Color (Baugh, 2017; Johnson et al., 2017). Another shortcoming associated with many understandings of formal "pre"-schooling is an incomplete view of this engagement as connected to life-wide learning, where instead of focusing on the ways "pre"-school learning facilitates a smooth transition into school, these knowledge, skills, and abilities could and should be conceptualized as supporting and embracing for the ways they build and facilitate young peoples' broader interest in the world, skill development, engagement with their families and others, and enjoyment or happiness. Only certain outcomes and connections to academic learning are deemed legitimate (Akiva et al., 2020). This view of the role of families in learning or schooling experiences is a frequent a shortcoming of school-based understandings of caregiver engagement throughout child development, where families are posited as most engaged when they are supporting the school's agenda—including though not limited to homework and PTO meetings—rather than the recognition that familial support of learning extends far beyond that. In addition, this research and positioning typically focuses on families supporting children in becoming "school-ready" rather than locating families and young people in context and recognizing behaviors and the need for schools and all learning environments to be child and family ready. In short, families are often described as either aligning with learning successes or as a barrier to be overcome.

The concepts of both "funds of knowledge" and "community cultural wealth" (Yosso, 2005) offer useful perspectives of the resources and engagement that racially and ethnically marginalized families and communities bring to their children's L&D ecosystems. Funds of knowledge (González et al., 2006) refers to the cultural knowledge and practices of Families of Color that are accumulated over time and through their everyday lived realities that they engage to build their children's educational and social capacities. Relatedly, community cultural wealth recognizes that communities imbue resources in their young people that are not always recognized by formal learning institutions, including familial, linguistic, and navigational capital (Yosso, 2005). These are critical aspects of knowledge and practice for racially and ethnically marginalized young people that OST leaders may also overlook.

Considering life-wide education and young people's learning experiences as couched in overlapping ecosystems (as discussed in a variety of ways throughout this volume) offers the opportunity to reframe learning in ways that truly center young people, but further offers the opportunity to see the fundamental roles that familial caregivers play and build upon their funds of knowledge (González et al., 2006). As Lovatt et al. (2017) offered, in thinking about early childhood learning through the framework of funds of knowledge, "Funds of knowledge incorporates the bodies of knowledge, including information, skills, and strategies, which underlie household functioning, development, and well-being." (p. 101). This includes shopping lists and recipes in literacy, as well as knowledge of cultural practices and routines—extending well beyond conceptualizations that focus on schools. Funds of knowledge align strongly with the learning that occurs outside of school but is more deliberately taken up in OST (Civil, 2016). An emphasis on the funds of knowledge—the beliefs and practices— that minoritized families bring to support their young people's learning offers potential for the development of relationships between schools, OST programs and spaces, families, and communities (Moll et al., 1992). This connects closely with the role that minoritized families play in their young people's L&D ecosystems through activism and resistance (Cooper, 2009; Mazama & Lundy, 2012). This extension of the idea of funds of knowledge brought by familial adults and connected to youth experiences of learning can extend from birth and early childhood learning to older youth as a way to more fully connect their understandings and worlds, as well as a way to support young people in not only bolster academic learning and school achievement, but rather to support young people in self and social knowledge and development, as well as justice endeavors (Paris, 2012).

DISPARITIES IN FAMILIES' LEARNING OPPORTUNITIES

Although all families have funds of knowledge on which to draw and build, families' access to learning opportunities varies greatly, and familial engagement in education is acknowledged and validated in very different ways based on families' race, ethnicity, language, and SES. Black, Indigenous, Latinx, Asian, and other Families of Color, families that do not speak English as a first language, and those living below the poverty line face a variety of barriers, and access to learning looks dramatically different for these families than their white, middle-

and upper-class counterparts. Further, these barriers connect with disparities and access gaps in childhood and beyond and the separation (rather than integration) across in and out of school spaces (Akiva et al., 2020). The types of learning opportunities available, the associated pathways, and the connection of these learning opportunities to familial support often looks dramatically different from the experiences and connections of white, middle- and upper-class families. In this section, I discuss the obstacles that families may face in accessing learning opportunities for their children, in particular as they intersect with families' race and socioeconomic status. Although these disparities may manifest differently, they exist across L&D ecosystems.

Obstacles to Family Connections to Learning

Structural Barriers

Structural barriers are those aspects of the external environment and systems that govern educational opportunities that may prevent the participation of families and young people in aspects of possible L&D ecosystems. For both schools and OST they are connected to the availability and access of programs across space, as they pertain to families. This connects with timing, cost, transportation; and the challenges associated with these barriers are often borne most heavily by families. These barriers are both material and psychic barriers. For instance, not being able to afford or access learning opportunities are material barriers; however, if families do not feel they or their children are the intended recipients of the programs or opportunities or that they are able to access such opportunities, those psychic barriers function just as effectively. Parents across incomes invest the same levels of time in their children, but there are disparities in financial expenditures, with wealthier parents able to access more across activity types for their children (Schneider et al., 2018).

Navigational Challenges

Another major barrier to participation facing Black, Indigenous, Latinx, Asian, and other Families of Color and those living in economic poverty is understanding how to navigate systems of education—both formal and nonformal settings. The ways this navigation is ultimately regarded further impacts learning opportunities that families engage. Research points to families as the drivers of connecting to other OST learning beyond the home in a practical sense because caregivers are often responsible for the processes associated with finding (information gathering), connecting to, and selecting nonformal learning experiences, particularly for younger children. They further provide the resources required to participate in these voluntary experiences, whether these activities connect to school or not. Recent work has tied to this to the challenges associated with growing neoliberal policy and practice in education—in particular, in the ways that nonformal learning opportunities require information, skills and abilities to select, and resources to pay (Levey-Friedman, 2013; Meier et al., 2018). For instance, to participate in an OST program, families need to know it exists, must have the time and understanding to find and complete any associated application materials, and the associated resources (time, financial, etc.) that allow their children to participate. As families seek to gather information, they are limited (or supported) by their networks, and their ultimately quality and outcomes in access is associated with the networks to which families belong. As DiSalvo et al. (2016) found, online information gathering for learning resources—lower SES families did not use technology resources as frequently and their electronic searches were not as effective due to limited skills with the technologies, as well as feelings of inability to engage the technology. In addition, low-SES families focused more on in-school performance and improving poor performance than on enrichment and supplementation of learning (DiSalvo et al., 2016). Families may also be persuaded or forced to consider OST opportunities that align directly with school learning to compensate for the environments in which their children are educated—either from their own assessment or outside policy (McNamara et al., 2018). This connects strongly to the intersection between barriers to learning and the reproduction of social inequalities.

Racialization of Educational Spaces

Another barrier to participation in L&D ecosystems comes from the ways that formalized educational spaces may be racialized to exclude and marginalize Black, Indigenous, Latinx, Asian, and other Families of Color. Racialization of education and OST aligned with schools, organizations that adhere to these logics may manifest whiteness and be both exclusionary and undesirable for Black, Indigenous, Latinx, Asian, and other Families of Color. Rather than seeking these formalized spaces, that have historically excluded or marginalized, Black, Indigenous, Latinx, Asian, and other Families of Color may seek out community opportunities.

Racialization of spaces goes beyond demographics, as Diamond and Lewis (forthcoming) pointed out; in particular, whiteness shapes spaces even when the people in them are not overwhelmingly white—forced assimilation, white racial projects and white supremacy; whiteness as power and a set of ideas; white cultural styles. As it connects to the influences of families on schooling and learning opportunities, white families often have influence on both structures and policies, whereas Black families' efforts are resisted or not deemed valuable (Diamond & Gomez, 2004; Howard & Reynolds, 2008). For instance, Diamond and Gomez (2004) noted the ways working class Black parents in low-income schools were engaging in the schools, but in ways that were focused on reform and often perceived as oppositional and thus devalued. Black parents may—in turn— operate and teach their children about schools and educators' antagonism toward them (Reynolds, 2010). The logics that define and animate these spaces whiten the spaces themselves. Relatedly, these expectations focus on individual children and families rather than on communities, despite understandings that minoritized communities historically and contemporarily may centralize communal experiences as part of both navigation and resistance (Cooper, 2009; Fields-Smith, 2005; Williams & Baber, 2007).

Similarly, OST spaces may be engaged by racially minoritized families to compensate for learning opportunities not available in their children's school, not as an expansion of topics or opportunities, but as a way to access opportunities available to children in economically well-resourced schools. The ways this engagement and cultivation is positioned as "good parenting" and particularly associated with mothering.

FAMILIES MAY EXACERBATE
BROADER EDUCATIONAL INEQUALITIES

Because learning experiences both in and outside of schools are inequitable, families' capacity to engage in them may work to further exacerbate those disparities. In this section, I discuss the ways that families may navigate learning that—despite their individual approaches—collectively work to further disadvantage others.

Recent data point to an unmet demand for afterschool programming in the U.S., with over 24 million young people interested in, but unable to access OST (Afterschool Alliance, 2020). In particular, families point to issues of cost (programs are too expensive), safety (there is no safe way to get to and from programming) and lack of available programming for not enrolling their children, with low-income, and in particular Black and Latinx families most likely to face these barriers to their children's OST access and participation (Afterschool Alliance, 2020). Rather than simply a barrier, the ways higher income families and, in some cases, white families across income levels may construct and engage in nonformal learning may itself harm *other* young people's life chances and access. Families may deliberately engage learning opportunities in ways that support their children in maintaining and building upon the social advantages they already possess (Levey-Friedman, 2013; Vincent & Ball, 2007). Concerted cultivation (Lareau, 2003) explains the ways that middle and high SES families are able to use their understanding of longer-term success—college and career, social, cultural outcomes—to foster both the development of their children's interests and talents and support them in maximizing these to achieve success. This understanding is class-based and has faced some challenges as it does not apply equally to Black, Indigenous, Latinx, Asian, and other Youth of Color and their families (Delale-O'Connor et al., 2020; Dow, 2019; Lewis-McCoy, 2014, 2016). However, it brings up clear barriers of access including information networks, financial resources, and alignment with gatekeeping activities for college and career. For instance, research points to continuous increase in both resources spending and investment of time spent with children in the U.S. (Kornrich & Furstenberg, 2013; Moore et al., 2014; Ramey & Ramey, 2009). Wealthy families spend considerably more money on outside of school enrichment than their counterparts earning less income—a gap which has always existed, but that nearly tripled between 1972/3 school year and 2005/6 school year (Duncan & Murnane, 2016). These differentials are seen most markedly on travel, music lessons and summer camps (Kaushal et al., 2011), as well as time spent in "novel" places among high income families (Phillips, 2011), activities which enhance children's background knowledge and vocabulary—areas that are connected to their in-school academic success.

Research points to the ways that OST can follow a "Matthew effect"—connecting young people and families with access to high quality learning opportunities to increasingly more opportunities and activities; young people in middle and upper middle class are more likely to participate in both school-based and non-school based extracurriculars and in more varied types of activities (Meier et al., 2018). OST learning in the summer correlates with academic achievement outcome gaps seen during the school year across SES (Alexander et al., 2007) and prompt a cumulative advantage connected to exposure, skill, and continued access. In addition, wealthier families are more likely to access free opportunities and online information regarding these than their less resourced counterparts (DiSalvo et al., 2016).

Families attribute meanings of well-being and future success—both educational and personal—to children's participation in extracurricular learning opportunities; this may stand as a way to try out/apprentice for future roles. This connects further with the ways outside of school learning helps families and children demonstrate the importance of "busyness" as preparation for middle class life (Gutiérrez et al., 2010).

There are negative impacts of this continual cultivation of children's learning on parents, as well as sometimes on children. "Good parenting" connects strongly with learning as framed in the rootedness of purchasing activity (Vincent & Maxwell, 2016) and family consumption with children's enrichment (Gutiérrez et al., 2010), but the benchmarks set by the most economically privileged families are unattainable by most. Some of the disparity is also centered on the individualistic focus of these opportunities—seeing one child or one family as navigating learning, rather than collectives and broader societal implications.

OST AS A WAY TO ADDRESS DISPARITIES

In contrast to the concerted cultivation and associated opportunity hoarding that may occur, families—particularly, Black, Indigenous, Latinx, Asian, and other Families of Color and those living in economic poverty—may work to not only compensate for disparate learning experiences but engage OST programs as a way to supplement and supplant in-school learning and as a way to consider broader community improvement. This is, at least in part, connected to the resources their schools may lack, as well as the erasure that occurs in the curricula their children experience both in and outside of schools. For instance, Black families may engage OST as a way to address African American history and Black experiences more generally that are not taken up in school (Huguley et al., 2021). Racialized compensatory cultivation (Delale-O'Connor et al., 2020) is a way that families seek to both mitigate racist structures and practices associated with schools and support children's academic and social development both inside and outside of school. Black families may actively seek these experiences through OST programs when such programs are available, or they may foster it through family activities, such as engaging with different media, attending festivals, or traveling (Delale-O'Connor et al., 2020). Black and other Families of Color may engage in homeschooling, unschooling, or other forms of education specifically to engage this heritage and future-facing orientation in their childrens' education and avoid the harms perpetuated by learning spaces that erase them.

Similarly, families who face systemic concerns about their children's physical safety may engage learning spaces for different reasons. For families, whose children are not safe in their neighborhoods due to racial identity or who feel that their children may deliberately engage in what they believe are socially undesirable activities, OST programs—regardless of type—may offer a safe location to send their children outside of school hours (Delale-O'Connor et al., 2020). Connected to state sanctioned racialized violence at the hands of the police, families of color, particularly Black families may see these spaces as ways to protect their children from the police and policing.

Related to both accessing better culturally connected experiences as well as safety, Black, Indigenous, Latinx, Asian, and other Families of Color may see OST learning based in their communities as a way to support the learning of children beyond their own families. Collective engagement and concern look different than the ways learning is often conceptualized—as an individualized effort; rather, families sometimes see themselves as part of a larger community and as such responsibility for the learning and development of children beyond those they are directly raising/caring for.

Families influence learning systems in a variety of ways on behalf of and in conjunction with young people. They are certainly part of the supportive relationships that propel youth experiences, and they are impacted by the same sectors that concurrently influence youth. Ideally schools, programs, and learning opportunities should draw from family culture and practices.

IMAGINING L&D ECOSYSTEMS AS CULTURALLY SUSTAINING SPACES THAT INCLUDE AND ENGAGE FAMILIES

Inclusion of families in learning involves communication, deliberate engagement, and centering of their experiences. In addition, it involves recognizing and dismantling the barriers that families face in accessing and engaging in learning opportunities for their young people. In response to family wants and needs for themselves and their young people, many programs and opportunities respond directly to the barriers discussed above. For instance, OST aimed at teaching young people about their heritage may directly provide the connections that schools do not (Delale-O'Connor et al., 2020; Lee & Hawkins, 2008). Although OST cannot reasonably be expected to address all of the disparities of school systems, programs, and learning opportunities can avoid further exacerbating and reinforcing/ replicating the inequalities perpetuated by schools. They can create spaces and interactions that serve as exemplars—connecting with families in ways that schools believe they cannot or have not (Allen et al., 2020; Lee & Hawkins, 2008). Familial caregivers remain a constant source connected to young people's experiences and development, and deliberate connections to families offers the opportunity to both better center children and support them in the fullest expression of their humanity. Below, I outline three broad ideas for OST leaders and other adults in the allied youth fields to better support families as an important part of L&D ecosystems.

1. Recognize the impacts of race, culture, and SES to build upon families' knowledge and goals for their children

Families' racial and cultural identities influence the way they and the young people within them see the world, the activities they encourage their young people to engage in, their trust of outside entities—in short, many factors that shape how they engage learning broadly. It is critical for educators across domains to not only understand this, but engage it across all aspects of programming from recruitment to hiring to curriculum to activities. These understandings are necessarily place and space related—as the context of each aspect of a L&D ecosystem matters. These practices will support family engagement. This can occur practically by offering opportunities for families to share information about who they are—through surveys, interviews, participation in programs, and projects that engage familial culture.

The goals of education across L&D ecosystems should be to support young people in both being their full selves and critically understanding the world around them. This includes not just knowledge of but inclusion and building upon their familial ways of being and knowing. It may mean direct inclusion of families in programs or complementary programming for families in shared sites, such as language classes, job training, or adult courses, thus providing holistic, "one-stop-shop" opportunities that support both family and children's needs. Opportunities for families to build skills they may not feel they have to support their children's learning or augment/connect to family experiences, as well as recognizing funds of knowledge that the families bring allows them (Hensley, 2005).

2. Design learning opportunities for access, connection, and freedom of movement

One of the barriers for marginalized families discussed above is navigating learning opportunities—connecting in-school learning and supporting young people in finding the "next" thing to help them build on and connect their learning experiences. City-wide networks (such as those developing in STEM Ecosystems, https://stemecosystems.org) allow families to not just access one space or opportunity, but make those connections in thinking about the ways learning can build upon and further more learning. This requires information resources that support parental navigating what can sometimes be complicated systems.

Supporting families through access and connections draw upon what Pinkard (2019) referred to as freedom of movement—that is the "degree with which youth and families can engage in planning and participation in learning opportunities" (p. 45). "Freedom of movement" involves a constellation of connections including opportunities that families can access via a variety of modes of transportation, activities that can be done in the home, and understanding and support parental of boundaries. This means asking and getting answer to questions such as: Are families comfortable with their child engaging with people and ideas with which they are not familiar? How can learning spaces and the people in them break down potential barriers? This goes beyond individual programs and extends to truly consider learning as something that happens within ecosystems.

3.   Deliberately value and support in-family learning

Finally, connected with the ideas above, is the focus on fostering high quality learning opportunities at home and in conjunction with families. COVID-19 has fostered opportunities for young people to learn online in their homes but doesn't necessarily mean that families are included in these learning opportunities. Kits, extensions, available across barriers (literacy, numeracy, and language challenges can be addressed, as well as the use of commonly found rather than purchased items). Games can be used across spaces as a way to support learning and encourage family connection to a variety of forms of learning (Kliman, 2006). Further, for families who may have children across ages, how can programs think about connecting learning across siblings/connected children? How can learning opportunities foster access to resources that families may need—such as growing food, cleaning water; conducting family narratives; learning to cook/bake? All of the suggestions require connection to communities and the knowledge of the histories and presents of these communities and how those things intersect with learning.

CONCLUSION AND REFLECTIONS

Although a lot of learning during COVID-19 has found its center in homes and among familial caregivers, the need to center families in young people's life-wide learning is not always recognized. Families are a critical part of all L&D ecosystems. The role of families in L&D ecosystems—as fostering, facilitating, and connecting children's learning and positioning the adults as learners themselves—both historically and contemporarily should not be overlooked. Families offer the opportunity to see young people holistically because they have a connection to each aspect of the ecosystems in which their young people function. In the best aligned learning opportunities, families are recognized as sites of learning the opportunity to build upon, connect to and foster familial connections and growth. Increasingly connecting the spaces of learning, including families allows us to shift away from school-centric models of learning and education and focus on the ways that learning happens across spaces and in ways that are embedded in young people's experiences.

REFERENCES

Addi-Raccah, A., & Arviv-Elyashiv, R. (2008). Parent empowerment and teacher professionalism: Teachers' perspective. *Urban Education, 43*(3), 394–415.

Afterschool Alliance. (2020). America after 3PM: Demand grows, opportunity shrinks. http://afterschoolalliance.org/documents/AA3PM-2020/AA3PM-National-Report. pdf

Akiva, T., Delale-O'Connor, L., & Pittman, K. J. (2020). The promise of building equitable ecosystems for learning. *Urban Education.* https://journals.sagepub.com/doi/full/1 0.1177/0042085920926230?casa_token=FsDXK72tRusAAAAA%3AH9cEfgS7-nGJtl5I3bWs9URY4u25JvoIWYHT7FCIJNyhxK--DkkDm9dSH85aseSQ3vjCpvo sQ6XGLbA.

Alexander, K. L., Entwisle, D. R., & Olson, L. S. (2007). Lasting consequences of the summer learning gap. *American Sociological Review, 72*(2), 167–180.

Allen, A., Ball, M., Bild, D., Boone, D., Briggs, D., Davis, D., Delale-O'Connor, L., Gonda, R., Iriti, J., Legg, A. S., *Long, C., Matthis, C., Sherer, J., & Stol, T. (2020). *Leveraging out-of-school STEM programs to meet the needs of youth and families during COVID-19.* Connected Science Learning. https://www.nsta.org/connected-science-learning/connected-science-learning-october-december-2020/leveraging-out-school

Baquedano-López, P., Alexander, R. A., & Hernández, S. J. (2013). Equity issues in parental and community involvement in schools: What teacher educators need to know. *Review of Research in Education, 37,* 149–182.

Barnyak, N. C., & McNelly, T. A. (2009). An urban school district's parent involvement: A study of teachers' and administrators' beliefs and practices. *School Community Journal, 19*(1), 33–58.

Barton, A. C., Drake, C., Perez, J. G., St. Louis, K., & George, M. (2004). Ecologies of parental engagement in urban education. *Educational Researcher, 33*(4), 3–12.

Bassok, D., Finch, J. E., Lee, R., Reardon, S. F., & Waldfogel, J. (2016). Socioeconomic gaps in early childhood experiences: 1998 to 2010. *AERA Open, 2*(3), 1–22. DOI: 2332858416653924.

Bassok, D., Gibbs, C. R., & Latham, S. (2019). Preschool and children's outcomes in elementary school: Have patterns changed nationwide between 1998 and 2010? *Child Development, 90*(6), 1875–1897.

Baugh, J. (2017). Meaning-less differences: Exposing fallacies and flaws in "the word gap" hypothesis that conceal a dangerous "language trap" for low-income American families and their children. *International Multilingual Research Journal, 11*(1), 39–51.

Blyth, D. A., & LaCroix-Dalluhn, L. (2011). Expanded learning time and opportunities: Key principles, driving perspectives, and major challenges. *New Directions for Youth Development, 131,* 15–27.

Carter, S. A. (2020, September) Learning at home has an unexpected history. *Washington Post,* https://www.washingtonpost.com/outlook/2020/09/09/learning-home-could-have-benefits-americas-students/

Castro, M., Expósito-Casas, E., López-Martín, E., Lizasoain, L., Navarro-Asencio, E., & Gaviria, J. L. (2015). Parental involvement on student academic achievement: A meta-analysis. *Educational Research Review, 14,* 33–46.

Child Trends Databank. (2019). *Preschool and prekindergarten.* Child Trends. https://www.childtrends.org/?indicators=preschool-and-prekindergarten

Civil, M. (2016). STEM learning research through a funds of knowledge lens. *Cultural Studies of Science Education, 11*(1), 41–59.

Cooper, C. W. (2009). Parent involvement, African American mothers, and the politics of educational care. *Equity & Excellence in Education, 42*(4), 379–394.

Dauber, S. L., & Epstein, J. L. (1989). *Parent attitudes and practices of parent involvement in inner-city elementary and middle schools.* Report No. 33.

Delale-O'Connor, L., Huguley, J. P., Parr, A., & Wang, M. T. (2020). Racialized compensatory cultivation: Centering race in parental educational engagement and enrichment. *American Educational Research Journal, 57*(5), 1912–1953.

Diamond, J. B., & Gomez, K. (2004). African American parents' educational orientations: The importance of social class and parents' perceptions of schools. *Education and Urban Society, 36*(4), 383–427.

Diamond, J. B., & Lewis, A. E. (in press). Opportunity hoarding and the maintenance of white educational space. *American Behavioral Scientist.* http://www.johnbdiamond.com/uploads/6/5/0/7/65073833/american_behavioral_scientist_paper_opportunity_hoardingfinal_7-27-20.edited.pdf

DiSalvo, B., Khanipour Roshan, P., & Morrison, B. (2016, May). Information seeking practices of parents: Exploring skills, face threats and social networks. In *Proceedings of the 2016 CHI Conference on Human Factors in Computing Systems* (pp. 623–634). Association for Computing Machinery Digital Library

Dow, D. M. (2019). *Mothering while Black: Boundaries and burdens of middle-class parenthood.* University of California Press.

Duncan, G. J., & Murnane, R. J. (2016). Rising inequality in family incomes and children's educational outcomes. *RSF: The Russell Sage Foundation Journal of the Social Sciences, 2*(2), 142–158.

Dunst, C. J., Hamby, D., Trivette, C. M., Raab, M., & Bruder, M. B. (2000). Everyday family and community life and children's naturally occurring learning opportunities. *Journal of Early Intervention, 23*(3), 151–164.

Ellenbogen, K. M. (2002). Museums in family life: An ethnographic case study. In G. Leinhardt, K. Crowley, & K. Knutson (Eds.), *Learning conversations in museums* (pp. 81–101). Lawrence Erlbaum Associates.

Elliott, L., & Bachman, H. J. (2018). How do parents foster young children's math skills? *Child Development Perspectives, 12*(1), 16–21.

Fields-Smith, C. (2005). African American parents before and after Brown. *Journal of Curriculum and Supervision, 20,* 129–135.

González, N., Moll, L. C., & Amanti, C. (Eds.). (2006). *Funds of knowledge: Theorizing practices in households, communities, and classrooms.* Routledge.

Gutiérrez, K. D., Izquierdo, C., & Kremer-Sadlik, T. (2010). Middle class working families' beliefs and engagement in children's extra-curricular activities: The social organization of children's futures. *International Journal of Learning, 17*(3), 633–656.

Harris, A., & Goodall, J. (2008). Do parents know they matter? Engaging all parents in learning. *Educational Research, 50*(3), 277–289.

Hensley, M. (2005). Empowering parents of multicultural backgrounds. In N. González, L. Moll, & C. Amanti (Eds.), *Funds of knowledge: Theorizing practices in households, communities and classrooms* (pp. 143–151). Routledge.

Hill, N. E., & Tyson, D. F. (2009). Parental involvement in middle school: a meta-analytic assessment of the strategies that promote achievement. *Developmental Psychology, 45*(3), 740.

Howard, T. C., & Reynolds, R. (2008). Examining parent involvement in reversing the underachievement of African American students in middle-class schools. *Educational Foundations, 22*, 79–98.

Huguley, J. P., Delale-O'Connor, L., Wang, M. T., & Parr, A. K. (2021). African American parents' educational involvement in urban schools: Contextualized strategies for student success in adolescence. *Educational Researcher, 50*(1), 6–16.

Jeynes, W. H. (2007). The relationship between parental involvement and urban secondary school student academic achievement: A meta-analysis. *Urban education, 42*(1), 82–110.

Johnson, E. J., Avineri, N., & Johnson, D. C. (2017). Exposing gaps in/between discourses of linguistic deficits. *International Multilingual Research Journal, 11*(1), 5–22.

Kim, Y. (2009). Minority parental involvement and school barriers: Moving the focus away from deficiencies of parents. *Educational Research Review, 4*(2), 80–102.

Kliman, M. (2006). Math out of school: Families' math game playing at home. *School Community Journal, 16*(2), 69–90.

Kornrich, S., & Furstenberg, F. (2013). Investing in children: Changes in parental spending on children, 1972–2007. *Demography, 50*(1), 1–23.

Kaushal, N., Magnuson, K., & Waldfogel, J. (2011). Parents supplement children's in-school educational activities and promote children's learning through a wide variety of investments. For preschool-age children, family income may be invested in early care and education programs as well as enrichment activities and items such. *Whither opportunity?: Rising inequality, schools, and children's life chances*, 187.

Lareau, A. (2003). *Unequal childhood: Class, race, and family life*. University of California Press.

Lareau, A., & Muñoz, V. L. (2012). "You're not going to call the shots" structural conflicts between the principal and the PTO at a suburban public elementary school. *Sociology of Education, 85*(3), 201–218.

LaRosa, L. (Ed.). (2013). *Families as learning environments for children*. Springer Science & Business Media.

Lareau, A. (2018). Unequal childhoods: Class, race, and family life. In *Inequality in the 21st century* (pp. 444–451). Routledge.

Lawson, M. A. (2003). School-family relations in context: Parent and teacher perceptions of parent involvement. *Urban Education, 38*(1), 77–133.

Lee, S. J., & Hawkins, M. R. (2008). "Family is here": Learning in community-based after-school programs. *Theory into Practice, 47*(1), 51–58.

Levey-Friedman, H. (2013). *Playing to win: Raising children in a competitive culture.* University of California Press

Lewis-McCoy, R. H. (2014). *Inequality in the promised land: Race, resources, and suburban schooling.* Stanford University Press.

Lewis-McCoy, R. (2016). Boyz in the 'burbs: Parental negotiation of race and class in raising Black males in suburbia. *Peabody Journal of Education, 91,* 309–325.

Lopez, M. E., & Caspe, M. (2014). Family engagement in anywhere, anytime learning. *Family Involvement Network of Educators (FINE) Newsletter, 6*(3), 1–9.

Lovatt, D., Cooper, M., & Hedges, H. (2017). Enhancing interactions: Understanding family pedagogy and funds of knowledge "on their turf." In A. Gunn & C. Hruska (Eds.) *Interactions in Early Childhood Education* (pp. 99–112). Springer, Singapore.

Mancilla-Martinez, J., & Lesaux, N. K. (2011). Early home language use and later vocabulary development. *Journal of Educational Psychology, 103*(3), 535.

Mazama, A., & Lundy, G. (2012). African American homeschooling as racial protectionism. *Journal of Black Studies, 43*(7), 723–748.

McNamara, A. R., Akiva, T., & Delale-O'Connor, L. (2018). Opportunity gaps in out-of-school learning: How structural and process features of programs relate to race and socioeconomic status. *Applied Developmental Science,* 1–17.

Meier, A., Hartmann, B. S., & Larson, R. (2018). A quarter century of participation in school-based extracurricular activities: Inequalities by race, class, gender and age?. *Journal of Youth and Adolescence, 47*(6), 1299–1316.

Milner IV, H. R. (2015). *Rac (e) ing to class: Confronting poverty and race in schools and classrooms.* Harvard Education Press.

Milner, H. R., Murray, I. E., Farinde, A. A., & Delale-O'Connor, L. (2015). Outside of school matters: What we need to know in urban environments. *Equity and Excellence in Education, 48*(4), 529–548.

Missall, K., Hojnoski, R. L., Caskie, G. I., & Repasky, P. (2015). Home numeracy environments of preschoolers: Examining relations among mathematical activities, parent mathematical beliefs, and early mathematical skills. *Early Education and Development, 26*(3), 356–376.

Moll, L. C., Amanti, C., Neff, D., & Gonzalez, N. (1992). Funds of knowledge for teaching: Using a qualitative approach to connect homes and classrooms. *Theory Into Practice, 31*(2), 132–141.

Moore, K. A., Murphey, D., Bandy, T., & Copper, P. M. (2014). Participation in out-of-school time activities and programs. *Child Trends Research Brief Publication 2014,* 13.

Morris, B. J., Owens, W., Ellenbogen, K., Erduran, S., & Dunlosky, J. (2019). Measuring informal STEM learning supports across contexts and time. *International Journal of STEM Education, 6*(1), 40.

Napoli, A. R., & Purpura, D. J. (2018). The home literacy and numeracy environment in preschool: Cross-domain relations of parent–child practices and child outcomes. *Journal of Experimental Child Psychology, 166,* 581–603.

Osher, D., Cantor, P., Berg, J., Steyer, L., & Rose, T. (2020). Drivers of human development: How relationships and context shape learning and development. *Applied Developmental Science, 24*(1), 6–36.

Paris, D. (2012). Culturally sustaining pedagogy: A needed change in stance, terminology, and practice. *Educational Researcher, 41*(3), 93–97.

Phillips, M. (2011). Parenting, time use, and disparities in academic outcomes. In G. J. Duncan & R. J. Murnane (Eds.), *Whither opportunity? Rising inequality, schools, and children's life chances* (pp. 207–228). Russell Sage Foundation.

Pinkard, N. (2019). Freedom of movement: Defining, researching, and designing the components of a healthy learning ecosystem. *Human Development, 62*(1–2), 40–65.

Ramey, G., & Ramey, V. A. (2009). *The rug rat race* (No. w15284). National Bureau of Economic Research.

Reinke, W. M., Smith, T. E., & Herman, K. C. (2019). Family-school engagement across child and adolescent development. *School Psychology, 34*(4), 346.

Reynolds, R. (2010). "They think you're lazy," and other messages black parents send their Black sons: An exploration of critical race theory in the examination of educational outcomes for Black males. *Journal of African American Males in Education, 1*(2), 144–163.

Rogoff, B., Callanan, M., Gutierrez, K. D., & Erickson, F. (2016). The organization of informal learning. *Review of Research in Education, 40*(1), 356–401.

Schneider, D., Hastings, O. P., & LaBriola, J. (2018). Income inequality and class divides in parental investments. *American Sociological Review, 83*(3), 475–507.

Sénéchal, J., & LeFevre, A. (2002). Parental involvement in the development of children's reading skill: A five-year longitudinal study. *Child Development, 73*, 445–460.

Simpkins, S. D., Davis-Kean, P. E., & Eccles, J. S. (2005). Parents' socializing behavior and children's participation in math, science, and computer out-of-school activities. *Applied Developmental Science, 9*(1), 14–30.

Smith, T. E., Reinke, W. M., Herman, K. C., & Huang, F. (2019). Understanding family–school engagement across and within elementary-and middle-school contexts. *School Psychology, 34*(4), 363.

Tamis-LeMonda, C. S., & Rodriguez, E. T. (2008). Parents' role in fostering young children's learning and language development. *Encyclopedia on Early Childhood Development, 1*, 1–11.

Vincent, C., & Ball, S. J. (2007). 'Making up' the middle-class child: Families, activities and class dispositions. *Sociology, 41*(6), 1061–1077.

Vincent, C., & Maxwell, C. (2016). Parenting priorities and pressures: Furthering understanding of 'concerted cultivation'. *Discourse: Studies in the Cultural Politics of Education, 37*(2), 269–281.

Votruba-Drzal, E. (2003). Income changes and cognitive stimulation in young children's home learning environments. *Journal of Marriage and Family, 65*(2), 341–355.

Wilder, S. (2014). Effects of parental involvement on academic achievement: A meta-synthesis. *Educational Review, 66*(3), 377–397.

Williams, E. R., & Baber, C. R. (2007). Part I: advancing the conversation: Building trust through culturally reciprocal home-school-community collaboration from the perspective of African-American parents. *Multicultural Perspectives, 9*(2), 3.

Yeung, W. J., Linver, M. R., & Brooks–Gunn, J. (2002). How money matters for young children's development: Parental investment and family processes. *Child Development, 73*(6), 1861–1879.

Yosso, T. (2005). Whose culture has capital? A critical race theory discussion of community cultural wealth. *Race, Ethnicity and Education, 81*, 69–91.

CHAPTER 6

THE POWER OF SIMPLE, ORDINARY INTERACTIONS IN DEVELOPMENTAL RELATIONSHIPS ACROSS CONTEXTS

Junlei Li and Dana Winters

In our work over the last decade, we have found ourselves in conversations with youth-serving professionals across a wide range of cultural and institutional settings. We have worked in orphanages that institutionalized children with disabilities and a rural foster care village that de-institutionalized children of similar disabilities. We have shadowed hospital social workers who provided psychosocial care to children awaiting medical cures. We have observed and interviewed crossing guards on street corners in urban neighborhoods. We have spent time with staff and youth in residential youth care facilities, youth violence prevention programs led by former gang leaders, and youth summer programs for children from migrant labor camps. These activities have afforded us the opportunities to shadow youth workers in their day-to-day work lives and hear their stories and reflections about what these interactions mean in the context of their communities. By serving as program evaluators, ethnographical observers, and professional learning facilitators, we have made incremental progress towards understanding

It Takes an Ecosystem: Understanding the People, Places, and
Possibilities of Learning and Development Across Settings, pages 109–124.

and appreciating authentic, everyday relational practices from the professionals who serve children, youth, and families.

As we followed staff and youth with our eyes and video cameras, we captured relational moments in seemingly routine interactions between staff and youth on almost any ordinary day. The most striking commonality across these developmental contexts is the visible and observable impact such small moments had on the youth and the adults. When we would play back these edited recordings for each local staff community and ask, "What do you notice?," the staff would readily describe the quality of relationships in such small moments—diaper change in the orphanage, calming a child during morning assembly, walking a youth from house to gym in residential care—and identify such interactions as core to their values and practices.

Our experience of facilitating conversations to *bring focus to* human relationships across developmental contexts opened our eyes, minds, and hearts to the common threads that bind together these professionals across the vast array of developmental contexts. Among the adults who serve youth, the academic and professional preparations vary greatly (e.g., teachers, artists, counselors) along with their institutional contexts (e.g., community-based programs, libraries, formal education). Yet, they are all developing the core competency of integrating the "content" of their work (e.g., teaching science, making art, community organizing) with the relational practice that build and sustain their connections with youth. These threads of their work weave together a rich, dynamic, and unifying mosaic of the allied youth fields (see Robinson & Akiva, Chapter 1 in this volume).

In our efforts to seed such conversations across the practice, program, and policy levels of the developmental ecosystem that encompasses professionals, youth, and families, we have posed three questions to engage people in reflecting about the power of human relationships across developmental contexts. Here, we describe each of these questions in the hopes that they may collectively offer a framework for relationship-focused conversations across the varying and expanding youth fields.

WHAT MAKES A DEVELOPMENTAL RELATIONSHIP?

Human relationships touch upon every stage of every domain of learning and development, whether it is language development in toddlers (Tamis-LeMonda et al., 2014), school-age learning (Hamre, 2014; Osher et al., 2018), or resilience development (Masten, 2014) and self- and co-regulation during adolescence (Center on the Developing Child, 2015; Immordino-Yang et al., 2018).

In developmental science, there are frequent mentions of relationships but relatively few comprehensive descriptions of what it means to build a "developmental relationship"—the kind of human relationship that supports the learning and development of one or more people in it. Depending on the theoretical or practical vantage point, the corresponding description and operationalization of relational processes often place a narrow emphasis on a particular dimension, phase, or domain of learning and development.

Attachment theorists such as John Bowlby and Mary Ainsworth focused on the mechanisms and measures of intense bonds between mothers and young children (Ainsworth et al., 1978; Bowlby, 1988). By carefully observing young children's patterns of behavior during separation and reunification with parents, they linked the security of a child's attachment to a primary caregiver to learning behaviors like exploration of novel environments. Cognitive theorists such as Jean Piaget focused on the mechanisms of conceptual development driven by adult and child interactions (Piaget, 1954). Through interactions with adults or other trusted sources of knowledge, children learn through a process of equilibration, where they find balance between adopting new knowledge into established mental structures or adapting established mental structures to integrate new knowledge. This relational process becomes the core mechanism for learning to restructure one's conceptual understandings. Social learning theorists such as Vygotsky (1978) emphasized the processes by which adults help push and scaffold children's learning. Introducing the concept of the "zone of proximal development," Vygotsky emphasized the intentional design of instruction to place optional challenges—neither too far nor too close to a child's present competency—as the iterative process of learning progress. Identity theorists such as Erik Erikson (1968) elaborated on the connections between relational experience and various stages of identity formation—for example, autonomy vs. doubt, industriousness vs. inferiority. Learning is not just intellectual or technical, according to this theoretical framework, but immensely personal and driven by one's striving to establish an integral identity. Collectively, these theoretical traditions laid the relationship-focused foundation for the emergence of the science of learning and development.

Ecological theorist Urie Bronfenbrenner (1979) attempted to integrate these social, emotional, and cognitive notions of learning and development in relational terms in the definition of the parent-child "developmental dyad" :

> Learning and development are facilitated by the participation of the developing person in progressively more complex patterns of reciprocal activity with someone with whom that person has developed a strong and enduring emotional attachment and when the balance of power gradually shifts in favor of the developing person. (p. 60)

The strengths of this definition are in its integration of participation, progressive complexity (akin to Vygotsky's successive Zone of Proximal Development), reciprocity, attachment, and power balance into relational processes. The limitations of Bronfenbrenner's ecological model and its subsequent elaboration and illustration is the notion of "individualized developmental ecosystem" (placing the child at the center of layers of concentric circles) rather than the much more interconnected, "center-less" learning and development ecosystem proposed by the editors of this volume (Robinson & Akiva, Chapter 1 in this volume; Akiva et al., Chapter 2). Nevertheless, we can today extend the intimate, dyadic processes at the "center" of Bronfenbrenner's model towards understanding the multi-directional relationships among children, families, and professionals throughout the

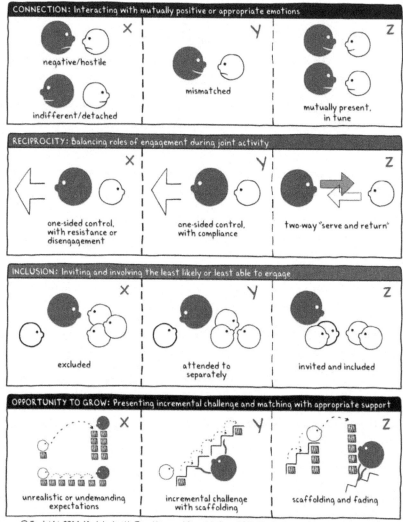

SIMPLE
INTERACTIONS
www.simpleinteractions.org

FIGURE 6.1. The Simple Interactions Tool, available for sharing, duplication, and adaptation through an Attribution, Non-commercial, Share-Alike Creative Commons 4.0 International License. Accessed from www.simpleinteractions.org.

entire ecosystem. There are dynamics of participation, progression, reciprocity, and connection in all relationships, influenced by and influencing the balance of power within each corner of the larger system.

To support this integrated understanding of what developmental relationships are and when (any time) and where (anywhere) they can take place, we believe that we need observational, descriptive, and learning tools that do not separate learning from feeling or connection from participation. For that purpose, we have developed the "Simple Interactions Tool" (Figure 6.1) that illustrates the commonly occurring modes of interaction along four interdependent dimensions: connection, reciprocity, opportunity to grow (these first three are very much inspired by the aforementioned dyadic definition by Bronfenbrenner), and inclusion (which considers the extent to which *all* children, including those who are most likely to be excluded, have access to the richness of relational interactions that embody the other three dimensions). The intent of this tool is to offer a flexible framework to facilitate the description, rather than the evaluation, of everyday practices. Over the past decade, we have made incremental adjustments to the tool to adapt to observed relational practices across the wide array of settings we described earlier. For example, within each dimension, the lines of division were modified from solid lines to dotted lines, reflecting the dynamic flow of the X, Y, Z modes within any interaction rather than using X, Y, Z as static labels.

We have used this tool in professional learning sessions for frontline staff as well as in the development of trainers, facilitators, staff coaches, supervisors, and researchers. Our intent is to expand the staff capacity to notice and describe relational interactions in everyday contexts and support the intentional reflections of relational practices that may already feel intuitive or instinctive (and thus often left unarticulated) to staff. By drawing attention to "interactions," we tried to de-mystify "relationship" from a state of being where one either "has or don't have one" to something that can be intentionally constructed from the small, incremental building blocks of everyday interactions. Such learning within communities of professional learning can affirm and expand our understanding of the role of relational practice across allied youth fields. We believe that is the essential task of growing our collective profession of serving children, youth, families, and communities.

WHY ARE DEVELOPMENTAL RELATIONSHIPS ESSENTIAL TO PRACTICE, PROGRAM, AND POLICY?

As the theories and science of developmental relationships evolved, the way relationships are defined, understood, measured, and assessed in practice settings needs to move from fragmentation to integration.

While most traditional conceptualizations of youth-serving practice include relational dimensions, relationships are often understood as having to do with interpersonal feelings of connection and overall positive climate in a setting, relatively separate from the activity content and skill-building aspects of youth programming. While relationships are thought to contribute to the development of skills, they are more frequently associated with social-emotional skills, such as self-regulation and help-seeking. Relationships are often not considered as integral to the development of cognitive and academic skills, such as creativity, problem-solving, or mastering writing or algebra.

Correspondingly, across program quality assessment tools from early childhood to youth development, from classrooms to informal learning contexts, staff-child relationships are often assessed as a separate dimension or domain of quality, apart from items that assess instructional or program activities (Granger, 2010; Mashburn et al., 2008; Pianta et al., 2012). In the hierarchy of program goals valued by those with significant decision-making power (e.g., funding, staffing), relationships most often remain a process indicator of *how* the program is operating, and not as one of the measurable outcomes to justify to the external world *why* the program is needed. Requests for proposals frequently feature academic and behavioral outcomes as the important accountability measures for funding, and rarely include relational metrics as *outcomes*.

The influence and pressure of such narrowly construed measures and funding requirements cascade to the program and practice level. We detect similarly compartmentalized understandings of the impact of relational practices when we first encounter program leaders and staff in conversation. Using the approximate distinctions of formal, informal, and nonformal learning settings (Blyth & LaCroix-Dalluhn, 2011), while staff would readily talk about the importance of building relationships with young people, the instances and examples they offer would often take place in informal settings. Teachers would talk about giving their students hugs in the hallway. Youth staff would talk about running into the program attendees in the neighborhood. Even those who are reluctant to embrace relational practices reflect such siloed views in their very resistance. On numerous occasions, we have heard some staff and leaders frame instructional and relational practices as a mutually exclusive choice, "I am not here to be their friend, I am here to teach (or coach)." While there are indeed wonderful opportunities for relationship building "on the sidelines" of formal teaching or programming, such understanding short-changes the richness of what teachers and youth staff actually do day to day, or at least, what they can actually offer from within their professional and personal capacity.

In our field observations, relational practices enrich everyday moments with real opportunities for belonging, learning, and growing in every aspect of learning and development. They transcend the distinctions and permeate the boundaries of formal, informal, and nonformal learning settings. We have captured moments of developmental interactions between adults and youth in transition time as well as in instructional time, during playful times, and during serious moments of disciplining and counseling. Consider a teacher finding and reflecting a sense of progress to a student after a mundane and mandated reading assessment, an out-of-school staff offering a few open-ended questions to challenge a group of children and watches them continue their tinkering with maker materials, and a residential care staff instructing a young man on how to brush a horse while listening to his struggles earlier in the school day. Separating relationship-building from measurable learning or developmental outcomes seems more externally imposed than internally driven by people who work closely with youth. When we replay such moments of interactions, captured on video, to staff and program leaders, they can readily recognize that relational practices deliver far more than "good feelings" between adults and youth.

Interactions like these also forge staff-child relationships that offer opportunities to break down barriers to access and support for youth across contexts, and especially for historically marginalized and excluded youth. It is not enough to merely extend access to nonformal and informal youth environments, but those environments must be intentional and equitable in their inclusion and support of youth. An equitable relational practice extends not only opportunity for interactions, but the support necessary for youth to engage in interactions with adults and other youth in ways that bring belonging, mattering, and agency (see Carey, 2019 for a thoughtful discussion about these social processes for Black youths in particular). By extending equitable relational practices, adults create environments that value the unique lived experiences of youth—remembering that each youth is more than just one thing (e.g., whether it is race, gender, academic performance, or athletics) and that there is more than one way for the adult to show up authentically to engage and connect with youth in daily interactions and support youth through sustained relationships.

Understanding relational practice as the central driver for a holistic range of learning and developmental outcomes has implications for practice, program, and policy across youth fields. While there are numerous studies and even meta-analyses of studies (in a recent writing effort, we counted over 50 reviews of studies in just the last 10 years!) about the importance of human relationships in development, we are particularly drawn to comparisons of relationships to the "active ingredient," or "essential ingredient" (Hamre, 2014; National Scientific Council on the Developing Child, 2004; Osher et al., 2018). This framing not only affirms the centrality of relational practices, but also clarifies the interdependencies of relational practice with other components of programs and policies (Li, 2019).

From our earliest to most recent writing (Li & Julian, 2012; Li & Winters, 2018; Winters & Li, 2018), we invoked the metaphor of fluoride inside a tube of toothpaste to describe what it means to be the "active ingredient." Most toothpastes list one single active ingredient—sodium fluoride. Toothpastes may vary greatly in packaging, flavor, texture, and additional features (e.g., whitening, breath-freshening), but its most critical function—cavity prevention—is accomplished by this one active ingredient. By analogy, we describe human relationships as the fluoride of developmental work. The critical function of supporting human development is accomplished by creating sufficient and sustained access for young people to the developmental relationships they need, whether it is instructional, coaching, mentoring, or even with older, younger, and same-age peers (Cantor et al., 2018; Center on the Developing Child, 2015; Immordino-Yang et al., 2018; Li & Julian, 2012; Rogoff et al., 2015). Colleagues at the Search Institute were also able to build on this "toothpaste" framing (Pekel et al., 2018) to elaborate how this general framework of "developmental relationships" applies in youth-serving contexts. Subsequently, through collaboration with the communication analysts at the Frameworks Institute, they adopted the "roots and trees" metaphor to match an ecological understanding (Frameworks Institute, n.d.).

To sharpen this focal point, we further extend this analogy by proposing a stronger hypothesis: that programs support development *if and only if* they enhance the quality of such relationships surrounding young people. Such supports may be direct, as in recruiting and developing staff who can effectively build relationships with young people. We saw this in the urban youth-violence prevention programs that intentionally recruited well-respected, former gang members to be youth staff. Such supports can also be indirect, as in creating fair and equitable working conditions to retain youth staff and lessen the life stressors on them, allowing them to be more fully present for the children they serve.

The corollary of this hypothesis would be: if programs undermine, dilute, or obstruct the quality of relationships between staff and youth, then the programs are not going to be effective. Here are two real and not-so-uncommon scenarios that we have observed in the course of our work. In response to external pressure to increase science and technology programming, an afterschool program rushed to introduce high-tech gadgets and curriculum. Without adequate professional development, the staff's attention and time were diverted from the existing activities that engaged youth and supported the relational practices. Staff then began to internalize the idea that the technology was the most important resource (instead of themselves) and referred to time with youth distinctly as "technology instruction time and relationship time." Separately, a residential care program struggled with persistently high staff turnover and absenteeism. Instead of addressing the root cause, the administrators pressured overworked staff to extend working hours to stay in compliance with mandated "staff to youth ratio." Stressed and demoralized, the remaining staff found it increasingly difficult to maintain relationships with youth.

In our work, we have found this way of analogical thinking to be helpful to dispel the perception or practice of treating relationships as a mere "check-list" item of program quality. For example, while the intent of approaches like Search Institute's "40 Developmental Assets" (Search Institute, n.d.) is to integrate numerous considerations in thinking of youth development, the shallow interpretation or implementation of such "list"-based frameworks can easily turn it into checklists of separate items and miss the interconnections, causal dependencies, and relative priorities within these items. We believe the "active ingredient" and "inactive ingredient" distinction can bring coherence to disconnected checklists. In the absence of fluoride, a tube of toothpaste can have all of its other ingredients and packaging, but still fail its core function of cavity prevention. For example, child-friendly flavoring does not equate in function as the active ingredient, even if it is helpful as an "inactive ingredient" to make the toothbrushing experience more pleasant or tolerable. Inactive ingredients may be exchangeable with substitutes (again, as in the example of flavoring), but there are no substitutes for the active ingredient—certainly not for human relationships in youth-serving programs. But just as simply holding fluoride in your mouth is not an ideal way to fight cavities, the active ingredient works better when supported by other inactive, yet useful ingredients (e.g., like the baking soda that foams and helps to distribute the fluoride, or the toothbrush that clears away the plaque). In youth-serving programs, staff training, resources, space, and partnerships can collectively support and strengthen the active ingredient of relational practices. In this way of thinking, we need not throw out the baby (e.g., checklists) with the bathwater (disconnected understanding of youth development). Using 40 Developmental Assets (Search Institute, n.d.) as an example, the lists of external assets (churches, youth program, school, safe neighborhoods) can remind us of all the places and opportunities where we can look to strengthen relational connections, and the list of internal assets (motivation, engagement, competence, decision-making) can remind us of all the developmental growth that can spring from the foundation of strong relationships.

In summary, we hope to cultivate an understanding that relational practices are embedded and intertwined in every aspect of program design and management. The active ingredient metaphor allows us to articulate and create consensus around what is indispensable and without substitutes—the active ingredient of relational practice. It also clearly illustrates what is necessary but flexible—the inactive yet supporting ingredients, such as program features that attract and engage youth or professional learning opportunities that affirm and encourage adults.

HOW DO WE GROW DEVELOPMENTAL RELATIONSHIPS?

By treating developmental relationship as the "active ingredient" that protects and promotes development across a learning and developmental ecosystem, we believe one question becomes essential to any effort to create a healthier learning and development ecosystem, "How does this practice improvement, program feature, or policy decision help to encourage, enrich, and empower the human relationships around the youth and those who are serving youth?"

So far, we have focused much of our discussion on the impact of relational practice in the development of youth. In our workshops, after staff and program leaders spend time examining the multi-faceted richness of staff-youth relational practices, they almost invariably start to wonder about the parallel processes of staff-staff, director-staff, and other human relationships in their setting. Here, we extend beyond the "youth-centered" lens to look at the broader ecosystems in which both youth and the youth-serving adults across youth fields are learning, growing, and connecting.

In an ecosystem that does not have a singular center, we can identify numerous "touchpoints" (possibilities) where human beings (people) and human organizations (places) come into relational contact with each other. At each touchpoint, human interactions take place through routines and rituals or by intentional design. For example, if we were to organize our thinking around the front-line staff who serve youth—the "keystone species" of this ecosystem (Akiva et al., Chapter 2 in this volume)—we might ask: "What are their touchpoints of interaction?" With youth, the staff interact in recruitment, program implementation, teaching, playing, counseling, and more other direct and immediate moments. With each other, the staff share ideas, resources, stories, frustrations, and encouragements. With their supervisors, the staff report successes, challenges, and expect and receive support. With the youths' families and communities, the staff foster engagement, build partnerships, maintain trust and communication. The quality of interactions at each of these touchpoints contributes to the overall quality of the developmental experience of youth, of staff, and of entire programs and communities.

Within such an ecosystem, we imagine that each adult—regardless of their professional role as staff, director, coach, researcher—is like the center of a series of overlapping ripples. We can picture what the surface of a small pond looks like as rain has just begun to fall. Each raindrop sends forth a series of concentric circles, covering an ever-widening area, and the increasingly complex and overlapping intersections of ripples will gradually reshape the entire surface and may even create larger waves or currents. In a similar way, what one person does relationally with others through the touchpoints they have immediately impacts those human beings nearby and has a rippling impact on others farther away. One powerful illustration of such mechanism is documented in the empathy intervention (Okonofua et al., 2016), where math teachers (and only math teachers) in low-income middle schools with predominantly students of color went through a short exercise of "empathy" that reminded them of their relationships with students. No additional staff or students received any intervention. Subsequently, the suspension rates of these schools were reduced to half of what they were, even though the study found that the math teachers themselves did not "discipline" the students any less. The impact stemming from just changing one person's relational touchpoint with students (who are unlikely going to be interacting with two different math teachers in the same school year) rippled out schoolwide. The lead author Jason Okonofua commented in an interview about the study, "The most interesting and inspiring part is that we only intervened with one of the students' teachers, and it affected their interactions with every other teacher. Just having one better relationship with a teacher at school—just one—can serve as a buffer for all the other struggles and challenges at school." (Sparks, 2016)

The rippling metaphor can contribute to our understanding of the larger effort of equity and social justice through the lens of relational practice within the learning and developmental ecosystem. Who are included in the ripples created by our practices, programs, and policies? As illustrated by the empathy intervention described above, it is necessary but not sufficient for low-income, predominantly minority students to have access to the schools, the math curriculum, or the math teachers. They need to access a kind of developmental relationship with the teacher, described above (Okonofua et al., 2016), a relationship that offers empathic interactions even in cases of performance or behavioral difficulties. Through that, students may start to develop a more relational engagement with the learning processes within the math classroom as well as the broader learning environment at school. When we have an unequal and unjust environment, children and youth are often denied opportunities to access touchpoints where they could interact constructively with helpful and trusted adults and mentors. At the level of programming and policy, intentional efforts to increase and make available such touchpoints through the equitable allocation of resources, facilities, and staff would expand such access. Yet access alone is a necessary but insufficient condition for relationship building. When children and youth reach these touchpoints, the actual interactions that take place—at the practice level—need to convey a genuine sense of welcome and inclusion and provide scaffolding to nudge them towards greater participation and engagement. If systemic and structural support can sustain and support the ongoing and mutual engagement of both youth and those who serve them, we then have the possibilities of expanding and strengthening both the quantity and quality of relationships. In an intentional equitable ecosystem, touchpoints, interactions, and relationships are available, abundant, and consistent for those who have historically been marginalized, including both youth themselves and those who serve them. By understanding and promoting equitable access to touchpoints, interactions, and relationships within the learning and development ecosystem, we can make progress towards equity and justice in such a system.

Thus, seeing the entire ecosystem as consisting of human relationships that take place across many touchpoints can lead to two actionable and iterative ideas to improve the overall health of learning and development ecosystems.

First, we can engage the members of the learning and developmental ecosystem to identify the most important interaction touchpoints among youth, adults, families, and communities. While it is important to identify both the presence and absence of touchpoints in any historically inequitable developmental context, it is equally important to highlight naturally occurring touchpoints in low-material-resource and historically marginalized communities. Some of these touchpoints may be what is traditionally or organizationally valued (e.g., classroom instruction), some may be unexpected or even overlooked (e.g., hallway and playground encounters). For example, an unglamorous but critical touchpoint in the lives of institutionalized young children with severe disabilities and their caregivers can be moments of daily, routine care—changing, bathing, and feeding. Such moments offer not only connection, but important therapeutic rehabilitation—beyond the set hours dedicated to medically defined "therapy" delivered by certified professionals. Or, a commonplace but influential touchpoint for children in a school day may well be with the crossing guard, bus driver, and cafeteria worker, rather than just with the instructional staff. In our work with crossing guards on the street, both the children and the crossing guards consider the few seconds that it took to cross an intersection safely to be important social and emotional rituals in the beginning and end of each school day. In short, we can look for the presence and absence of such touchpoints across formal, informal, and nonformal learning contexts.

Second, we can observe and describe the dynamics and quality of interactions as they currently exist at these important touchpoints. Such inquiry starts with observation and description—with an eye towards appreciation—rather than with the conventional goals of evaluation, scoring, and measurement. Such an inquiry also needs to be grounded in awareness of equity, such that we are not simply looking for and striving for "the best relationships and interactions" with *some* youth (e.g., the talented, gifted, well-behaved, privileged by race or class or gender), but looking for and striving for "equitable access to rich relationships and interactions" with *all* youth, especially those from historically and presently marginalized groups. Long before we can judge whether an interaction warrants a score of 3 or 5 or 7 on a program or staff quality scale, we need to understand the situational, relational, and power context of such interactions. It requires us to forego simplistic dichotomies, such as youth-led vs. adult-led or instruction vs. discovery. Rather, we need to acknowledge that the adult staff must become available to share their experience and expertise with youth, while at the same time creating space for youth to develop and acknowledge their own emerging experience and expertise (see Delpit, 1988 for a thoughtful discussion about such dynamics in the classroom). We can do that by engaging and listening to the community of people—adults and youth alike—on both sides of the interactions—so that we might create meaning collectively from inside out, rather than assign meaning to interactions from outside in.

In our work, we have facilitated these discussions using video recordings of interactions within the staff community. Our colleague Tom Akiva (one of the editors for this volume) has done the same with both staff and youth in out-of-school time programs. This can be one important learning mechanism within the community of practice, especially among the adult staff (Snyder & Wenger, 2010; Wenger et al., 2002). By identifying touchpoints and finding meaning within even the most routine and overlooked moments of interactions, these learning experiences can serve as a powerful reminder of both the self-efficacy of individual staff, whose roles (or ripples) are pivotal in such systems, and the collective efficacy within the community (Bandura, 1994, 2000).

CONCLUSION: DEVELOPING OUR COLLECTIVE CAPACITY TO SEE, UNDERSTAND, AND GROW RELATIONAL PRACTICES ACROSS CONTEXTS

In this chapter, we laid out our thinking about the power of human interactions and relationships within the learning and developmental ecosystem framework. We reflected on three questions:

- What makes a developmental relationship?

- Why are developmental relationships essential to practice, program, and policy?
- How do we grow developmental relationships?

Much of what we shared here about growing the "ripples" of human interactions across ecological touchpoints emerged from our engagements with communities and partners, sometimes over workshops, and sometimes in multi-year relationships. Our colleagues have collected some systemic data to identify the opportunities, challenges, and impacts of such efforts (Akiva et al., 2017; Akiva et al., 2020; McNamara et al., 2018; Wanless & Winters, 2018). We share these ideas here not as some pre-packaged "evidence-based" model to be replicated, but as promising directions for adoption and adaptation (Coburn, 2003; Morel et al., 2019).

Engaging communities and stakeholders in reflecting on these questions have helped us and communities see relationships in terms of the building blocks of simple, ordinary, everyday interactions. This way of thinking has placed relationships as the essential driver—rather than a check-list item—of program quality across child- and youth-serving fields. By engaging in this dialogue, we hope to create opportunities to support the growth of developmental relationships in at least three ways. One, we draw the attention of participants in the ecosystem towards what matters most—the relational practice among the people in the environment. We facilitate a deeper and more integrated understanding of where relationships occur, how they develop, and why they matter. Two, in the course of such discussions, we sow and nurture the seeds of a community of "relational practice" in which each person can recognize their active role and positive impact on the relationships touched by their "ripples." Such professional affirmation may extend to many more touchpoints within each person or group of persons' circle of influence. Three, unlike theories or external interventions, touchpoints are always located in socially, geographically, and culturally proximal settings. When a community gathers to examine the interactions, they build a bridge between the development of individual self-efficacy in relational practice to the growth of collective efficacy and trust across the whole community (Bandura, 2000; Bryk & Schneider, 2002).

Using an accessible and adaptive relational framework as a lens has helped us see more clearly the power of developmental interactions across such a diverse range of youth development settings. The "active ingredient" metaphor of articulating and analyzing the essential role of relational practice is a consensus-building way of talking about relationships. Regardless of role or occupation, those in the helping professions like to know for themselves (not simply be told by outsiders) that the authentic, ordinary, and common things they do can have intrinsic value to other human beings. We believe that building communities of relational practice, in a learning-focused and non-evaluative context, is a worthy endeavor in and of itself. To the extent that we can consider the adult staff as "keystone species" that keep the entire ecosystem healthy, their relational practices are the core mechanisms that make it happen.

Ultimately, we believe that the health and strengths of the youth fields, as well as the potential for allied youth fields, are determined by the collective sense of identity and purpose shared by the helping professionals and volunteers. At the heart of that identity and purpose is how and why we build relationships with young people and with one another. We need to understand what it is that we are actually doing in simple, daily touchpoints, why it matters, and how we can have more of it. There is no substitute.

REFERENCES

Ainsworth, M. D. S., Blehar, M. C., Waters, E., & Wall, S. (1978). *Patterns of attachment: A psychological study of the strange situation.* Lawrence Erlbaum.

Akiva, T., Li, J., Martin, K. M., Horner, C. G., & McNamara, A. R. (2017). Simple Interactions: Piloting a strengths-based and interaction-based professional development intervention for out-of-school time programs. *Child & Youth Care Forum, 46*(3), 285–305. https://doi.org/10.1007/s10566-016-9375-9

Akiva, T., White, A. M., Colvin, S., DeMand, A., & Page, L. C. (2020). Simple Interactions: A randomized controlled trial of relational training for adults who work with young people across settings, *Applied Developmental Science,* 1–14. http://doi.org/10.1080/10888691.2020.1819809

Bandura, A. (1994). Self-efficacy. In V. S. Ramachaudran (Ed.), *Encyclopedia of human behavior* (Vol. 4, pp. 71–81). Academic Press. (Reprinted in H. Friedman [Ed.], Encyclopedia of mental health. Academic Press, 1998).

Bandura, A. (2000). Exercise of human agency through collective efficacy. *Current Directions in Psychological Science, 9*(3), 75–78. https://doi.org/10.1111/1467-8721.00064

Blyth, D. A., & LaCroix-Dalluhn, L. (2011), Expanded learning time and opportunities: Key principles, driving perspectives, and major challenges. *New Directions for Youth Development, 2011,* 15–27. https://doi.org/10.1002/yd.405

Bowlby, J. (1988). *A secure base.* Basic Books.

Bronfenbrenner, U. (1979). Chapter 4: Interpersonal structures as contexts of development. In U. Bronfenbrenner (Ed.), *The ecology of human development: Experiments by nature and design* (p. 60). Harvard University Press.

Bryk, A., & Schneider, B. (2002). *Trust in schools: A core resource for improvement.* Russell Sage Foundation.

Cantor, P., Osher, D., Berg, J., Steyer, L., & Rose, T. (2018). Malleability, plasticity, and individuality: How children learn and develop in context. *Applied Developmental Science, 23*(4), 307–337. http://doi.org/10.1080/10888691.2017.1398649

Carey, R. L. (2019). Imagining the comprehensive mattering of Black boys and young men in society and schools: Toward a new approach. *Harvard Educational Review, 89*(3), 370–396. https://doi.org/10.17763/1943-5045-89.3.370.

Center on the Developing Child at Harvard University. (2015). *Supportive relationships and active skill-building strengthen the foundations of resilience: Working paper No. 13.* www.developingchild.harvard.edu.

Coburn, C. E. (2003). Rethinking scale: Moving beyond numbers to deep and lasting change. *Educational Researcher, 32*(6), 3–12. https://doi.org/10.3102/0013189X032006003

Delpit, L. D. (1988). The silenced dialogue: Power and pedagogy in educating other people's children. *Harvard Educational Review, 58*(3), 280–299. https://doi.org/10.17763/haer.58.3.c43481778r528qw4

Erikson, E. (1968). *Identity: Youth and crisis.* Norton.

Frameworks Institute. (n.d.). *Reframing developmental relationships: a communications toolkit.* https://www.frameworksinstitute.org/toolkit/reframing-developmental-relationships/

Granger, R. (2010). Understanding and improving the effectiveness of after-school practice. *American Journal of Community Psychology, 45*, 441–446. https://doi.org/10.1007/s10464-010-9301-5

Hamre, B. K. (2014). Teachers' daily interactions with children: An essential ingredient in effective early childhood programs. *Child Development Perspectives, 8*(4), 223–230. https://doi.org/10.1111/cdep.12090

Immordino-Yang M. H., Darling-Hammond, L., & Krone, C. (2018). *The brain basis for integrated social, emotional, and academic development: How emotions and social relationships drive learning.* Aspen Institute. https://www.aspeninstitute.org/publications/the-brain-basis-for-integrated-social-emotional-and-academic-development/

Li, J. (2019). Achieving quality with equity: Recognizing and supporting high quality practices and professionals in low-resource communities. *Zero to Three Journal, 40*(2), 5–9.

Li, J., & Julian, M. (2012). Developmental relationships as the active ingredient: A unifying working hypothesis of "what works" across intervention settings. *American Journal of Orthopsychiatry, 82*(2), 157–166. https://doi.org/10.1111/j.1939-0025.2012.01151.x

Li, J., & Winters, D. (2018). Simple, everyday interactions as the active ingredient of early childhood education. *Child Care Exchange, 41*(1), 60–65.

Mashburn, A. J., Pianta, R. C., Hamre, B. K., Downer, J., Barbarin, O. A., Bryant, D., & Howes, C. (2008). Measures of classroom quality in pre-kindergarten and children's development of academic, language and social skills. *Child Development, 79*, 732–749. https://doi.org/10.1111/j.1467-8624.2008.01154.x

Masten, A. (2014). Global perspectives on resilience in children and youth. *Child Development, 85*(1), 6–20. https://doi.org/10.1111/cdev.12205

McNamara, A., Akiva, T., Delale-O'Conner, L. (2018). Opportunity gaps in out-of-school learning: How structural and process features of programs relate to race and socioeconomic status. *Applied Developmental Science*, 24 (4), 360–375. https://doi.org/10.1080/10888691.2018.1513794

Morel, R. P., Coburn, C., Catterson, A. K., & Higgs, J. (2019). The multiple meanings of scale: Implications for researchers and practitioners. *Educational Researcher, 48*(6), 369–377. https://doi.org/10.3102/2F0013189X19860531

National Scientific Council on the Developing Child. (2004). *Young children develop in an environment of relationships.* (Working paper no. 1). http://developingchild.harvard.edu/resources/wp1/

Okonofua, J. A., Paunesku, D., & Walton, G. M. (2016). Brief intervention to encourage empathic discipline cuts suspension rates in half among adolescents. *Proceedings of the National Academy of Sciences, 113*(19), 5221–5226. https://doi.org/10.1073/pnas.1523698113

Osher, D., Cantor, P., Berg, J., Steyer, L., & Rose, T. (2018). Drivers of human development: How relationships and context shape learning and development. *Applied Developmental Science, 24*(1), 6–36. https://doi.org/10.1080/10888691.2017.1398650

Pekel, K., Roehlkepartain, E. C., Syvertsen, A. K., Scales, P. C., Sullivan, T. K., & Sethi, J. (2018). Finding the fluoride: Examining how and why developmental relationships are the active ingredient in interventions that work. *American Journal of Orthopsychiatry, 88*(5), 493–502. https://doi.org/10.1037/ort0000333

Piaget, J. (1954). *The construction of reality in the child.* Basic Books. https://doi.org/10.1037/11168-000

Pianta, R. C., Hamre, B. K., & Allen, J. P. (2012). Teacher-student relationships and engagement: Conceptualizing, measuring, and improving the capacity of classroom interactions. In S. Christenson, A. Reschly, C. Wylie (Eds.), *Handbook of research on student engagement* (pp. 365–386). Springer. https://doi.org/10.1007/978-1-4614-2018-7_17

Rogoff, B., Mejía-Arauz, R., & Correa-Chávez, M. (2015). A cultural paradigm: Learning by observing and pitching in. In R. M.-A. & B. R. Maricela Correa-Chávez (Eds.), *Advances in child development and behavior* (Vol. 49, pp. 1–22). Academic Press. https://doi.org/10.1016/bs.acdb.2015.10.008

Search Institute. (n.d.). *The developmental assets framework.* https://www.search-institute.org/our-research/development-assets/developmental-assets-framework/

Snyder, W. M., & Wenger, E. (2010). Our world as a learning system: A communities-of-practice approach. In Blackmore C. (Ed.), *Social learning systems and communities of practice.* Springer. https://doi.org/10.1007/978-1-84996-133-2_7

Sparks, S. (July 13, 2016). One way to reducing school suspension: a little respect. *Education Week.* https://www.edweek.org/leadership/one-key-to-reducing-school-suspension-a-little-respect/2016/07

Tamis-LeMonda, C. S., Kuchirko, Y., & Song, L. (2014). Why is infant language learning facilitated by parental responsiveness? *Current Directions in Psychological Science, 23*(2), 121–126. https://doi.org/10.1177/0963721414522813

Vygotsky, L. (1978). Interaction between learning and development. In M. Cole, V. Jolm-Steiner, S. Scribner, & E. Souberman (Eds.), *Mind in society: Development of higher psychological processes.* (pp. 79–91). Harvard University Press. https://doi.org/10.2307/j.ctvjf9vz4.11

Wanless, S., & Winters, D. (2018). A welcome space for taking risks. *The Learning Professional Magazine, 39*(4), 41–44.

Wenger, E., McDermott R., & Snyder, W. (2002). *Cultivating communities of practice.* Harvard Business Review Press.

Winters, D., & Li, J. (2018). Appreciating and growing the active ingredient in early childhood education. *Child Care Exchange, 41*(1), 63–65.

CHAPTER 7

WHO ARE THE ADULTS WHO WORK WITH YOUTH?

Unpacking the Occupational Identities of Library and Afterschool Workers in the Context of Learning and Developmental Ecosystems

Sharon Colvin and Annie White

Who are the adults who work with youth? We often think of teachers, but there are so many other adults that work with young people. Society makes a lot of assumptions about these adults, especially those who work outside of school. Images of babysitters and tutors might come to mind for afterschool workers. Stereotypes about unkind older women, perhaps with their hair in a tight bun, who shush people all day, are still prevalent for librarians. Why do societal stereotypes about people who work with youth matter? We suggest that in a learning and development ecosystem, the adults who work with young people play a crucial role and that their wellbeing is essential for the wellbeing of the entire ecosystem. We also suggest that assessing these adults' professional identities is one way to assess their wellbeing, and by extension, the health of the entire ecosystem. After all, adult wellbeing affects the wellbeing—and the learning and development—of the youth with whom they work.

It Takes an Ecosystem: Understanding the People, Places, and
Possibilities of Learning and Development Across Settings, pages 125–141.
Copyright © 2022 by Information Age Publishing
All rights of reproduction in any form reserved.

The Learning & Development Ecosystem

In this chapter, we focus specifically on adults who work with youth and how they fit into the learning and development ecosystem. The learning and development ecosystem concept, as framed by Hecht and Crowley (2019), is based on biological ecosystems. Species from microorganisms to predators interact with one another and the health and wellbeing of each impacts the entire system. Similarly, each aspect of the learning and development ecosystem—teachers, youth, schools, libraries, etc.—is important in various ways to the health of the entire system. In biological ecosystems, *a keystone species* is critical to the wellbeing of other species' survival. A *keystone species* helps balance the ecosystem so that all organisms flourish—all the way down to the microbes in the soil. Hecht and Crowley (2019) propose that adults who work with youth are the keystone species which make them essential to the learning and development ecosystem. In fact, in their model, the health of these adults drives the health of the entire system. Consider what would happen if all the adults who work with young people in one city all stopped working. We have seen recent examples of this during Chicago teacher strikes in 2019, and when youth workers were forced to pause in-person programming in response to the COVID-19 pandemic. These moments had meaningful, and sometimes negative, impacts on youth, families, and the education system more broadly.

Youth Workers as Keystone Species

We use the term "youth worker" broadly, to refer to adults who work with young people in a variety of learning and developmental contexts. More specifically, Yohalem et al. (2006) define youth workers as all individuals who "facilitate [youth] personal, social and educational development and enable them to gain a voice, influence and place in society as they make the transition from dependence to independence" (p. 6). These adults include afterschool workers, coaches, library workers, teachers, tutors and many more. Teachers and others who work in the formal education system are important to learning and development of young people, but we will focus here on the adults who work outside the formal education system in out-of-school time.

In this chapter, we focus on youth workers in afterschool programs (specifically, Boys and Girls Clubs of America and YMCA) and in public libraries. Our research has found that these youth workers engage in very similar work related to learning and connecting with youth (Colvin et al., 2020). Learning in these settings may look different than that which happens in classrooms, but is just as important (Baldridge et al., 2017; Durlak et al., 2010; Hurd & Deutsch, 2017). In addition to supporting school-related learning, libraries and afterschool programs emphasize learning skills that may not be explicitly taught in school such as social-emotional skills, STEM (Science, Technology, Engineering, Math), and social justice (Akiva et al., 2017; Baldridge, 2020; Durlak et al., 2010; Vossoughi & Bevan, 2014).

We are concerned with the health and wellbeing of youth workers because they can be considered a keystone species and their health deeply affects the health of the entire learning and development ecosystem (Hecht & Crowley, 2019). When we think of professional health and wellbeing, we suggest looking at how strongly youth workers feel they are connected to the learning and development ecosystem. We know from previous studies (and from experience with the media) that educators are often disrespected and disenchanted and at risk for burnout (Colvin et al., 2020; Zee & Koomen, 2016). We have also found considerable friction between how youth workers feel they are perceived and how they see themselves. This is concerning because it could have negative consequences on their work (Mckimmie, 2015; Phelan & Kinsella, 2009; Skorikov & Vondracek, 2011). One way to understand how strongly connected youth workers feel to the learning and development ecosystem and any existing friction is to look at their occupational identities.

A MODEL OF YOUTH WORKER OCCUPATIONAL IDENTITY

In order to understand how youth workers feel they are connected to the ecosystem, we need to understand how they think they are perceived and if that matches with their internal identities. We draw on identity research to understand youth workers' professional identities and their role as keystone species in the ecosystem. The field of identity research is vast. After all, humans have many identities throughout their lives including race, gender, sexual orientation, occupation, religion and culture (Skorikov & Vondracek, 2011). These identities change over time and some identities are more or less important at different times of life or within certain contexts. For example, when young people get their first jobs, they may not identify strongly with the work or the workplace. But, as they start making more active, informed choices about jobs, they may start to identify more strongly with the work and associated profession.

Occupational identity is an important facet of most adults' identities because adults spend a great deal of time at work. Some are lucky enough to have a calling or a vocation that closely aligns with their internal values, while others have a job and occupational identity that is just one part of their overall identity (Billett, 2011a). There are many different approaches to understanding occupational identity. Psychology tends to focus on the individual while sociology focuses on the social context in which people develop. Institutions also play into identity as they frame a person's actual work. Beyond the institution, professional and organizational standards set expectations for workers. Figure 7.1 illustrates how these perspectives might fit together.

Notice that the social context influences all parts of the model in Figure 7.1. In some cases, social expectations turn into stereotypes (Ashforth & Schinoff, 2016). These stereotypes can affect occupational identity both positively and negatively.

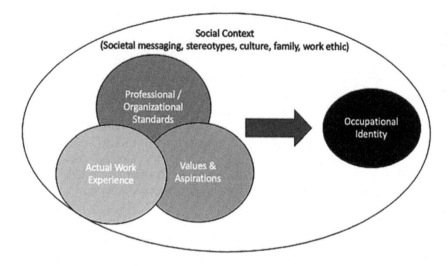

FIGURE 7.1. Occupational Identity Model

For example, school teachers struggle with stereotypes about controlling students, being subject specialists, and having an identity entirely defined by teaching (Beijaard et al., 2004; Smith, 2015; Weber & Mitchell, 1996). Library workers tend to be stereotyped as quiet, conservative rule-followers (Walter, 2008). Everyone deals with stereotypes differently. Some people opt into certain stereotypes as a way to define themselves while others go to great lengths to separate themselves from expectations (Spears, 2011).

Values & Aspirations. In the field of psychology, occupational identity is seen as a goal or an achievement of development (Hammack, 2015; Kroger & Marcia, 2011). People develop identities through experience and context such as structural inequities, economic circumstances, and cultural expectations (Côté, 1996; Côté & Levine, 2002, 2014). In this way, social validation is an important part of identity. Part of adulthood involves choosing which expectations to follow and which incentives are valued (Ashforth & Schinoff, 2016). This feedback loop is key to self-validation and success in a job.

Identity researchers explain that callings, or vocations, are work that is deeply tied to individual values, aspirations, and self-worth (Ashforth & Schinoff, 2016; Billett, 2011b). This kind of deeply personal work can create a scenario where youth workers feel they need to take on more work than they can handle and where setting boundaries is discouraged (Ettarh, 2018). The problem is that when work is so deeply tied to personal values, struggle and failure may also feel deeply personal. Job creep (Van Dyne & Ellis, 2004), or the gradual inclusion of additional tasks and responsibilities can add to the stress of youth workers.

There may also be link between youth work being an aspirational "calling" to help people. Fobazi Ettarh coined a term, "vocational awe" which describes the library profession as a calling and library work as inherently sacred work and is above reproach (2018). In a historical context, library work started with monks and religious texts (Maxwell, 2005) and libraries, like afterschool programs can also be traced back to the desire to help white immigrants assimilate into American life (Brady & Abbott, 2015; Halpern, 2003; Jones, 1999). The idea of youth workers as shepherds and brokers of knowledge continues today as programs are framed to enrich youth that society may consider "disadvantaged" or lacking resources which reflects the historical deficit framework of education in general (Baldridge, 2020). White saviorism reinforces this systemic racism and creates an environment where youth workers are there to "save" or "fix" youth who do not know any better (Albright et al., 2017; Baldridge, 2019; Walsh, 2020). While not every youth worker experiences the pressures of callings and buys into deficit mindsets, the system seems to perpetuate these ideas. In this way, values and aspirations may be affected by systemic values.

- **Professional/Organization Standards.** Occupational identity is also tied to the standards set by organizations and professions. While the work that afterschool and library workers engage in with youth is similar, the professional contexts and standards with which they are associated is quite different. While libraries are supported by a large and established profession, afterschool programs are largely independent. Neither group has mandated access to professional development or training on how to work with young people. In both contexts, we found that the individual organizations at which the youth worker was employed played a large role in their experiences and how they talked about their occupational identity (Colvin et al., 2020). Library workers faced strong, specific social stereotypes whereas afterschool workers described their social standing in much more vague terms.
- **Libraries.** Public libraries are part of the large profession of librarianship. The American Library Association (ALA) professionalized libraries in 1876 and is the oldest and largest professional organization in the United States (American Library Association, 2020). ALA tightly controls the guidelines for Masters in Library/Information Science programs across the country. Each library and its associated system or state agency works a little differently (Colvin et al., 2020). The library system we worked within for our research had 18 branches with children's and teen services in each one. In order to better understand the context of this library system, we interviewed the Teen Services Coordinator, who, along with the Children's Service Coordinator, provides onboard training and mentorship to youth services staff in all 18 branches. She described the strategic plan and its emphasis on "Interest Based Learning" which involves encouraging young

people to pursue interests and to acquire skills and knowledge to reach mastery, feel independent and gain career skills. Under this plan, the library is to be a space for informal learning for anyone at any time. There is an emphasis on youth services staff being mentors to youth, but this mentorship seems very much tied to interest and skill development. The emphasis is less on social-emotional skills and more on "practical" skill acquisition. The professional development available to youth services staff revolves around skill building. This institutional view is supportive of staff in a very specific, skill-related way.

- **Afterschool.** Afterschool workers are part of a very different professional setting. Afterschool workers tend to be part time and underpaid (Yohalem & Pittman, 2006; Yohalem et al., 2006). Compared to libraries, there is a lack of cohesion and recognition (Pozzoboni & Kirshner, 2016). In 2011, the National Afterschool Association (NAA) published core competencies for youth workers (National AfterSchool Association, 2011) that included curriculum, assessment, interactions, relationships, and more. NAA continues to update these competencies and support the work of afterschool workers, but afterschool organizations do not have to follow them (Starr & Gannett, 2016). The work of afterschool employees and their training is therefore most likely shaped by the organization that employs them rather than by an overarching profession (Emslie, 2013; Fusco, 2012).
- **Actual Work Experience.** Occupational identity is also defined by youth workers' actual work. As mentioned, the work of afterschool and library workers is similar (Colvin et al., 2020). Researchers and thought leaders have proposed the term, allied youth field, to unite adults that work with youth across contexts based on these similarities (Pozzoboni & Kirshner, 2016; Yohalem & Pittman, 2006). The idea of the allied youth fields is that many fields, including afterschool and libraries, may share skills and practices that support youth development, regardless of their other professional backgrounds and organizational homes. For example, across the allied youth fields, youth workers prioritize relationship building with children and youth (Colvin et al., 2020). In addition, youth workers often have to balance the needs of the youth with the goals and/or funding of the overarching organization.

A key part of youth workers' actual work is also tied to the organization and profession in which they work. There are no overarching organizations that support the training and development of afterschool workers. Rather, afterschool workers' job duties are impacted by the expectations of the program at which they work. For library workers, the American Library Association (ALA) maintains a loosely coupled control over local libraries (Scott & Davis, 2007); however, although they control training and guidelines for librarianship, local boards and governments provide the funding for the library services. So, like afterschool programs, libraries are very much molded by their local communities. Local management is therefore important to consider in what day-to-day practice and expectations look like.

UNDERSTANDING YOUTH WORKER OCCUPATIONAL IDENTITY

Measuring Identity

In order to better understand the occupational identities of youth workers, we have been developing an approach to stimulate conversations about identity. The idea is based on a popular internet meme that circulated a few years ago and illustrated (sometimes humorously or ironically) "what my friends think I do," "what my parents think I do" and "what other people think I do." The last two boxes are always the same: "what I think I do" and "what I really/actually do." We used the Public School Teacher meme (Figure 7.2) as an example in several interview-based studies. We then gave youth workers a blank grid with their own prompts, shown in Figure 7.3. Boxes were left open so that youth workers could write or draw in response to each prompt. We then analyzed the verbal and written responses. For this chapter, we focus on *What the community thinks I do, What I think I do* and *What I actually do.*

This tool gives us a way to consider multiple facets of youth worker identity and how they are connected to the learning and development ecosystem. Youth

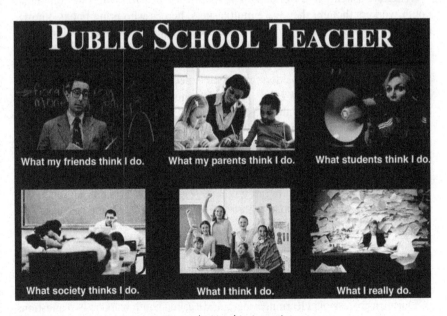

FIGURE 7.2. Internet Meme Example Used in Interviews

	What the community thinks I do.	What (adult) library patrons think I do. (library staff only) What parents think I do. (afterschool staff only)	What the kids think I do.
External Perceptions			
Internal Expectations/ Perceptions	What I think I do.	What I actually do.	

FIGURE 7.3.   Prompts for Identity Interviews

workers are connected to fellow youth workers, coworkers, the children and youth that they serve, caregivers, other educators, the organizational leadership, and the community. This is just one way to look at identity, but we think we gathered important insights about the health and wellbeing of youth workers.

Values, Aspirations, and Stereotypes

When we asked youth workers, "*What Do You Think You* Do?," we found that youth workers thought they were multitaskers, heroes who bring books, knowledge and learning to children and brokers of happiness. In a national study of library workers, we found that 25% of youth workers described themselves as being overwhelmed with work while 28% described themselves as heroes (Colvin et al., 2021). When considering societal expectations using the prompt, *What Does the Community Think I Do?*, both afterschool and library workers felt that the community thought of them as stereotypical. Library workers thought they were perceived as an older white lady with a bun, a scowl, and a book, while afterschool workers felt that they were seen as "glorified babysitters" who did not warrant much respect (Colvin et al., 2020). Even more concerning is that a substantial number of the library and afterschool youth workers thought that the community saw them as not doing anything of any importance at all, bringing up images of clock watching, relaxing, and, for library workers especially, being "extinct." We found similar stereotypical answers to *What Does the Community Think I Do* in a national study of library workers (Colvin et al., 2021). These stereotypes are in the media, society and in conversation all around youth workers. It is possible that the aspirations that youth workers internalize are a reaction to these stereotypes. The community thinks I do nothing of importance, but I actually do everything!

During a professional learning program, we asked youth workers two questions about their aspirations: "What do you want youth to get out of your program?"

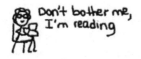 

FIGURE 7.4.   Examples of Drawn Responses to Prompt: What the Community Thinks I Do

and "What drives the work you do with kids?" In response, a majority of youth workers said they wanted to help youth with abstract goals such as feeling agency, becoming confident, learning and growing, reaching their potential, and having a bright future. Fewer shared specific ways they might do this such as building relationships, setting high expectations, and creating a safe environment (Akiva et al., 2020; Akiva et al., under review). It is interesting (and also expected) that the aspirations were large, lofty goals for youth. While abstract goals are good, we worry that this might set youth workers up for friction when these aspirations meet daily life and the stereotypical assumptions of the community.

Professional/Organizational Standards and the Allied Youth Field

Our research has found that organizational work often got in the way of engaging with youth (Colvin et al., 2020). In response to, *What I Actually Do,* 21 of the 34 youth workers we asked mentioned administrative work of some kind. The fact that the jobs entailed administrative tasks and meetings was not a problem on its own. The friction appeared when administrative tasks got in the way of engaging with youth. One afterschool worker commented, "Sometimes I do feel like it's very much focused on the behind-the-scenes stuff, which is fine because that's necessary to have this run. But I want to do more of just the hanging out with kids part. So sometimes I feel the emphasis and the importance is placed on have the employees be perfect, have these programs be perfect, let's spread yourself as thin as you can doing all these programs instead of just let's go hang out with kids. Let's play a game. Let's play cards." To the outside, "hanging out with kids" may seem like an unimportant part of youth work, but it is actually a key part of building relationships with youth and relationships are a key part of learning (Li & Julian, 2012; Rhodes, 2004). This may point to a general misunderstanding about the importance of youth work.

Management is an important consideration because managers can help mediate the stress of youth workers; decreased stress is associated with healthier, more satisfied employees (Maslach et al., 2001; Rhoades & Eisenberger, 2002; White et al., 2020). We found that directors tended to take two different approaches: they either enforced compliance to top-down mandates or they buffered staff from top-down mandates. Staff that worked for compliance-oriented directors stated feeling disconnected from management and frustrated by rules and regulations they had to follow (White et al., under review). Staff that worked at organizations whose management took a buffering approach described having agency in their jobs and choosing to use their time with children to build relationships and support social and emotional learning. Management practices can support staff and play a role in the occupational identity and health of the keystone species (Baldwin et al., 2015; Devaney et al., 2012; Smith et al., 2014).

Actual Work Experience & Stress

The closest perspective to youth worker occupational identity is daily practice, or the work they actually do. In Akiva et al. (under review), we describe a professional development program (Simple Interactions, 2021) that affirms youth workers' daily practice. The program focuses on interactions and relationships between youth and youth workers. In the program, youth workers connect with other youth workers and build a community of practice. One way this happens is by watching videos of one another working with youth and discussing videos using strengths-based language. The underlying idea is that we can learn from the great work youth workers already do (Marsh et al., 2004). Through interviews, youth workers' responses to this program were overwhelmingly positive. One of the program features youth workers found most useful was the opportunity to become more intentional about their everyday interactions and to be active in their own learning. One youth worker explained, "I think there's value in the way that other people have interactions and you can see things that work really well for other people that maybe you wouldn't have taken that course of action, but seeing somebody else do it and do it successfully can translate back into your work as well;" Another youth worker added that the program was "just absolutely a positive, supportive space." Through this professional development program, we found that youth workers are thirsty for education and training. They explained that they really need connection with other youth workers who are engaged in similar work.

While we heard youth workers talk about strengths of their daily practice in the professional development program, youth workers shared the stress they felt in their actual practice in our interviews (Colvin et al., 2020). Afterschool workers were stretched thin doing administrative tasks rather than the work they aspired to do, such as building relationships with youth (Colvin et al., 2020). Afterschool workers described a lot of "running around," engaging in behavior management, cleaning, "putting out fires," and changing plans. One afterschool educator described being a "jack of all trades," and that she never gets to focus because "I was the front desk coordinator, I'm homework help, I used to teach dance, I'm a summer camp counselor." This was in addition to the negative feeling of being disrespected and misunderstood. One afterschool worker shared: "I just feel like we could be doing more in terms of teaching because we are an enrichment program, but the parents call us aftercare." Another youth worker described feeling frustrated that the community did not understand the true impact of his actual work. He said: "What they don't see is that if I am playing ping pong, I'm also probably talking to the kid about how their day was, and how was school, or why are they tired."

Similarly, library workers described their daily work as overwhelming. They mentioned feeling pulled in many directions and "being bombarded by questions" (Colvin et al., 2020). In particular, almost half of library worker youth workers talked about the overwhelming amount of work they were required to do. There was a clear sense of distress with comments like, "I lead a life of quiet desperation" and "there's not enough time in the day" and "I pull my hair out ever so gently while smiling." The differences between youth workers' aspirational and actual work are troubling because it seems that reality is not matching up with goals. This could lead to burnout and distress (Maslach et al., 2001; Skorikov & Vondracek, 2011).

CONCLUSIONS & TAKEAWAYS

Friction Between Aspirations and Actual Work

Across these studies, we saw friction between youth workers' aspirations and their descriptions of actual work. As Ettarh (2018) argues, a culture where youth workers aspire to do more and where boundary setting is discouraged sets them up for burn out and taking on more work duties that will never be compensated appropriately (Van Dyne & Ellis, 2004). While it may be fun to see youth workers as superheroes in capes (as one youth worker depicted in Figure 7.8), ready to save the day, the trope could be harmful. We found that many of the afterschool and library workers described themselves as super-human either as an aspiration or in daily practice (Colvin et al., 2020) which could be a reflection of the deficit perspective we mentioned earlier. A recent article from the National Afterschool Association pointed out that seeing youth workers as heroes undermines their professional skills and creates an unrealistic image of a human who can do anything (Ham, 2020). From an identity point of view, we wonder if the narrative of "I am a superhero" might be a reflection of unrealistic expectations for themselves. If youth workers expect that they can do anything, even save the world, reality will always be disappointing. The image of youth workers as super-human also puts distance between them and their community which can strain their connections with youth. When work is mismatched with personal goals and expectations, burnout is a serious result (Skorikov & Vondracek, 2011). This may point to a more systemic issue and perpetuate the idea that youth workers should continue to be underpaid and undervalued.

In a field that struggles with burnout and turnover, this is something that we should address. One strategy might be to offer youth workers opportunities to participate in professional learning experiences. The first step would be to offer time and compensation signaling recognition and value of youth work. Additionally, by establishing professional learning communities, like the Simple Interactions approach described earlier, youth workers may remind themselves and one another that they are already doing good work. In other words, by reflecting with one another, youth workers may see that rather than trying to be a superhero (an impossible task) their actual work is what they can aspire to. This may help youth workers set themselves up for success.

Disrespect

Our analysis of these studies highlights some troubling trends in the occupational identities of youth workers; this may give us insight into the health of youth workers as keystone species. The most striking is the deep disrespect that youth workers feel from the community. Stereotypes are pervasive in these studies and youth workers seem to feel misunderstood by the community at large. The general misunderstanding that youth workers are "just playing" or "doing nothing" is not only harmful to the identities of the youth workers, it completely undermines the work they do.

When youth work is seen as unimportant or easy, all of the time, effort, and energy they put into their work is disrespected and erased. In the context of a learning and development ecosystem, this kind of disrespect has ripple effects. Youth workers rely on the community for monetary and structural support and on other educators for support and collaboration. If youth work is ignored or disrespected, the connections between youth, adults, and the community are weakened, and the organizations may miss out on opportunities to collaborate and help each other.

Implications for the Learning and Development Ecosystem

The tension we find between the external and internal occupational identities is likely a sign of friction and an unhealthy keystone species. Society and the ecosystem itself have set unrealistically high expectations (and huge workloads) for youth workers. At the same time, youth workers feel that the community disrespects and disregards all of their hard work. They are in a precarious situation because the reality of daily practice seems to be overwhelming and disappointing at the same time. If the keystone species is living in a culture where job creep, vocational awe, and disrespect prevail, there seems to be no end to the high turnover and low pay that affects the field (Yohalem & Pittman, 2006). But in the face of

FIGURE 7.5. Examples of Drawn Responses to Prompt: What Do You Think You Do?

all of this stress, youth workers show up to work every day and continue to inspire and teach youth. We had youth workers in our studies who have showed up for 50 years and continue to do so. While the health of the keystone species looks poor, the persistence of youth workers looks strong.

Next Steps

These forgotten helpers have told us through focus groups, interviews and surveys, what they need to survive. Youth workers need time to reflect, connect with peers, build networks and share ideas. Above all, they need legitimacy and recognition. There are arguments for and against credentialing in the allied youth field at large (Starr & Gannett, 2016), but legitimacy within the local learning and development ecosystem could be much simpler.

Organizations can adapt practices that support youth workers with the professional development and other tangible and intangible supports that they need. For example, youth workers in this study mentioned the usefulness of having a teen services coordinator position in the library system. In addition, many cities have intermediary organizations that serve afterschool programs with these kinds of supports. Furthermore, organizations can use continuous improvement approaches, like the Youth Program Quality Intervention (Smith et al., 2012), that build time for reflection into the rhythms of an organization. Both intermediaries and CQI approaches are described in other chapters in this volume (see Chapter 10 by Little and Donner and Chapter 9 by Wilson-Ahlstrom and Martineau in this volume).

This chapter focuses on only two examples of youth workers: afterschool and library youth workers. There are many other youth workers in many other unique learning and development ecosystems such as coaches, camp counselors, corrections counselors, social workers, and more. There is no one-size-fits-all approach to learning and development ecosystems (Hecht & Crowley, 2019). However, there is an opportunity to build alliances across the allied youth field. Given our findings that librarians and afterschool workers engage in similar work with young people, we might look across diverse youth-serving settings and find connections among youth workers engaged in similar practices. One approach that we have seen succeed in our professional development program was giving youth workers time to reflect on their own work and to affirm the good work they are already doing. This legitimizes their daily practice and the practice of their colleagues (Akiva et al., 2020). Connecting youth workers to each other for support and morale also creates a community of practice which has been shown to be positive for many different groups (Graff et al., 2013; Hatch et al., 2016; Lave & Wenger, 1991). In addition, providing a space to set meaningful and attainable goals would help youth workers calm internal occupational friction.

REFERENCES

Akiva, T., Carey, R. L., Cross, A. B., Delale-O'Connor, L., & Brown, M. R. (2017). Reasons youth engage in activism programs: Social justice or sanctuary? *Journal of Applied Developmental Psychology, 53*(February), 20–30. https://doi.org/10.1016/j.appdev.2017.08.005

Akiva, T., White, A. M., Colvin, S., DeMand, A., & Page, L. C. (2020). Simple Interactions: A randomized controlled trial of relational training for adults who work with young people across settings. *Applied Developmental Science.* https://doi.org/10.10 80/10888691.2020.1819809

Akiva, T., White, A. M., Colvin, S., Li, J., & Wardrip, P. (under review). *Simple Interactions: A design study of a relationship-based professional learning program.*

Albright, J. N., Hurd, N. M., & Hussain, S. B. (2017). Applying a social justice lens to youth mentoring: A review of the literature and recommendations for practice. *American Journal of Community Psychology, 59*(3–4), 363–381. https://doi.org/10.1002/ajcp.12143

American Library Association. (2020). *American Library Association: About ALA.* Retrieved March 31, 2017, from http://www.ala.org/aboutala/

Ashforth, B. E., & Schinoff, B. S. (2016). Identity under construction: How individuals come to define themselves in organizations. *Annual Review of Organizational Psychology and Organizational Behavior, 3,* 111–137. https://doi.org/10.1146/annurev-orgpsych-041015-062322

Baldridge, B. J. (2019). *Community-based youth work in uncertain times.* Stanford University Press.

Baldridge, B. J. (2020). The youthwork paradox: A case for studying the complexity of community-based youth work in education research. *Educational Researcher, 89*(8), 618–625. https://doi.org/10.3102/0013189X20937300

Baldridge, B. J., Beck, N., Medina, J. C., & Reeves, M. A. (2017). Toward a new understanding of community-based education: The role of community-based educational spaces in disrupting inequality for minoritized youth. *Review of Research in Education, 41*(1), 381–402. https://doi.org/10.3102/0091732X16688622

Baldwin, C. K., Stromwall, K., & Wilder, Q. (2015). Afterschool youth program design and structural quality: Implications for quality improvement. *Child and Youth Services, 36*(3), 226–247. https://doi.org/10.1080/0145935X.2015.1046592

Beijaard, D., Meijer, P. C., & Verloop, N. (2004). Reconsidering research on teachers' professional identity. *Teaching and Teacher Education, 20*(2), 107–128. https://doi.org/10.1016/j.tate.2003.07.001

Billett, S. (2011a). Vocational education. *Vocational Education,* 59–82. https://doi.org/10.1007/978-94-007-1954-5

Billett, S. (2011b). Vocational Education. *Vocational Education,* 83–109. https://doi.org/10.1007/978-94-007-1954-5

Brady, H., & Abbott, F. (2015). *A history of U.S. public libraries.* https://dp.la/exhibitions/exhibits/show/history-us-public-libraries

Colvin, S., White, A. M., & Akiva, T. (2021). Learning in the library: A national study of youth services public library workers. *Journal of Community Psychology, 49*(6), 2040–2058.

Colvin, S., White, A. M., Akiva, T., & Wardrip, P. S. (2020). What do you think youth workers do? A comparative case study of library and afterschool workers. *Children and Youth Services Review, 119.* https://doi.org/10.1016/j.childyouth.2020.105537

Côté, J. E. (1996). Sociological perspectives on identity formation: the culture-identity link and identity capital. *Journal of Adolescence, 19*(5), 417–428. http://www.ncbi.nlm.nih.gov/pubmed/9245295

Côté, J. E., & Levine, C. (2002). *Identity formation, agency, and culture: A social psychological synthesis.* L. Erlbaum Associates.

Côté, J. E., & Levine, C. (2014). Integrating sociological and psychological perspectives on identity: Toward a social psychology of identity. *Identity Formation, Agency, and Culture, a Social Psychological Synthesis, 2001,* 47–69.

Devaney, E., Smith, C., & Wong, K. (2012). Understanding the "how" of quality improvement: Lessons from the Rhode Island Program Quality Intervention. *Afterschool Matters, 16,* 1–10. http://files.eric.ed.gov.cupdx.idm.oclc.org/fulltext/EJ992132.pdf%5Cnhttp://eric.ed.gov/?q=Continuous+quality+improvement+hybrid+learning&id=EJ992132%5Cnhttp://files.eric.ed.gov/fulltext/EJ992132.pdf

Durlak, J. A., Weissberg, R. P., & Pachan, M. (2010). A meta-analysis of after-school programs that seek to promote personal and social skills in children and adolescents. *American Journal of Community Psychology, 45*(3–4), 294–309. https://doi.org/10.1007/s10464-010-9300-6

Emslie, M. (2013). Toward a youth work profession. *Child and Youth Services, 34*(2), 125–138. https://doi.org/10.1080/0145935X.2013.785880

Ettarh, F. (2018). Vocational awe and librarianship: The lies we tell ourselves. *In The Library with The Lead Pipe.* http://www.inthelibrarywiththeleadpipe.org/2018/vocational-awe/

Fusco, M. (2012). *Advancing youth work: current trends, critical questions.* Routledge.

Graff, R., Korum, K., Randall, S., & Simmons, T. (2013). From youth worker professional development to organizational change. *New Directions for Youth Development, 139,* 27–57. https://doi.org/10.1002/yd

Halpern, R. (2003). *Making play work: The promise of after-school programs for low-income children.* Teacher's College Press.

Ham, H. (2020). *Skilled professionals, not superheroes.* Retrieved August 23, 2020, from https://naaweb.org/professional-development/item/1342-skilled-professionals-not-superheroes?fbclid=IwAR1az077PCB91X1X3v_1fUTvFnAUhly4XgcVFQyXSN-_7yY-u3RUOWOPfcs

Hammack, P. L. (2015). Theoretical foundations of identity. In K. C. McLean & M. Syed (Eds.), *Oxford handbook of identity development* (pp. 11–30). Oxford University Press.

Hatch, T., Hill, K., & Roegman, R. (2016). Investigating the role of instructional rounds in the development of social networks and district-wide improvement. *American Educational Research Journal, 53*(4), 1022–1053. https://doi.org/10.3102/0002831216653205

Hecht, M., & Crowley, K. J. (2019). Unpacking the learning ecosystems framework: Lessons from the adaptive management of biological ecosystems. *Journal of the Learning Sciences, 29*(2), 264–284.

Hurd, N., & Deutsch, N. (2017). SEL-focused after-school programs. *The Future of Children, 27*(1), 95–115.

Jones, P. A. (1999). *Libraries, immigrants, and the American experience*. Greenwood Press.

Kroger, J., & Marcia, J. E. (2011). The identity statuses: Origins , meanings , and interpretations. In S. J. Schwartz, K. Luyckx, & V. L. Vignoles (Eds.), *Handbook of identity theory and research* (pp. 31–53). Springer. https://doi.org/10.1007/978-1-4419-7988-9

Lave, J., & Wenger, E. (1991). *Situated learning: Legitmate peripheral participation*. Cambridge University Press.

Li, J., & Julian, M. M. (2012). Developmental relationships as the active ingredient: A unifying working hypothesis of "what works" across intervention settings. *American Journal of Orthopsychiatry, 82*(2), 157–166. https://doi.org/10.1111/j.1939-0025.2012.01151.x

Marsh, D. R., Schroeder, D. G., Dearden, K. A., Sternin, J., & Sternin, M. (2004). The power of positive deviance. *British Medical Journal, 329*(7475), 1177–1179. https://doi.org/10.1136/bmj.329.7475.1177

Maslach, C., Schaufeli, W. B., & Leiter, M. P. (2001). Job burnout. *Annual Review of Psychology, 52*, 397–422.

Maxwell, N. K. (2005). *Sacred stacks: The higher purpose of libraries and librarianship*. ALA Editions.

Mckimmie, B. M. (2015). Cognitive dissonance in groups. *Social and Personality Psychology Compass, 9*(4), 202–212. https://doi.org/10.1111/spc3.12167

National AfterSchool Association. (2011). *Core knowledge and competencies for afterschool and youth development professionals*. NAA. https://naaweb.org/resources/core-competencies

Phelan, S., & Kinsella, E. A. (2009). Occupational identity: Engaging socio-cultural perspectives. *Journal of Occupational Science, 16*(2), 85–91. https://doi.org/10.1080/14427591.2009.9686647

Pozzoboni, K. M., & Kirshner, B. (2016). The changing landscape of youth work: Theory and practice for an evolving field. In K. M. Pozzoboni & B. Kirshner (Eds.), *The changing landscape of youth work: Theory and practice for an evolving field* (pp. 1–8). Information Age Publishing.

Rhoades, L., & Eisenberger, R. (2002). Perceived organizational support: A review of the literature. *Journal of Applied Psychology, 87*(4), 698–714. https://doi.org/10.1037//0021-9010.87.4.698

Rhodes, J. E. (2004). The critical ingredient: Caring youth-staff relationships in afterschool settings. *New Directions for Youth Development, 101*, 145–161. https://doi.org/10.1002/yd.75

Scott, R. W., & Davis, G. F. (2007). *Organizations and organizing: Rational, natural, and open system perspectives*. Pearson Education, Inc.

Simple Interactions. (2021). *Simple interactions*. https://www.simpleinteractions.org/

Skorikov, V. B., & Vondracek, F. W. (2011). Occupational identity. In S. J. Schwartz, K. Luyckx, & V. L. Vignoles (Eds.), *Handbook of identity theory and research* (pp. 693–714). Springer. https://doi.org/10.1007/978-1-4419-7988-9

Smith, C., Akiva, T., McGovern, G., & Peck, S. C. (2014). Afterschool quality. *New Directions for Youth Development, 2014*(144), 31–44. https://doi.org/10.1002/yd.20111

Smith, M. J. (2015). It's a balancing act: The *good* teacher and *ally* identity. *Educational Studies, 51*(3), 223–243. https://doi.org/10.1080/00131946.2015.1033517

Spears, R. (2011). Group identities: The social identity perspective. In S. J. Schwartz (Ed.), *Handbook of identity theory and research* (pp. 201–224). Springer. https://doi.org/10.1007/978-1-4419-7988-9

Starr, E., & Gannett, E. (2016). Credentialing for youth work. In K. M. Pozzoboni & B. Kirshner (Eds.), *The changing landscape of youth work: Theory and practice for an evolving field* (pp. 31–49). Information Age Publishing.

Van Dyne, L., & Ellis, J. B. (2004). Job creep: A reactance theory perspective on organizational citizenship behavior as over-fulfillment of obligations. In P. Appleman (Ed.), *The employment relationship: examining psychological and contextual perspectives*. Oxford University Press.

Vossoughi, S., & Bevan, B. (2014). *Making and tinkering: A review of the literature.* National Academy of Sciences, Committee on Successful Out-of-School STEM Learning.

Walsh, G. M. (2020). Challenging the hero narrative: Moving towards reparational citizenship education. *Societies, 10*(34), 1–16.

Walter, S. (2008). Librarians as teachers: A qualitative inquiry into professional identity. *College and Research Libraries, 69*(1), 51–71. https://doi.org/10.5860/crl.69.1.51

Weber, S., & Mitchell, C. (1996). Drawing ourselves into teaching: Studying the images that shape and distort teacher education. *Teaching and Teacher Education, 12*(3), 303–313. https://doi.org/10.1016/0742-051X(95)00040-Q

White, A. M., Akiva, T., Colvin, S., & Li, J. (under review). *Social and emotional learning in afterschool programs: Creating space for educator expertise.*

White, A. M., DeMand, A., McGovern, G., & Akiva, T. (2020). Understanding youth worker job stress. *Journal of Youth Development, 15*(1), 47–69. https://doi.org/10.5195/jyd.2020.817

Yohalem, N., & Pittman, K. (2006). *Putting youth work on the map: Key findings and implications from two major workforce studies.* Forum for Youth Investment.

Yohalem, N., Pittman, K., & Moore, D. (2006). *The human services workforce initiative: Growing the next generation of youth professionals.* Forum for Youth Investment.

Zee, M., & Koomen, H. M. Y. (2016). Teacher self-efficacy and its effects on classroom processes, student academic adjustment, and teacher well-being: A synthesis of 40 years of research. *Review of Educational Research, 86*(4), 981–1015. https://doi.org/10.3102/0034654315626801

CHAPTER 8

ORGANIZING FOR EQUITY

Addressing Institutional Barriers and Creating Learning Opportunities

Fatima Brunson, DaVonna Graham,
Tanja Burkhard, and Valerie Kinloch

In this chapter, we enter into an ongoing, longstanding discussion of ecosystems and the importance of understanding the people, places, and possibilities of learning and development across settings" (the very subtitle of this book) at a crucial moment in the United States and around the world. From increased economic instability, educational inequities, and health disparities to political upheaval and social inequalities, the lives of millions of people are being negatively impacted by the conditions of this present moment. This moment is being shaped heavily by the COVID-19 global pandemic and ongoing racial violence directed at Black, Indigenous, Latinx, and other People of Color.[1] It is also being defined by increased disconnections within and across the multiple learning systems in which children,

---

[1] We also intentionally acknowledge and stand against the harm that this present moment (as connected to the past and as will be impacted by the future) continues to inflict onto "Black queer and trans folks, disabled folks, undocumented folks, folks with records, women, and all Black lives along the gender spectrum" (see https://blacklivesmatter.com/about/).

It Takes an Ecosystem: Understanding the People, Places, and
Possibilities of Learning and Development Across Settings, pages 143–160.
Copyright © 2022 by Information Age Publishing

youth, and adults participate. As we recognize these difficult times and their impact on learning, we suggest that we need new forms and examples of leadership to meet this moment—forms and examples that are collaborative, collective, and based in cultural knowledge.

We turn our attention to how two educational leaders—Mr. Blackwell, a Black man who is a high school principal, and Dr. Kinloch, a Black woman who is a university dean of a school of education—organize for equity. We selected these two leaders because of their commitments to equity and justice, as well as their particular positions as Black educators and educational leaders within the contexts they navigate. Mr. Blackwell is a Black man leading a school community in which he has close community ties. His vision for enacting equity centers on formal and informal strategies for "building culturally responsive pedagogy from the ground up." Dean Kinloch is the first Black woman Dean leading an academic school, including the School of Education, on the university campus where she works. She accepted her position specifically because of her explicit desire to create culturally responsive and sustaining spaces. Both leaders seek to eliminate institutional barriers and foster sustainable, positive learning opportunities for educators and students, and in so doing, their leadership practices have significant implications for those working in the allied youth field. In this chapter, we discuss how their leadership practices inform the shaping of learning and development of ecosystems. Drawing on the public school and higher educational contexts in which Mr. Blackwell and Dr. Kinloch work, we consider the following question, "How is culturally responsive leadership defined, enacted, and sustained within their practices?"

To address this question, we discuss how Mr. Blackwell and Dr. Kinloch demonstrate commitments to culturally responsive and sustaining leadership. Their respective approaches to engaging people in addressing and eliminating institutional barriers, as marked by how they center equity in their interactions with colleagues, in their leadership dispositions, and in the enactment of transformative visions of education, highlight the valuable role of culturally responsive leadership. Such leadership, we contend, is necessary if we are to create and sustain learning contexts and communities that are critical, nurturing, and relevant. It goes without saying that educational and community leaders (e.g., superintendents, principals, teachers, deans, out-of-school time leaders, community advocates, families, etc.) play important roles in shaping equitable learning environments that, in turn, must be sustained. We need culturally responsive and sustaining leadership to organize systems that support *all* youth.

Thus, we are driven by our collective desire to better understand how Mr. Blackwell and Dr. Kinloch embody equitable, culturally responsive leadership commitments as they address institutional barriers and encourage others to enact equitable strategies within teaching and learning environments. To frame this discussion, we turn to literature in culturally relevant, responsive, and sustaining practices to think through leadership that is grounded in commitments to equity.

Then, we discuss storying as "the convergence of theory and method, and theory and practice" (Kinloch & San Pedro, 2014, p. 22). Doing so allows us to explore the leadership approaches of Mr. Blackwell and Dr. Kinloch by sharing vignettes from aspects of their leadership experiences. In our conclusion, we emphasize the significance of organizing for equity by addressing institutional barriers and creating positive learning opportunities for all.

CULTURALLY RESPONSIVE AND SUSTAINING PRACTICES

Our focus on Mr. Blackwell and Dr. Kinloch is informed by critical scholarship about stories of transformation—within learning systems and in educational practices—through enactments of equity. Most notably, to address our guiding question, we rely on research in culturally responsive and sustaining practices to build on how leaders can begin their journey in organizing for equity (Gay, 2002; Khalifa, 2013; Ladson-Billings, 1995; Paris & Alim, 2017). Collectively, this body of research provides a necessary and humanizing foundation for investigating *how* and *why* learning systems (e.g., youth programs, libraries, faith-based organizations, schools, and universities) must work to eliminate institutional barriers such as ineffective policies, practices, pedagogies, and procedures that disadvantage some people and that prevent rich educational opportunities from being fully realized. It also provides a framework by which to center equitable educational opportunities, co-construct critical learning spaces, assert sociopolitical commitments, deepen cultural competence, affirm the lives of students and educators, and develop critical consciousness.

Insofar as educational leaders are concerned, an explicit focus on culturally responsive and sustaining practices offers tangible strategies for enacting a vision of equity through the (re)design of systems that are, to borrow the words of Geneva Gay (2000), "*validating, comprehensive, multidimensional, empowering, transformative,* and *emancipatory"* (pp. 31–37). Although Gay is referencing culturally responsive teaching, we contend that her approach connects to culturally responsive leadership that seeks to transform learning environments into liberatory spaces of equity, justice, and freedom. Within such spaces, we believe it is necessary that both school and out-of-school time leaders embody critically conscious dispositions as they strive to always "honor and respect humankind and the multiple cultures, knowledges, languages, and literacies of learners" (Willis et al., 2008, p. 49).

In these ways, effective education and community leaders, particularly those who are willing to lead systems level change efforts, must commit to fostering learning environments that are equitable and just, which points to a rootedness in culturally responsive leadership. We are aware that countless education scholars have referred to culturally responsive school leadership (Khalifa, 2013; Khalifa et al., 2016) as culturally relevant (Horsford et al., 2011), culturally proficient (Terrell et al., 2018), and as cross cultural (Shields, 2002). Our decision to use the phrase *culturally responsive leadership* is intentional. We believe it includes a commitment to cultural awareness, critical listening, and collective forms of engagement, which are key to implementing action and change efforts that are responsive. Culturally responsive leadership connects to, and, in many ways, can become, culturally sustaining leadership in its serious attention to, and valuing of, cultures, identities, and critical engagements. In *becoming* culturally sustaining, this type of leadership must also demonstrate an ongoing commitment to *not* conforming to traditional leadership approaches that embody patriarchal, authoritarian, exclusionary, men-dominated, and monolithic stances. It must not reproduce assimilationism, but advocate for, and center, equity and justice. Actualizing this vision necessarily requires disruption of oppressive policies and practices within educational and community contexts.

Educational leaders who are innovative in their pursuit of culturally sustaining leadership often come from minoritized backgrounds, have themselves experienced schooling within faulty dominant educational settings, and/or are gravely underrepresented in educational leadership spaces (Santamaría & Santamaría, 2016). Echoing this notion, Hattori (2016) notes that her own "mainstream" leadership training often conflicted with her Indigenous (Chamoru) ways of knowing. The word mainstream, here, refers to the pervasiveness of dominant culture and policies used to organize learning spaces. She describes the approach she has developed over time as follows, "Mobilizing my Chamoru identity in an effective leadership practice has enabled me to realize Paris' ideal of culturally sustaining pedagogy in leadership, respecting both my native culture and that of my organization" (p. 2). Culturally sustaining leaders and a culturally sustaining leadership approach embrace collectivism rather than individualism, collaboration rather than competition, and decision-making processes steeped in cultural traditions rather than the fast-paced decisions that often result from business-like approaches to educational leadership. Such leaders are willing to examine and change deeply entrenched historical ideologies that permeate in many learning environments and community organizations. To do so, they work at designing, developing, and enacting culturally sustaining practices, policies, and procedures that "foster…linguistic, literate, and cultural pluralism" (Paris & Alim, 2014, p. 88).

Additionally, culturally responsive leadership that becomes culturally sustaining leadership does not emphasize corporate-style approaches focused on business and best-evidence models (Lytle, 2012). Instead, it centers justice for minoritized and marginalized communities; cultural, racial, and linguistic identities and heritages of educational leaders; cultural competence for educators; and asset-based, humanizing models that recognize the promise and potential of people, especially, to borrow the words of Kinloch et al. (2017), Black and other minoritized folks. Culturally responsive and sustaining educational leaders who are invested in transformative change must be able to do (or learn to do) the following things, among others:

- Critically self-reflect on their preconceptions and their practice, which is foundational to any efforts at positively impacting and transforming learning systems. This can lead to continuous improvement efforts that take seriously learning, teaching, and leading as connected to (and that really do honor) the cultural knowledges, multiple contexts, and the development of critical consciousness of self and others (Bird et al., 2012; Raffo, 2014). In the vignette of Mr. Blackwell, we highlight how he engaged in critical self-reflection, which led him to institute opportunities for educators to learn from and with each other.
- Support other educators to become culturally responsive and/or to deepen their existing practices in cultural responsiveness. In other words, culturally responsive school leaders must encourage other educators to always seek ways to strengthen their capacities in culturally responsive pedagogy (Voltz et al., 2003) while also providing culturally responsive professional development opportunities (Ginsberg & Wlodkowski, 2000). Their support of others reflects their own commitments to critical self-reflection. As we discuss later, we observed these ways of leading with the work that Mr. Blackwell and Dr. Kinloch individually facilitate.
- Cultivate culturally responsive learning environments in which human lives, identities, experiences, and opportunities for culturally responsive interactions can emerge and be sustained (Howard-Hamilton, 2000; Khalifa, 2020). Learning about educators and opening up spaces for them to learn about each other as they considered their organization's priorities is one action we noted in the vignette about Dr. Kinloch.
- Develop meaningful, positive relationships/collaborations with communities inside and beyond their current learning environments and remain invested in advocating for equitable learning experiences for others (Cambron-McCabe & McCarthy, 2005; Gardiner & Enomoto, 2006). Mr. Blackwell, for instance, not only sought ways to engage with educators in the high school context in which he worked, but also with members in the communities surrounding the school.
- Provide genuine opportunities for others to be reflective and, as Gay and Kirkland (2003) describe in their examination of preservice teacher education students developing cultural critical consciousness, "to understand how cultural hegemony and racism are manifested in school programs and practice" (p. 186). This requires that we support educators "to practice modifying curriculum content, instructional strategies, and learning climates to make them more responsive to ethnic and cultural diversity" (p. 186). This applies to how culturally responsive leaders lead change efforts within systems that are inherently traditional and, in most cases, steeped in racism and exclusion. The vignette about Dr. Kinloch refers to her efforts to reorganize academic departments and programs by inviting members

of the school of education to reflect on their collective priorities through a humanizing, culturally relevant and sustaining lens.

In other words, culturally responsive and sustaining educational and community leaders are aware of the challenges of transforming complex systems in order for those very systems to not reproduce inequities and inequalities. Across organizations, these leaders must not only facilitate change, but collaborate with others to implement new visions of, and structures for, educational equity that foster cultural responsiveness, critical consciousness, and creativity in learning.

A BRIEF NOTE ABOUT METHODOLOGY AND METHODS

As we (Fatima, DaVonna, Tanja, and Valerie) collaborated on this chapter, we exchanged many stories about leadership. We used stories to grapple with meanings of change within educational systems. And, we recounted some of our own stories of witnessing change that, in some cases, did not appear to result in positive outcomes, and, in other cases, that produced increased forms of collaboration, especially for those who are often positioned on the outside of change efforts. As we exchanged stories, we became compelled to question and grapple with how stories are central to human life, human experiences, and to human connections to places (e.g., home, work, schools, communities, etc.) and to people (e.g., others and self). Stories and storying, as Kinloch and San Pedro (2014) explain, embody our pains, struggles, triumphs, hopes, and joys. Stories capture and contain our various ways of being in relation to self, others, and the world. Even those stories that do not get told and/or that we intentionally keep secret or in silence within ourselves remain necessary parts of our human existence.

Storying, the telling and retelling of stories as well as the creation of new ones, requires that we listen to one another in ways that invite us to be open to differences and in ways that ask us to be vulnerable with others. We believe there is, however, a distinction between storying and storytelling. Whereas storytelling is typically a method through which People of Color narrate or tell their experiences with racism and other forms of violence, storying is deliberately dialogic, experiential, and multi-directional (e.g., Delgado & Stefancic, 2017). In fact, storying does not require that we "limit ourselves to the vitality of oral language to fully communicate our streams of consciousness" (Kinloch & San Pedro, 2014, p. 21). The telling of stories is indeed a valuable part of coming to consciousness, though stories can be told in myriad forms and do not always involve the nuanced elements of storying. Instead, storying is an exchange between people wherein they enter into relationship with one another while listening carefully to not only words, but attempting to tune into tone, apprehensions, body language, silences, and all other manners of embodiment.

Thus, our commitment to carefully listen to, recognize, and center human stories in this chapter, especially from two Black educational leaders in two different yet interconnected contexts: a high school (Mr. Blackwell) and a university school of education (Dr. Kinloch). As we listen to their stories of organizing for equity, we connect them with humanization; thus, our methodological approach is informed by projects that are humanizing (see Kinloch & San Pedro, 2014, for writings on *Projects in Humanization, or PiH;* see also Irizarry & Brown, 2014; Paris & Winn, 2014; San Pedro & Kinloch, 2017). *PiH,* a philosophical approach to educational research that emphasizes the significance of stories and storytelling, represents "life projects that are collaborative, intentional, and purposeful and that are just as much social as they are political and educational" (San Pedro & Kinloch, 2017, p. 390S). When we connect *PiH* with stories of culturally responsive and sustaining leadership, we get closer to understanding human interactions and relationship-building. We also get closer to understanding how such interactions and relationships inform (and are informed by) the types of decisions culturally responsive and sustaining leaders make to continuously improve, reimagine, and even rebuild educational contexts into humanizing, inclusive, equitable learning spaces.

Our focus on stories, storying, and humanization informs the research vignettes we share in this chapter. Developed through a collaborative effort to understand what makes a leader culturally responsive and sustaining, we—Fatima Brunson, a postdoctoral fellow; DaVonna Graham, a doctoral student; Tanja Burkhard, an assistant professor; and Valerie Kinloch, a professor and dean—intentionally focused on Mr. Blackwell and Dr. Kinloch for particular reasons.[2] As Black women in higher education, we wanted to learn more about the leadership stances and dispositions of other People of Color and, in this case, Black people in positions that can effect positive institutional change. This motivated us to examine how Mr. Blackwell's and Dr. Kinloch's leadership decisions get enacted organizationally and structurally to create more just and equitable systems. During the span of three years, DaVonna, Tanja, and Valerie met upwards of two times per week to examine research in Black life, literacies, and languages, and to explore institutional strategies for supporting diversity, equity, and justice work within university settings. Our ongoing work led to our current focus with Fatima on the pursuit of equity and justice in educational contexts with multiple stakeholders (e.g., principals, superintendents, students, deans, community members, families, etc.).

For our current work, some of which is reflected in this chapter, we met two times per week during the course of one academic semester to discuss institutional barriers and opportunities that surface in our work, in the lives of our collaborators, and in our various communities. We engaged in storying as a humanizing act through conversational interviewing (Burgess-Limerick & Burgess-Limerick, 1998). This allowed us to organically listen to stories not just from ourselves, but also from a principal (Mr. Blackwell, in Fatima's case) and a dean (Dr. Kinloch,

---

[2] We note that Dr. Kinloch is both a co-author on this chapter and featured in the second vignette. We (DaVonna, Tanja, and Fatima) asked her to be interviewed and DaVonna and Tanja analyzed data from our interviews and conversations with her to craft her vignette. We sought to distinguish and complicate her dual roles in this chapter.

in DaVonna and Tanja's case) who are organizing for equity. Our listening led us to wonder about how their leadership reflects culturally responsive and sustaining stances. Thus, we decided to audio record our storying conversations, individually take notes, read literature about transformative leadership, and examine aspects of Mr. Blackwell's and Dr. Kinloch's leadership.

In the remainder of this chapter, we turn our attention to these two educational leaders and how they individually take up the call to lead in responsive and sustaining ways. Their stories, as presented in the following vignettes, encourage us to think deeply about institutional barriers and opportunities that are present in organizing for equity within learning environments.

TWO VIGNETTES OF CULTURALLY RESPONSIVE LEADERSHIP

Vignette 1: Focusing on Mr. Blackwell

Mr. Blackwell has spent his entire 15-year career as an administrative leader at Wells High School (WHS), a suburban district in the U.S. Midwest where he was born and raised. Interview and observational data show that the overwhelming majority of the teaching staff at WHS is white.[3] The demographic divide (Gay & Howard, 2000) is highly visible at WHS, with just over 70% of the students identifying as Black, and less than 25% of the students identifying as Hispanic. Mr. Blackwell spent five years as an academic counselor at a neighboring school in the district, and 10 years as the principal at WHS. A Black man in his mid-forties who, at the time of data collection, was enrolled in a doctoral program in education, Mr. Blackwell calls himself a servant leader and is known for his close ties to the school's surrounding community.

Moving Beyond "Mainstream Mandates"

Our analysis of Mr. Blackwell begins with how he critically self-reflects on his leadership behaviors, while inviting his leadership team to do the same. This regular reflection is important because it can, as Theoharis and Haddix (2011) remind us, help leaders "challenge hegemonic epistemologies and whiteness in their school" (p. 12). As Mr. Blackwell reflects on his work as a leader, especially within the contexts of standardization and reform, he acknowledges the importance of attending to the political and cultural contexts in which educators work and students attend school. He is honest about how district and state level measures have made WHS look like "a failure" by requiring "unrealistic expectations." He highlighted that the pressures of accountability have increased since the inception of the law, No Child Left Behind, which served to label schools, like WHS, as failing. Thus, he challenges hegemonic discourses within educational systems; he highlights how NCLB

---

[3] We prefer not to capitalize "white" because it is our explicit attempt to decenter whiteness in humanizing ways. In doing so, we aim to push back against the norms of academic writing and publishing that have always capitalized white and not any other descriptor, like Black.

used unrealistic benchmarks, set by people who are not educators, to measure academic progress. In meetings with staff, he refers to district aligned state standards as "mainstream mandates" that narrowly focus on raising math and reading scores and do not focus on promoting equitable teaching environments. Because of this awareness and the tension that it creates, he develops formal and informal systems to support educators to determine what is truly "relevant" and "needed" at WHS.

Mr. Blackwell's commitment to promoting equitable teaching environments is also connected to his desire to reverse the public narrative about the school's poor teacher quality and pedagogical engagements, hence, the low test scores. Reversing the narrative starts with his investment in changing teachers' mindsets about themselves, their students, and their practice. He finds that teachers, particularly those who work with Black and Latinx students and families, are subjected to "the blame game" where educational narratives often attack educators in schools for much of what is going wrong in society and social institutions. Mr. Blackwell makes sure to provide educators with multiple ways to see themselves and to honor their practices outside of "mainstream mandates." Recognizing hegemonic epistemologies within state and district policies and committing to reversing WHS's narrative serve as an important way to begin developing an equitable environment and taking up equitable teaching and learning strategies.

Culture as a Resource

Mr. Blackwell is very creative when developing teachers' capacity for engaging equitable concepts and strategies (Ginsberg & Wlodkowski, 2000; Voltz et al., 2003). Given the pervasive cultural mismatch between staff and students at WHS, it is impossible to ignore the dire need to deepen teachers' cultural knowledges and strengthen their pedagogical approaches and teaching dispositions. Supporting the types of knowledges and dispositions that lend themselves to equity means increasing educators' instructional capacities to work with students, and in this case, with majority Black and Latinx students. Mr. Blackwell realizes this and has decided to implement culturally responsive approaches to strengthen educators' instructional capacities. One way that this materializes in practice is with bi-monthly professional development drop-in sessions he initiated in which teachers were supported to observe their colleagues enacting culturally responsive lessons inside classrooms.

Developing teachers' capacity for equity also includes getting educator buy-in. He highlighted that enacting equity only works when everyone understands its purpose and significance and commits to it; thus, he acknowledged the racial demographics of his staff as he considered, "...will a staff of 75, 78% white teachers embrace culturally responsiveness holistically?" As he grapples with this question, he devotes time in staff meetings to openly discussing the importance of culture in the curriculum, and to critically examine strategies for dealing with feelings of uncertainty and/or efficacy with a majority of white teachers. These actions have led to the creation of a culturally responsive teaching committee that works to align Mr. Blackwell's vision for equitable environments and practices with enhancing educators' critical consciousness and cultural responsiveness in partnering with students. Teacher leaders who are culturally responsive pedagogues, who have an explicit commitment to justice, and who teach through a culturally responsive and equity framing lead the committee.

Addressing Cultural Mismatches

Recognizing the range of differences between educators and students supports Mr. Blackwell's focus on inclusive school level policies and practices. Previous research on the topic (Khalifa, 2013) highlights that leaders who promote inclusive workplaces do so by acknowledging, valuing, and relying on the cultural and social capital of students and staff. Cultural differences between staff and students include racial differences and, among others, socioeconomic status, which acts as another cultural difference that divided students and staff. The socioeconomic status of many of WHS's Black and Latinx educators and staff do not match the socioeconomic realities of students. Therefore, it is imperative that training on culturally responsiveness include honest conversations about the multiple realities and positionalities of the school population.

Over time, WHS administrative leaders are becoming more aware of the nuances inherent within the school's demographic divide. A heightened focus on cultural identities, to also include the identities of educators and staff, remains a priority. This focus, in fact, connects to attempts by Mr. Blackwell to increase educators' levels of consciousness, support student engagement, and restructure the curricula in more relevant and responsive ways. Enacting largescale equitable strategies and addressing the cultural mismatches at WHS are ongoing endeavors that Mr. Blackwell has an outright commitment to fulfilling.

Enacting Equity Through Advocacy

Mr. Blackwell often refers to himself as an advocate and social activist for community-based causes within the contexts of WHS and the surrounding community. His advocacy and activist efforts allow him to support, encourage, and mentor other educators to become advocates for students and families. In this way, then, enacting equity, for Mr. Blackwell, includes supporting educators to learn about, recognize, and honor the cultural knowledges, histories, and identities of other people within and beyond our learning environments. Even as they learn to become culturally responsive advocates, educators have a responsibility to develop and utilize relevant, responsive, and sustaining strategies with students. Effective practice can ensue when educators adopt a mindset that understands, as Mr. Blackwell would regularly reference, the proliferation of injustices experienced by students. He states:

> But, if we make teachers understand that most of our student deficiencies are derived from social injustices, just in their communities alone, then guess what? Just addressing those issues alone, advocating for those issues alone, will help them in their classroom ultimately…What they're being asked to do is teach students who may seem deficit from being denied certain things, socially and academically, over the years.

We do seriously question Mr. Blackwell's language of "our student deficiencies" and wonder what additional understandings are needed to nuance his discussions about systems of inequities, inequalities, and racism. Relatedly, we are aware of his own deepening commitment to social justice and his investment in ensuring that educators at WHS are afforded opportunities to learn and organize for equity.

Vignette 2: Focusing on Dr. Kinloch

Dr. Kinloch is dean of the University of Pittsburgh (Pitt) School of education in the U.S. Northeast. She has been dean since summer 2017, and before becoming dean, she spent approximately 17 years as a university professor at other universities, including some years as a chief diversity officer, an associate dean, and an associate department chair. We asked her to share her perspectives, beliefs, and approaches to culturally responsive leadership, social justice, transformation, and equitable learning environments for faculty, staff, and students. In short, we learned that for Dr. Kinloch, bold goals and a co-constructed vision are essential components to her leadership stance, which we believe is critically reflective and humanizing in nature.

Radical Possibilities in Leadership

Dr. Kinloch began her tenure as dean of Pitt's School of Education after having served as Professor of Literacy Studies and Associate Dean for Diversity, Inclusion and Community Engagement at The Ohio State University. Pitt is centrally planted in a rustbelt city that in some ways still laments the loss of the once booming steel industry while simultaneously experiencing a burgeoning technology sector. The city is made up of roughly 90 unique and individual neighborhoods, which tend to be racially, ethnically, economically, and generationally segregated. The largest school district in the area has been critiqued for its historic and contemporary racial segregation and "low performing" low-income schools. Amidst this landscape of segregation and another wave of gentrification, school closings, and declining population (particularly of Black residents), Dr. Kinloch's appointment as Dean was more than a breath of fresh air in this former steel town, for the entire School of Education and the surrounding out-of-school community. She is not only the first Black woman Dean of the Pitt School of Education, but she is also the first Black woman to hold a deanship in any school or college across the entire university. This makes her presence in such a position a *radical* possibility that has been finally actualized. For us (DaVonna, Tanja, and Fatima), *radical* characterizes her ways of being both in her role as Dean and as interwoven throughout her identities more broadly.

Cultivating a Culturally Responsive Learning Environment

During what many might consider the *settling in* period, Dr. Kinloch began to build and strengthen relationships among faculty, staff, students, and community partners. She did so by establishing networks for sharing with, and learning from, one another. Frequent convenings, with flexible and open agendas called "Conversations with the Dean," were held at least monthly. These provided a venue for students, faculty, and staff to think and learn with her, and for her to do the same with them. People were invited to bring questions and suggest recommendations for programmatic initiatives, strategic priorities, and overall school improvements. More importantly, they were invited to just think and talk with each other. Such access, responsiveness, and visibility of someone in the role of dean was in itself radical. Dr. Kinloch shared with us that faculty, staff, and students began to rely on these regular opportunities to connect with her in ways that had not been expected or typical before.

Additionally, Conversations with the Dean presents a continuous opportunity that allows Dr. Kinloch to learn about the teaching, research, and engagement interests of colleagues and about the projects in which they were engaged. These also served as a space for students, faculty, and staff to talk through institutional, structural, and other challenges that exist(ed) within the school and at the university. We should also note that as people exchanged ideas and considered additional opportunities for collaboration, they were also invited to talk about their families, communities, and hopes for themselves and each other.

Foundational in her approach to transformation (Cooper, 2009; Shields, 2010), Dr. Kinloch also enacted culturally responsive leadership in the ways she facilitated the construction of a new mission-vision statement for the school. We believe the creation of a new mission-vision statement as well as a new strategic plan, new bylaws, and a new governance structure all serve as important lenses through which initiatives and programming are created and evaluated. She held in high regard the values, perspectives, and desires of students, faculty, staff, community members, and other partners at each phase of the creation of the new mission-vision and strategic plan. As a necessarily collaborative project, the mission-vision statement has become so vastly imbibed that it has begun to shift the conceptual framework of the school of education to a space that is becoming more committed to educational equity and justice. We believe that a commitment to equity and justice requires continual opportunities to share knowledge and to challenge one's assumptions. As stated in the mission-vision, Dr. Kinloch is unapologetic in her intention to "innovate and agitate" with others, and this is indeed radical. She is innovative in her restructuring of departments, development of training divisions, and creation of new roles such as an Associate Dean for Equity and Justice and an Assistant Dean for Student Engagement. From our interview and our daily observances of her within and beyond the school, we have come to witness someone who agitates norms by directly interrogating policies that are rooted in systemic racism. And she inspires faculty, staff, and students to do the same.

Critically Reflective Leadership Practices

We asked Dr. Kinloch to talk about her process of critical self-reflection and how she cultivates this practice with others. Included in her contemplation were myriad experiences she had while in the role of Associate Dean of the Office of Diversity, Inclusion and Community Engagement at Ohio State University. Many of those experiences informed her approach as she assumed her role as Dean of Pitt's School of Education. While at Ohio State, she was able to have focused conversations with a variety of people about diversity, inclusion, equity, and engagement. As she critically listened to and reflected with them, many people (including Dr. Kinloch, herself) were inclined to question their own assumptions and beliefs—of other people, of long-held practices and procedures, and of irrelevant policies. We have seen for ourselves how Dr. Kinloch models this type of critical self-reflexivity as a leadership practice and how she encourages others to engage in the same sort of practice (Khalifa et al., 2016).

As previously referenced, another example that surfaces of her efforts to reflect and respond to organizational change and the needs of educators (e.g., faculty, staff, students, and communities)[4] is her design and creation of senior level positions. For example, shortly after arriving to Pitt, she created the position of Associate Dean for Equity and Justice. Then, she reorganized the school's student support services and created an Assistant Dean for Student Engagement position to interface with all prospective, new, and current students in the school. Designing and creating these positions, for Dr. Kinloch, served as explicit ways to upend traditional, hierarchal structures that perpetually miscategorized equity and justice work as easy diversity and inclusion tactics. In fact, the naming of the Associate Dean for Equity and Justice position, for instance, was an intentional and non-negotiable decision that represented a different way of operating within a once traditional organizational structure.

Finally, acknowledging her own identities, positionalities, and epistemological and ontological standpoints, Dr. Kinloch says confidently that she is "just being Valerie." For us, Valerie is relentless in her pursuit of equity and justice. She advocates and agitates for humanity in every aspect of her life. In her role as Dean Kinloch, she approaches leadership, research, teaching, and service with rigor, accountability, collaboration, and radical transformation.

IMPLICATIONS FOR THE ALLIED YOUTH FIELDS

Both Mr. Blackwell's and Dr. Kinloch's visions of leadership are deeply embedded in the central aspects of culturally responsive (Khalifa et al., 2016) and culturally sustaining leadership (Santamaría & Santamaría, 2016). These visions include: (1) Critical reflection and action; (2) Collaboration, dialogue and democratic decision-making processes that center ethnicity, race, gender, class, amongst others; (3) Commitments to challenging structural inequities and deficit-based ideologies, particularly as they relate to People of Color; and (4) Leading by example by attending to the needs and hopes of other people within and beyond their own communities. In other words, the goals of the organization should also reflect the goals of its sur-

---

[4] Dr. Kinloch is intentional in her decision to broaden how we think of educators. For her, educators are not only people who teach students. They are also teachers and professors, students and staff, families and community leaders, advocates and activists who have a commitment to providing others and to receiving themselves educational experiences and learning opportunities.

rounding community. According to Raffo (2014), self-reflection and mindfulness are at the core of authentic leadership, as "the leader's ability to be self-reflective and mindful helps encourage greater authenticity. Self-reflection leads to mindful attention to one's identity, values, strengths and weaknesses, purpose, and core beliefs" (p. 181).

Raffo continues, "This mindful attention allows a person to be authentic and develop a deeper clarity that becomes wisdom" (p. 181). Both vignettes illustrate how this aspect of leadership is enacted by Mr. Blackwell and Dr. Kinloch to further a leadership agenda that organizes for equity and that is rooted in justice. Their individual agendas seek to support educators (to include, as Dr. Kinloch described, "teachers and professors, students and staff, families and community leaders, advocates and activists") in creating culturally responsive, culturally sustaining, and equity-driven educational spaces, pedagogies, and curricula. Their engagements in critical reflection, and for Dr. Kinloch, critical listening, impact how they create and sustain spaces for collaborative opportunities in which the voices of stakeholders are heard. In these spaces, Mr. Blackwell and Dr. Kinloch both demonstrate their ongoing professional development and leadership commitments within systems that need to be changed for the better.

Cambron-McCabe and McCarthy (2005) highlight the ways in which collaboration (particularly among urban schools, universities, and community organizations) can play a central role in redefining leadership in ways that emphasize justice. Both Mr. Blackwell and Dr. Kinloch highlight the importance of collaboration, dialogue, and democratic processes in their respective contexts. They know that their culturally responsive leadership that is rooted in justice requires the buy-in of a large portion of stakeholders (e.g., students, teachers, staff, faculty, etc.). As described earlier, their leadership stories and experiences point to scholarship in culturally responsive and sustaining educational leadership that is innovative, collaborative, reflective, and attentive to cultural identities and multiple ways of being.

However, this type of leadership orientation is not simply a nod to diversity. As Santamaría and Santamaría (2016) note, "[b]eyond bringing diverse (e.g., race, ethnicity, linguistic, sexual orientation, class) perspectives into the practice of leadership, representative of the communities served by schools locally, nationally and globally; culturally sustaining leadership requires greater attention and appropriate critical action toward naming challenges associated with equity and diversity for the groups of the communities impacted" (p. 5). Mr. Blackwell and Dr. Kinloch have both recognized this need and they encourage members in their communities to work toward reflective action as well. They invite people to think with each other, to talk, to collaborate, and to reimagine possibilities in order to reinvent learning environments. In their efforts, they both embody growing levels of critical consciousness that attend to cultural identities, race, and ways of being for educators, students, and themselves within schools and communities. This embodiment, we believe, can lead to new types of interactive systems, or ecosystems, that truly center the lives, learnings, and developments of people within multiple contexts. It is this type of embodiment that must also work to eliminate pervasive systems-level forms of inequities and inequalities within multiple learning systems—from our public schools, universities and colleges, to our youth programs, libraries, and faith-based community organizations.

Building on their prior conceptualizations of Culturally Sustaining Pedagogy (CSP), Paris and Alim (2017) note, "In essence, by proposing schooling as a site for sustaining the cultural ways of being of communities of color rather than eradicating them, CSP is responding to the many ways that schools continue to function as part of the colonial project" (p. 2). Culturally sustaining approaches to leadership, then, must extend this response to pedagogies by actively seeking to disrupt the various manifestations of coloniality within educational spaces by supporting students, families, faculty, teachers, and staff in their pursuits of sustaining the languages and cultures of minoritized peoples. Doing so also requires that we cast a critical gaze at dominant and oppressive structures, institutions, and policies if we are to ever decenter the "panoptic White Gaze" (Morrison, 1998) that sees people, and particularly Black, Indigenous, Latinx, and other Communities of Color, through deficit perspectives. As Kinloch (2017) writes, "CSP disrupts dominant narratives that superficially affirm differences and diversities while maintaining the status quo" (pp. 28–29). When CSP gets mapped onto educational leadership, then a reinvention of learning systems as equitable, as just, and as humanizing becomes more possible.

Our examples of Mr. Blackwell and Dr. Kinloch show the many ways in which they enact this work in their leadership. For instance, Mr. Blackwell's provision of a professional development program that brings together the school community to observe enactments of CSP is one way to disrupt the superficial inclusion of topics related to diversity and to move toward community-based, critical education. At the same time, Dr. Kinloch's involvement of the entire School of Education community in crafting a new vision-mission statement (let alone a new strategic plan, bylaws, and governance structure) that centers the pursuit of social justice is a similar approach, in its collaborative, community-engaged nature.

SHAPING LEARNING AND DEVELOPMENT ECOSYSTEMS

The two vignettes, or sets of stories we share, reveal the significance of leading that privileges listening, criticality, and care. Although our focus in this chapter is not explicitly on building the allied youth fields, which is an overarching goal of this book, we do emphasize some of the ways two educational leaders are working to refigure institutions into more equitable learning spaces. Their uptake of culturally responsive and sustaining leadership practices is reflective of their belief that institutions such as public schools and university schools of education (and the people within) must address institutional barriers that hinder just, equitable, and collaborative learning opportunities. In this way, they provide insight into how we can (re)shape learning and educational spaces, including schools as well as the allied youth fields, in humanizing ways. It remains important that these strategies are used across youth serving organizations. Worthwhile attempts to create equitable learning environments engage leaders in multiple types of youth serving organizations as a way to meet the varied needs of children and families within communities. We believe this is essential in any pursuit of equity and justice.

Within the stories that Mr. Blackwell and Dr. Kinloch shared surfaced commitments to how diversity, equity, and justice provide critical opportunities to support learning and development. Their stories revealed strategies for organizing for equity within institutions such as: (1) Increasing connections, alignments, and complementarities within and across learning systems; (2) Supporting the professional development and learning of educators and self by centering cultural responsiveness; (3) Focusing on the people, practices, and policies within systems in order to impact sustainable change; and (4) Relying on stories in order to engage in a paradigm shift in how people lead, teach, collaborate, and organize for equity. Their stories also revealed strategies for organizing for equity within communities and the allied youth fields such as: (1) Engaging in leadership practices that inform the shaping of learning and development ecosystems; (2) Working to de-center learning in traditionally formal educational spaces by being attentive to how young people learn, thrive, and survive in out-of-school spaces (e.g., youth programs, libraries, faith-based organizations, etc.); and (3) Expressing expanded notions of education beyond formal institutions by always working to de-center schools. This is an important point, as Hal Smith (Chapters 3 and 16 in this Volume) describes, because de-centering schools allows us to better understand how "communities have schools." Ultimately, these strategies for organizing for equity within institutions and in the allied youth fields involve noticing, acknowledging, and disrupting current social norms and harmful policies that negatively impact young people's learning experiences and opportunities.

If we are to design and cultivate culturally responsive and sustaining learning environments, then we must consider the possibilities of learning and development in the spaces where we teach, learn, live, and work. We must listen to and learn from one another. We must welcome and exchange stories. We must cultivate relationships. We must work to eliminate institutional barriers. We must learn from the stories of Black educational leaders. We must de-center traditional schooling. We must realize that communities are sites of learning, already. We must know that communities are already the schools that we need. And, we must foster sustainable, positive, critical, and creative learning opportunities for educators and students, for families and communities wherever we are. Thus, we must organize for equity within and across multiple types of learning spaces.

REFERENCES

Bird, J. J., Wang, C., Watson, J., & Murray, L. (2012). Teacher and principal perceptions of authentic leadership: Implications for trust, engagement, and intention to return. *Journal of School Leadership, 22*(3), 425–461.

Burgess-Limerick, T., & Burgess-Limerick, R. (1998). Conversational interviews and multiple-case research in psychology. *Australian Journal of Psychology, 50*(2), 63–70.

Cambron-McCabe, N., & McCarthy, M. M. (2005). Educating school leaders for social justice. *Educational Policy, 19*, 201–222.

Cooper, C. W. (2009). Performing cultural work in demographically changing schools: Implications for expanding transformative leadership frameworks. *Educational Administration Quarterly, 45*(5), 694–724.

Delgado, R., & Stefancic, J. (Eds.). (2017). *Critical race theory: An introduction* (3rd ed.). New York University Press.

Gardiner, M. E., & Enomoto, E. K. (2006). Urban school principals and their role as multicultural leaders. *Urban Education, 41*(6), 560–584.

Gay, G. (2000). *Culturally responsive teaching: Theory, research, & practice.* Teachers College Press.

Gay, G. (2002). Preparing for culturally responsive teaching. *Journal of Teacher Education, 53*(2), 106–116.

Gay, G., & Kirkland, K. (2003). Developing cultural critical consciousness and self-reflection in preservice teacher education. *Theory Into Practice, 42*(3), 181–187.

Ginsberg, M. B., & Wlodkowski, R. J. (2000). *Creating highly motivating classrooms for all students: A schoolwide approach to powerful teaching with diverse learners. The Jossey-Bass education series.* Jossey-Bass.

Hattori, M. T. P. (2016). Culturally sustaining leadership: A Pacific islander's perspective. *Education Sciences, 6*(1), 4.

Horsford, S. D., Grosland, T., & Gunn, K. M. (2011). Pedagogy of the personal and professional: Toward a framework for culturally relevant leadership. *Journal of School Leadership, 21*(4), 582–606.

Howard-Hamilton, M. F. (2000). Creating a culturally responsive learning environment for African American students. *New Directions for Teaching and Learning, 2000*(82), 45–53.

Irizarry, J., & Brown, T. (2014). Humanizing research in dehumanizing spaces: The challenges and opportunities of conducting participatory action research with youth in schools. In D. Paris & M. Winn (Eds.), *Humanizing research: Decolonizing qualitative inquiry with youth and communities* (pp. 63–80). SAGE.

Khalifa, M. (2013). Creating spaces for urban youth: The emergence of culturally responsive (hip-hop) school leadership and pedagogy. *Multicultural Learning and Teaching, 8*(2), 63–93.

Khalifa, M. (2020). *Culturally responsive school leadership.* Harvard Education Press.

Khalifa, M. A., Gooden, M. A., & Davis, J. E. (2016). Culturally responsive school leadership: A synthesis of the literature. *Review of Educational Research, 86*(4), 1272–1311.

Kinloch, V. (2017). "You ain't making me write": Culturally sustaining pedagogy and Black youths' performances of resistance. In D. Paris & H. S. Alim (Eds.), *Culturally sustaining pedagogies: Teaching and learning for a changing world* (pp. 25–41). Teachers College Press.

Kinloch, V., Burkhard, T. , & Penn, C. (2017). When school is not enough: Understanding the lives and literacies of Black youth. *Research in the Teaching of English, 52*(1), 34.

Kinloch, V., & San Pedro, T. (2014). The space between listening and storying: Foundations for projects in humanization. In D. Paris and M. Winn (Eds.), *Humanizing research: Decolonizing qualitative inquiry with youth and communities* (pp. 21–42). SAGE.

Ladson-Billings, G. (1995). Toward a theory of culturally relevant pedagogy. *American Educational Research Journal, 32*(3), 465–491.

Lytle, J. H. (2012). Where is leadership heading? *Phi Delta Kappan, 93*(8), 54–57. https://doi.org/10.1177/003172171209300813

Morrison, T. (1998, March). *From an interview on Charlie Rose.* Public Broadcasting Service. http://www.youtube.com/watch?v=F4vIGvKpT1c

Paris, D., & Alim, H. S. (2014). What are we seeking to sustain through culturally sustaining pedagogy? A loving critique forward. *Harvard Educational Review, 84*(1), 85–100.

Paris, D., & Alim, H. S. (2017). *Culturally sustaining pedagogies: Teaching and learning for justice in a changing world.* Teachers College Press.

Paris, D., & Winn, M. (Eds.). (2014). *Humanizing research: Decolonizing qualitative inquiry with youth and communities.* SAGE.

Raffo, D. (2014). Reflection and authentic leadership. In K. D. Schuyler, J. E. Baugher, K. Jironer, & L. Lid-Falkman (Eds.), *Leading with spirit, presence, and authenticity: A volume in the international leadership association series, building leadership bridges* (pp. 179–197). Jossey-Bass.

San Pedro, T., & Kinloch, V. (2017). Toward projects in humanization: co-creating and sustaining dialogic relationships. *American Educational Research Journal, 54*(1S), 373S–394S.

Santamaría, L., & Santamaría, A. (2016). Toward culturally sustaining leadership: Innovation beyond 'school improvement' promoting equity in diverse contexts. *Education Sciences, 6*(4), 33. https://doi.org/10.3390/educsci6040033

Shields, C. M. (2002). Cross-cultural leadership and communities of difference: Thinking about leading in diverse schools. In *Second international handbook of educational leadership and administration* (pp. 209–244). Springer.

Shields, C. M. (2010). Transformative leadership: Working for equity in diverse contexts. *Educational Administration Quarterly, 46*(4), 558–589.

Terrell, R. D., Terrell, E. K., Lindsey, R. B., & Lindsey, D. B. (2018). *Culturally proficient leadership: The personal journey begins within.* Corwin Press.

Theoharis, G., & Haddix, M. (2011). Undermining racism and a whiteness ideology: White principals living a commitment to equitable and excellent schools. *Urban Education, 46*(6), 1332–1351.

Voltz, D. L., Brazil, N., & Scott, R. (2003). Professional development for culturally responsive instruction: A promising practice for addressing the disproportionate representation of students of color in special education. *Teacher Education and Special Education, 26*(1), 63–73.

Willis, A. I., Montavon, M., Hall, H., Hunter, C., Burke, L., & Herrera, A. (2008). *On critically conscious research: Approaches to language and literacy research.* Teachers College Press.

SECTION III

POSSIBILITIES: TOOLS AND STRUCTURES FOR
SHAPING LEARNING AND DEVELOPMENT
ECOSYSTEMS

CHAPTER 9

JUST QUALITY

How Youth Justice Programs Can Inform Program Quality Efforts to Support Equitable Learning & Development Ecosystems

Alicia Wilson-Ahlstrom and David J. Martineau

While working at HighScope Education Research Foundation twenty years ago,[1] we convened teen leaders and staff from out-of-school time (OST) programs across Metro Detroit and from Kalamazoo, Michigan for four-day retreats we called Youth-Adult Training Institutes (YATI). The participating programs varied in mission, catchment, size, and budget, and represented much of the ecosystem supporting youth outside the school day: libraries, social service organizations, museums, diversion programs, support groups, civic engagement, and creative

[1] Given our opening vignette, it seems important to share our positionality related to the organizations we mention. Alicia Wilson-Ahlstrom is an independent consultant who worked at the Forum for Youth Investment for 15 years after leaving HighScope. She continues to consult with the Forum on projects related to youth work and equity. David Martineau is the Director of Design & Innovation at the Forum's Weikart Center. Prior to joining the staff, he was Executive Director for the National Conference for Community & Justice of Metropolitan St. Louis, a nonprofit organization that delivered training for adults and youth on inclusion, equity, and social justice. The David P. Weikart Center for Youth Program Quality began as the adolescent division at the HighScope Educational Research Foundation and now is a unit at the Forum for Youth Investment.

It Takes an Ecosystem: Understanding the People, Places, and
Possibilities of Learning and Development Across Settings, pages 163–181.
Copyright © 2022 by Information Age Publishing
163

arts initiatives. Participants from those diverse programs lived together at High-Scope's camp facility for four days of learning-in-community. They participated in a range of activities designed to promote team building, problem-solving, and leadership development. The goal of the YATI was to prepare participants to experience and adapt positive youth development practices for use with other young people in their OST programs. These same practices later became the foundation for the Youth Program Quality Assessment, or Youth PQA, the training and continuous quality improvement framework created by the David P. Weikart Center for Youth Program Quality (Weikart Center; see www.forumfyi.org/weikartcenter).

During one activity, small groups of participants were asked to develop and execute a plan to build a tower out of an assortment of craft supplies and scrap materials, against criteria of height, stability, and aesthetics. The point of the activity was to create a fun, shared experience of engaging in planning and reflection, and to support participants in understanding how those activities support goal accomplishment and executive function. In addition to discussing adult staff practices that facilitate planning and reflection, Black youth from an OST program hosted in Detroit's public housing contributed an entirely different set of insights. Their commentary centered on a more critical analysis of the activity itself and how it reproduced the structures and expressions of social inequality at small scale: The activity provided unequal distribution of resources for groups to build towers, discouraged sharing resources with other groups, and encouraged unquestioned acceptance of externally imposed criteria for success.

Their critical analysis of the tower building activity was rich and nuanced, beyond the planned learning objectives for the activity and eye-opening for white participants and staff in programs from more affluent communities. These observations were borne of a different set of life experiences, offered by youth who were programmatically engaged in exploring issues of inequity, racism, and poverty—youth from a program that had recently and successfully petitioned the city government to reconsider plans to close the program they represented at the YATI. Their perspectives reflected youth engagement in activities beyond the walls of their OST program, the centrality of a critical social analysis to the programmatic approach, and to the real-world implications of programmatic choices about which perspectives are included, acknowledged, and centered in conversations of what makes for good youth programming. All of these have implications for what it looks like to advocate and promote quality youth program practices, and the degree to which such practices might speak to all audiences.

This vignette illustrates some of the questions, tensions, and dilemmas that can arise when the prevailing approach to youth program quality—rooted in the positive youth development approach—meets programs that are, by mission or by community, focused more squarely on issues of social justice, racial equity, and social action. The insights provided by these young people challenge efforts to promote interventions that aim to benefit learning and development of all youth, in a "color-neutral" or "non-political" framework, and also point out the opportunities and connections missed by not making race, power, and justice explicit. They affirm the value of youth voice, in programs and in community more broadly, as not only critical, but also as expressly political. They lead us to believe that programs with an equity and justice focus bring new perspectives on youth learning and development, and these perspectives provide a critical lens for understanding not only how quality is constructed within such programs, but also questions for conceptualizations of quality for all programs.

This chapter explores the conversation between youth program quality, a powerful influence on the growth of the youth development field, and youth justice and equity programs, which have a long history of engaging with young people in meaningful ways in their communities and in society. We follow the opening story with some background and perspective on the efforts of the Weikart Center to impact the quality of opportunities for young people, efforts which flourished in OST program spaces. We continue with an overview of types of youth programs that explicitly focus on social justice in a variety of ways, and present some challenges and opportunities they present for youth programs and quality improvement efforts that may lend themselves to building just and equitable learning and development ecosystems. We animate this theoretical presentation by sharing examples from a statewide intermediary currently engaged in promoting program quality while also centering racial equity and social justice. We close with some reflections on what this means for the allied youth fields and ecosystems that promote equitable learning and development for young people. *How can what we know—from youth program quality efforts and from youth justice and equity practices—inform efforts to promote equitable ecosystems for young people to learn and grow?*

PROGRAM QUALITY AND CONTINUOUS QUALITY IMPROVEMENT IN ECOSYSTEM CONTEXT

The David P. Weikart Center for Youth Program Quality was launched in 2008 as a joint venture of High/Scope and the Forum for Youth Investment, becoming part of the Forum a year later. At that time, grant-funded projects had supported the dissemination of a professional development training program for practitioners in the OST field—now called "youth work methods workshops." Based on the approach to working with teenagers developed at High/Scope's summer camp program, the Institute for IDEAS, which David P. Weikart started in 1963, prepared program leaders to use practices (e.g., active learning, planning and reflection, reframing conflict) that foster positive youth development. Another grant-funded project had validated the Youth Program Quality Assessment (PQA), a standardized observational tool that measures the degree of high-quality practices in youth programs.

The Weikart Center combined these assets into a program of continuous quality improvement, called the Youth Program Quality Intervention (YPQI). Using an assess-plan-improve sequence, in a repeating, cyclical process, the intervention involves collecting data using the Youth PQA, facilitating data-informed improvement planning, and targeted training and coaching for site managers and staff to improve practice. The YPQI was shown in a randomized controlled trial to improve practice in OST programs (Smith et al., 2012) and is currently implemented in more than 135 youth networks or systems, training over 31,000 staff members in 4700+ individual sites and impacting an estimated 406,000 children and youth.

The Weikart Center's success in the field—both in promoting high-quality youth programs and in scaling the continuous quality improvement intervention to support staff in pursuing it—has built on a multilevel systems approach to the field. The relationships with early adopters—local program leaders in Southwest Michigan and across Metro Detroit—were supported by local intermediary organizations and networks. These experiences paved the way for replication with other municipal/regional systems, as well as expansion with state departments of education (who administer federally funded 21st Century Community Learning Centers), statewide intermediaries (e.g., School's Out Washington in Seattle), and national organizations with local affiliate programs embedded in communities across the country (e.g., Boys and Girls Clubs of America).

Program quality efforts flourished with supportive government policies, dedicated funding, and support for assessment and evaluation. Compared to bureaucracy of school districts, new OST networks were relatively open and receptive to training and professional development for youth program staff as well as solutions for assessing and improving how programs could best support youth development. These combined efforts helped define youth work as a field and a profession, and supplied a knowledge base and methodology, the absence of which undervalued the learning and development that occurs in OST programs. At the same time, a more formalized OST system can unintentionally replicate systemic inequities, serving as "place[s] of containment" (Baldridge, 2019, p. 16) for youth of color framed as at-risk. In navigating such a system, OST programs can face structural impediments to being responsive to the youth and the communities they serve (a charge often leveled at schools). What Hal Smith of the National Urban League reminds us about schools is also true for OST programs: "Schools don't have communities; communities have schools" (Riback & Smith, 2021, 6:07).

Program quality furthered by the Youth PQA and the YPQI process are built on a construct that centers the idea that youth development is driven by the nature of adult-child interactions and the level of youth engagement (Eccles & Gootman, 2002; Larson et al., 2009; Li & Julian, 2012; Pianta & Hamre, 2009) in a context that provides physical and emotional safety (Marzano, 1998; Maslow, 1943; Pianta, 2007; Ryan & Deci, 2000). This framework for quality in youth development initially drew from the knowledge base on school-day instructional practices (Bransford et al., 1999; Eccles & Midgley, 1989; Marzano, 2001) and the emerging literature on afterschool practices (Grossman et al., 2010; Miller, 2005), and was recently consolidated by the SoLD Alliance (Darling-Hammond, et al., 2020) in its synthesis of the literature on the science of learning and development.

Relationships, context, and engagement are themes for quality that nearly all youth-focused programs deem important. These themes, however, are culturally bound, and the scientific research that produces our knowledge base is embedded in a social order and its attendant biases and limitations. This truth is acknowledged by the SoLD Alliance, inviting important critical reflection on the application of this work to advance the fields. This echoes the caution that many who work with young people have voiced when it comes to defining quality, summed up by Zaretta Hammond (2019), who asks "How will we understand and apply the science of learning and development within the current socio-political context of education systems that are still inherently inequitable?"

We are reflecting on quality and equity at the close of 2020, a year that brought heightened awareness to the racial and social inequity embedded in our society. Taken together, these prominent news stories—the disparate health outcomes of COVID-19 pandemic based on race, the inequitable social and economic impact of the public health policies put in place in response to it, and the protests against racialized police violence following the police killings of George Floyd and Breonna Taylor—have activated a renewed commitment to centering issues of racial and social justice, civil rights, and equity across youth-serving contexts. They demand that definitions of quality and efforts to improve it must simultaneously address social justice and equity if they are indeed to be quality improvement efforts of any efficacy and validity for all youth.

As we consider how youth programs can align practices that address youth program quality and the knowledge base on learning and development with core commitments to social justice and racial equity, we recognize that there are programs that offer insight into how to reconcile these. Those programs organized around a set of goals and pedagogical approaches not directly addressed in the YPQI, approaches that are central to their organizational identities and key strategies. These strategies may be oriented around cultural identity development, youth organizing, or civil rights. For such organizations, quality improvement cannot be decoupled from strategies that center and amplify cultural, equity, or social justice aims. In the next section, we look more closely at these programs and explore the challenges and opportunities their approaches to youth learning and development present to quality in the field.

CHALLENGES AND OPPORTUNITIES THAT YOUTH JUSTICE ORGANIZATIONS BRING TO PROGRAM QUALITY

To gain insight about how social justice-focused youth programs—including, youth organizing, cultural identity development, or civil rights-oriented programs—might frame and approach quality and improvement, we briefly describe the features often shared by these programs, examining the common characteristics that likely inform their understanding of quality. Further, we examine the challenges that such equity and justice-oriented youth organizations bring to the conceptualization of quality in an ecosystem framework, and the opportunities that emerge for reconceptualizing what the aims of a continuous quality improvement process might be.

Such programs facilitate opportunities for adolescents to develop political commitments through a process in which they develop social responsibility and agency, understand social issues within a broader ecosystem with increasing complexity, and "reflect on the political and moral ideologies used to understand society" (Yates & Youniss, 1998, p. 499). Specifically, youth organizing merges traditions of youth development and "social justice strategy that trains young people in community organizing and advocacy" toward meaningful institutional and social change (Funders Collaborative on Youth Organizing, 2003, p. 9). Organizations such as the Future Coalition and Black Youth Project 100 stand in this tradition.

Cultural identity development programs, including programs like Assata's Daughters in Chicago or La Plazita Institute in Albuquerque, promote youths' development through culture-specific approaches that promote positive identity-related socialization and opportunities for meaningful interpersonal interaction. Such programs are expressly guided by specific acknowledgement of the larger macrosystems that young people must navigate, particularly those that operate as systems of oppression and impede positive identity development (Loyd & Williams, 2017). Finally, civil rights organizations, including longstanding organizations like UnidosUS, the National Urban League, and the NAACP work to upend political, educational, and social inequities in the broader ecosystem for their various constituencies. Many such organizations have a youth development arm aligned to its broader mission. In such organizations, youth programming serves to advance the rights of historically marginalized groups through leadership development for youth and young adults.

While important to acknowledge both conceptual and practice differences between these three approaches, the common orientation of each of these programmatic approaches is the central concern that each has with promoting identity development and social engagement in the context of engaging young people in activities to actively counter inequitable and oppressive conditions in their broader environment. Many of these programs, focused on equity and justice, directly engage youth whose lives have been racially, economically, and situationally marginalized in justice-oriented activities as an essential element of healthy self-identification, social support, and a core feature of healing-centered practice (Akiva et al., 2017; Cammarota, 2011; Ginwright, 2011). Further, such programs create spaces for youth to disrupt various forms of inequality within their schools and neighborhoods (Ginwright & Cammorota, 2007; Kirshner, 2015) and challenge discourses about the deficiency of youth of color (Baldridge, 2014; Kwon, 2013). The "praxis" that develops within these programs—opportunities for transformation through critical reflection and action in relation to the broader social environment (Freire, 2000)—serves as a catalyst in transformative learning and development and has important implications for how they also might understand and construct quality.

These orientations suggest that youth programs focused on equity and justice challenge traditional conceptualizations of program quality. It is reasonable to assume that equity and justice-focused programs view quality as distinctly inseparable from elements of social justice. This inseparability brings critical questions to bear on the understanding and framing of quality and how a continuous improvement process can support organizations in actualizing their goals.

While virtually no literature links a quality improvement process specifically to the aims of social justice and equity-focused youth programs, there is both an emerging knowledge base and growing call suggesting that conceptualizations of quality explicitly include greater consideration of the cultural assets and identities of all participants, the community context which informs the experiences of participants, and an active commitment to countering systems of bias and oppression in the design and quality execution of programs (Baldridge, 2014; Ginwright, 2011; Gonzalez et al., 2020; Kirshner, 2015; Osher et al., 2020).

CHALLENGES

With this backdrop in mind, we raise three challenges and two opportunities that equity and justice-oriented youth programs present to the conceptualization of quality and a continuous quality improvement process.

Challenge 1: Positive youth development approaches have largely developed in a race-neutral way and have potential to reproduce the harms of a neoliberal, color-blind approach

Tools like the Youth PQA, which were developed to codify best practice in youth development were largely developed using "color-blind" constructs (Baldridge, 2017; Tuck & Yang, 2011), similar to parallel practices in schools. Recent criticisms of common school pedagogies suggest that the framing of best practices through a "race-neutral" or "color-evasive" lens produces an underpowered set of tools for understanding and assessing quality. They are also potentially harmful as a model focused on "the ethics of care and caring relations with little or no attention to inequalities and power dynamics" (Johnson, 2021, p. 11). These power dynamics are particularly experienced by Black, Indigenous, Latinx, LGBTQI, and other marginalized youth populations. This challenge raises an essential question, For a quality construct that begins with the existence of a safe and supportive environment, for whom is it safe and supportive?

Scholars who have raised such criticisms suggest that race-conscious, explicitly political, and historically rooted frameworks are more appropriate for attending to the full social and psychological safety needs—and assessing the quality of learning environments that serve them—of youth from marginalized identities (Duncan-Andrade, 2009; De Royston, et al., 2017; Roberts, 2010; Valenzuela,

1999; Ware, 2006). A quality construct built on framing that does not address these dimensions is also problematic for optimizing development and fails to fully address who determines which practices are best.

Challenge 2: A quality construct that does not explicitly name and target systems of oppression and promote spaces for healing and collective action misses opportunities to shape environments for optimal learning and development

A youth program quality construct undergirded by the principles of safety, support, interaction, and engagement must not only address these elements of quality "within the walls of the program," but reach beyond those walls to help young people engage the realities of systems of oppression in the larger ecosystem. Gonzalez and colleagues (2020) raise this criticism when they suggest that traditional positive youth development constructs lack a framework that brings a critical understanding of the role and impact of power, privilege, and oppression and their impact on young people's development. They further advocate that critical consciousness be added as integral to learning and healthy socioemotional development.

As Osher et al. (2020) propose, across contexts, robust equity-oriented strategies must serve as "the intentional counter to inequality, institutionalized privilege and prejudice, and systemic deficits and the intentional promotion of thriving" (p. 28) for those who experience inequity and injustice. Learning settings that promote robust equity must engender optimal development by giving voice to young people's social realities, provide opportunities to name those realities, address systems of oppression, and develop solutions that draw on individual and collective strengths.

This second challenge suggests that not only must high-quality learning environments be free from bias, demonstrate cultural competence, and actively affirm the identities of participants (elements that are currently documented in the Youth PQA), but also be intentionally liberatory as a counter to deep inequity, oppression, and the negation of youths' identities (Osher et al., 2020). In liberatory environments, quality constructs would expand to reflect proactive measures that acknowledge and counter forces within a larger ecosystem that serve to perpetuate inequity and oppression. Features of such environments include proactive inclusion of the marginalized experiences of youth; developmental strategies that draw on and amplify the full cultural assets and adaptive strengths that young people bring such as the social-emotional assets that many BIPOC youth possess in countering racism; and intentional practice of political care and critical consciousness work to actively disrupt oppressive systems in ways that center the knowledge of marginalized communities (Vossoughi & Tintiangco-Cubales, 2021). As Osher et al. (2020) suggest, a model to "move toward liberated learning" is connected to developing critical consciousness, which has been tied to a developmental systems perspective on youth thriving. Again, an essential question is raised, If quality improvement does not lead to liberatory experiences, is the framework right for the kind of growth and improvement we seek?

Challenge 3: Youth justice organizations raise a challenge to a construction of quality that is not structurally connected to the health of the broader ecosystem

This third challenge highlights the need to address the constraints that the ecosystem places on quality within the learning and development program context. This challenge foregrounds the interconnectedness of the elements of the ecosystem and validates the importance of addressing a policy and resource climate that incentivizes and pressures programs to narrow their approaches (e.g., tying funding in community-based programs to narrow achievement aims in education or risk diversion aims in areas of justice or public health) in ways that compromise overall quality (Baldridge, 2019; Kwon, 2013), and especially and perniciously for marginalized young people who have been historically cut off from their broader cultural knowledge and community wisdom in formal learning settings (Bang et al., 2016).

Although schools–more so than OST programs—may be perceived as much more institutionally entrenched in models that are detached from community ways of knowing, the criticisms above remind us that, detached from these cultural and human-centered elements, quality can be (and too often has been) narrowed to fit a particular construction that fails to mitigate or even reproduces other elements in the ecosystem that work against healthy youth development, even in more flexible organizational contexts. Further, this challenge underscores the inequitable social and resource landscape in which various programs operate, a landscape that under-resources programs that serve communities of color (Baldridge, 2014; Kwon, 2013; Quinn, 2012), further limiting the options for operationalizing quality in the expansive and robustly equitable manner highlighted in the second challenge. A conceptualization of quality that structurally acknowledges the health of broader ecosystem compels us to think not just about the quality of individual program settings in which learning occurs, but about the structural opportunities and constraints in the ecosystem that expand or limit how quality is conceptualized.

Bianca Baldridge (2019) explains this development in outlining the separate histories around which youth programs designed for white children and those designed for Black and Brown children have each developed, guided by different assumptions and experiences within a broader ecosystem—experiences which matter quite significantly for the construction of quality. Because of these separate histories, programs that had been designed around the needs of Black youth, though historically under-resourced, had been grown to celebrate culture and community. Most recently, however, what Baldridge terms as neoliberal currents in the wider ecosystem have served to slowly undermine and chip away at many deeply culturally and community-rooted approaches, in favor of program models to serve "at-risk" youth that are often stripped of the cultural celebration and deep roots. Further, these models have been expanded with the rise of newer sources of federal and other funding (e.g., 21st Century CLC funds), while many homegrown programs have seen a decline in support.

This history suggests that we might push current conceptualizations of quality to acknowledge a much broader set of inputs that shape quality, and how the quality of various settings is experienced. Further, it suggests that we embrace the deeply rooted cultural systems that have not been historically valued by formal systems (even though many of these cultural histories predate the formal systems that are now positioned to "legitimize" them), but are tied to youths' sense of culture, belonging, and connectedness (Osher et al., 2020).

OPPORTUNITIES

The challenges that equity and justice-oriented youth programs present to the conceptualization of quality raises two opportunities for strengthening quality and improving a process of continuous quality improvement:

Opportunity 1: The model for conceptualizing quality must expand to include race-conscious frameworks, explicitly name and target systems of oppression, and support youth engagement in broader ecosystem

An expanded view of a quality construct can be valuable not just for programs focused on equity and justice (though they might be the programs most inclined to demand it), but for all programs. Specifically, the opportunities that a race-conscious, community-rooted approach to framing quality present for modeling and demonstrating partnerships that expand what is counted and valued as learning, as adult expertise, and as potentially developmentally transformative for youth, particularly marginalized youth, contribute to and strengthen quality.

This can be accomplished through centering the intergenerational, linguistic, and cultural perspectives that align with the lived experience of the young people being served, and providing guidance and tools for how communities can build those perspectives into their conceptualizations of quality. Ishimaru et al. (2018) echo the tremendous restorative potential of a movement to proactively partner with families and community-rooted teachers as co-pedagogues and designers of intergenerational approaches has for transformative learning and development. Such partnerships can demonstrate how quality practices can both support continuous improvement and position young people and their communities to act within and advocate for change in the broader ecosystem.

Opportunity 2: Robust learning and development ecosystems must more intentionally and effectively merge a powerful technology and set of continuous improvement tools.

Finally, we point to a second opportunity to more intentionally and effectively apply the powerful technology that is reflected in the set of continuous improvement tools to learning and development ecosystems more broadly (not just for OST programs). This opportunity recognizes that learning and development systems are dynamic and require constant monitoring and adjustment to meet the changes that reality brings. In response, learning and development settings must adopt an adaptive management approach. Adaptive management is a concept that has attracted attention as a means of linking learning with policy and implementation and is compatible with a continuous improvement process.

The dramatic illustration of the COVID-19 pandemic and the most recent renewed calls for racial justice illuminates what the evidence suggests—too few organizational spaces have adapted to the needs of the most marginalized youth and that these youth are the least well-served across learning and development contexts (Gaylord-Harden et al., 2020; Kijakazi et al., 2019). Adaptive management can be a useful concept to help learning ecosystem designers and managers of continuous quality improvement prepare for the inevitable, and dramatic, shifts that this moment—and beyond—demands. Adaptive management can help designers expand on a continuous improvement process to increase the field's recognition and adaptability to include evolving understandings of quality that are fully inclusive of the lived experiences and perspectives of the most marginalized youth (Akiva, et al., 2020).

A growing awareness and emphasis on program quality, continuous improvement, as well as many professional development efforts are merging with an equally growing call for social justice and institutional change. In the allied youth fields, equity and justice-focused youth programs may lead the way—leading the charge for evolving quality improvement in ways that can more robustly inform the health of the ecosystem and guide the next set of adaptations.

JUSTICE, EQUITY & PROGRAM QUALITY IN THE OST FIELD

To examine more fully what it can look like in practice to engage with these opportunities and challenges—addressing racial equity and social justice while pursuing youth program quality—we turned to the experiences of a longtime partner of the Weikart Center. For more than a decade, School's Out Washington (SOWA) has promoted and supported "expanded learning opportunities" (i.e., OST programs) across the state of Washington. SOWA provides the infrastructure to support quality practices for youth programs across the state, while also making grants to programs and advocating for the field. The close partnership between SOWA and the Weikart Center has allowed for many conversations centering structural racism and the cultural relevance of the program quality framework and assets to promote it in their work. We engaged in a structured conversation around the themes outlined in this chapter with one of the Weikart Center's embedded trainers at SOWA to see how they resonated with their experience.[2]

---

[2] The authors would like to thank our partners at School's Out Washington for continued insistence that we infuse our program quality work with a racial equity lens, and especially Sheely Mauck for her consultation and review of this chapter. May this serve as a tangible next step.

As a statewide intermediary, SOWA recognizes the diversity of its stakeholders, including place-based programs led by people of color to serve young people in culturally specific ways (e.g., Somali Youth and Family Club, Filipino Community of Seattle, East African Community Services). SOWA sees its responsibility to support these programs in ways that are culturally responsive and to make sure that their efforts more broadly promote not only quality, but also promote anti-racist, anti-bias work. In this way, the systems SOWA builds better promote quality for all youth. SOWA has made a strong commitment to advance racial equity in its work, including heavy investment in supporting place-based initiatives and in supporting organizations led by people of color. To honor that commitment, SOWA undertakes regular internal training and planning efforts to bridge quality and equity. In 2013, they created and began delivering specialized training on structural racism and cultural responsiveness for youth organizations. They also launched a training-of-trainers for this content in 2016. This provides a common anti-racist, anti-bias framework for SOWA and the programs it serves, facilitating the ability for SOWA trainers, coaches, and consultants to make program quality relevant in different communities and for youth from marginalized racial identity groups.

Cultural responsiveness is a guiding tenet of SOWA's work to support quality practices with youth programs they serve, as they are embedded in diverse communities with diverse cultural perspectives. Quality coaches are a key conduit for SOWA to promote quality in ways that are responsive to the programs they serve. Coaches represent many of the communities that SOWA services, and act as both translators and advocates as they promote quality. As translators, they integrate program quality and the quality improvement process with the perspectives and lived experiences of the young people and program staff. As advocates, they bring observations of and critical reflections on how well suited the quality construct and improvement processes are to non-dominant youth, families, and communities.

Coaches enter relationships with a clear presentation of the quality construct reflected in the Youth PQA, and an acknowledgment that baked into it are not only research and literature, but also attendant cultural values. Some of these values and the accompanying practices may or may not resonate culturally with their program. Next, they can engage in conversation about the program's goals for the young people they serve, so they can identify what from the quality framework can help them achieve these goals, what can be adapted to fit, and what they can set aside. This allows for flexible engagement with the quality improvement model based on shared goals for young people. It also provides a window into where and how quality fits (or does not fit) in the communities they serve, bringing critical perspectives back to SOWA, the Weikart Center, and the field to improve this work through praxis.

Some examples shed light on what praxis looks like in coaching. One scale in the Youth PQA focuses on staff practices to support youth in building skills.

In some programs, the practices as outlined, which include staff naming learning objectives and breaking activities into smaller goals, differ from more culturally resonant pedagogy rooted in pure discovery, where young people are left to name their own learning goals. Coaches support staff from programs where this is the case to assess whether or what from the practices might help them meet their goals for youth, and to leave what does not. A different example centers on items related to youth-adult interactions, such as using a warm tone of voice with young people and explaining the reasons underlying requested behavior. When program staff voice that yelling is necessary to get young people to do what they are asked to do, or that youth need to learn to do it because an adult said to, coaches validate that, while also gently inviting critical conversation to unpack those practices in terms of colonization and white supremacy. Further, they relay this feedback back into to the system, proposing changes to the item and to assessor training, since the quality description includes a relative term ("warm") that is difficult to observe reliably and objectively. Bias on the part of assessors and trainers on quality may judge behaviors in communities as low quality because they do not match what this looks like in their own cultural framework.

In advocating for the diverse communities it serves, SOWA engaged the Weikart Center to build into its continuous quality improvement process an additional set of Youth PQA items that reflect the importance of the families they serve and the communities that surround them. These additional items are added to the standard "Form B" of the Youth PQA, which outlines organization-level or administrative factors that impact quality. SOWA's Form B includes items that assess family engagement in program planning, implementation, and evaluation, to ensure they are responsive. Another set of items specifically examines cultural competency and responsiveness, which includes addressing barriers to access, promoting safe, unbiased environments, and ensuring that activities draw upon and reflect the young people's heritage and culture. Finally, to assess connections to the community, Form B also looks at connections with other organizations to enhance what they offer in their programs, to make referrals to other resources, and to help youth engage in the larger community. The Weikart Center is now also promoting this set of items to its clients in other communities.

Partnerships with families, caregivers, schools, and other organizations have grown closer during the COVID-19 pandemic, focused on strengthening supports for young people. Many programs have initiated protocols to facilitate communication between their staff and parents/guardians, and with their permission, with the young people themselves. Programs are also partnering with school meal locations to provide take-home activities for young people, while also responding to requests from caregivers for training and coaching to better support young people at home. SOWA is considering how they might open workshops and coaching to families post-pandemic, training and supporting caregivers in effective, responsive strategies for supporting young people outside their OST program.

Supporting more transformative, liberatory outcomes for youth programs reflects an underlying value and long-term outcome of program quality construct: the importance of youth voice and a model of partnership between staff and young people that fosters youth-driven spaces. SOWA staff strive to model this developmental approach in their coaching and support, modeling a process that is owned and implemented by the program staff in ways that work for their communities. The hope is that the youth program partners that SOWA supports take and use the information and skills to further their goals for the young people they serve in ways that make sense for them, in the same way that the quality construct prepares staff to engage youth to set and carry out their own plans and goals.

Some other ways that SOWA staff model and support this liberatory approach include engaging young people from community-based youth programs as presenters at its annual statewide conference. Youth, alongside SOWA staff allies, have both presented during plenary sessions and led substantive, content workshops on topics like restorative practices and cultural competency. SOWA also serves as the fiscal sponsor for SOAR-KC, a policy and advocacy coalition that includes the King County Youth Advisory Council an "activism-oriented learning community" comprised of 15–20 young people (profiled in Chapter 10 of this volume by Little and Donner) and the Seattle affiliate of Opportunity Youth United. These are tangible ways that SOWA staff support young people to interrogate the broader ecosystem, setting them up to effectively navigate, give critique, and act upon the world around them.

At the same time, SOWA staff are humble about where they are in their process. They strive to hold SOWA as an organization, and themselves as individuals working within it, accountable to its quality mission and its racial equity and justice mission. They engage in their own intentional praxis—taking action and critically reflecting on how it goes—so that SOWA continues to grow its ability to advance youth program quality across the state of Washington with equity and justice in mind.

STEPS TOWARD JUST QUALITY FOR LEARNING AND DEVELOPMENT ECOSYSTEMS

SOWA, and organizations like it, present ways to approach program quality and social justice together. Just Quality reflects a belief in the quality construct and its utility in creating strong supports, relationships, and opportunities for young people to grow. But it also engages with the challenges and meet the opportunities we outline in this chapter. Just Quality operates within intentionally race-conscious frameworks, explicitly acknowledges the impact of systems of oppression, promotes ways to engage youth and others in efforts to change unjust systems, and centers connection to the health and resources of the broader ecosystem. This approach can also improve quality improvement tools and technologies in ways that reach beyond individual programs, using them to impact ecosystems more broadly. It reflects the spirit of humility and partnership necessary for an equity and justice lens we need for quality. Just Quality embodies the idea that quality and equity are not only a destination, but also a journey, and that the process by which we navigate that is important. It also illustrates some of the tangible ways that other youth programs and networks can realize the promise of integrating what youth social justice programs offer the allied youth fields and an ecosystems framework, which we summarize in a few closing points.

First, the way that youth program quality is constructed (and the tools to support it) is useful, rooted as it is in the science of learning and development. That said, Myles Horton and Paulo Freire (1990) reminds us that, "There's no science that can't be used for good or for evil. Science could be used by whoever has the power to use it and desire to use it" (p. 105). Bringing theory, knowledge, and strategies into practice requires integration with a community's wisdom and ways of knowing. The frameworks that youth social justice programs employ provide models for thinking about how to integrate important practices for youth of color and other marginalized young people—practices that center healing from the traumas of injustice and that promote critical consciousness around structural power and institutional violence. A quality construct that works for all young people must be politically engaged and explicitly race conscious, lest it runs the risk of reifying institutional power dynamics that advantaged privileged groups at the expense of the young people they serve.

Second, methods for promoting youth program quality that co-construct how it applies in the context of their ecosystem neighborhoods, programs, schools, and communities can help build a common language for young people's learning and development. This sets the stage for engaging families and communities surrounding young people as resources, countering the common framing of them as deficits. The idea offered by youth justice programs—that natural teachers in the lives of young people should be celebrated—can coexist with school teachers, whether in formal educational settings or in ever more systematized youth programs. These natural teachers and mentors offer a different and important mooring for marginalized young people, rooted in shared identity and experience. This is not well captured in current conceptualizations of quality experiences for young people. A recognition of the assets surrounding young people is necessary for engaging ecosystems to support not only young people's learning and development, but also thriving and liberation.

Finally, because youth social justice programs compel us to consider the question of quality improvement toward what end, continuous quality improvement tools must reflect liberatory aims. These tools must help program designers better position their programs to disrupt narrower conceptualizations of quality in favor of those that broaden the pedagogical and developmental imagination within and across learning settings and help programs more adeptly embrace disruptive, transformative conceptualizations of quality (Bang & Vossoughi, 2016; see also Chapter 3 by Pittman et al. in this volume). Doing so will not only involve an expansion of the quality construct to include processes to engage critical consciousness, adoption of healing-centered practices, and a much more integrated commitment to community partnerships that center the cultural and community assets of greatest importance to youth, but also a willingness to disrupt processes and environments that do not optimally serve young people, engaging a collective social imagination in bold and unapologetic ways in service of more liberatory aims.

REFERENCES

Akiva, T., Carey, R., Brown Cross, A., Delale-O'Connor, L., & Brown, M. (2017). Reasons youth engage in activism programs: Social justice or sanctuary? *Journal of Applied Developmental Psychology, 53,* 20–30. //doi.org/10.1016/j.appdev.2017.08.005

Akiva, T., Delale-O'Connor, L., & Pittman, K. (2020). The promise of building equitable ecosystems for learning. *Urban Education. OnlineFirst,* 1–27. //doi.org/10.1177/0042085920926230

Baldridge, B. (2014). Relocating the deficit: Reimagining Black youth in neoliberal times. *American Educational Research Journal, 51,* 440–472.

Baldridge, B. (2017). Toward a new understanding of community-based education: The role of community-based educational spaces in disrupting inequality for minoritized youth. *Review of Research in Education, 41,* 381–402.

Baldridge, B. (2019). *Reclaiming community: Race and the uncertain future of youth work.* Stanford University Press.

Bang, M., Faber, L., Gurneau, J., Marin, A., & Soto, C. (2016). Community-based design research: Learning across generations and strategic transformations of institutional relations toward axiological innovations. *Mind, Culture, and Activity, 23*(1), 28–41.

Bang, M., & Vossoughi, S. (2016). Participatory design research and educational justice: Studying learning and relations within social change making. *Cognition and Instruction, 34*(3), 173–193. https://doi.org/10.1080/07370008.2016.1181879.

Bransford, J., Brown, A. L., & Cocking, R. R. (1999). *How people learn: Brain, mind, experience, and school.* National Academy Press.

Cammarota, J. (2011). From hopelessness to hope: Social justice pedagogy in urban education and youth development. *Urban Education, 46*(4), 828–844. doi:10.1177/0042085911399931

Darling-Hammond, L., Flook, L., Cook-Harvey, C., Barron, B., & Osher, D. (2019). Implications for educational practice of the science of learning and development. *Applied Developmental Science, 24*(2), 97–140. //doi.org/10.1080/10888691.2018.1537791

De Royston, M. M., Vakil, S., Nasir, N. S., Ross, K. M., Givens, J., & Holman, A. (2017). 'He's more like a "brother" than a teacher': Politicized caring in a program for African American males. *Teachers College Record, 119*(4), 1–40.

Duncan-Andrade, J. M. R. (2009). Note to educators: Hope required when growing roses in concrete." *Harvard Educational Review, 79*(2), 181–194.

Eccles, J., & Gootman, J. A. (2002). *Community programs to promote youth development.* The National Academies Press. National Research Council and Institute of Medicine. //doi.org/10.17226/10022.

Eccles, J. & Midgley, C. (1989). Stage/environment fit: Developmentally appropriate classrooms for young adolescents. In R. E. Ames, & C. Ames (Eds.), *Research on motivation and education* (Vol. 3, pp. 139–186). Academic Press.

Friere, P. (1990). We *make the road by walking: Conversations on education and social change.* Phildelphia Temple University Press.

Freire, P. (2000). *Pedagogy of the oppressed.* Continuum. (Original work published 1979).

Funders Collaborative on Youth Organizing. (2003). *An emerging model for working with youth: Occasional paper series on youth organizing, No. 1.* //fcyo.org/uploads/resources/8141_Papers_no1_v4.qxd.pdf

Gaylord-Harden, N., Adams-Bass, V., Bogan, E., Francis, L., Scott, J., Seaton, E., & Williams, J. (2020, September). *Addressing inequities in education: Considerations for Black children and youth in the era of COVID-19.* Statement of the Evidence. Society for Research in Child Development.

Ginwright, S. (2011). Hope, healing, and care: Pushing the boundaries of civic engagement for African American youth. *Liberal Education, Spring 2011,* 34–39.

Ginwright, S., & Cammarota, J. (2007). Youth activism in the urban community: Learning critical civic praxis within community organizations. *International Journal of Qualitative Studies, 20,* 693–710.

Gonzalez, M., Kokozos, M., Byrd, C., & McKee, K. (2020). Critical positive youth development: A framework for centering critical consciousness. *Journal of Youth Development, 15*(6), 24–43.

Grossman, J. B., Goldsmith, J., Sheldon, J., & Arbreton, A. J. A. (2010). Assessing afterschool settings. In N. Yohalem, R. Granger, & K. Pittman (Eds.). *New directions for youth development: Theory, practice, and research—Assessing Quality Across Settings.* Jossey-Bass

Hammond, Z. (2020) Looking at SoLD through an equity lens: Will the science of learning and development be used to advance critical pedagogy or will be used to maintain inequity by design? *Applied Developmental Science, 24*(2), 152–158. //doi.org/10.1080/10888691.2019.1609733

Ishimaru, A. M., Rajendran, A., Nolan, C. M., & Bang, M. (2018). Community design circles: Co-designing justice and wellbeing in family-community-research partnerships. *Journal of Family Diversity in Education, 3*(2), 38–63.

Johnson, D. W. (2021). *Liberatory possibilities: Reimagining developmental relationships in school contexts.* Framework for Liberatory Education: First Installment. University of Chicago Consortium on School Research, CASEL, and the National Equity Project.

Kijakazi, K., Brown, K. S., Charleston, D., & Runes, C. (2019, May). *What would it take to overcome the damaging effects of structural racism and ensure a more equitable future? Next 50 catalyst brief.* Urban Institute. 2019.05.12_Next50 structural racism finalized (1).pdf (urban.org)

Kirshner, B. (2015). *Youth activism in an era of education inequality.* New York University Press.

Kwon, S. (2013). *Uncivil youth: Race, activism, and affirmative government mentality.* Duke University Press.

Larson, R. W., Rickman, A. N., Gibbons, C. M., & Walker, K. C. (2009). Practitioner expertise: Creating quality within the daiiy tumble of events in youth settings. *New Directions for Youth Development, 121,* 71–88.

Li, J., & Julian, M. M. (2012). Developmental relationship as the active ingredient: A unifying working hypothesis of "what works" across intervention settings. *Ameri-*

can Journal of Orthopsychiatry, 82(2), 157–166. https://doi.org/10.1111/j.1939-0025.2012.01151.x

Loyd, A. B., & Williams, J. V. (2017). The potential for youth programs to promote African American youth's development of ethnic and racial identity. *Child Development Perspectives, 11*(1), 29—38.

Marzano, R. J. (1998). *A theory-based meta-analysis of research on instruction.* Mid-continent Regional Educational Laboratory. //www.teachit.so/index_htm_files/Marzano_1998.pdf

Marzano, R. J. (2001). *Designing a new taxonomy of educational objectives.* Corwin.

Maslow, A. H. (1943). A theory of human motivation. *Psychological Review, 50,* 370–396.

Miller, B. M. (2005). *Pathways to success for youth: What counts in after-school: Massachusetts After-School Research Study (MARS): Report.* Intercultural Center for Research in Education & National Institute on Out-of-School.

Osher, D., Pittman, K., Young, J., Smith, H., Moroney, D., & Irby, M. (2020). *Thriving, robust equity, and transformative learning & development: A more powerful conceptualization of the contributors to youth success.* American Institutes for Research and Forum for Youth Investment.

Pianta, R. C. (2007). *Developmental science and education: The NICHD study of early child care and youth development: Findings from elementary school* [Report]. National Institute of Child Health and Human Development Early Child Care Research Network.

Pianta, R. C., & Hamre, B. K. (2009). Conceptualization, measurement, and improvement of classroom processes: Standardized observation can leverage capacity. *Educational Researcher, 38*(2), 109–119.

Quinn, J. (2012). Advancing youth work: Opportunities and challenges. In D. Fusco (Ed.), *Advancing youth work: Current trends, critical questions* (pp. 207–215). Routledge.

Riback, C. (Host), & Smith, H. (Guest Contributor). (2021, March 2). We can't just do the same things we've always done. In *The 180 Podcast.* Turnaround for Children. //turnaroundusa.org/the-180-podcast-we-cant-just-do-the-same-things-weve-always-done-with-hal-smith/

Roberts, M. (2010). Toward a theory of culturally relevant critical teacher care: African American teachers' definitions and perceptions of care for African American students. *Journal of Moral Education, 39*(4), 449–467. https://doi.org/10.1080/03057241003754922.

Ryan, R. M., & Deci, E. L. (2000). Self-determination theory and the facilitation of intrinsic motivation, social development and well-being. *American Psychologist, 55*(1), 68–78.

Smith, C., Akiva, T., Sugar, S., Lo, Y. J., Frank, K. A., Peck, S. C., & Cortina, K. S. (2012). *Continuous quality improvement in afterschool settings: Impact findings from the youth program quality intervention study.* David P. Weikart Center for Youth Program Quality at the Forum for Youth Investment. www.cypq.org/ypqi

Tuck, E., & Yang, K. W. (2011). Youth resistance revisited: New theories of youth negotiations of educational injustices. *International Journal of Qualitative Studies in Education, 24,* 521–530.

Valenzuela, A. (1999). *Subtractive schooling: U.S.-Mexican youth and the politics of caring.* SUNY Series, the Social Context of Education. State University of New York Press. http://pi.lib.uchicago.edu/1001/cat/bib/4068416.

Vossoughi, S., Tintiangco-Cubales, A. G. (2021). *Radically transforming the world: Repurposing education and designing for collective learning and well-being. Equitable Learning Development Project. Framework for Liberatory Education: First Installment.* University of Chicago Consortium on School Research, CASEL and the National Equity Project.

Ware, F. (2006). Warm demander pedagogy: Culturally responsive teaching that supports a culture of achievement for African American students. *Urban Education, 41*(4), 427–56. https://doi.org/10.1177/0042085906289710.

Yates, M., & Youniss, J. (1998). Community service and political identity development in adolescence. *Journal of Social Issues, 54*(3), 495–512.

CHAPTER 10

THE ROLE OF OUT-OF-SCHOOL TIME INTERMEDIARIES IN CONTRIBUTING TO EQUITABLE LEARNING AND DEVELOPMENT ECOSYSTEMS

Priscilla Little and Jessica Donner
with Wokie Weah, Mike Snell, LaRon Henderson,
Jessica Werner, and Eddie Cleofe

While grappling with the impact of the pandemic, the entire country has been challenged to address the structural racism that has, for too long, negatively impacted the lives, health and economic conditions of communities of color.... While we do not know the long- and short-term impact of the current challenges faced by the afterschool [OST] field, this study gives us reason to believe that cities with coordinated afterschool [OST] programs, which bring together stakeholders from multiple sectors to provide supports to children and youth will be in a better position to weather these times because of their shared vision, collective wisdom, standards of quality, and ability to collect and use data to assess needs and plan for the future (Simkin et al., 2021).

It Takes an Ecosystem: Understanding the People, Places, and
Possibilities of Learning and Development Across Settings, pages 183–205.
Copyright © 2022 by Information Age Publishing

In the past 20 years, many communities have implemented a strategy to improve access to quality out-of-school time (OST) programming by focusing on coordination—engaging OST providers, government leadership and agencies, private funders, higher education, and a myriad of other community-based learning and development settings in coordinated efforts to reduce the fragmentation that has generally characterized the OST sector. Indeed, communities that have taken a coordinated approach to OST programming have been shown to improve access to quality OST programs and facilitate the development of management information systems that yield data for planning and improvement (Kauh, 2011; Bodilly & McCombs, et al. 2010).

Transforming a patchwork of disconnected service providers operating in the out-of-school hours into a cohesive coordinated system is a critical step towards the goal of having allied youth fields. This is because, unlike school systems, social services systems, and even youth employment systems, OST providers are linked not by a specific shared outcome (e.g., academic success, summer employment) but by a shared time commitment (afterschool and summer). OST providers include public agencies (e.g., parks and recreation, libraries, public housing), non-profit service providers, businesses, faith and civic organizations, and schools. Giving these providers and their staff a way to transcend their individual systems—to make a shared commitment to help young people feel more connected to school, explore their interests, build confidence in their abilities as learners, make connections with caring adults, and make real contributions in their communities—is a concrete way to build alliances across the learning and development ecosystem.

Weaving optional programs and services into a coherent system is also a concrete way to address inequities in learning and development opportunities. Once established, these coordinating system have the capacity to compile community-level (and neighborhood or population specific) supply and demand data, identify service deserts, give families a much-needed entry point for finding quality afterschool and summer learning opportunities, advocate for funding, and help level-out resource distribution across a diverse provider network. They do all this by harnessing the power of partnership and collaboration among a myriad of public, private, and non-profit institutions and organizations across a community.

OST coordination requires staffing and resources to perform a set of functions that connect public and private funders with direct service providers, serving as the nucleus and guiding coordinator within a community's multifaceted network of government, schools, practitioners, and front-line OST programs (CBASS, 2007). Many intermediaries also manage data and quality improvement systems. These functions are often bundled together and housed in *OST intermediaries,* the general term used to describe the role of being the connector—mediating, connecting, facilitating, brokering, coordinating—with an eye towards bringing disparate parties together in support of the common goal of creating more equitable community-based learning and development opportunities for all young people.

As such, OST intermediaries are a much-needed tool to help broker relationships and make connections among and across the many macrosystems where young people spend their time.

Most importantly, OST intermediaries are inclusive of many types of community programs and agencies that work together to promote greater equity across the many formal, informal, and nonformal learning settings in a community. As such, they have the potential to not only improve quality and visibility of OST programs, they also have the potential to address some of the glaring disparities in availability, access, quality, and funding. Namely:

- There is documented unevenness in the availability of OST opportunities across the country. National survey data reveals that almost 25 million children and youth aren't able to access an OST program in their community, with a disproportionate number of those children and youth being low-income Black and Latinx children (Afterschool Alliance, 2020).
- The unevenness in availability is often directly linked to a family's ability to pay for OST experiences. Too often, there is s systemic pattern of "winners and losers" when it comes to participation in quality OST experiences, with higher income families spending almost seven times more on enrichment activities for their children than low-income families (Duncan & Murnane, 2011).
- This access gap is coupled with an outcomes gap. The combination of lack of availability due to structural inequities often means that even when programming is available to low-income, Black, and Latinx youth it may not be the kind of programming that fosters the developmental experiences with peers and adults that enable young people to foster essential social and emotional skills (Nagaoka et al., 2015).
- Although out-of-school time programs are sometimes deployed to address inequity evidence suggests they also can serve to reflect and replicate inequity. In particular, both in-school and out-of-school settings may enact narrowed views of success and deficit framings of children from marginalized racial and economic backgrounds (Akiva et al., 2020).
- As noted by Pittman et al. in Chapter 3 of this volume, researchers and advocates alike highlight the need to increase both quantity and quality. Low income, Black and Brown youth not only have less access to OST programs, they are more likely to be enrolled in OST programs that, because of an emphasis on addressing academic deficits, mirror rather than mitigate their school systems' priorities and approaches.

This chapter examines the role that OST intermediaries can play in contributing to equitable learning and development ecosystems to help mitigate the disparities listed above. We draw on national survey data to describe the various kinds of intermediaries that exist in communities across the country. Next, we describe the specific functions that OST intermediaries can perform to contribute to the mesosystem of supports for young people, shining a spotlight on the role that OST intermediaries can play in building the capacity of all adults to support optimized learning and development for all young people. We then conclude with a set of four vignettes that illustrate different ways that OST intermediaries are contributing to healthy, anti-racist, learning and development ecosystems.

OST INTERMEDIARIES COME IN ALL SHAPES AND SIZES

In 2011 Every Hour Counts conducted the first-ever national survey of OST intermediaries, with 212 in the sample. It targeted nonprofit OST intermediary organizations whose primary functions included grant-writing, training, advocacy, policy, and/or program oversight for OST programs. The survey examined: what organizations are trying to build the capacity of OST programs, what impact they are having on services and policies in their communities, what kinds of support they need to build on their progress.

Findings reveal that intermediaries come in all shapes, sizes, and places (CBASS, 2012). OST intermediaries vary in terms of where they are housed. OST intermediary structures include stand-alone nonprofits dedicated to a network of providers, community-based multi-service agencies, multi-site national providers such as Boys and Girls Clubs of America and the YMCA, community foundations, and universities. Most in the sample operated with budgets of $500,000 per year or less, on average depending equally on public and private funding. A full 40% of the intermediaries who responded to the survey had been working in the OST field for at least 15 years. The survey also revealed that OST intermediaries grew organically out of local planning efforts to respond to community conditions and needs. Depending on those conditions, OST intermediaries serve multiple varied functions across communities, as described in the next section.

Many intermediaries do not run programs themselves but *manage networks of OST providers* that are dedicated to improving access to and engagement in quality OST experiences. For example, the *Expanded Learning Opportunities Network* in Grand Rapids is a membership-based community collaboration that includes over 60 organizations and community stakeholders representing schools, higher education, police, faith-based organizations, youth-serving non-profits, foundations, United Way, businesses, and individuals.

Other OST intermediaries are *dedicated to supporting the OST workforce*. The *Youth Development Resource Center* in Detroit supports a network of hundreds of youth development providers to strengthen their individual and collective impact on youth by equipping them with the tools they need to increase program quality and collect actionable data. The *California Teaching Fellows Foundation* (featured later in this chapter) trains ethnically diverse college undergraduates to be instructors in K–12 after school, tutoring and summer programs, serving as mentors and role models for college success, thereby increasing the diversity of the OST workforce.

Every Hour Counts is a coalition of more than 20 local intermediaries that represent longstanding partnerships with more than 3,500 schools, districts, community-based organizations and local leaders, that provide quality after-school and summer programming aimed at supporting the whole child. Its members reflect the diversity of OST intermediaries whose common mission is to support thriving youth. Every Hour Counts was formed in 2005 to serve as a collective voice for the OST field to make the case for the value of coordinated OST systems that coordinate the work of service providers, public agencies, funders and schools, so more young people are served with transformative learning opportunities.

Some intermediaries *offer direct services to youth and families. After School Matters* in Chicago, for example, provides programming to over 19,000 teens each year, in public spaces as well as community organizations and arts institutions. The *Nashville After Zone Alliance,* housed at the Metro Nashville Public Library, focuses on increasing middle school youth's access to free, high-quality afterschool programing in order to create positive relationships with peers and adults, develop a sense of belonging, and have access to safe and supporting environments outside of school hours.

The diversity of providers, combined with specific community needs, helps shape what the local intermediary does to contribute to the learning and development ecosystem. As noted by Akiva, Hecht, and Blyth in Chapter 2 of this volume, schools, businesses and nonformal learning programs –and the staff that make them possible in a community change every day. With those changes come changes in the existence, nature, quality, and accessibility of the people, places and possibilities that shape learning and development of all younc people in a community. OST intermediaries take an "adaptive management" approach, ensuring that the full learning and development ecosystem is being responsive to and supportive of the specific needs of each young person as community context changes.

HOW INTERMEDIARIES CONTRIBUTE
TO EQUITABLE LEARNING ECOSYSTEMS

Despite the varied approaches that OST intermediaries take to supporting equitable learning and development ecosystems, they have many commonalities that define them as a critical part of a learning ecosystem. To use Bronfenbrenner's terms (see description in Chapter 2 of this volume by Akiva, Hecht, & Blyth), OST intermediaries operate at the *mesosystem* level, where a young person's individual microsystems interconnect and assert influence upon one another. They help to foster connections by brokering direct interaction among the people in the microsystems (e.g., community-based practitioners talking with teachers and school administrators, shared professional development to support consistent experiences across settings). Not all communities have OST intermediaries, and not all OST intermediaries perform the same functions in every community. But research and experience converge on a set of functions that, when in place, support more equitable learning and development ecosystems—functions that many OST intermediaries perform.

Expand and Improve Access to OST Opportunities

First and foremost, it is essential to expand access to quality programs and learning opportunities across a community. By mapping the provider landscape against the zip codes where youth live, OST intermediaries can even out distribution of programming so that more youth have access to programs in their own neighborhoods with a focus on communities that lack access. For example, at the system level, Philadelphia's OST system utilized data on youth poverty, early childhood risk factors and School District of Philadelphia data including school dropout rates and school progress scores, and overlaid OST data in the form of maps and other easy to understand visual formats in order to understand progress toward its goal of improving literacy. Known as The Community Snapshot, it sorted by zip code and included the number of students ages 5–9 who had two or more early childhood risk indicators, and then compared this against the number of known OST slots available in each zip code. In addition, the School District of Philadelphia elementary schools were mapped based on their K–2 Reading Scores and the number of OST slots at each school. Examining these data helped the city improve access to OST literacy supports.

OST intermediaries can also address transportation barriers by helping youth access public transportation passes and negotiating with school districts to use their buses to help with safe transport to afterschool sites and home at the end of the day. *Sprockets*, the OST intermediary in St. Paul, has its roots in a pilot program that provided children on St. Paul's East Side with free transportation between various afterschool activities during the summer and school year. What began in 2005 as an attempt to level the playing field for youth with less access to quality programming has become a citywide system of coordination among community organizations, city government, and the school district. Improving access is the first step on the path toward supporting the whole child because if youth aren't in a program, they can't reap its benefits.

Improve Program Quality

OST intermediaries do more than just expand and improve access to programs. They can improve access to *quality* programs, which we know from decades of research is critical to youth outcomes (Durlak et al., 2010; Kauh, 2011; Springer & Diffily, 2012; Vandell et al., 2007). OST intermediaries often manage a continuous program quality improvement system, offering supports to OST providers that help them: set common program quality standards; use program-level assessment tools to measure quality; help program staff create improvement plans; and engage staff in ongoing professional development. Establishing research-based quality processes across a wide variety of community-based settings helps ensure that all the many settings where young people spend their time maximizes the likelihood they will have a positive impact (For more on how OST intermediaries support program quality, see Singer, Newman, & Moroney, 2018).

The diversity of the OST workforce, which draws from a broad range of adults across the community and varies in: age (anywhere from teens through older adults); education levels (high school coursework through graduate school); and compensation levels (volunteers to part-time to full-time staff). This means that young people are interacting with adults from different backgrounds and with different capacities across a number of settings. Taking a systems approach to program quality and professional development provides some consistency in how the adults across settings work with young people so that regardless of where a young person chooses to spend their time outside of school, what zip code that young person lives in—they are assured a positive learning and developmental experience.

One way to ensure that youth have quality experiences that are consistent and responsive across settings is to make joint capacity building the norm so that adults across learning and development ecosystems have access to and engage in common professional development resources and trainings. There is mutual benefit in sharing professional expertise and content and, indeed, many efforts exist to co-train educators and youth development professionals. However, in most communities these efforts are primarily school-driven, designed, and delivered. Youth development and other community-based learning settings have a history of supporting aspects of whole child design, namely: building relationships with caring adults and fostering supporting learning environments. With the advocacy and support of intermediary organization, community-based organizations can contribute to professional learning.

Get and Use Reliable Information

In addition to supporting geo-mapping to understand supply, demand, and access issues intermediaries can get and use reliable information to understand where, when, and how learning happens. Some OST intermediaries conduct market research to assess where community programs are needed in a learning ecosystem, uncovering gaps in services for a specific neighborhood, age group, or type of programming. Extensive market research in Providence revealed a dearth of programming for middle schoolers across the city and so the *Providence After School Alliance* was launched to fill a much-needed opportunity gap for middle school youth.

Many OST intermediaries invest in data systems so they can collect, store, and analyze data from their partners in one shared management information system (MIS) that tracks youth participation, the characteristics of the youth who participate, and some commonly agreed to youth outcomes. Having these data is essential to creating an equitable learning ecosystem because it helps identify patterns of participation, experiences, and outcomes across different groups of youth. Data on where, when, and with whom youth spend their time can be used to reexamine opportunities in a learning ecosystem with an equity lens.

A study of data use among nine OST intermediaries found that developing the capacity to use data well depends as much on the people and the processes as it does on the technology used (Spielberger et al., 2016). *People* includes the stakeholders involved in the operation of the OST system and the dynamic connections among them. The social capital that emerges from the network of relationships among the people in the OST system is critical to establishing the trust needed for data sharing across partners. *Processes* are the routines, norms, and practices that evolve and are repeated over time and include collecting, organizing, analyzing, interpreting, and using data. Initially, processes help people know how to use the data system but over time the processes established also support strategies that facilitate meaning-making with the date across all the stakeholders. *Technology* refers to the means by which the data are organized and accessed to inform the operation of the OST system, including the hardware and software systems, commonly referred to as a management information system (for more information on the steps OST intermediaries can take to ensure effective data planning, analysis and use, see Yoo et al., 2019).

Promote Partnerships

By nature, OST intermediaries are collaborative and interact with other systems, thereby also contributing to diversity in the larger community ecosystem at the mesosystem level. In a 2013 random sample survey of cities of over 100,000 people, about three-quarters reported they were coordinating afterschool efforts (FHI360, 2013). When asked how many agencies and organizations (not specific OST sites) were engaged in the coordination effort, the median number of organizational partners in the effort was 20 (with a range of 1–700), indicating that OST intermediaries tend to work with a broad group of organizations across a community. In recent years, OST intermediaries in some communities have become trusted partners with school districts to support young people's social, emotional, academic, and cognitive development.

In the spring of 2020, as the COVID-19 pandemic descended on our country and out-of-school time became all the time, in many cities, OST intermediaries stepped in to partner with schools to provide critical family supports such as meal distribution, connecting to services, and checking in with young people. During the pandemic, some OST intermediaries created entire online virtual program options to complement school activities. For example, *NextUp* is an intermediary in Richmond, VA dedicated to providing opportunities for middle school youth to continue their learning beyond the school day. To help OST providers continue to deliver enrichments as a critical learning and development support over the summer of 2020, it created an online portal with both synchronous and asynchronous elements. Middle schoolers subscribed to the portal where they selected from four to six live learning enrichments happening every day. Topics ranged from sports and wellness, to arts and humanities, to leadership and careers—all topics that support the development of the whole child.

Help with Scale and Saturation Across a Community

An analysis of information from 45 scaled social programs, including OST programs, describes strategies for scaling up social programs (Larson et al., 2017). It defines "scaling up" as a process for significantly increasing the number of sustained implementations of a successful program, thereby serving more people with comparable benefits. But, what does "scale" look like when an OST intermediary supports a diverse set of OST providers, with varied program models, varied staffing configurations, diverse funding sources, and that serve different populations of youth?

Thinking about scale in the context of a citywide learning and development ecosystem broadens definitions of scale to include saturation. Defined as "*a state when no more of something can be absorbed*," saturation in the context of OST is when all young people across a community are getting access to and participating in as many rich developmental OST experiences as they feel they need for their own growth and development—regardless of the program "brand" they participate in. Data are essential to understanding saturation—coupling program location information with participation at the individual youth level enables OST leaders to monitor and analyze opportunities for each young person to be sure that they have affordable, accessible, and engaging options.

THE ROLE OF OST INTERMEDIARIES IN PROMOTING OPTIMIZED DEVELOPMENT, LEARNING AND THRIVING FOR EVERY CHILD AND ADOLESCENT

A robust learning & development ecosystem framework embraces the mantra that *learning happens everywhere* and that each and every adult from teachers to non-school personnel to community partners to family members, in each and every setting where a young person spends their time—-classrooms, cafeterias, playgrounds, playing fields, youth development programs, and families—is responsible for helping youth to thrive. Although K–12 education has long been considered the main setting accountable for learning and development, science tells us that learning can happen anywhere there are relationship-rich environments that offer a sense of safety and belonging, challenging content, intentional development of skills and mindsets, and the recognition that each and every young person has their own unique pathway toward thriving (Darling-Hammond et al., 2019). Unlike school districts that support K–12 settings, OST intermediaries that support networks of OST programs and opportunities have less accountability for specific standardized results and greater flexibility to support the whole child.

As described by Pittman et al. in Chapter 3 of this volume, the multi-disciplinary science findings on developmental potential shine a spotlight on the role that OST programs and settings can and do play in supporting thriving youth. While diverse in terms of where, when, how, and with whom they operate, the ties that bind community programs together are the very components that science tells us are the five "non-negotiables" of optimal conditions for learning and development. Specifically, OST learning and development opportunities:

- **Lead with safety and belonging**, creating consistent routines and expectations in a culturally affirming context;
- **Foster positive developmental relationships** among peers as well as with the adults who staff the program and with family members;
- Offer **engaging content-rich, culturally responsive learning environments** that celebrate the unique identities of all learners, while building on their diverse experiences to support rich and inclusive learning;
- Help youth **master critical skills, habits, and mindsets** by integrating social and emotional learning in an environment that incorporates healing centered practices and nurtures a growth orientation mindset;
- Offer **integrated systems of supports** to help children and youth access supplemental learning opportunities that contribute to academic growth and promote access to other supports and opportunities that foster health and well-being (Forum for Youth Investment et al., in press).

OST practitioners and organizations have a long history of emphasizing relationships, safety, and belonging, as well as creating learning experiences that match youth interests, helping them build skills and habits, all while working to affirm, if not meet, youth and family needs for comprehensive supports. It is validating that what OST practitioners have a history of doing is now being affirmed by science. The unique application of these components is to build them in reinforcing and integrated ways to truly support learner needs, interests, talents, voice, and agency. The aim is a culture and context that is greater than the sum of its parts.

Given the functions of OST intermediaries described above, they are well-poised to build the capacity of all adults across their OST networks to create developmentally rich OST settings and experiences that integrate these five "non-negotiables" of optimized learning settings. Further, local coordination of OST programming can pave the way for school-community partnerships that align developmental experiences across school and OST settings. For example, as part of Denver's Social Emotional Academic Learning (SEAL) Initiative, the Denver Afterschool Alliance (DAA), Denver's OST intermediary intentionally aligns professional learning strategies with its district partner, Denver Public Schools (DPS). It created "bite-sized" professional learning opportunities, which they promote as

SEAL U. These sessions are designed to zoom in on a particular SEAL strategy, practice, or competency and to be delivered to both school and out-of-school time staff in tandem so that adults across settings have a shared understanding of and capacity to implement, science-informed developmental practices.

OST INTERMEDIARIES AS LEVERS OF CHANGE TO PROMOTE RACIAL EQUITY

A commitment to aggressively expand access to equitable learning environments is a targeted and effective way to accelerate individual and collective thriving of all young people by focusing explicitly on creating opportunities and conditions that support the learning and development of our most marginalized young people. In both school and community settings, this commitment must focus on thriving, optimize transformative learning, enhance development, and address multiple determinants of inequity (Osher et al., 2020, p. 3).

The quote above acknowledges that expanding access to equitable learning environments is an effective way to address inequity. Indeed, OST intermediaries and their partners generally have a common goal of making high-quality OST programming accessible to underserved youth in order to raise their rate of participation and engagement—a first step in creating opportunities and conditions that support the learning and development of marginalized young people. While necessary, this first step is insufficient to address the multiple determinants of inequity, chiefly structural racism. An inherent challenge is that structural inequities are pervasive across our country. This became even more clear when, in spring 2020 COVID-19 ripped away the curtain on deep-seated racial inequities embedded within our country's systems and institutions—exposing the dual pandemics of COVID and systemic racism—both of which are connected and hurt BIPOC (Black, Indigenous, People of Color) communities more than others.

Many OST intermediaries fight against structural racism and work to increase access to quality learning opportunities for young people, modeling strategies organizations can take to mitigate inequities in their communities, such as empowering youth through advocacy, leading advocacy campaigns, and convening community stakeholders (Margolis, 2020). Some help the OST programs in their networks conduct diversity audits to ensure representatives of the communities served are reflected in staffing, board members, and leadership roles. This section of the chapter offers case examples of the ways four OST intermediary leaders, in their own words, describe how their intermediary works to contribute to a healthy, anti-racist learning and development ecosystem. The four OST intermediaries featured in this section vary in terms of how they set themselves up to address racial equity, and illustrate that there is no "right approach" to being an OST intermediary and that different OST intermediaries perform different ecosystems functions:

- **Youthprise** in Minneapolis, Minnesota is a statewide OST intermediary that serves as a resource for OST programs and provides leadership opportunities for young people. It centers its racial equity work with a commitment to meaningful youth voice and engagement by empowering authentic youth voice, which is a key component of optimal learning environments.

- **California Teaching Fellows** in Fresno, California hires young adults of color who are pursuing degrees in education to work as staff and mentors in OST programs. As a capacity-building intermediary it works to improve racial equity by supporting career pathways and workforce development for Black and Brown educators and community practitioners.
- **The Collective for Youth** in Omaha, Nebraska leads and supports a network of quality OST programs and is working with them to change the community narrative around race.
- **Youth Development Executives of King County** (YDEKC) is a coalition of over 100 non-profit youth serving agencies. It centers antiracist policies and practices in its coalition work to ensure that leaders across the OST system have opportunities to strengthen their skills and peer networks to advance racial equity.

Youthprise: Putting Youth at the Center to Dismantle Systemic Inequities. Wokie M. Weah, President & CEO of Youthprise

If there is one piece of advice I have for those working with young people that ranks high it is this: *the voice of the youth matters and should be heard and acted upon.* That is the philosophy that Youthprise employs in all that it does to improve and advance the lives of the youth it serves. Established in 2010 by the McKnight Foundation to increase the quality, accessibility, sustainability and innovation, Youthprise has served as a leader in Minnesota, providing OST opportunities across the state. Youthprise's mission is to "increase equity *for and with* indigenous, low income, and racially diverse *youth.* It sits at the intersection of mobilizing and reinvesting in youth, advocating for change, and sharing knowledge."

Youthprise is an intermediary organization specifically formed to help youth programs in our region become youth-centered, equitable and self-sustainable. To accomplish its mission, Youthprise built a web of grassroots relationships with community, government, counties, cities, foundations, school districts, youth leaders, and policy makers. This was done to accelerate leadership and innovation, catalyze action, and trigger new investments in the communities they serve. Youthprise is intentional and unapologetic about elevating youth voice, advancing racial equity and disrupting systems, especially systems like policy, research, and philanthropy that all have great impacts on the lives of youth.

Our vision is a Minnesota where every young person, regardless of race, zip code, or economic status has access to a reliably excellent out-of-school system. Our intention is to disrupt inequity by offering a new story about the promise and potential of Minnesota youth. Important to our work is to recognize that young people have the capacity to transform inequitable systems, but often lack the opportunity to do so. Our investment portfolio focuses on investing in youth as decision makers, youth-serving organizations, city and statewide systems, and youth themselves. For example, in the wake of COVID-19, the organization's youth leaders mobilized to rectify the digital divides they were experiencing. Youth leader Salma Abdi shared, "*The way distance learning is going is not equitable, but equal, so it's like putting everyone on the same scale when in reality some people's parents have different education levels, more access to tutoring and other services, and have the time.*"

Youthprise teamed up with other local nonprofits to address gaps in digital access in a letter to state officials and at a virtual town hall event where youth leaders shared the challenges and inequalities surrounding virtual learning and advocated for a new set of priority recommendations. State Representative Adri Arquin seemed to agree, identifying the first step as ensuring everyone has access to education, and next figuring out how to catch up those who have fallen behind because of inequitable access.

We have learned a lot about how to upend racial inequity working with youth:

- *Advancing the twin engines of racial equity and youth leadership is a compound, complex phenomenon.* Deep investments are required when leading with racial equity and youth leadership including investments in organizational learning, accountability, and actively practicing anti-racism.
- *Championing a Youth/Adult Board model includes a youth and adult co-chair of the Board as well as at the committee level.* We highly recommend this approach to energize the mission and growth of OST intermediaries but caution that asking young people to step into an adult driven, transactional world doesn't always work. Young people are relationship driven, and therefore training adults and youth for mutually beneficial relationships is key to successful youth engagement on boards and committees.
- *Promoting culturally informed and responsive programming for BIPOC youth to reach their full potential is critical.* Years of youth work have taught us that young people care deeply about racial justice, social justice, environmental justice, and economic justice. They are keenly aware that systems are designed to replicate themselves. High quality youth programming can provide opportunities to explore their own cultural identities and authentic leadership development.
- *To be successful, OST intermediaries interested in youth leadership must support programs with training, tools, and assistance.* It is also critically important to consider *when* you are involving young people. Youthprise had a team of youth innovators from the outset who encouraged us to think about how the role of youth would grow as the organization and its investment in young people also grew.
- *Amplifying youth voice through podcasts and other virtual platforms applying community organizing principles elevates the voice of youth and energizes the field.* The myriad of social media platforms presents unprec-

edented opportunities to respond to the urgency of now and creative wealth that young people bring to the work.

- *Pivoting is important to organizational relevancy, to remain adaptive, nimble, and willing to make mid-course corrections is needed.* An important mid-course correction for Youthprise was to add economic opportunity and health and safety to our impact areas. Intermediaries that embrace innovation have to also be willing to try new and different things.

At Youthprise we lean into the future confident, that the next generation will dismantle systems of inequity. For more information about Youthprise visit its website at: https://youthprise.org/.

California Teaching Fellows Foundation: Addressing California Teacher Quality, Quantity and Diversity Through Expanded Learning Systems. Mike Snell, Chief Executive Officer

California is in the midst of a statewide teacher shortage that is disproportionately impacting communities with large populations of low-income students and students of color. The gap between the number of qualified, well-prepared teachers needed in the classroom and the number of new teachers entering the field must be closed to avoid far-reaching consequences for both the individuals involved and the communities in which they live. California Teaching Fellows Foundation (CTFF) is addressing the challenge by expanding the pipeline of diverse and well-prepared teachers. As a capacity-building intermediary based in Fresno, CTFF has recruited and prepared future teachers for the classroom since 1999 using expanded learning programs (the term the state of California uses to refer to OST programming) and a network of strategic partnerships as levers of change.

The main way that CTFF works to improve racial equity is by ensuring that teaching fellows reflect the student populations in which they serve, which has the effect of introducing students from traditionally underserved communities to young leaders from their own neighborhoods, cultures, and backgrounds. In CTFF's home of Fresno, for example, 82% of K–12 students come from non-white ethnic backgrounds (California Department of Education, 2017), which is similar to the Teaching Fellows population of 85%. For a statewide comparison, California's teachers are predominately white (65%), whereas the state's student population is 54% Hispanic and only 25% white (Ed-Data, 2016). Each semester, dozens of Teaching Fellows graduate and matriculate into teacher credential programs, other careers in education, or leadership roles in our community, further helping our community elevate leaders of color and diversity in our teaching population.

CTFF employs three complementary strategies to prepare future teachers for the classroom:

1. Pre-service Teaching Experience: CTFF Expanded Learning Programs

CTFF is the leading expanded learning capacity-builder in the Central Valley, providing supervised pre-service teaching experiences for more than 2,000 Teaching Fellows spread across 350 schools, 50+ school districts, and five counties. Teaching Fellows are college students who are trained as instructors in OST programs, providing homework help and leading enrichment activities for more than 30,000 K–12 students daily.

The benefits of the Teaching Fellows program are two-fold. First, Teaching Fellows are placed in schools that qualify for Title I funding, which means that at least 40% of the students come from low-income households. In addition to tutoring and leading enrichment activities, Teaching Fellows are mentors and role models to thousands of young people, including many who will be the first in their family to graduate from high school or attend college. Second, Teaching Fellows on a path to a teaching credential receive supervised early field experiences, ongoing professional development, and holistic support to help navigate school and life challenges. Future teachers have the opportunity to observe the instructional practices of experienced teachers and make connections with district and school administrators.

2. *Ongoing Professional Development: Teaching Fellows Academy*

Every Teaching Fellow participates in monthly professional development through Teaching Fellows Academy, a series of monthly trainings, hosted by Fresno State's Kremen School of Education, that prepares Teaching Fellows for their current work in an OST program and their future work as a California classroom teacher. Workshops are facilitated by experts in the field of OST, education and equity.

3. Holistic Support: The Dream Initiative

One of the goals of CTFF is a preservice teacher workforce that mirrors the school and neighborhood populations they serve. However, because Teaching Fellows come from these same underserved and under-resourced communities, they often encounter obstacles that impede their own educational progress, from a lack of good transportation options to health problems, financial insecurity or overwhelming family responsibilities.

To help Teaching Fellows not only overcome these obstacles but to realize their dreams, CTFF has invested in the design and implementation of the Dream Initiative, an organization-wide strategy to provide individual and small group coaching, and life skills workshops to increase the well-being, satisfaction, and retention of Teaching Fellows, which will further expand the pipeline of future teachers. Structured support is especially critical for first-generation college students, who often lack adult role models who can help guide them through the thicket of the postsecondary systems and to a college degree (Deil-Amen & Rosenbaum, 2003).

To learn more about the California Teaching Fellows Foundation visit: http://www.ctff.us/

*Collective for Youth: Reimagining Community Conversations
on Racial Equity. LaRon Henderson, Program Quality Director,
Collective for Youth*

Throughout our country's history, white supremacy has played a significant role in creating a mindset of believing you are either a valuable part of society or your life is insignificant depending on the color of your skin. This mindset is based on a false narrative that white people are genetically superior to Black people. We have been taught throughout our academic journey that the ancestors of Black people were all slaves and systems like Affirmative Action were created to benefit minorities. We listened to stories about Pocahontas thinking it was about the romance between Pocahontas and John Rolfe; in reality, we were not being taught the truth, but a made up, glorified, glamourized, monetized lie intended to "make people in white American culture feel good about [their] history" (Mansky, 2017, para. 10).

Committed to upending racial inequity, it is the mission of Collective for Youth to lead and support a network of high-quality OST programs that inspire and engage youth, while stimulating academic and personal growth that promotes racial equity. We serve as an intermediary between our state government and the largest public school district in Nebraska. Our network includes nine separate agencies, 37 schools, serving over 7,000 students annually.

In order to address the issue of racial equity, we designed a series of conversations to start chipping away at the old mindset and ideology around the narrative we have all been presented throughout our educational journey. Depending on the area of the country you were born in, the lens from which you see life is important, so it was essential to stay away from the emotional impact this subject could have on people. Although we felt we knew what the problem was, getting to the root or the "why" was important, so we convened our network to participate in a training led by the Racial Equity Institute, based out of North Carolina. The goal of the Institute was to bring awareness and analysis to the root causes of disparities and disproportionality in order to create racially equitable organizations and systems. In that workshop we learned about seven expectations that were adopted from the work of Bryan Stevenson, the founder/executive director of the Equal Justice Initiative. These include getting proximate to the problem and changing the narrative while staying committed and engaged, even during uncomfortable conversations, in a safe and confidential environment.

Reflecting on the Community Conversations, it is easy to combine the conversation about racial equity with diversity or inclusion, but we have learned these are different topics. Our conversations have opened the door for individuals to intentionally destroy their ignorance and bias without destroying another person. It has been amazing to watch how such a diverse group of individuals have come together around this topic. The cross generational make up of our network has been represented throughout this process. Executive directors, CEO's, site directors, principals, school administrators, frontline staff, and providers have all joined the conversations. Rather than us as the OST intermediary recruiting new participants, we have encouraged folks to invite friends to join us and we continue to grow each new topic. We don't believe we are close to the end but will continue to lay the foundation for the next person to explore their own journey.

As an OST intermediary, we have initiated a process of destroying ignorance around racial equity and learned some tips that might help other OST intermediary who want to do so as well:

- Base your conversation on historical facts, not human emotion. We have found this to be a very emotionally driven topic and you don't always know the back story from those participating. So, we have intentionally kept the focus on destroying ignorance with brutal facts.
- Don't confuse racial equity and diversity/inclusion.
- Make a commitment to do the work when it is not socially popular. Just because the news media isn't writing stories or someone has not been killed, doesn't mean this work is not important.
- We are not waiting for Superman to show up and save the day. Each person around to table has a voice and a circle of influence, a united voice delivered by many individuals can go a long way.

For more information about Omaha's Collective for Youth visit: https://collectiveforyouth.org/

Youth Development Executives of King County (YDEKC): Centering People of Color in OST Systems Design. Jessica Werner, Executive Director with Eddie Cleofe, YDEKC Database and Communications Coordinator

Youth Development Executives of King County (YDEKC) is a diverse coalition of more than 100 youth-serving community based and nonprofit organizations across King County, WA. With a focus on equity, our members embrace a youth development approach to support young people—especially Black, Indigenous and young people of color—to reach the future they envision. Our members are an essential part of the ecosystem of supports that young people need to learn, grow, and thrive. YDEKC strives to center antiracist policies and practices in our work to ensure that leaders at every organizational level have opportunities to strengthen their skills and peer networks to advance along their own pathway.

Racial equity work addresses root causes of inequities not just their manifestation. This includes the elimination of policies, practices, attitudes, and cultural messages that reinforce differential outcomes by race or fail to eliminate them. As a coalition of youth-serving organizations working to support young people to thrive, we must be explicit and committed to centering People of Color in our programs and activities—not only for the youth of color that we collectively serve, but also with and for the leaders of color among us. We have three levers for focusing on racial equity:

1. *We advocate* for policies, funding streams and recognition for the organizations on the ground that are supporting thriving youth—especially young people of color—who have been failed over and over again by systems built on white supremacy and racist practice, even if unintentionally.

2. *We support* our nonprofit member leaders to dig deep into their own organizations and practices to create more equitable environments internally, from their boards of directors to their front line-staff.

3. *We offer trainings and formal and informal opportunities* to learn in community with peers to deepen ability to provide socially and emotionally rich, and equity focused learning environments for the young people that our members and our partners in K–12 support.

In Spring 2017, YDEKC launched our Racial Equity Community of Practice (CoP)—a group of 15 leaders from nine youth-serving non-profit professionals who came together monthly for a year to discuss the ongoing racial equity work in our organizations. The experience was eye-opening, challenging, and an important step in our ongoing goal of making systems more equitable for young people of color—starting with our own organizations. This is what we learned about working to upend racism:

- *This will take longer than you think.* Racism affects everything in our lives, including how we perceive time. Unspoken norms of white supremacy create a sense of urgency, the feeling that decisions have to be made and action has to be taken now. This sense of urgency is often the root of decisions that are less inclusive. Through the community of practice, we learned to take more time to connect with, listen to, argue with, and get to know one another. Eventually, through integrating separate People of Color and white caucuses, the community of practice found a rhythm, one that included taking the time to be people with one another.

- *A tool is just a tool.* One of the major goals of the project was to surface resources, tools, and tactics that our peers knew of or were actively using to help all of us improve our own practice. It's a great goal, but it ignores what so often gets ignored because of racism: context. A well-designed tool, such as a workshop on talking about race at work, can cause more harm than good if not facilitated well and/or not designed with the audience's wants and needs factored in.

- *Goals are a moving target.* At launch, our goals were: To create a multicultural professional learning community to surface resources tools and tactics that leaders could learn from one another to strengthen the organizational capacity of each participating organization to deepen their racial equity practice, policies and internal structures. Although we were mostly able to meet our goals, more importantly, our goals shifted to be more responsive to the wants and needs of participants. By responding to emergent issues, our facilitators refocused our goals from ones based solely in 'the work' to ones based in understanding ourselves both personally and professionally.

- *Relationships come first.* No racial equity work can be done if the people doing it aren't in authentic relationship with one another. One of racism's functions is to dehumanize all of us; only by working to understand, learn from, and take action with each other can we make headway into a more just world.
- *Wearing many hats can cause lots of headaches.* YDEKC had the tricky position of being both a participant and the convener of the community of practice. We hired Fostering Real Opportunities to facilitate the CoP, to honor our goal of supporting POC led organizations that have been doing this work for a long time. This relationship then meant that not only were racial power dynamics at play, but power dynamics too. With time, and getting past norming to storming, we allowed the silences to be longer, the conflicts more spoken, and the relationships to become deeper.

We are committed to deepening our antiracism lens and learning and leading alongside our members and community, as the journey is long. The goal of a society that fully honors the humanity of every one of us and where we all can thrive is worth it.

To learn more about YDEKC visit: https://ydekc.org

***

Central to a commitment to racial equity for these four OST intermediaries is a willingness and openness to ask hard questions about their contribution to equitable learning and development ecosystems:

- Are we doing enough?
- When we look at our OST systems now and other systems in our community that were designed to rectify inequities and injustices, or to create solutions to problems that disproportionately affect communities of color, are we asking ourselves whether we are doing all we can to work towards these ends?
- Are we leading our ecosystems with a youth centered, asset-based approach?
- Are we engaging youth, family and community partners in leadership roles on non-profit boards, advocating with elected officials, informing program design and evaluation efforts?

- Are we looking to our young people to help design the learning ecosystem they experience every day?
- Are we supporting a youth workforce that reflects the field with sustainable jobs and career pathways that break cycles of poverty?
- Are we reflecting on and rectifying deep-seeded white supremacy cultures that marginalize voices of color?

Now, more than ever, all actors and institutions across learning and development ecosystems have a responsibility to address these questions.

CONCLUSION

The last two decades have seen the emergence of OST intermediaries that are working to transform a patchwork of disconnected service providers operating in the out-of-school hours into a cohesive coordinated system. As such, they are an important tool in creating and managing a learning and development ecosystem, brokering relationships and making connections among and across the many macrosystems where young people spend their time. Weaving this patchwork of optional programs and services into a coherent system is also a concrete way to address inequities in learning and development opportunities that are exacerbated in the afterschool and summer periods due to structural inequities.

This chapter described that many ways that OST intermediaries and their network of partners can contribute to more just, equitable learning ecosystems, tackling the pervasive inequities that exist across communities. They can commit to improving access for Black, Indigenous and other youth of color, not just those who can afford to pay, or live in the right zip code. They can strive to ensure that all adults across the ecosystem are trained to implement science-informed practices. They can use data to drive their efforts to upend inequity. They can take the approach that the way to get to saturation of quality practices across the learning ecosystem is to commit to partnerships. And finally, like the four intermediaries featured in this chapter, they can create an explicit and intentional focus on addressing racial equity in a way that meets their partner's and community's needs. While they can do all these things will they be able to?

> Balanced and equitable learning systems require balanced and equitable funding. To be effective partners in supporting social, emotional, cognitive, and academic development, the youth development sector needs increased and stable funding. (Little & Pittman, 2018, p. 12)

Currently, the promise of OST intermediaries to contribute to equitable learning and development ecosystems is not matched by investments in them nor in the OST programs they work with. Historically, OST programs and intermediaries have been substantially under-funded, relying primarily on short-term, unstable resources. Stable funding would allow OST intermediaries to build capacity of all adult practitioners to deepen their practice and improve quality by accessing critical professional development supports to help them implement science-aligned practices alongside school day professionals. More funding would also help address the documented unevenness of access to and participation in quality OST programs experienced by many Black and Brown young people across our communities. Funding would also help intermediaries analyze and reflect on structural inequities in their communities and design approaches to disrupt centuries of systemic injustices.

Increasing and stabilizing funding alone will be insufficient to fulfill the promise of OST intermediaries. Coupled with funding, the OST sector needs more reflection and attention to the capacity of how systems can dismantle structural racism, with research, policy and practice. It also needs more and better documentation of how OST intermediaries are contributing members of equitable learning and development ecosystems. This chapter is a down payment on that documentation.

REFERENCES

Afterschool Alliance. (2020). *America after 3PM*. Author. http://www.afterschoolalliance. org/AA3PM/

Akiva, T., O'Connor, D., & Pittman, K. (2020). The promise of building equitable ecosystems for learning. *Urban Education*, 1–27. Sage Publications.

Bodily, S., McCombs, J., Orr, N., Scherer, E., Constant, L., & Gershwin, D. (2010). *Hours of opportunity: Lessons from five cities on building systems to improve after-school, summer school, and other out-of-school time programs*. RAND Education. https://www.rand.org/pubs/monographs/MG1037.html

California Department of Education. (2017). *DataQuest*. https//: data1.cde.ca.gov/Dataquest

Collaborative for Building After-School Systems. (2007). *Shaping the future of afterschool: The essential role of intermediaries in bringing quality after-school systems to scale*. Author. https://www.expandinglearning.org/sites/default/files/Shaping%20the%20Future%20of%20After-School.pdf

Collaborative for Building After School Systems. (2012). *Making the connections: A report on the first national survey of out-of-school time intermediary organizations*. Author. https://www.wallacefoundation.org/knowledge-center/Documents/Making-the-Connections-Report-First-National-Survey-of-OST.pdf.

Darling-Hammond, L., Flook, L., Cook-Harvey, C., Barron, B., & Osher, D. (2019). Implications for educational practice of the science of learning and development. *Applied Developmental Science*, 24(2), 97–140. https://www.tandfonline.com/doi/full/10.1080/10888691.2018.1537791.

Deil-Amen, R., & Rosenbaum, J. (2003). The social prerequisites of success: Can college structure reduce the need for social know-how? *The ANNALS of the American Academy of Political and Social Science*, 580, 120–143.

Duncan, G. J., & Murnane, D. (2011). *Wither opportunity? Rising inequality, schools, and children's life chances*. Russell Sage Foundation.

Durlak, J. A., Weissberg, R. P., & Pachan, M. (2010). A meta-analysis of after-school programs that seek to promote personal and social skills in children and adolescents. *American Journal of Psychology, 45*, 294–309.

Ed-Data. (2016, February 15). *Teachers in California*. https://www.ed-data.org.

FHI360 and The Wallace Foundation. (2013). *Is citywide afterschool coordination going nationwide? An exploratory study in large cities*. Authors. https://www.wallacefoundation.org/knowledge-center/documents/is-citywide-afterschool-coordination-going-nationwide.pdf.

Forum for Youth Investment, Learning Policy Institute & Turnaround for Children. (2021, in press). *Design principles for community-based settings: Putting the science of learning and development into action*. The Science of Learning and Development Alliance.

Kauh, T. J. (2011). *AfterZone: Outcomes for youth participating in Providence's citywide after school system*. Public Private Ventures. https://www.wallacefoundation.org/knowledge-center/Documents/AfterZone-Outcomes-Youth-Participating-Providences-Citywide-After-School-System.pdf.

Larson, R., Dearing, J., & Backer, T. (2017). *Strategies to scale up social programs: Pathways, fidelity, and partnerships*. Diffusion Associates. https://www.wallacefoundation.org/knowledge-center/Documents/Strategies-to-Scale-Up-Social-Programs.pdf

Little, P. M., & Pittman, K. (2018). *Building partnerships in support of where, when, and how learning happens*. National Commission on Social, Emotional and Academic Development.

Mansky, J. (2017). The true story of Pocahontas. *Smithsonian Magazine*wwwwwwwww-wwwwwwwwwwwwwww. https://www.smithsonianmag.com/history/true-story-pocahontas-180962649/.

Margolis, A. (2020). *The disparate impacts of COVID-19 require dismantling more than the virus: How intermediaries are centering racial equity in their responses*. Every Hour Counts. https://everyhourcounts.medium.com/the-disparate-impacts-of-covid-19-require-dismantling-more-than-the-virus-how-intermediaries-are-41d5707f286a

Nagaoka, J., Farrington, C. A., Ehrlich, S. B., & Heath, R. D. (2015). *Foundations for young adult success: A developmental framework*. University of Chicago Consortium on Chicago School Research. https://consortium.uchicago.edu/publications/foundations-young-adult-success-developmental-framework

Osher, D., Pittman, K., Young, J., Smith, H., Moroney, D., & Irby, M. (2020). *Thriving, robust equity, and transformative learning & development: A more powerful conceptualization of the contributors to youth success*. Forum for Youth Investment. https://forumfyi.org/knowledge-center/thriving-robust-equity-and-transformative-learning-development/

Simkin, L., Charner, I., Dailey, R., Khatri, S., & Thapa, S. (2021). *Stability and change in afterschool systems, 2013–2020*. FHI360. https://www.wallacefoundation.org/knowledge-center/pages/stability-and-change-in-afterschool-systems-2013-2020-a-follow-up-study-of-afterschool-coordination-in-large-cities.aspx.

Singer, J., Newman, J., & Moroney, D. (2019). Building quality in out-of-school time. *The growing field of out-of-school time* (pp. 195–210). Information Age Publishing.

Spielberger, J., Axelrod, J., Dasgupta, D., Cerven, C., Spain, A., Kohm, A., & Mader. N. (2016). *Connecting the dots: Data use in afterschool systems*. Chapin Hall at the

University of Chicago. https://www.wallacefoundation.org/knowledge-center/Documents/Connecting-the-Dots-Data-Use-in-Afterschool-Systems.pdf.

Springer, K., & Diffily, D. (2012). The relationship between intensity and breadth of afterschool program participation and academic achievement. *Journal of Community Psychology, 40*(7), 785–798.

Vandell, D. L., Reisner, E. R., & Pierce, K. M. (2007). *Outcomes linked to high-quality afterschool programs: Longitudinal findings from the study of promising afterschool programs.* Charles Stewart Mott Foundation. https://www.researchgate.net/publication/237263207_Outcomes_Linked_to_High-Quality_Afterschool_Programs_Longitudinal_Findings_from_the_Study_of_Promising_Afterschool_Programs.

Yoo, Y., Whitaker, A., & McCombs, J. (2019). *Putting data to work for young people: A ten-step guide for expanded learning intermediaries.* The RAND Corporation. https://www.rand.org/content/dam/rand/pubs/tools/TL300/TL350/RAND_TL350.pdf.

CHAPTER 11

FROM SYSTEM TO (ECO)SYSTEM

Policy Examples that Foster Cross-Sector Collaboration

Michelle J. Boyd-Brown, Jill Young, and Deborah Moroney

Policies and their related systems impact young people's learning and development (L&D) ecosystem, and thus young people's capacity to thrive. A policy is "a law, regulation, procedure, administrative action, incentive, or voluntary practice of governments and other institutions" (Centers for Disease Control and Prevention, n. d.). As our colleagues shared in Chapter 2 (see Akiva, Hecht, and Blyth, this volume), a healthy L&D ecosystem is defined as effective and positive co-actions between and among ecosystem elements, such as all the people, places, and possibilities in young people's lives, that support learning and development. These coactions are the relational, bidirectional actions involved in processes for learning and development including the mutual influences between young people and the contexts they grow up in (Gottlieb & Halpern, 2008; Overton & Lerner, 2014). Such coaction between and among ecosystem elements happens regardless of whether we choose to manage those transactions actively and intentionally. Designing and managing healthy L&D ecosystems requires making science-informed decisions and drawing on our best knowledge from the science of learning and development—including to inform the design and implementation of policies

It Takes an Ecosystem: Understanding the People, Places, and
Possibilities of Learning and Development Across Settings, pages 207–226.
Copyright © 2022 by Information Age Publishing
207

at all levels (e.g., local, state, federal) and across all sectors that support healthy L&D ecosystems.

The Science of Learning and Development

The science of learning and development draws from diverse disciplines to describe the biological, neurobiological, social, emotional, cognitive, cultural, and behavioral processes, among others, that influence and affect human learning and development. This multidisciplinary body of science suggests that all young people have the potential to thrive (Osher et al., 2017; Science of Learning and Development [SoLD] Alliance, 2020). There is recent and ongoing work to synthesize the large and diverse bodies of science and research on learning and development and consider its application for policy and practice (e.g., Alliance for Excellent Education, 2019; Nagaoka et al., 2015; National Commission on Social, Emotional, and Academic Development, 2018; Osher et al., 2017). This work includes the efforts of the SoLD Alliance, which is a group of scholars working to compile research on learning and development and advance its translation and application to transform youth-serving systems.

The SoLD Alliance identifies five practice components that support young people's learning, development, and capacity to thrive (Darling-Hammond et al., 2020). They include: 1) positive developmental relationships; 2) environments filled with safety and belonging; 3) rich learning experiences; 4) development of critical knowledge, skills, habits, and mindsets; and 5) integrated support systems. Integrated support systems speak to the idea that learning and development happen wherever young people, live, learn, work, and play—including recognition of and coordination across all the formal and nonformal settings in which learning and development occur.

Application of the Science of Learning and Development to Policymaking

The emphasis on integrated support systems in the science of learning and development tells us that it is the job of the adults who design, manage, and make up those systems to coordinate their operations and efforts to support young people. Thus, to actualize the promise of these scientific findings, young people need access to the right opportunities, experiences, and relationships, which requires thoughtful and well-implemented policies and user-centered systems for youth that are grounded in the latest knowledge on how young people learn and develop (SoLD Alliance, 2017). The science of learning and development provides important lessons that we can apply to better design and manage L&D ecosystems. The science also provides insights for shaping L&D ecosystems to be responsive to inevitable changes and create high-quality, equitable conditions and opportunities for contemporary youth.

When informed by these multidisciplinary science findings, policy decisions can provide supportive infrastructures for healthy L&D ecosystems across multiple sectors, including out-of-school time (OST). These policy decisions can also determine investments of people, time, and resources that uphold or advance equity in circumstances and outcomes for all young people, especially those who are growing up in under resourced or developmentally unfavorable contexts. For example, policy decisions can include laws that establish summer and mentoring programs for young people who have fallen behind or become disconnected and disengaged during the COVID-19 pandemic; regulations to monitor and disaggregate data for groups of young people at risk of inequitable and disparate treatment; and incentives to provide educational and employment opportunities for youth and young adults in low-income communities.

Systems are influenced, and in some cases created, by policies. That is, policymakers create federal, state, and local policies that establish rules and priorities, create structures and procedures, allocate resources, and create and enforce norms of behavior (SoLD Alliance, 2017). For example, policymakers can allocate resources to programs within systems that explicitly support youth learning and development in a variety of educational settings (such as OST, community-based settings, and enrichment programs). Thus, policies can be a mechanism for building young people's strengths and assets as well as addressing critical challenges that affect young people—to contribute to healthy L&D ecosystems. Furthermore, policies and their implementation are key levers to address the inequities in youth-serving systems.

However, policies can also inadvertently undermine young people's success and capacity to thrive. For instance, policies and related systems that are not well aligned with one another—which is often the case in youth-serving systems—can make it hard for young people and their families to navigate those systems and benefit from policies (e.g., Changing the Odds for Disconnected Youth, 2014; Interagency Working Group on Youth Programs, 2016). In addition, policies and associated systems that do not reflect the latest science findings on how young people learn and develop run the risk of being developmentally inappropriate or even harmful (e.g., a policy that arbitrarily ends the supports and services a young person can access when they turn 18, which is contradictory to what we know from developmental science about young people's maturation and ongoing developmental opportunities and challenges).

Youth-serving systems can enhance support for young people when policymakers crafting policies and adults working within systems implementing those policies apply scientific evidence on how young people learn and develop. Policies can transform systems and create conditions for practitioners to serve young people holistically and equitably when informed by science (Darling-Hammond et al., 2020). Policymakers and practitioners can use information grounded in the science about young people's potential for thriving to ensure that youth-serving systems are developmentally affirming and equitable and serve the whole young person. Doing so requires taking into consideration the various dimensions of young people's health, well-being, readiness, and success, as well as the interrelationships among all elements of young people's L&D ecosystems. Policymakers can then use this information about youth to shape policies and practices that support young people across settings, systems, and developmental periods (Darling-Hammond & Cook-Harvey, 2018).

This chapter focuses on how policies and related systems can impact young people's L&D ecosystems and thus support or hinder youth's capacity to thrive. We provide an overview of some major federal public policies that affect youth-serving systems and programs that are part of many young people's L&D ecosystems. We then describe several elements of policies, with national, state, and local examples, that have the potential to build and transform systems to better serve youth.

EXAMPLES OF FEDERAL PUBLIC POLICIES THAT SUPPORT YOUTH-SERVING PUBLIC SYSTEMS

Several systems and related institutions make up the L&D ecosystems in which youth live, learn, work, and play. L&D ecosystems are made up of these multiple systems in which adults engage with young people. From childhood to young adulthood, young people interact with systems that may include child welfare, education, health, juvenile justice, and workforce systems. Youth also engage in programs and experiences outside of the school day, for example, afterschool and summer programs, enrichment and tutoring, mentoring, and clubs. These activities are traditionally grouped together and collectively called OST programs.

In this chapter we focus on OST broadly and the related youth-serving systems. These systems are shaped by policy choices and outputs (including legislation, regulations, and programs) that set the systems' priorities, practices, and strategies for supporting young people. Practitioners and programs within OST fields operate within L&D ecosystems that are broader than a particular type of OST program or organization. Therefore, OST practitioners should be knowledgeable of the types of policies and systems (e.g., child welfare, juvenile justice) that affect young people. This knowledge is valuable given how policies and systems intersect and interact, compounding the effects (both positive and negative) that they have on the lives of youth. Increased awareness provides practitioners with a more complete picture of the multitude of young people's experiences within and outside of schools, including their engagement with multiple youth-serving systems—thus, providing a fuller understanding of the implications of their program- or organization-specific decisions for youth.

Attention to these issues is also important for ensuring equitable access to the relationships, conditions, and opportunities that support optimal learning and development. For instance, certain groups of young people, including based on their race/ethnicity, sexual orientation, gender identity, and disability status, experience unequal treatment and disparities within and disproportional contact with certain systems (e.g., exclusionary discipline within the formal education system; involvement with the juvenile justice and child welfare systems), contributing to short- and long-term negative outcomes (National Academies of Sciences, Engineering, and Medicine [NASEM], 2019b).

This section briefly describes several federal laws that shape youth-serving systems. The descriptions of these key laws here and later in the chapter provide information on how they can impact young people's learning and development and provide equitable access to the formal and nonformal contexts and opportunities that promote their capacity to thrive. Moreover, the summary of these laws provides background information for a discussion on how to improve policy actions.

Affordable Care Act (2010)

The Patient Protection and Affordable Care Act, also known as the Affordable Care Act (ACA), is a health care reform law administered by the U.S. Departments of Health and Human Services, Labor, and Treasury. The ACA supports young people in two primary ways. First, the policy includes initiatives specifically intended to support young people, such as funding for school-based health centers, teen pregnancy prevention programs, and community-school health partnerships and community health centers (NASEM, 2019b; Vaughn et al., 2013). Second, the ACA requires insurers to extend the coverage of dependents on a family plan until age 26 (HealthCare.gov, n.d.). This extension promotes healthy development and well-being as it provides young people with stable access to health care during major points of life transition, and through a life phase that includes, for example, the typical age of onset for many mental health disorders (e.g., de Lijster et al., 2017; Kessler et al., 2007; NASEM, 2019b; Schwartz & Sommers, 2012).

Child Abuse Prevention and Treatment Act (2018)

The Child Abuse Prevention and Treatment Act (CAPTA) is the main federal legislation that addresses child abuse and neglect, and it is the first federal law governing the child welfare system. The Act, administered by the U.S. Department of Health and Human Services, provides federal funding to states to provide supports and protection for children and youth safety and well-being (e.g., physical, social, emotional), so that young people grow up protected from harm. Young people who enter the child welfare system often have had adverse and traumatic experiences, increasing their potential vulnerabilities (Beyerlein & Bloch, 2014; Greeson et al., 2011). Through legislation including CAPTA, there has been an increasing focus on prioritizing well-being and equity within the child welfare system through, for example, the promotion of screenings and assessments and guidance and assistance for jurisdictions (e.g., Administration for Children and Families, 2012; Children's Bureau Express, 2020; Institute for Child and Family Well-Being, 2016).

Child Care and Development Block Grant (2014)

The Child Care and Development Block Grant (CCDBG) reauthorized the Child Care and Development Fund (CCDF) program (Office of Childcare, 2020). CCDBG provides working parents with access to affordable childcare and after-school opportunities for children up to age 13 while parents work or attend training or an educational program—offering access to opportunities that can reinforce a young person's learning and development including opportunities based on the science of early childhood development (Center on the Developing Child, 2007; Deans for Impact, 2019; Garcia et al., 2016; Yoshikawa et al., 2013). CCDBG also provides support for low-income families receiving or transitioning from the Temporary Assistance for Needy Families program, a federal cash assistance program for low-income families with children. Families receive vouchers to purchase OST services specifically before-school, afterschool, or summer programming or care for their school-age children.

Every Student Succeeds Act (2015)

The U.S. Department of Education administers the Every Student Succeeds Act (ESSA); ESSA reauthorized the Elementary and Secondary Education Act. ESSA is the main federal education law for all public schools, and it holds states and school districts accountable for providing quality education. ESSA has increased flexibility in how states and school districts account for achievement and academic performance. Some states have used ESSA as an opportunity to focus on areas of work related to the science of learning and development and the advancement of educational equity including by prioritizing social and emotional learning and development, positive conditions for learning, and whole child supports (NASEM, 2019a; Young & Webb, 2019). ESSA also reauthorized the 21st Century Community Learning Centers (21st CCLC) program, which provides federal funding focused on before- and afterschool, summer, and OST learning programs.

Juvenile Justice and Delinquency Prevention Act (2018)

The Juvenile Justice and Delinquency Prevention Act (JJDPA) supports local and state efforts to prevent delinquency and improve the juvenile justice system (OJJDP, n.d.). JJDPA's guiding premise is "that youth who offend should be treated differently and separately from adults who offend, that juvenile offending is preventable, and that youthful offenders should receive individualized treatment and services" (National Research Council, 2013, p. 318). In recent years, Congress has embraced developmentally informed juvenile justice system reforms including by requiring federal and state policies and plans to reflect the science of adolescence learning and development (NASEM, 2019b). Additionally, JJDPA recognizes existing inequities in the juvenile justice system and further strengthens and outlines states' obligation to decrease racial and ethnic disparities, which is particularly important given persistent and increasing inequities within the system (NASEM, 2019b). JJDPA provides funding of delinquency prevention programs such as OST experiences including but not limited to leadership and youth development activities; assistance in the development of job training skills; youth mentoring programs; and afterschool programs (Hanson & Finklea, 2021; 34 U.S.C. §11313).

Workforce Innovation and Opportunity Act (2014)

The U.S. Departments of Education and Labor administer the Workforce Innovation and Opportunity Act (WIOA). Policymakers designed WIOA to "strengthen and improve our nation's public workforce system and help get Americans, including youth and those with significant barriers to employment, into high-quality jobs and careers and help employers hire and retain skilled workers" (U.S. Department of Labor, n.d.). WIOA funds three job training and employment services specifically for youth, including Youth Workforce Investment Activities program, Job Corps, and Youth Build (Fernandes-Alcantara, 2020). Such programs aid youth ages 14 to 24 who encounter barriers to education, training, and employment. Services for youth include educational assistance (e.g., tutoring and dropout prevention strategies and recovery services) and employment assistance (e.g., paid and unpaid work experiences, skills training) for youth who are in school (14 to 21 years of age) or those who have left school (16 to 24 years of age) and meet other eligibility criteria (e.g., low income; Fernandes-Alcantara, 2020; Urban Institute, n.d.).

The federal laws that we presented above shape youth-serving systems and provide broad examples of the various ways in which federal policymakers are attempting to consider issues of young people's learning and development across formal and informal settings and experiences. These examples as described above and later in the chapter also provide a snapshot of some policy responses for working towards identifying and addressing disparities and advancing equity.

Building on the previous section's background information about aspects of the current federal policy landscape, the remaining sections of this chapter focus on policy elements that have the potential to: 1) build on the science of learning and development and 2) transform disparate systems into integrated ones that contribute to healthy L&D ecosystems that are designed and managed to better and equitably meet the developmental strengths and needs of young people across settings (e.g., OST programs and education systems). We explore more detailed examples of youth-focused policy initiatives at the federal, state, and local level to illustrate each policy element.

SYSTEM COORDINATION AND ALIGNMENT

Across sectors, there is a collective responsibility to build systems focused on young people and use current knowledge on learning and development to best align with their development strengths and meet their developmental needs in childhood, adolescence, and young adulthood (e.g., NASEM, 2019b). Doing so requires supporting their learning and development across the diverse and sometimes siloed systems and settings with which they interact. Systems often operate with distinct priorities, requirements, and functions, which can result in fragmented and uncoordinated actions in serving young people. Thus, navigating policies and systems that are intended to support youth can become challenging for providers, families, and young people. Decisionmakers should continue to explore and employ collective initiatives and cross-system coordination and collaboration to address these burdens and barriers and increase access and improve outcomes for young people. For instance, the ACA's emphasis on comprehensive school health centers and care coordination can play a role in supporting learning and academic success including by reducing a student's time away from school and formal instruction (McClanahan & Weismuller, 2015; Murray et al., 2007).

Coordinated and aligned efforts involve articulating clear frameworks for coordination as well as providing the necessary infrastructure and incentives for coordination and alignment (e.g., by allowing funding flexibility). This may also involve transforming underlying structures—such as funding, reporting, and regulatory structures and processes—to better align them with each other. A policy emphasis on coordination and alignment has the potential to reduce fragmentation, better leverage available resources, and minimize burdens and barriers for young people.

Clear Frameworks for Coordination and Alignment

Given how policies and systems inevitably intersect and interact, it is ideal for stakeholders to be intentional and strategic in designing and managing healthy L&D ecosystems to benefit young people. Leaders, policymakers, and practitioners must first have clear frameworks to provide a foundation for how systems are intended to coordinate to better serve youth, families, and communities in a holistic and equitable way. Establishing a clear framework requires creating a shared vision and goals, articulating aligned and complementary strategies, setting standards for mutual responsibility, and identifying methods and metrics for collective accountability.

One example of a policy effort with a clear framework is the Interagency Working Group on Youth Programs (IWGYP). The IWGYP is, as of 2021, a collaboration of 21 federal agencies and departments that support youth-focused programs and services. The U.S. Department of Health and Human Services serves as the Chair of the IWGYP, with the U.S. Department of Justice serving as Vice-Chair. Congress directed the Working Group to develop an overarching strategic plan in the 2009 Omnibus Appropriations Act. In 2016, the Working Group released the final version of its strategic plan for federal collaboration (Pathways for Youth: Strategic Plan for Federal Collaboration). Their framework aligns with strengths-based approaches, applies the knowledge on how young people best learn and develop, acknowledges the range of settings and systems young people engage with, and prioritizes youth in vulnerable circumstances.

A clear framework, like the one created by the IWGYP, articulates the shared vision and goals of the group or system. The common vision and goals then drive policy choices and outputs, including decision-making concerning structures, processes, investments, and incentives. For instance, the IWGYP's strategic plan for federal collaboration includes a strengths-based vision for youth, and goals and associated objectives. The vision and goals outlined in the plan serve as a roadmap for the IWGYP's policy work in service of youth.

Children's Cabinets provide another example of a coordinating body that is founded on a clear framework. Like the IWGYP, Children's Cabinets (also known as commissions or councils) operate at the state and local levels and involve the heads of the government agencies that are responsible for child- and youth-serving programs. Children's Cabinets convene regularly to coordinate services (FYI, n.d.a). Each cabinet describes the purpose for and functions of the cabinet with specificity and clarity. Doing so informs the cabinet's structure and work, ensuring that its efforts are coordinated to serve young people and equipping it to make systemic improvements and reinforce positive outcomes for and the well-being of young people (Gaines et al., 2008).

Children's Cabinets determine a shared set of outcomes and collaboratively select strategies and activities and execute them to achieve desired results for young people (FYI, n.d.a). Children's cabinets in Rhode Island and Denver, Colorado offer examples of using their goals to guide budgetary decisions; these cabinets used fiscal resource mapping efforts to link spending with their priorities for children and youth (Denver Children's Cabinet, n.d.; Rhode Island, n.d.). Fiscal mapping exercises allow decisionmakers and other stakeholders to systematically identify, analyze, and align existing and potential funding streams and resources to leverage funds efficiently and effectively (FYI, n.d.b; Jobs for the Future, n.d., 2016, 2018).

Opportunities for Coordination and Alignment

The IWGYP and Children's Cabinets are examples of efforts to promote cross-system coordination and alignment but have limited reach to meet the needs of all young people given their focus, structure, and involved stakeholders. For instance, the IWGYP membership reflects a subset of federal agencies and departments that support youth-focused programs and services. Similarly, despite their benefits for designing systems for youth and families, Children's Cabinets and related bodies are not a mechanism employed by all states, localities, and communities. However, coordinated and collaborative actions and inclusive decision making should be employed at all levels (e.g., federal, state, local) and across all sectors to maximize impact.

Accordingly, federal, state, and local governments should develop comprehensive, sustained, and transparent policies and processes for helping youth access and navigate systems and services. For example, NASEM's *The Promise of Adolescence* specifically calls out the need for greater coordination and alignment across child welfare, juvenile justice, education, and health systems (NASEM, 2019b). The report recommends that systems work together to, for example, create an integrated data system (to be discussed more below) that links information so they can provide effective and integrated services to young people. Similarly, a cross-cutting recommendation within the National Research Council's (NRC's) *Investing in the Health and Well-Being of Young Adults* involves coordinating and integrating services for young adults for improved efficiency and effectiveness (IOM and NRC, 2015). Additionally, the science of learning and development findings emphasize the importance of integrating all relevant and critical systems to better support young people and strengthen families (Darling-Hammond et al., 2020; SoLD Alliance, 2017).

Furthermore, there is a need for a broader national vision for young people that articulates priorities for addressing issues concerning youth and outlines strategic activities and opportunities to sustain young people's development. This need for national vision and agenda setting could be met by the establishment and functions of a central, coordinating federal department or agency that focuses on the holistic health, well-being, learning, and development of children and youth such as a recently proposed White House Office on Children and Youth (Federal Leadership for Children and Youth, 2021). This vision must be anchored by the science of learning and development and advance a whole child, equity-focused policy agenda. In some cases, the IWGYP's strategic plan has been framed as the nation's youth policy; however, that was not its intended purpose (e.g., Youth Policy Labs, n.d.). Thus, federal priority setting and directives on pursuing the interests of youth that can influence federal, state, and local thinking and action which is essential.

Incentives for System Coordination and Alignment

Successful policy efforts also include an emphasis on and incentives for system coordination and alignment of services, to be intentional and strategic in designing and maintaining L&D ecosystems. Too often, research, services, and programs to serve certain populations of young people—for example disconnected or opportunity youth—are uncoordinated, misaligned, and fragmented (Treskon, 2016; White House Council for Community Solutions, 2012). One federal policy response to this lack of alignment is the Performance Partnership Pilots for Disconnected Youth (P3; P3, n.d.; Rosenberg & Brown, 2019). The P3 program provides flexibility to states, localities, and tribal communities in coordinating discretionary program funds from several participating federal departments and agencies to design pilots serving opportunity youth. This flexibility provides an incentive, and a mechanism, for improved services. Similarly, WIOA, a primary federal funding source for workforce development, emphasizes coordination and alignment of programs that serve out-of-school youth—including through collaboration with the American Job Center network—to ensure that these young people obtain critical skills for educational and career readiness and success (U.S. Department of Labor, 2017).

Offering stakeholders a benefit—something they want or need—provides an incentive for coordination and alignment of services. For example, the Connecticut After School Network launched a collaborative effort called Social Emotional Learning Alliance for Connecticut (SEL4CT) to support social and emotional learning (SEL) policies and practices throughout the state. SEL4CT aims to build statewide awareness for SEL and related approaches; advocate for state and local SEL-related policies and funding; provide opportunities for various SEL stakeholders to learn about and share SEL advocacy, research, and best practice; and connect a broad range of SEL stakeholders to coordinate and support implementation across the state (SEL4CT, n.d.). SEL4CT members come from various types of organizations, including K–12 education, afterschool, higher education, and the state education department. The Connecticut After School Network incentivizes participation in policy efforts such as SEL4CT (e.g., volunteer on policy committees, write policy related blog posts) by providing access to trainings and resources that support adult practice that can promote for example, capacity building and opportunities to adopt common approaches and framing for pursuing the work. For example, Connecticut's state department of education and the Yale Center for Emotional Intelligence provide free online training and certification on SEL for teachers. Connecticut After School Network was able to advocate for the training to be made available to afterschool professionals in the state as well.

Grounding in the Science of Learning and Development

To succeed, youth-serving policies must be grounded in the science of learning and development and must take into account the specific developmental opportunities and supports in childhood, adolescence, and young adulthood. For example, consider the steps states have taken to adopt developmental approaches to juvenile justice including through the previously described federal JJDPA. In addition, in 2017, Washington State began requiring schools to take multiple steps to address the underlying issues leading to multiple unexcused absences before involving the justice system (ACLU Washington, 2017; Santos, 2016). In the same year, California expanded the Transitional Age Youth Pilot Program to allow eligible youth convicted of felonies to receive additional services, including developmentally appropriate educational and vocational programs and mental health services (Chief Probation Officers of California, n.d.). Efforts like these ensure that the goals of systems and programs as well as young people's experiences within them are suited to youth and young adults' growth and maturation—harnessing their developmental potential and promoting positive trajectories while addressing their needs and challenges.

Applying the lessons learned from the science of learning and development to policymaking also requires explicitly addressing issues of equity. For instance, the ACA promotes health equity including reductions in socioeconomic and racial and ethnic disparities in some key health outcomes (e.g., health care access and coverage; Chaudry et al., 2019; Griffith et al., 2017; Lantz & Rosenbaum, 2020). In addition, the need for childcare and afterschool opportunities may be pronounced for families headed by young parents (18 to 24 years old), who themselves are youth attempting to navigate the education and workforce systems (Dodkowitz et al., 2018). As previously mentioned, CCDBG can promote equity through access to stable, affordable, and high-quality childcare to low-income families. Concerning P3 and WIOA, system coordination and alignment have the potential to advance equity by aiding young people in reconnecting to meaningful educational and career pathways. WIOA reporting requirements and flexibility in performance targets and indicators can identify disparities, allow for innovation in helping those who encounter barriers, and further advance equity in academic and employment opportunities (Pham, 2018).

Policymakers can also use data to understand, monitor, and promote equity of their policies. Data are a powerful tool; they provide information that can be used to redesign systems and programs to be more results-driven and more effective in benefitting young people. For instance, creating data infrastructure (like cross-sector data-sharing and integration efforts) allows institutions to focus specific attention on measures of racial equity, transparency, and community engagement, and monitor progress on those measures throughout different phases of program implementation (Hawn Nelson et al., 2020). This can involve the sharing of data and findings in user-friendly formats among key stakeholders (including families and communities), providing guidance on interpretation and use, disaggregating the data by demographics, and monitoring the data for groups of young people who are at risk of disparate treatment.

For example, the Children's Services Council (CSC) of Broward County, Florida, has implemented the Building Power and Equity Together project, which emphasizes that "sharing data is also about sharing power and seeing each other as partners with assets and expertise, with government workers and the people they serve creating policies and practices together" (Annie E. Casey Foundation, 2019). Thus, the CSC is employing data-focused efforts and creating data systems that will build awareness and provide information for reflection, action, and collaboration by and between the various stakeholders.

There is sufficient theory and science, especially on young people's learning and developmental processes, to take purposeful action towards improving policies so that they advance equity and are in the best interest of young people (Osher et al., 2020). But less is known about effective policies that ensure their health, well-being, readiness, and success across domains of life. This gap in knowledge is particularly acute for certain populations of young people who may be growing up in vulnerable circumstances, such as disconnected or opportunity youth, youth with disabilities, and specific subpopulations within these broader categories (e.g., IOM and NRC, 2015; Treskon, 2016).

Addressing these knowledge gaps—including what works for certain young people and under what conditions—will involve more comprehensive and strategic research and evaluation. These efforts would involve collecting and reporting data by age (while sampling sufficiently across distinct age groups) and on a diverse set of demographics, issues, and outcomes of relevance for young people. Furthermore, there will always be new and evolving scientific advancements, inquiries, and opportunities coupled with inevitable changes and disturbances within L&D ecosystems; therefore, whether there is emerging or more established evidence of program effectiveness in an area, decisionmakers will still need to continually, intentionally, and strategically identify remaining gaps and prioritize investments towards addressing them including to design and manage healthy L&D ecosystems in an intentional, strategic, and responsive manner. This identification and prioritization will involve determining how best to innovate and test promising approaches as well as replicate and scale evidence-based models. Collectively, these efforts can build the knowledge base that decisionmakers can draw upon to design effective policies that reinforce healthy L&D ecosystems (e.g., NASEM, 2019b; IOM and NRC, 2015).

INCLUSION OF DIVERSE STAKEHOLDER GROUPS

Policymakers can better serve young people by harnessing the voices of varied stakeholders to inform public policies. Decisionmakers can foster inclusion through, for example, participatory action research as well as engagement of and partnerships with youth and young adults with lived experience. For instance, the IWGYP was already responsible for a website on youth issues, youth.gov, that targets an audience of youth-serving professionals and organizations. The group added to this by launching a microsite with information for and by youth audiences (Youth Engaged 4 Change [YE4C], engage.youth.gov); it recently recruited 10 young people for an inaugural YE4C editorial board (YE4C, n.d.b). In addition, the Capacity Building Center for States, a technical assistance provider for the Children's Bureau, within the U.S. Department of Health and Human Services, hires and compensates young people with lived experience in the foster care system to work with the Center as "Young Adult Consultants" on technical assistance projects (YE4C, n.d.a).

These efforts also align with research on young people's normative learning and development including their needs and desires for respect, feeling valued, autonomy, and voice especially during adolescence (NASEM, 2019b). The science of learning and development highlights the importance of relationships and meaningfully engaging young people and ensuring voice and choice or agency to make certain that young people have authentic experiences where they can, for example, build skills and competencies and explore their sparks and interests (Osher et al., 2019). Policy efforts at the national, state, and local level should actively engage young people, their families, and their communities to ensure these efforts reflect the lived experience of the people the policy efforts are intended to support. A recent report highlights youth engagement strategies and practices at the federal level including youth consultants, grant reviewers, service, councils, listening sessions, and conferences (Irons et al., 2020). Effective partnership with youth, families, and communities may require a reframing and cultural shift for some agencies, organizations, and actors to fully understand and value the assets and contributions of young people, families, and communities. Policy implications also include but are not limited to building the capacity of young people, adults working within systems, families, and community members to effectively partner with each other and promoting cultural and linguistic competence and responsiveness. The goal should be to maximize opportunities to engage, collaborate, share decision-making power, and integrate youth, families, and community members' voices and perspectives into policies and practices.

A state-level example of inclusion of diverse stakeholder groups involves Afterschool for Children and Teens (ACT Now), a statewide coalition in Illinois that works to ensure young people in the state have access to quality, affordable afterschool and youth development programs (ACT Now, n.d.). The coalition works with a diverse group of stakeholders—families, educators, business leaders, afterschool providers, community advocates, youth organizations, and policy makers—to support its mission. In 2016, an Illinois state budget impasse cut off funding to Teen Responsibility, Education, Achievement, Caring and Hope, or Teen REACH, a comprehensive initiative that provides afterschool programs to high-risk youth ages 6 to 17 (Illinois Department of Human Services, n.d.). ACT Now partnered with other supporters as well as Teen REACH providers, families, and youth to share impactful stories about Teen REACH, testify at hearings, reach out to voters, and mobilize supporters to contact legislators. ACT Now and its partners' actions amplified the voices of Teen REACH providers, participants, and families to make the case for reinstating funding for Teen REACH. These efforts contributed to the eventual reinstatement of Teen REACH's funding.

Furthermore, policymakers can use Youth Participatory Evaluation and Youth Participatory Action Research methods to engage and partner with youth and young adults on policy efforts and accurately reflect their lived experience. To elevate young people's insights and expertise, decisionmakers can also convene youth advisory boards, provide official positions on governance boards, and employ them in leadership and advisory roles (Blakeslee & Walker, 2018). Inclusion of young people's voices also provides an opportunity for policymakers to partner with youth-led groups to further support their efforts and understand their perspectives. For example, decisionmakers in Chicago's city government partner with Mikva Challenge youth councils to formulate, implement, and evaluate public policy (Mikva Challenge, 2020). The youth council members serve as policy experts and work closely with the CEO of Chicago Public Schools and with county and city leaders to make policy decisions that significantly impact youth citywide (Mikva Challenge, 2020).

CONCLUSION

Young people interact with multiple systems and are affected by various policies in their everyday lives. Policies and the systems through which policymakers implement them have the potential to support or hinder young people's capacity to thrive. Examples of policies that are supportive of young people's success exist at the federal, state, and local levels. But opportunities remain to build on the science of learning and development and transform disparate systems into integrated ones that contribute to healthy L&D ecosystems that are designed and managed to better and equitably meet the developmental strengths and needs of young people across settings, including OST. In addition to prioritizing cross-sector coordination and alignment, policies that benefit healthy L&D ecosystems also ground decisions in the science of learning and development. That is, they must be driven and informed by our current knowledge about how young people best learn and develop including the relationships, conditions, and experiences that increase their capacity to thrive. Furthermore, policymakers should utilize the collective contributions and voices of varied stakeholders to inform the design and implementation of programs and policies that are relevant and impactful. Decisionmakers should employ coordinated and collaborative methods with an overarching strengths-based vision as a guide. Policymakers should build upon the progress of policies and further improve, innovate, and test for effective policy models to expand the evidence base on what is effective for improving the lives of young people. Decisionmakers must create policies that undergird healthy L&D ecosystems by reflecting the real-world experiences of young people and supporting equitable opportunities for learning and development that build upon their strengths while being responsive to their developmental needs and concerns. Many impactful public policy efforts already exist; others can be improved, and even the best-designed policies and programs can be expanded in scope and scale—and these policy elements have the potential to build and transform systems that holistically and equitably support young people.

REFERENCES

ACLU Washington. (2017). https://www.aclu-wa.org/docs/parents-guide-truancy-washington

ACT Now Coalition. (n.d.). *About us.* http://www.actnowillinois.org/about-us/who-we-are/

Administration for Children and Families. (2012). *Information memorandum: Promoting social and emotional well-being for children and youth receiving child welfare services.* https://www.acf.hhs.gov/sites/default/files/documents/cb/im1204.pdf

Alliance for Excellent Education. (2019). *Science of learning: What educators need to know about adolescent development.* https://mk0all4edorgjxiy8xf9.kinstacdn.com/wp-content/uploads/2019/09/05-SAL-What-Educators-Need-to-Know-About-Adolescent-Development_FINAL.pdf

Annie E. Casey Foundation. (2019). *Incorporating racial equity in data sharing in Broward County, Florida.* https://www.aecf.org/blog/incorporating-racial-equity-in-data-sharing-in-broward-county-florida/

Beyerlein, B. A., & Bloch, E. (2014). Need for trauma-informed care within the foster care system: A policy issue. *Child Welfare, 93*(3), 7–21.

Blakeslee, J., & Walker, J. (2018). *Assessing the meaningful inclusion of youth voice in policy and practice: State of the science.* Research and Training Center for Pathways to Positive Futures, Portland State University. https://pdxscholar.library.pdx.edu/cgi/viewcontent.cgi?article=1230&context=socwork_fac

Center on the Developing Child (2007). *InBrief: The science of early childhood development.* https://46y5eh11fhgw3ve3ytpwxt9r-wpengine.netdna-ssl.com/wp-content/uploads/2007/03/InBrief-The-Science-of-Early-Childhood-Development2.pdf

Centers for Disease Control and Prevention; (n.d.). *Definition of policy.* https://www.cdc.gov/policy/analysis/process/definition.html

Changing the odds for disconnected youth: Initial design considerations for performance partnership pilots. (2014). https://youth.gov/docs/P3_Consultation_Paper_508.pdf

Chaudry, A., Jackson, A., & Glied, S. A. (2019). *Did the Affordable Care Act reduce racial and ethnic disparities in health insurance coverage?* Commonwealth Fund. https://doi.org/10.26099/d8hs-cm53

Chief Probation Officers of California. (n.d.). *Governor Brown signs transitional age youth pilot program legislation relying on mounting brain research of treatment options for youthful offenders age 18–21.* https://www.cpoc.org/post/governor-brown-signs-transitional-age-youth-pilot-program-legislation-relying-mounting-brain

Children's Bureau Express. (2020). *Thriving families, safer children.* https://cbexpress.acf.hhs.gov/index.cfm?event=website.viewSection&issueID=219&subsectionID=101

Darling-Hammond, L., & Cook-Harvey, C. (2018, September). *Educating the whole child: Improving school climate to support student success.* Learning Policy Institute. https://learningpolicyinstitute.org/sites/default/files/product-files/Educating_Whole_Child_REPORT.pdf

Darling-Hammond, L., Flook, L., Cook-Harvey, C., Barron, B., & Osher, D. (2020). Implications for educational practice of the science of learning and development. *Applied Developmental Science 24*(2), 97–140. https://doi.org/10.1080/10888691.2018.1537791

de Lijster, J. M., Dierckx, B., Utens, E. M. W. J., Verhulst, F. C., Zieldorff, C., Dieleman, G. C., & Legerstee, J. S. (2017). The age of onset of anxiety disorders: A meta-analysis. *The Canadian Journal of Psychiatry / La Revue Canadienne de Psychiatrie, 62*(4), 237–246. https://doi.org/10.1177/0706743716640757

Deans for Impact. (2019). *The science of early learning.* Deans for Impact. https://deansforimpact.org/wp-content/uploads/2017/01/The_Science_of_Early_Learning.pdf

Denver Children's Cabinet. (n.d.). *Denver children's cabinet.* https://www.arcgis.com/apps/MapSeries/index.html?appid=939edc78fa0e4c799089f233ff07395a

Dodkowitz, A. D., Park, Y., & Spaulding, S. (2018). *Strategies to meet the needs of young parent families: Highlights from interviews with 14 programs.* Urban Institute. https://www.urban.org/sites/default/files/publication/99011/strategies_to_meet_the_needs_of_young_parents.pdf

Federal Leadership for Children and Youth. (2021). *Charter for a White House Office and conference.* https://www.nemours.org/content/dam/nemours/wwwv2/childrens-health-system/documents/white-house-office-on-children-and-youth-charter.pdf

Fernandes-Alcantara, A. L. (2020). *Vulnerable youth: Employment and job training programs.* Congressional Research Service. https://crsreports.congress.gov/product/pdf/R/R40929

Forum for Youth Investment. (n.d.a). *Children's cabinets networks.* https://forumfyi.org/work/ccn/

Forum for Youth Investment. (n.d.b). *Fiscal mapping tools.* https://forumfyi.org/fiscal-mapping-tools/

Gaines, E., Faigley, I., & Pittman, K. (2008, August). *Elements of success issue 1: Structural options.* State Children's Cabinet and Councils Series. The Forum for Youth Investment. https://forumfyi.org/wp-content/uploads/2018/08/Elements_of_Success1_Structure.pdf

Garcia, J. L., Heckman, J. J., Leaf, D. E., & Prados, M. J. (2016). *The life-cycle benefits of an influential early childhood program* (NBER Working Paper No. 22993). National Bureau of Economic Research. https://www.nber.org/system/files/working_papers/w22993/w22993.pdf

Gottlieb, G., & Halpern, C. T. (2008). Individual development as a system of coactions: Implications for research and policy. In A. Fogel, B. J. King, & S. G. Shanker (Eds.), *Human development in the twentyfirst century: Visionary ideas from system scientists* (pp. 41–47). Cambridge University Press.

Greeson, J. K. P., Briggs, E. C., Kisiel, C. L., Layne, C. M., Ake III, G. S., Ko, S. J., Gerrity, E. T., Steinberg, A. M., Howard, M. L., Pynoos, R. S., & Fairbank, J. A. (2011). Complex trauma and mental health in children and adolescents placed in foster care: Findings from the National Child Traumatic Stress Network. *Child Welfare, 90*(6), 91–108.

Griffith, K., Evans, L., & Bor, J. (2017). The Affordable Care Act reduced socioeconomic disparities in health care access. *Health Affairs, 36*(8), 1503–1510. https://doi.org/10.1377/hlthaff.2017.0083

Hanson, E. J., & Finklea, K. (2021). *Juvenile justice funding trends.* Congressional Research Service. https://crsreports.congress.gov/product/pdf/R/R44879

Hawn Nelson, A., Jenkins, D., Zanti, S., Katz, M., Berkowitz, E., et al. (2020). *A toolkit for centering racial equity throughout data integration. actionable intelligence for social policy.* University of Pennsylvania. https://www.aisp.upenn.edu/wp-content/uploads/2020/08/AISP-Toolkit_5.27.20.pdf

HealthCare.gov. (n.d.). *Affordable Care Act.* https://www.healthcare.gov/glossary/affordable-care-act/

Illinois Department of Human Services. (n.d.). *Teen responsibility, education, achievement, caring and hope (Teen REACH).* https://www.dhs.state.il.us/page.aspx?item=30777

Institute for Child and Family Well-Being. (2016). *Issue brief: Assessing well-being in child welfare.* https://uwm.edu/icfw/wp-content/uploads/sites/384/2016/06/AssessingWellBeing.pdf

Institute of Medicine and National Research Council. (2015). *Investing in the health and well-being of young adults.* The National Academies Press. https://doi.org/10.17226/18869

224 • MICHELLE J. BOYD-BROWN, JILL YOUNG, & DEBORAH MORONEY

Interagency Working Group on Youth Programs. (2016). *Pathways for youth: Strategic plan for federal collaboration.* https://youth.gov/sites/default/files/IWGYP-Pathways_for_Youth.pdf

Irons, A., Kates, A., & Reid. R. (2020). *Youth engagement at the federal level: A compilation of strategies and practices.* U.S. Department of Health and Human Services. https://youth.gov/sites/default/files/YES-Report.pdf

Jobs for the Future. (n.d.). *Fiscal mapping case study series.* https://www.jff.org/resources/fiscal-mapping-case-study-series/

Jobs for the Future. (2016). *Opportunity youth.* https://jfforg-prod-prime.s3.amazonaws.com/media/documents/Opportunity_Youth_0823161.pdf

Jobs for the Future. (2018). *Connecting the dots: A Guide to leveraging federal funding streams.* http://application.jff.org/lffs/

Kessler, R. C., Amminger, G. P., Aguilar-Gaxiola, S., Alonso, J., Lee, S., & Üstün, T. B. (2007). Age of onset of mental disorders: A review of recent literature. *Current Opinion in Psychiatry, 20*(4), 359–364.

Lantz, P. M., & Rosenbaum, S. (2020). The potential and realized impact of the Affordable Care Act on health equity. *Journal of Health Politics, Policy & Law, 45*(5), 831–845. https://doi.org/10.1215/03616878-8543298

McClanahan, R., & Weismuller, P. C. (2015). School nurses and care coordination for children with complex needs: An integrative review. *Journal of School Nursing, 31*(1), 34–43. https://doi.org/10.1177/1059840514550484

Mikva Challenge. (2020). *Youth-led advocacy.* https://mikvachallenge.org/our-work/programs/youth-led-advocacy/

Murray, N. G., Low, B. J., Hollis, C., Cross, A. W., & Davis, S. M. (2007). Coordinated school health programs and academic achievement: A systematic review of the literature. *The Journal of School Health, 77*(9), 589–600.

Nagaoka, J., Farrington, C. A., Ehrlich, S. B., & Heath, R. D. (2015, June). *Foundations for young adult success: A developmental framework* (Concept Paper for Research and Practice). University of Chicago Consortium on Chicago School Research. https://consortium.uchicago.edu/publications/foundations-young-adult-success-developmental-framework

National Academies of Sciences, Engineering, and Medicine. (2019a). *Monitoring educational equity.* The National Academies Press. https://doi.org/10.17226/25389

National Academies of Sciences, Engineering, and Medicine. (2019b). *The promise of adolescence: Realizing opportunity for all youth.* The National Academies Press. https://doi.org/10.17226/25388

National Commission on Social, Emotional, and Academic Development. (2018). *How learning happens: Supporting students' social, emotional, and academic development.* The Aspen Institute. https://assets.aspeninstitute.org/content/uploads/2018/01/2017_Aspen_InterimReport_Update2.pdf?_ga=2.172917541.762802214.1594147383-452436439.1569938308

National Research Council. (2013). *Reforming juvenile justice: A developmental approach.* The National Academies Press. https://doi.org/10.17226/14685

Office of Childcare. (2020). *OCC Fact Sheet.* U.S. Department of Health & Human Services. https://www.acf.hhs.gov/occ/fact-sheet

Office of Juvenile Justice and Delinquency Prevention. (n.d.). *Legislation.* https://ojjdp.ojp.gov/about/legislation

Osher, D., Cantor, P., Berg, J., Steyer, L., & Rose, T. (2017). *Science of learning and development: A synthesis.* American Institutes for Research. https://www.air.org/sites/default/files/downloads/report/Science-of-Learning-and-Development-Synthesis-Osher-January-2017.pdf

Osher, D., Cantor, P., Berg, J., Steyer, L., & Rose, T. (2019). Drivers of human development: How relationships and context shape learning and development. *Applied Developmental Science 24*(1), 6–36. https://doi.org/10.1080/10888691.2017.1398650

Osher, D., Pittman, K., Young, J., Smith, H., Moroney, D., & Irby, M. (2020, July). *Thriving, robust equity, and transformative learning & development: A more powerful conceptualization of the contributors to youth success.* Forum for Youth Investment. https://forumfyi.org/wp-content/uploads/2020/07/Thriving.Equity.Learning.Report.pdf

Overton, W. F., & Lerner, R. M. (2014). Fundamental concepts and methods in developmental science: A relational perspective. *Research in Human Development, 11*(1), 63–73. DOI: 10.1080/15427609.2014.881086

Performance Partnership Pilots for Disconnected Youth (P3). (n.d.). Youth.gov. https://youth.gov/youth-topics/reconnecting-youth/performance-partnership-pilots

Pham, D. (2018). *Advancing racial equity through career pathways.* Center for Law and Social Policy. https://www.clasp.org/sites/default/files/publications/2018/10/2018.10.30%20Career%20Pathways%20Racial%20Equity%20.pdf

Rhode Island. (n.d.). *Children's budget.* https://files.constantcontact.com/f1015ff6001/5461ef4c-8e6b-4610-a0ac-09a76dd743fd.pdf

Rosenberg, L., & Brown, E. (2019). *Early experiences of the performance partnership pilots for disconnected youth (P3): Cohort 1 pilots.* Mathematica Policy Research. https://mathematica.org/publications/early-experiences-of-the-performance-partnership-pilots-for-disconnected-youth-p3-cohort-1-pilots

Santos, M. (2016). New truancy law aims to keep kids out of court, juvenile detention. *Bellingham Herald.* https://www.bellinghamherald.com/news/state/washington/article77899377.html

Schwartz, K., & Sommers, B. D. (2012). *Young adults are particularly likely to gain stable health insurance coverage as a result of the Affordable Care Act.* U.S. Department of Health and Human Services. https://aspe.hhs.gov/system/files/pdf/76421/rb.pdf

Science of Learning and Development Alliance. (2017). *The role of policy in advancing the science of learning and development.* https://www.soldalliance.org/what-weve-learned

Science of Learning and Development Alliance. (2020). *How the science of learning and development can transform education: Initial findings.* https://www.soldalliance.org/what-weve-learned

SEL4CT. (n.d.). *About us.* https://sel4ct.org/about/about-us/

Treskon, L. (2016, February). *What works for disconnected young people: A Scan of the evidence.* MDRC. https://disconnectedyouth.issuelab.org/resources/25634/25634.pdf

U.S. Department of Labor. (n.d.). *About WIOA.* https://www.dol.gov/agencies/eta/wioa/about

U.S. Department of Labor. (2017). *Training and employment guidance letter one-stop operating guidance for the Workforce Innovation and Opportunity Act.* https://wdr.doleta.gov/directives/attach/TEGL/TEGL_16-16_Acc.pdf

Urban Institute. (n.d.). *The public workforce system.* https://workforce.urban.org/topics/public- workforce-system

Vaughn, B., Princiotta, D., Barry, M., Fish, H., & Schmitz, H. (2013). *Schools and the Affordable Care Act.* National Center on Safe Supportive Learning Environments. https://safesupportivelearning.ed.gov/sites/default/files/1953_Schools%20Afford-able%20Care%20Brief_d3%20lvr.pdf

White House Council for Community Solutions. (2012). *Final report: Community solutions for opportunity youth.* https://assets.aspeninstitute.org/content/uploads/files/content/docs/resources/White_House_Council_For_Community_Solutions_Final_Report.pdf

Yoshikawa, H., Weiland, C., Brooks-Gunn, J., Burchinal, M., Espinosa, L., Gormley, W. T., Ludwig, J., Magnuson, K., Phillips, D., & Zaslow, M. (2013, October). *Investing in our future: The evidence base on preschool.* Society for Research in Child Development. https://www.srcd.org/sites/default/files/file-attachments/mb_2013_10_16_investing_in_children.pdf

Young, K., & Webb, E. (2019). *Social and emotional learning and development, conditions for learning, and whole child supports in ESSA state plans.* Council of Chief State School Officers. https://ccsso.org/sites/default/files/2019-04/EC_CCSSO%20ESSA%20SEL%20Brief-FINAL.pdf

Youth Engaged 4 Change [YE4C]. (n.d.a). *Being a youth consultant.* https://engage.youth.gov/inspiring-stories/being-youth-consultant

Youth Engaged 4 Change [YE4C]. (n.d.b). *The Young Adult Consultant Program of the Children's Bureau.* https://engage.youth.gov/opportunities/young-adult-consultant-program-childrens-bureau

Youth Policy Labs. (n.d.). *National youth policy overview.* https://www.youthpolicy.org/nationalyouthpolicies/

SECTION IV

PLACES: CASE STUDIES OF LEARNING AND
DEVELOPMENT ECOSYSTEMS

CHAPTER 12

THE ROLE OF PHILANTHROPY, RESEARCH, AND EVALUATION IN SHAPING LEARNING AND DEVELOPMENT ECOSYSTEMS

The Case of Creative Learning in Pittsburgh

Mac Howison, Esohe Osai, and Thomas Akiva

What does it take to engage in ecosystem management toward a more equitable and just society? In this chapter, we address one aspect of that pursuit, the current and potential role of philanthropic organizations, along with researchers and evaluators, in shaping learning and development (L&D) ecosystems. We define equity as all young people getting the opportunities and supports they need to thrive. Within L&D ecosystems, inequities often exist related to race, resources, and reach, as higher concentrations of historical harms, power imbalances, and outright policies disproportionately impact people of color, those with constrained economic mobility, and those who experience barriers limiting access to opportunity.

The authors of this chapter are part of an ongoing collaborative project, which we call a *research practice philanthropy partnership* (RP3). We have worked together across several phases of the initiative we describe in the chapter's case

It Takes an Ecosystem: Understanding the People, Places, and
Possibilities of Learning and Development Across Settings, pages 229–247.
Copyright © 2022 by Information Age Publishing
229

study, focused on youth arts education in nonformal settings (i.e., programs outside of school) or, more simply, the creative learning ecosystem in Pittsburgh. We apply a critical perspective to the relationships among research, evaluation, practice, and philanthropy and we argue that philanthropic partnerships may productively engage in ecosystem management toward equity and justice, but that this requires a re-imagining of roles and practices—especially given the power imbalances inherent in grantor-grantee relationships. Alongside our exploration of RP3, we consider what happens when we shift the focus from individual programs to ecosystems and attempt to shape the ecosystem via a partnership approach.

One way to visualize the philanthropic role is that of *directing energy* in the L&D ecosystem. In physics, energy is defined as the capacity for doing work; for example, electricity is a form of energy that does the work of powering lights, appliances, etc. In a natural ecosystem, energy flows from the sun and transfers through the ecosystems to sustain life (Odum, 1988). In a L&D ecosystem, financial resources, along with their associated conditions (e.g., grant stipulations), can serve as a form of energy. This energy flows to some organizations and programs, which can then grow and thrive, whereas those without this energy may wither or discontinue operations. Funders have the ability to shape this energy flow and they do this with varying levels of intentionality. Funding priorities, requests for proposals, and conversations with grantees all affect how energy flows through the ecosystem—which organizations, programs, and ideas get the energy they need and which ones don't get what they need. With intention and community participation, the directing of this energy has the potential to shape the learning ecosystem in positive and equitable ways.

The direction of energy in L&D ecosystems can be particularly powerful when the beneficiaries of a funding strategy are actively consulted in the strategic program design and the distribution of funds, an approach sometimes referred to as activist or participatory grantmaking. Nazir and Apgar (2019) described the profundity of this approach: "The act of philanthropists transferring power and control over funds to the communities they seek to serve is an unapologetic form of social activism and can lead the field to innovate with bigger and bolder ideas" (p. 1). When implemented authentically, the results can be highly satisfactory for both constituents and funders, in spite of or perhaps because of the much higher time and resource commitment required by all participants.

An example of authentic success in this approach can be seen in the Boston Youth Arts Evaluation Project, a three-year initiative funded by the Barr Foundation to create a comprehensive set of evaluation tools designed specifically for youth arts organizations. Evaluators and foundation staff in this project developed a partnership with an exemplary Boston youth arts program. Working together, they developed a framework and logic model, and a powerful set of evaluation tools that were made available for other youth arts programs (Boston Youth Arts Evaluation Project, 2012). This locally-developed and funded program serves as an example of how a place-specific ecosystem initiative can impact other L&D

ecosystems with related characteristics in different geographic regions. By 2014, the Creative Youth Development (CYD) field convened in Boston for the first National Summit for Creative Youth Development. Collective action from that summit generated a movement of overlapping and complementary RP3 approaches in regions where CYD learning ecosystems were already established or emerging outside of Boston, including San Diego, Austin, Pittsburgh, Detroit, Seattle, and the Bay Area. This spreading happened through a national partnership model that included practitioners, funders, researchers and youth (Montgomery, 2017).

The direction of energy in L&D ecosystems does not always lead to positive outcomes. When philanthropy overstates its knowledge and perspective on learning ecosystems, the intentional direction of energy can have negative outcomes among the organizations making up the ecosystem, as seen in the example of the Intensive Partnerships for Effective Teaching initiative, funded by the Bill and Melinda Gates Foundation. This seven-year (2009–2016), nearly $1 billion project had no measurable effect on its goals of improved access to effective teaching to improve student achievement (Stecher et al., 2018). Evaluators cited teacher resistance as an important factor for why this project did not yield results. The tremendous scale of energy deployed in this initiative was not effective in reaching its goals and the project failed to establish authentic partnerships with practitioners and philanthropy.

The concept of research-practice partnership (RPP) is an innovation in education research that has been promoted by several prominent funders, including the W.T. Grant Foundation (rpp.wtgrantfoundation.org), the Spencer Foundation (www.spencer.org), and even the federal Institute of Education Sciences (ies.ed.gov). Coburn et al. (2013) define RPP as "Long-term, mutualistic collaborations between practitioners and researchers that are intentionally organized to investigate problems of practice and solutions for improving district outcomes" (p. 2). The idea is that practitioners such as school leaders and teachers work together with researchers—over more than a single project—to tackle applied problems of practice. We extend this idea beyond formal education and add the third "P" for philanthropy because of the important role played by philanthropic foundations in the L&D ecosystem. A well-constructed RP3 benefits from more relational give-and-take and collaborative learning between partners—including foundation staff—than the conventional philanthropic approach of hiring a consultant to analyze a problem in a field of practice, receiving a summary recommendation or research paper, and implementing a funding strategy in response. In our local context, the coming together of researcher/evaluation, philanthropy, and practice makes for a particularly powerful partnership for intentionally directing energy in the learning ecosystem. However, we also recognize the power dynamics at play in such a partnership. In particular, funders, who financially support practitioners, inherently wield more power than practitioners and must be careful and intentional about working to avoid replicating inequities.

Program evaluators and researchers, depending on their involvement in an ecosystem, may also hold outsized power in the ways in which their priorities can direct energy in the ecosystem and their evaluations may affect the funding practitioners receive. Traditional summative, "does-it-work?" evaluation can affect how funders direct energy. This can be problematic as randomized controlled trials (the dominant tool of does-it-work evaluation) favor highly-specified interventions (such as scripted reading programs), and this research method is often a bad fit in areas such as creative learning. Like evaluators, researchers may or may not play an impactful role in the learning ecosystem, depending on their involvement in practical education and the degree to which universities and researchers overcome traditional university-community tensions. But again, with the right perspective and balance, perhaps research and evaluation alongside philanthropy may have productive roles in shaping L&D ecosystems.

This chapter presents the case of a Creative Learning-focused Research, Philanthropy, and Practice Partnership (RP3) in Pittsburgh. First, we'll provide a brief history of philanthropic organizations in the U.S., highlighting the role of funders as central to regional L&D ecosystems. We then include a specific local history of philanthropy in Pittsburgh, as specific insights into this region set up the phenomena that emerge in this chapter's case study. The section that follows is an exploration of the field of creative learning and how issues of equity have come to fore, leading community-based organizations to address the diminishing role of the arts in schools for youth of color. The chapter then segues into a description of the joint initiative in Pittsburgh that uses a transformative evaluation approach to identify effective strategies for youth engagement in the arts. We end with a discussion on what might be possible as place-based philanthropy and research partners coordinate with community-based programs to build equitable and just ecosystems.

Philanthropy in the United States

Philanthropy in the United States has roots in Puritan values and the founding of early institutions such as volunteer associations, ethnic and religious "benevolent society" groups, and private local contributions for community services where no strong government support existed (Bremner, 1960). Since the late 19th century, philanthropy has been a major source of income for religion, health care, arts, and education in the U.S. By the mid-20th century, the field of philanthropy included multi-billion-dollar private institutions such as Ford, Rockefeller, Mellon, and W. K. Kellogg, as well as hundreds of family foundations, endowments and trusts of varying sizes, charitable arms of for-profit corporations and banks, community foundations, and faith-based institutions. Advances in technology, data, media, and medicine led to the establishment of newer foundations towards the end of the century, and many of today's largest foundations are relatively young compared to their 20th century peers (e.g., The Bill & Melinda Gates Foundation was founded in 1994, Gordon & Betty Moore in 2000, Bloomberg Philanthropies in 2006).

Over the past twenty years, trends in educational philanthropy began to surface that addressed widening equity gaps in access to quality arts education and the resulting impacts on student well-being, academic performance, and social-emotional learning. The Wallace Foundation (wallacefoundation.org), as an example of a foundation with national reach, currently has initiatives in six areas: afterschool, arts education, building audiences for the arts, expanded learning, school leadership, and summer learning. These initiatives build on Wallace's work to support L&D ecosystems by delivering local benefits—often in the form of substantial multi-year grants to intermediary networks—and generating knowledge useful to the field as a whole in the form of reports (e.g., Montgomery et al., 2013). Wallace's commitment to knowledge sharing continues to influence local and regional L&D ecosystems as more foundations seek to inform their grant-making with the benefits of evidence-based practices, participatory research, and scalable models from other locales.

As new foundations have emerged and responded to the increasing complexity of national and global social problems, interrogation and critique of the nonprofit sector—with particular attention leveled on philanthropy—has also increased. In the United States, following the economic collapse of 2008 through the social upheaval of the 2016–2020 presidency, philanthropic leaders, social change activists, and critical theorists have challenged the conventions of the so-called "nonprofit industrial complex" through major publications, high-profile keynotes, op-eds, and reform-minded restructuring of institutions. Possibly the most influential of these critics from within the field of philanthropy itself is the President of the Ford Foundation, Darren Walker, who offers illuminating recommendations from behind the curtain of one of America's larger private foundations (Walker, 2019). Other critics are not nearly as diplomatic as Walker, as a host of publications from 2016–2020 include fierce indictments of philanthropy as dangerously elite, undemocratic, and harmful to the very constituents they claim to benefit (Giridharadas, 2018; Reich, 2018; Villanueva, 2018).

Historical and Regional Context for the Case Study

The history of philanthropy in Pittsburgh, the site of our case study, is intrinsically connected to the widely-cited American philanthropic manifesto "The Gospel of Wealth" by iconic steel industry pioneer Andrew Carnegie. Originally titled simply "Wealth," Carnegie's (1889) article is considered a foundational document in the field of philanthropy. Authored in his adopted hometown of Pittsburgh, Carnegie wrote that accumulated wealth should be given away with benevolent intention during one's lifetime. The essay unapologetically defines capitalist and individualist values as the highest form of human striving, and argues that in order to strengthen a community one must:

Place within its reach the ladders upon which the aspiring can rise—parks, and means of recreation, by which men are helped in body and mind; works of art, certain to give pleasure and improve the public taste, and public institutions of various kinds, which will improve the general condition of the people; in this manner return-ing their surplus wealth to the mass of their fellows in the forms best calculated to do them lasting good (Carnegie, 1889, p. 663).

The principles of this essay, and Carnegie's example of granting much of his own wealth to establish community institutions during his later years, defined philan-thropy as a philosophy and practice for the remainder of the 19th and throughout much of the 20th century.

Critical to the early development of learning ecosystems in the Pittsburgh re-gion, Carnegie's grantmaking created the modern American community library system starting in 1886 and established the Carnegie Institute which grew into a network of museums of fine arts, science, natural history, and venues for the per-forming arts (Gangewere, 2011). Notably, Pittsburgh contains the first Carnegie libraries ever donated by the philanthropist—and every library in Pittsburgh is a Carnegie library, owing to his personal connection to the area. Architectural critic Patricia Lowry (2003) calls them "Pittsburgh's most significant cultural export." A total of 2,509 Carnegie libraries were built between 1883 and 1929 worldwide, including some belonging to public and university library systems. Carnegie's grants were very large for the era, and his library philanthropy is one of the most costly philanthropic activities, by value, in history (Kevane et al., 2016). Carnegie Libraries were purpose-built as no-cost ("Free to the People") resource centers for industrial workers and their families, and acted as learning network hubs for ac-cess to literature, art, music, history, and science, as well as recreation and social gathering. The Carnegie Libraries in the Pittsburgh region still serve a similar purpose today, acting as important places and resources in the L&D ecosystem.

Following Carnegie's example, wealthy industrialists, inventors, publicists, and entrepreneurs established dozens of foundations in the early to mid-1900s that to this day play an outsized role in the regional funding landscape. For a city of its size, Pittsburgh boasts a relatively high density of foundation resources and an equivalently rich diversity of nonprofit organizations—likely in correla-tion. Historically, most foundations in the Pittsburgh region began with and have sustained their giving to large civic projects and public institutions such as parks, libraries, schools and universities, health and human service providers, neigh-borhood redevelopment efforts, and arts and cultural organizations. The region's philanthropic initiatives have tended to align with conventional nonprofit services and trends in response to social change movements already underway both locally and nationally, with some exceptional initiatives piloted over time in the fields of healthcare, medicine, sustainable development, environmental justice, regional learning networks for educators, out-of-school-time systems, and downtown arts and culture as a regional economic development strategy.

Pittsburgh is a mid-size American city (City population 300,000; metro region population of 2.4 million; 2019 estimate from U.S. census) that has much higher concentrations of racially segregated neighborhoods and dispiritingly worse economic, social, and health outcomes for Black families, especially Black women than comparable locales (Howell et al., 2019). Evidence of the disproportionality of foundation support for Black nonprofits is similarly evident as shown in a 2018 report on racial equity and arts funding (Greater Pittsburgh Arts Council, 2018). These reports, along with other data reflecting disproportionate negative outcomes for Black people in the criminal justice system and in education, confirmed what Black Pittsburghers have known for years and provided an uncomfortable revelation for many of the predominantly white institutions that occupy positions of power and influence. These inequities can extend to the foundation community in what is sometimes referred to as philanthropic redlining, "a discriminatory practice of inequitable distribution of philanthropic funds combined with neglect of justice-centered Black-led institutions, fueled by discriminatory notions that Black-led institutions are ineffective, inferior, and fraudulent" (Scott et al., 2020, p. 18). Nationally, this practice results in little as 8% of foundation funding going to people of color (Stone, 2019). In Pittsburgh, redlining as a housing and neighborhood segregation policy also heavily influenced the disproportionate outcomes for populations by race, which had a later, mid-20th century effect on Pittsburgh's population after many of Carnegie's libraries were already built.

Leading up to the present era of more widely-available research and accountability measures related to racial equity, several influential Pittsburgh-area foundations explored strategies to more intentionally diversify the impact of their giving by investing in Black, Indigenous, People of Color (BIPOC) leadership (e.g., Oliphant, 2016). The Heinz Endowments and The Pittsburgh Foundation in particular were early leaders in these efforts as they established funding streams and strategies such as the Multi-Cultural Arts Initiative in the 1990s, Advancing Black Arts in Pittsburgh (pittsburghfoundation.org/advancing-black-arts-pittsburgh), and the Transformative Arts Process (Cook, 2019). A few of these shifts in priority for the foundations were first piloted with arts and education initiatives that acknowledged the need for coordination and collaboration among networks—a nascent exploration of the learning ecosystem model. Some of the grantmaking by Pittsburgh-area foundations built support for creative learning in out-of-school time environments and often collaborated with in-school programs through local intermediary organizations for educators (See chapter 7 by Little and Donner in this volume). Over time other initiatives in support of networks and learning ecosystems began articulating goals that included a focus on racial equity.

The evolution of Pittsburgh's philanthropic sector's focus on racial equity in grantmaking has been a gradual process, with most foundations taking years to develop and premier their strategies. Influences on philanthropy during this period include a growing body of research, recommendations, and acknowledgements that frequently identify racial inequity as an underlying cause of many of the structural flaws and gaps in social fabric that foundations intend to address. By mid-2020, the COVID-19 pandemic, the economic bottoming out for already vulnerable populations, and an increased public awareness of American structural, systemic, and interpersonal racism accelerated the pace for foundations to address underlying and explicit issues of race in their funding strategies. For Pittsburgh's learning ecosystem, these factors contributed to increased awareness of, and more attention paid to fundamental goals of improving access to high quality creative learning experiences, especially for BIPOC youth.

Why Focus on Creative Learning?

Creative learning is a uniquely important space through which to examine L&D ecosystem management. Through an arts engagement lens, creative learning is a process and approach to learning that includes arts disciplines and practices, helping to spark new ideas and perspectives in children, youth, and their communities (Akiva et al., 2019). Creative learning builds on and promotes Creative Youth Development (CYD)—a recent term for a longstanding theory of practice that integrates creative skill-building, inquiry, and expression with positive youth development principles, supporting young people's creativity and building critical learning and life skills (Montgomery, 2017). Creative youth development refers to both a phenomenon and a growing field: the term refers to the developmental impacts associated with creative learning experiences as well as the larger ecology of practitioners and system-level leaders involved in making creative learning experiences accessible to young people (Jimenez, 2019).

The momentum with CYD is in direct response to problematic trends related to arts involvement for young people. Trends from the previous four decades reveal a dramatic decline in arts participation among young people (Rabkin & Hedberg, 2011). This decline is largely due to reductions in arts programs in public and private schools, lessening both exposure to and engagement with the arts. Due to education policy, arts funding has decreased as schools shifted to emphasize tested content in math, sciences, and literacy at the expense of formal arts programming in schools. Black and Latinx youth have disproportionately experienced the effects of the decline in arts opportunities. Rabkin (2011) reports that the percentage of African American and Latinx youth involved in the arts in school declined from 50 to 30 percent between 1982 and 2008. Findings from Welch and Kim (2010) reveal that Black and Hispanic students have less exposure to arts learning experiences when compared to white and Asian students. The pronounced decline in arts involvement for young people of color can be attributed to curriculum narrowing that has had particularly harmful effects for youth of color. Such inequities can be linked to dehumanizing schooling practices that detrimentally affect the education of minoritized youth in urban schools (Love, 2019). These realities are even more pronounced in the dual pandemic inspired analysis of the racism inherent in our school systems.

Alongside this substantial and uneven reduction of arts in schools, several studies provide evidence that engagement in the arts can lead to a host of positive outcomes for young people (Catterall, 2002). Some of this evidence supports a link between arts education and academic success. For example, in an analysis from four large, longitudinal studies, Catterall (2012) found multiple indicators that youth in low socioeconomic status (SES) families who engage in in-depth arts activities have better academic outcomes than low-SES youth with less arts. They also found that students (regardless of SES) who had intensive art in high school were more likely to earn a bachelor's degree and to earn "mostly A's" in college. Catterall (2009) went on to analyze additional years of data following 12,000 youth and found additional evidence that low-SES youth do better in "art-rich" schools. Beyond the academic and psychologically adaptive aspects of involvement, arts participation can be valuable for youth as an outlet of creative expression and can lead to opportunities to enhance schools and communities (Heath, 2001). And the strong connections that many young people develop with teaching artists likely contribute to overall learning and development (soldalliance.org; Osher, et al., 2019).

In the absence of school-based creative learning opportunities, arts organizations and community-based programs have stepped in to fill the void, providing arts rich experiences for youth, often in the out-of-school time (OST) format. These organizations and programs—and the teaching artists who make them possible—have become vital to thriving creative learning ecosystems in many cities and regions (Bodilly et al., 2008). Arts organizations have a long history as informal education spaces that serve children and youth in communities. From the Renaissance era through today, informal learning has always been the primary method for arts learning (Ulbricht, 2005). Since the 1990s, we have seen a proliferation of arts programs, cultural districts, and professional organizations committed to arts learning and experiences for young people (Bodilly et al., 2008). These community-based arts programs have become a central part of learning ecosystems that serve youth from diverse communities, engaging the interests and creativity of young people.

The creative learning ecosystem case presents an instructional case through which to consider broader L&D ecosystem management because it highlights three important realities: 1) arts learning is a key facilitator of learning and development, especially as it relates to educational equity for Black and Brown children and youth; 2) the arts education space is a long existing informal learning network that is being professionalized with a uniquely situated role of the teaching artists—an important element of the allied youth fields; and 3) though arts learning ecosystems may have distinctly desirable outcomes, there is sometimes a misalignment between resources and goals.

THE CASE OF CREATIVE
LEARNING IN PITTSBURGH

This case study reflects several facilitative factors coming together at a particular time. The Heinz Endowments was seeking innovation and new directions to build on their previous work in arts and learning with an equity lens. The Endowments' has a long history of involvement in the arts, cultural anchors, and education, and has long promoted an inclusive racial equity vision ("Just Pittsburgh"; see heinz.org/equity). The researchers were interested in strengthening approaches to research-practice partnership and finding better ways to conduct participatory research. That is, we felt that although the idea of RPP was desirable, examples of true partnership (versus false packaging of researcher-centered design) were rare. We wondered whether we could achieve the right balance so that evaluation and research could support ecosystem management.

We carried out our ecosystem approach across three phases (see Figure 12.1). All three phases combined philanthropic and research tools and perspectives to shape the design of the ecosystem initiative. We included various participatory

Phase 1: Shaping

How should we define creative learning?

How can we improve access and equity in creative learning?

Philanthropic and research partners worked together, with practitioner focus groups, to get clear on the basic contours of the proposed strategic funding area.

(Data activities: 4 one-on-one interviews, 5 researcher/grant officer meetings, 4 90-minute focus groups with total of 20 practitioner-leaders, internal report)

Phase 2: Modeling

What does the local creative learning ecosystem look like?

We collected baseline survey data and held focus group meetings with key local practitioner-leaders. These 90-minute meetings involved collaborative ecosystem visualization and data for social network analysis.

(Data activities: 8 focus groups with 39 practitioner-leaders, surveys of organizational leaders [N=53] and teaching artists [N=83], public report available at tiny.cc/CLPgh)

Phase 3: Transformative Evaluation (ongoing)

What meaningful changes occur for participants in creative learning programs?

Across several group meetings, teens and adults share stories of change. The group conducts collaborative, thematic analysis of stories, culminating in greater understanding of each program's strengths and areas for improvement. During the COVID-19 pandemic, we launched a podcast with similar aims.

(Data activities: 3-session "story generation" meetings with teen and adults across multiple grantees, "Stories of Change" podcast, site reports and annual ecosystem report)

FIGURE 12.1. The Creative Learning Initiative Across Three Phases

methods in each phase to involve local creative learning practitioner leaders (e.g., directors or education directors of youth arts programs and museums). Across the project, we moved from defining the boundaries of the initiative (Phase 1), to better understanding the ecosystem (Phase 2), to deeper understanding of program processes and participant experiences (Phase 3).

We organized Phase 1 around the questions listed in Figure 12.1; we call the first phase "shaping" because the primary aim was to work as an RP3 to conceptualize creative learning and set its boundaries (what was within and beyond the scope of the initiative). This phase involved information gathering, consideration of access and equity, conversations about boundaries, and the development of a cohesive plan for moving forward. The phase included multiple RP3 working meetings and focus groups attended by practitioner-leaders. In these focus groups we specifically asked practitioner-leaders for their views on how the initiative should be shaped. At the end of this phase, the researchers produced a report that rooted the plan for the initiative in research (e.g., this report referenced the dramatic historical declines in access to arts education for BIPOC). This report enabled the philanthropic side of the partnership to move forward with an initial funding appropriation from The Heinz Endowments' trustees, and served as a sort of blueprint for later phases.

Phase 2 represented a more extensive effort that served both as baseline data collection as well as outreach for the not-yet-announced initiative. That is, alongside valuable data collection, we had rich discussions with local practitioner leaders—discussions that shaped the initiative and let the youth arts community know where the project might be headed. In a series of 90-minute focus group meetings, we asked practitioner-leaders first to nominate other organizations that were "important to creative learning in the region" and to describe their rationale for these nominations. This helped establish what participants valued in the ecosystem (e.g., access, representation, deep learning) and provided data for social network analysis (with youth arts organizations as the unit rather than individual people). We then asked each group to collaboratively depict the creative learning ecosystem using whiteboard and sticky notes.

Phase 2 led to several findings and ways of applying an ecosystem approach, which we summarized in a public report (available at tiny.cc/CLPgh). We found that from our sample of community-based programs: 59% of youth arts organizations deliver programming in schools and 75% of teaching artists do as well. We found it useful to categorize organizations by the degree to which they centered creative learning (CL) (by examining mission statements and websites). "CL Core" organizations provide direct programming with creative learning in their core mission; "CL Included" organizations provide direct programming but not all is creative learning, and "CL Supporters" do not provide direct programming but influence and support creative learning. We also found it useful to distinguish arts exposure (e.g., a school field trip to the symphony) and more advanced art experiences (e.g., multi-year learning in hip-hop music production). Both are important for a healthy ecosystem; organizations may excel at one or the other.

The phase led to several findings specific to Black Centered Arts programming (BCA). We developed a scheme for identifying the degree to which organizations focused on BCA based on their mission statements: "BCA centered" organizations mentioned Black or Africana arts in their missions; "BCA adjacent" used only vague words like "diversity"; and "BCA not specified" did not mention culture in their missions. BCA centered organizations tended to have smaller budgets than BCA adjacent or not specified organizations. Social network analysis suggested that although generally a single network existed, some sub-networks existed, including one focused on BCA.

Finally, we learned a good deal about the adult leaders who make creative learning possible. The majority of our sample (89% of educators) preferred the term "teaching artist." Most of these teaching artists identify with both being an artist and being a teacher. The vast majority practice their art as well as teach it. This is an important factor that makes creative learning distinct from most other youth programming in the learning and development ecosystem. It also highlights the importance of the allied youth fields concept described by Robinson and Akiva in Chapter 1 of this volume. That is, teaching artists represent an important type of adult in the ecosystem—they are distinct yet should be allied with other adults in the youth fields.

We are now in Phase 3, which takes a novel, transformative approach to evaluation. Based on protocols established in a multi-country study of youth work in Europe (Ord et al., 2018), we take a strengths-based approach to understanding creative learning organizations in the ecosystem. Transformative evaluation is designed to accomplish two goals: to provide evidence of program impacts for participating youth and to support teaching artists as they strengthen their educational practices. At the heart of the approach is working collaboratively with youth and educators over a series of meetings to systematically and rigorously collect and analyze stories of change. Before plans were put on hold due to the COVID-19 Pandemic, we piloted the process with several sites. Not only did it generate rich and useful data, multiple participants told us they found the process valuable. For example, one site identified four main themes: they appreciated the **home & family** like atmosphere of the program, and through their participation they experienced **self-discovery, hard work,** and **growth.** This group recorded a video of a song with stories in voice-over, which accompanied the report we provided. This approach shifts the typical role of evaluator—from outside judge to collaborator in accomplishing goals. The transformative evaluation is not just concerned with identifying effectiveness of parts; it's about helping the whole learning ecosystem grow and develop.

Takeaways from the Case Study

In this section we consider the lesson and ideas readers might take from this chapter, particularly the case study. We present these in three areas, listed in Figure 12.2: roles and partnership concepts related to RP3, management of L&D ecosystems in general, and more specific takeaways related to creative learning.

L&D Ecosystem Management

The ecosystem approach provided a birds-eye view through which we could see how diverse populations of teaching artists, youth of color, and BIPOC-led

---

Learning & Development Ecosystem Management

The shift to *ecosystem as unit of analysis* required us to change and innovate in terms of evaluation methods: focus groups with ecosystem elicitation activities, social network analysis, community metrics

Creative Learning

- The *special role of teaching artists* was apparent. Teaching artists liked the term, identify with both artistry and teaching, and need support—pay, benefits, professional learning—for the ecosystem to thrive.

- Examination of the network showed *one network with important subnetworks* (initiatives in other cities may have different findings). We found that the network valued access, representation, and rigorous, quality art.

- We developed *two taxonomies* that may be useful in other initiatives:
  - For Creative Learning programs (centered, included, supporter; see tiny.cc/CLPgh, page 8-9)
  - For Black-Centered arts programs (centered, adjacent, not specified; see tiny.cc/CLPgh, page 10-11)

- The *spectrum of engagement* was salient and consensus was that a healthy ecosystem needs both arts exposure programs *and* deep, multi-year learning opportunities.

Partnerships and roles

- Grant officers came to the partnership with a vision and direction but with *flexibility* and interest in rooting the initiative in research. Researchers/evaluators came to the partnership with interest but without fully-defined aims—so that *research/evaluation aims could be shaped* by the partnership.

- Several *meetings with researchers + grant officers* fully shaped evaluation/research design as well as the philanthropic initiative.

- The *participatory grantmaking* aspects (focus groups, interviews, surveys) both shaped the CL initiative and supported positive community relations.

FIGURE 12.2. Takeaways

organizations appear in and move through the ecosystem. The most profound shift we encountered was related to goals and outcomes of the initiative—which we began discussing at the very beginning of Phase 1. That is, shifting the unit of analysis from children, youth, or programs to the L&D ecosystem itself meant we kept the focus, during dialog-based activities, on the overall health of the system central. In RP3 conversations in Phase 1, this shaped every aspect of conceptualizing the initiative. In focus groups in Phase 2, we asked participants (most of whom were the directors of youth arts programs) to visualize the L&D ecosystem rather than only focus their program. These practitioner-leaders were able to do this and the dialog that followed was different than if we had focused on individual programs strengths and needs.

For example, an illustrative example relates to the depth of participation offered by creative learning programs (listed in Figure 12.2 under Creative Learning). This factor—whether programs offered brief or long-term engagements—was salient in most of the focus groups in Phase 2. That is, some programs primarily offer arts exposure, such as a 3rd grade field trip to the symphony; whereas other programs focus on deep learning, such as teens spending multiple years developing their craft as hip hop artists. A program-focused call for proposals might ask all programs to support deep learning. An ecosystem-focused call would recognize that some programs are well equipped for exposure and others for deep learning and that a diversity along this spectrum would support L&D ecosystem health.

In addition, through multiple surveys, focus groups, and interviews all designed with an ecosystem perspective, it became apparent that equity and access are priorities important for creative learning leaders in the Pittsburgh region. Back to the energy metaphor presented in the introduction, the clear focus of the community on equity and access can be transformed into energy in the form of calls for proposals that reflect this priority. As this effort was initiated by The Heinz Endowments with the intention of informing funding priorities in creative learning, the collaboration supports intentional redirection of resources to create a more just and equitable system.

Creative Learning

Primary findings from the three phases of this initiative revealed salient insights about the terrain of creative learning in Pittsburgh. These insights relate to the role of teaching artists in the ecosystem, the types of organizations that have influence in the ecosystem, and the ways that the system can reflect a more equitable space. Through engaging both teaching artists and creative learning organizations, we were able to identify avenues through which teaching artists represent a keystone species in the ecosystem (see Covin & White, Chapter 7 in this volume). Their role is unique, as teaching artists experience the ecosystem in a way that allows them to shape arts-related experiences through their direct work with youth, as well as through their entrepreneurial creative contributions (Chemi, 2015). Professional development experiences that can enhance support for teaching artists, especially teaching artists of color, will improve the ecosystem's ability to increase equity (Reeder, 2009).

Our surveys revealed that Black-Centered Arts (BCA) organizations make up a sizable group (16 out of 88 programs [18% of the sample] identified by 3 or more respondents), existing across several different subnetworks in the region. These BCA organizations have significant influence in Pittsburgh, as measured through social network analysis indicators of importance. However, the BCA organizations, which are typically BIPOC-led, tend to have smaller budgets. Teaching artists typically to work across multiple organizations, in salaried, contract and hourly positions. About 15% of teaching artists in our surveys identified as Black (compared to a Black population that is 26% of the city). Some are employed at BCA organizations and some at other organizations. When it comes to equity, creative learning program leaders identified factors that highlight race, resources, and reach, spanning across interpersonal, institutional, and structural dimensions of the need to address inequity.

Related to creative learning organizations, we found that the majority of the programs (54%) serve schools, while the vast majority (94%) deliver programming in out-of-school settings (57% deliver programming both in schools and OST). Black-Arts Centered (BAC) programs make up a significant and recognizable portion of the Pittsburgh creative learning ecosystem. The focus groups and surveys uncovered a strong desire to more reach youth of color, which may happen through the identification of mutually beneficial partnerships that could more effectively serve youth in historically marginalized communities.

Partnership and Roles

Using an equity-focused lens, our RP3 was built both to understand and to transform a youth arts learning ecosystem through a multi-phase collaboration between creative learning programs, funders, and researchers. RP3s have the distinct potential to bring thoughtful synergy between the *experiential knowledge of program providers*, the *technical expertise of researchers*, and the *thoughtful beneficence* of philanthropy, along with the energy—financial and other support—to make things happen. This unique synergy, paired with intentional listening and respect for these multiple ways of knowing, can be especially valuable in addressing system level inequities in the arts, which often disadvantage minoritized youth. Exposure to the arts can be beneficial for young people (Bowen & Kisida, 2019; Winner & Hetland, 2008); yet, due to diminishing school-based arts learning opportunities, youth from under-resourced communities tend to have less exposure to the creative learning opportunities and resources that spark interest and foster healthy development. Informal learning spaces, often in the form of community-based arts organizations, can offer arts havens for young people to explore creative outlets as well as supportive places for learning and development (Davis, 2010). In this case study, we focused on a regional creative learning ecosystem, highlighting opportunities to create partnerships that enhance equity in the arts.

Philanthropic organizations continue to seek innovative ways to transform their grantmaking from a transactional payment for nonprofit services into meaningful partnerships with the communities they serve. One way foundations can go beyond simply addressing the financial needs of nonprofits that serve young people is to employ an ecosystem-focused RP3 approach to new or revisited initiatives, especially in the creative learning and youth development fields. Foundations interested in RP3 should account for adequate time and resource investments in the approach—including foundation staff time, compensation for practitioners, and synchronous development of the initiative and the evaluation with researchers. The process of developing the Creative Learning initiative at The Heinz Endowments took approximately two years from the start of internal and field research by foundation staff through the endorsement of the strategy by the Endowments' trustees and subsequent funding of ecosystem partners. Foundations that invest in RP3 can benefit from this longer runway for initiative development by using the time spent in the process to build deeper relationships with current and prospective grantees, teaching artists, and youth; establish accountability to and reciprocal learning with peer funders locally and nationally; and, gain fluency in research and evaluation practices.

We hope that the implications from this work are useful to various city and regional networks that are aligning with the emerging Creative Youth Development field. Implications from our work can serve as a model for various cities and regional networks that are aligning with the emerging Creative Youth Development field. As CYD develops, we have an opportunity to build it on a framework that prioritizes the experiences of families from historically marginalized communities. Across the U.S., local philanthropic organizations have an opportunity to work intentionally with creative learning programs, as well as researchers, to pioneer innovative ecosystems that are inclusive and accessible to all families.

A Path Forward

The RP3 approach presented in this chapter provides a model for how learning ecosystems can benefit from meaningful partnership between researchers, practitioners, and philanthropy in the development of equitable creative learning opportunities for young people. Key insights gained from the Pittsburgh Creative Learning initiative development example reveal the value of partnering research and philanthropy in a way that shifts the unit of analysis from the program level to the ecosystem level. Tending to the healthy maintenance and management of a learning ecosystem requires care and attention from practitioners, partners, youth participants, evaluators, and funders—all of whom benefit from the reciprocity of engagement in what is fundamentally a fluid, evolving, and sometimes turbulent field of practice. For Creative Youth Development networks, the future of this work depends on the many elements of the ecosystem developing trusting give-and-receive relationships that can withstand small stresses and changes to conditions such as local and larger economic forces, trends in youth interests, funding, and policy shifts. Looking ahead, sustainable ecosystems aligned through the RP3 process will require mutual accountability to a set of goals that reflect values including youth-adult partnerships, anti-racism, support for teaching artists, and collective action in order to create the most favorable conditions for young people to equitably access creative learning experiences.

REFERENCES

Akiva, T., Hecht, M., & Osai, E. (2019). *Creative learning in Pittsburgh* (Issue September). University of Pittsburgh School of Education.

Bodilly, S. J., Augustine, C. H., & Zakaras, L. (2008). *Revitalizing arts education through community-wide coordination.* RAND Corporation.

Boston Youth Arts Evaluation Project. (2012). *Boston youth arts evaluation project handbook and workbook.* Boston Youth Arts Evaluation Project and Raw Arts Works.

Bowen, D. H., & Kisida, B. (2019). *Investigating causal effects of arts education experiences: Experimental evidence from Houston's arts access initiative.* https://kinder.rice.edu/research/investigating-causal-effects-arts-education-experiences-experimental-evidence-houstons-arts

Bremner, R. H. (1960). *American philanthropy.* The University of Chicago Press.

Carnegie, A. (1889). Wealth. *The North American Review, 148*(391), 653–664. https://doi.org/10.1215/00182168-39.1.173

Catterall, J. S. (2002). The arts and transfer of learning. In R. J. Deasy (Ed.), *Critical links: Learning in the arts and student academic and social development* (pp. 151–157). Arts Education Partnership.

Catterall, J. S. (2009). *Doing well and doing good by doing art: The effects of education in the visual and performing arts on the achievements and values of young adults.* CreateSpace Independent Publishing Platform.

Catterall, J. S. (2012). *The arts and achievement in at-risk youth: Findings from four longitudinal studies* (Research Report# 55). National Endowment for the Arts.

Chemi, T. (2015). The teaching artist as cultural learning entrepreneur: An introductory conceptualization. *Teaching Artist Journal, 13*(2), 84–94. https://doi.org/10.1080/15411796.2015.997114

Coburn, C. E., Penuel, W. R., & Geil, K. (2013). *Research-practice partnerships at the district level: A new strategy for leveraging research for educational improvement.* William T. Grant Foundation.

Cook, B. (2019). *The Heinz Endowments' transformative arts process: Final evaluation report.* Dragonfly Partners.

Davis, J. H. (2010). Learning from examples of civic responsibility: What community-based art centers teach us about arts education. *Journal of Aesthetic Education, 44*(3), 82–95. https://doi.org/10.1353/jae.2010.0001

Gangewere, R. J. (2011). *Palace of culture: Andrew Carnegie's museums and libraries in Pittsburgh.* University of Pittsburgh Press.

Giridharadas, A. (2018). *Winners take all: The elite charade of changing the world.* Knopf.

Greater Pittsburgh Arts Council. (2018). *Racial equity & arts funding in Greater Pittsburgh.* Greater Pittsburgh Arts Council.

Heath, S. B. (2001). Three's not a crowd: Plans, roles, and focus in the arts. *Educational researcher, 30*(7), 10–17.

Howell, J., Goodkind, S., Jacobs, L. A., Branson, D., & Miller, L. (2019). Pittsburgh's inequality across gender and race. In *Gender analysis white papers*. City of Pittsburgh's Gender Equity Commission.

Jimenez, R. (2019). *Creative youth development: Mapping a phenomenon , growing a field.* Harvard University.

Kevane, M. J., Sundstrom, W. A., & Kevane, M. (2016). Public libraries and political participation, 1870–1940. *Economics, Paper, 55,* 1–39.

Love, B. L. (2019). *We want to do more than survive: Abolitionist teaching and the pursuit of educational freedom.* Beacon Press.

Lowry, P. (2003, March 2). Carnegie's library legacy. *Pittsburgh Post-Gazette.* http://old.post-gazette.com/ae/20030302carnegie2.asp

Montgomery, D. (2017). The rise of creative youth development. *Arts Education Policy Review.* https://doi.org/10.1080/10632913.2015.1064051

Montgomery, D., Rogovin, P., & Persaud, N. (2013). *Something to say: Success principles for afterschool arts programs from urban youth and other experts.* The Wallace Foundation.

Nazir, R., & Apgar, M. (2019). *Are you ready to become an activist philanthropist?* Grantcraft. https://grantcraft.org/content/blog/are-you-ready-to-become-an-activist-philanthropist/

Odum, H. T. (1988). *Self-organization, transformity, and information. 242*(4882), 1132–1139.

Oliphant, G. (2016). *Just Pittsburgh.* https://www.heinz.org/blog-the-point/blog-detail?id=28

Ord, J., Carletti, M., Cooper, S., Dansac, C., Morciano, D., Siurala, L., & Taru, M. (2018). *The impact of youth work in Europe: A study of five European countries.* Humak University of Applied Sciences Publications.

Osher, D., Cantor, P., Berg, J., Steyer, L., & Rose, T. (2019). Drivers of human development: How relationships and context shape learning and development. *Applied Developmental Science, 24*(1), 6–36. https://doi.org/10.1080/10888691.2017.1398650

Rabkin, N., & Hedberg, E. C. (2011). *Arts education in America: What the declines mean for arts participation. Based on the 2008 survey of public participation in the arts. Research report# 52.* National Endowment for the Arts.

Rabkin, N., Reynolds, M., Hedberg, E., & Shelby, J. (2011). *Teaching artists and the future of education.* NORC at the University of Chicago.

Reeder, L. (2009). Hurry up and wait: A national scan of teaching artist research and professional development. *Teaching Artist Journal, 7*(1), 14–22.

Reich, R. (2018). *Just giving: Why philanthropy is failing democracy and how it can do better.* Princeton University Press.

Scott, K. A., Bray, S., & McLemore, M. R. (2020) First, do no harm: Why philanthropy needs to re-examine its role in reproductive equity and racial justice. *Health Equity, 4*(1), 17–22.

Stecher, B. M., Holtzman, D. J., Garet, M. S., Hamilton, L. S., Engberg, J., Steiner, E. D., Robyn, A., Baird, M. D., Gutierrez, I. A., Peet, E. D., De Los Reyes, I. B., Fronberg, K., Weinberger, G., Hunter, G. P., & Chambers, J. (2018). *Improving teaching effectiveness: Final report, the intensive partnerships for effective teaching through 2015–2016.* The RAND Corporation.

Ulbricht, J. (2005). What is Community-Based Art Education? *Art Education, 58*(2), 6–12. https://doi.org/10.1080/00043125.2005.11651529

Villanueva, E. (2018). *Decolonizing wealth: Indigenous wisdom to heal divides and restore balance*. Berrett-Koehler.

Walker, D. (2019). *From generosity to justice: A new gospel of wealth*. The Ford Foundation/Disruption Books.

Welch Jr., V., & Kim, Y. (2010). *Race/Ethnicity and Arts Participation: Findings from the Survey of Public Participation in the Arts*. National Endowment for the Arts.

Winner, E., & Hetland, L. (2008). Art for our sake school arts classes matter more than ever-but not for the reasons you think. *Arts Education Policy Review, 109*(5), 29–32. https://doi.org/10.3200/aepr.109.5.29-32

CHAPTER 13

CONNECTED LEARNING & LIBRARIES

An Essential Part of the Out-of-School Time Ecosystem

Linda W. Braun and Lance Simpson

In Tuscaloosa, Alabama, kids and families plant gardens with mentors and educators. They eat the food they grow and engage in mindfulness activities that help to ground and center them in the work of feeding themselves and their community (Dugat, personal communication, October 2020). In Chicago, Illinois, at the Chicago Public Library, teenagers work with mentors and educators to create new clothing from old in an effort to re-envision and redesign what they wear so it is free of gender categorization (Reyes, personal communication, October 2020). In communities across Massachusetts, youth engage with public library staff to create lawn signs that complete the prompts, "Freedom of...," "Freedom To...," "Freedom From...," and "Freedom For..." (Kirkland, 2019). Each of these activities fosters the interests of participating youth, connects them with opportunities to share and grow these interests in and with their communities, and supports building relationships around young people's personal interests. Each of the aforementioned moments is possible because of partnerships across multiple in-

It Takes an Ecosystem: Understanding the People, Places, and
Possibilities of Learning and Development Across Settings, pages 249–261.
Copyright © 2022 by Information Age Publishing

249

stitutions that share resources and collaborate. When participating in these ways, youth are engaged in connected learning (CL).

For youth to engage in CL in sustainable and meaningful ways, they need a learning ecosystem filled with mentors, educators, and peers all working together to create opportunities for them to learn and grow in their interests. As with a natural ecosystem, a learning ecosystem is an intentional coalition that recognizes the power of relationships and mutually beneficial collaboration. When the stakeholders in a learning ecosystem work as a whole, rather than as disparate parts, they effectively leverage their own resources to support each other and directly meet the learning needs of the youth they serve. In this chapter, through examples from public libraries and others in allied youth fields, we look specifically at the CL framework as a tool for expanding a thriving learning ecosystem.

WHAT IS CL?

Foundationally, the CL framework is built around research that says young people learn best at the intersection of their own interests and passions; through relationships with adult mentors, educators, and peers; and with opportunities to continue to engage by leveling up [improving skills through scaffolded experiences] and/or "geeking out" [showing excitement and passion for a particular area of interest] (Ito et al., 2020). The CL Framework provides guidance and structure for developing and maintaining responsive and creative spaces for youth across a learning ecosystem and ensures relationships with learning mentors and role models that cultivate and broker opportunities for the young people they serve. While in this chapter we primarily examine the value of facilitating CL in the spaces of out-

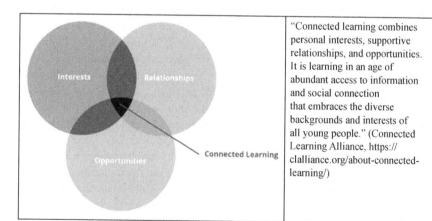

FIGURE 13.1.   Connected Learning Infographic

of-school time (OST), for an enhanced healthy learning ecosystem, connections across both formal and informal spaces of learning need to be recognized.

CL also highlights the value of shared purpose that connects all learning across a young person's spheres of influence from home to school, with friends, through online engagement, and especially at play (Widman, et al., 2019, p. 35). It builds on scholarship in the science of learning and development (see soldalliance.org) and acknowledges "a growing consensus in the learning sciences recognizes that learning is most robust when grounded in a learner's cultural identity, part of meaningful inquiry, supported by caring relationships, and reinforced across settings" (Ito et al., 2020, p. 26). The elements that comprise CL are not new to formal and informal education. John Dewey (1902) considered the context of learning based on the needs of the child. He noted that any exercises in education, be they academic in nature or not, were "[subservient] to the growth of the child," (p. 13) and that all education should solely support and encourage that growth. "The child is the starting-point, the center, and the end," of this process, and all learning should be connected and integrative, rather than separated out into disparate pieces (Dewey, 1991, p. 107). Nearly 90 years later, Seymour Papert argued for fostering and encouraging young people to want and love to learn, through the personal computer and through a connected society. Papert saw that technology would continue to bring opportunities to better the world, and envisioned that mentors and educators would encourage young people to connect with as many of these opportunities as possible (Papert, 1993). In the context of CL, this connected world that Papert envisioned is local, national, and even global with all learning ecosystem members acknowledging their purpose.

CL AND PUBLIC LIBRARIES

A relevant example of CL that reflects the ideas of Dewey and Papert can be seen in the work of the Providence, Rhode Island, Public Library (PPL). Through funding from the Institute of Museum and Library Services (IMLS), PPL was able to expand their CL-based teen programs. This included "learn to earn" programs in which teens were given the chance to work at the library as they gained skills in an area of interest. The teens were also mentored by peers and adults at the same time. In the summer of 2020, after the completion of the IMLS project, the library hosted a "Data for Good" learn to earn program. Paid Teen Associates, with the support of library staff, worked with the nonprofits on answering each organizations' specific data questions. As a part of the program, teens completed the Library's Data Navigators curriculum, learned how to work for and with a client, and participated in workforce development training (Providence Public Library, 2020). As the program was offered entirely virtually, teens who did not have technology tools to participate were given those tools as library staff delivered what was needed to teen's homes.

Based on research from the Digital Youth Network (digitalyouthnetwork.org/), CL found its home in practice and design with public libraries in the late 2000s and early 2010s through support from the MacArthur Foundation. This support enabled the development of YOUmedia Chicago at Chicago Public Library, and a subsequent expansion of a network of libraries and museums through the IMLS Learning Labs in Libraries and Museums initiative (Barron et al., 2014; Institute of Museum and Library Services, 2014). These libraries and museums utilized the CL framework to design spaces and develop collaborative relationships with community partners to provide opportunities for teens to pursue play and learning through the lens of their own interests and passions. "It's important...that we equip [teens] with the tools they need so they can be as good as they can be" (Benjamin L Hooks Central Library, 2018, p. 1:20).

The CL framework is grounded in empowering young people. When educators and mentors encourage youth to follow their interests, they shift the power dynamic between teacher and learner to acknowledge the learner's autonomy in pursuing knowledge and understanding of a world that is meaningful, and which makes sense to them. CL acknowledges the power of young people by leveraging opportunities for controlling their own education. This highlights the role of CL in an equity agenda, as young people are infrequently in control of anything in their lives. CL acknowledges the role and responsibility of adults and institutions as holders of power. By sharing power between learning facilitators, mentors, and youth CL becomes a robust way to ensure that diverse voices are represented and heard. For example, youth in York County, Pennsylvania, demonstrated an interest in facilitating conversations about the ways in which people in their area perceived each other. York County Library staff member Jennifer Johnson recognized this was important to these young people and worked with them to organize the conversations among peers and community members. Through this work teens were given the power to engage with each other and adults in ways that were meaningful to them within the context of their lived experiences (Johnson, personal communication, October, 2020).

CL as an actionable learning framework informs the development of youth-centered learning activities in libraries. It can also be operationalized at an institutional level to create community learning partnerships, and ensure the survival and sustained growth and health of a community's learning ecosystem. Public libraries across the United States have gravitated to the CL framework. One reason is that CL can readily be connected to practices already in place. Take for example, public library preschool story times. These activities, hosted regularly by many U.S. libraries, can frequently be deeply grounded in CL. Library staff select a theme for story time that is of interest to very young children—perhaps dinosaurs or pets. Staff collect materials—books, songs, crafts, etc.—for the children to engage with so as to learn more about their interests. And, these preschoolers are given the chance to talk with each other and adults about their love of the topic.

Among the array of frameworks used in allied youth fields, the four below are commonly cited as setting the stage for an organization's connections with and for youth. Each framework has a specific purpose and value and CL can be used with one or more to create a bridge between the broader ideas of youth and social emotional development and direct connections with youth through interests, relationships, and opportunities.

40 Developmental Assets

Published by the Search Institute, the 40 developmental assets lay out eight categories to consider when building youth assets. The categories are defined as what's needed externally, outside of themselves, and what's needed internally, personal skills, etc. Each of the eight categories: support, empowerment, boundaries & expectations, and constructive use of time is further defined through specific assets within each category (Search Institute, n.d.).

Hart's Ladder of Participation

Since its publication, Hart's Ladder of Participation has been used throughout allied youth fields as a cornerstone for describing and implementing activities that integrate youth voice and choice. At the lowest rungs of the ladder youth are manipulated, used for decoration, and tokenized. As a result, youth voice is non-existent and adults take the lead in all ways. At the top of the ladder, the highest rungs, child initiated and directed and child initiated shared decisions with adults focuses on truly centering youth voice by giving youth the chance to decide on activities and then work with adults to turn those activities into a reality (Hart, 1992, p. 8).

CASEL Social Emotional Learning (SEL) Framework

Divided into five competencies, the SEL framework highlights the skills and attitudes young people need to gain to achieve lifelong success. These competences are centered on real-world skills and behaviors including self-awareness, social awareness, responsible decision making, self-management, and relationship skills. (Collaborative for Academic, Social, Emotional, Learning, 2020)

Positive Youth Development

As stated on the Act for Youth website, "Positive youth development is a framework that guides communities in the way they organize services, opportunities, and supports so that young people can develop to their full potential." (Act for Youth, n.d.) Embedded in the framework are strengths and positive outcomes, youth voice and engagement, strategies that involve all youth, community involvement and collaboration, and long-term commitment.

FIGURE 13.2.   Selection of Frameworks Used in the Allied Youth Fields

CL BEYOND PUBLIC LIBRARIES

Public libraries are not the only providers of CL based activities; to truly harness the opportunity and power of CL, across allied youth fields with local institutions and community members is essential. As noted by Reich and Ito (2017), "When initiatives are co-developed and co-facilitated with stakeholders, they are more likely to be better attuned to important elements of social and cultural contexts, and learners are more likely to take ownership of these initiatives" (p. 3).

In 2020, CL researchers reflected on the first decade of CL research and learning and revised the CL framework based on learning from the previous decade. At that time Mizuko Ito, Professor in Residence at the University of California, Irvine, highlighted what makes CL unique from other frameworks and how this uniqueness is also why it's so important within the larger ecosystem of allied youth fields. Ito (2020) wrote, "Designing for CL takes an ecological and systemic approach, which emphasizes partnerships across sites of learning. It is not about implementing a particular technology or technique" (p. 64). Within the discussion presented here, this point by Ito is important. In our research, we discovered that while many other frameworks are used by allied youth fields, there is a strong desire for partnering to provide quality equitable learning experiences for youth.

HAVING A SHARED LANGUAGE

We've learned that allied youth fields facilitate activities that embed CL, however, that's usually not how those activities are described. In conversation with groups of out-of-school time staff and intermediaries, a number of other frameworks were mentioned as the basis for their work. These include the Search Institute's 40 Developmental Assets, the Collaborative for Academic, Social, and Emotional Learning (CASEL) Competencies, Positive Youth Development, and Hart's Ladder of Youth Participation. As a result of the multitude of frameworks used, it can be difficult for allied youth fields to work together to reach youth-focused collective impact. As Jennifer Brady, CEO of Development Without Limits, stated in a focus group, "We all call the same thing, different names, and so we can't quite always figure out what you're all talking about" (Brady, personal communication, October 2020). Eric Reyes, Digital Media Coordinator at the Chicago Public Library, explains this further, "It seems like in the time that I've been working in out-of-school time programming there seems to be trends and cycles of things that are the same things just branded in different ways. We hear people say for example, 'you should start a STEAM program' and we're like, 'We already do that, but it's called something else" (Reyes, personal communication, October 2020). If those working in allied youth fields intentionally work together to understand one another's language and guiding frameworks, the potential for a vibrant ecosystem increases. If that ecosystem intentionally includes CL (as an enhancement and extension of other frameworks) outcomes and opportunities for youth and communities expand. A sample of the variety of language used to describe similar ideas is

Connected Learning	CASEL SEL	40 Developmental Assets	Hart's Ladder
Interests: Learning is motivating when based on personal interests.	Self-awareness: Including developing interests and a sense of purpose.	Support: Youth are engaged in meaningful activities outside of school and home.	Child initiated and directed: Youth have the opportunity to decide what activities take place.
Opportunities: Learning is motivating when real-world connections are possible	Responsible Decision-making: Including the ability to use critical thinking and evaluate choices.	Empowerment: Youth are involved in activities that support the community, school, and home.	Child initiated, shared decisions with adults: Youth and adults together make decisions about activities.
Relationships: Learning is motivating when supported by peers and mentors	Relationship skills: Including the ability to "establish and maintain healthy and supportive relationships."	Support: Youth have meaningful relationships with at least three non-parental adults	Child initiated, shared decisions with adults: Youth and adults work together to design and implement activities

FIGURE 13.3. Language Comparisons Across Frameworks

shown in the chart below. CL's three main principles are listed first to demonstrate how they relate to and extend the ideas of the other frameworks highlighted.

When reviewing allied youth field offerings, it's readily apparent that CL principles are regularly embedded in the work. For example:

- Youth in Focus is a Seattle, WA based nonprofit with the mission of "Amplifying teen voice through photography and arts education" (Youth in Focus, n.d., para. 2). An example of the organization's focus on CL is clearly seen in the description of the Skate and Media course, "Skateboarding, photography and video have been linked together in a rebellious alliance for as long as there have been skateboards! Youth in Focus is partnering with CHILL Seattle for a highly interactive and hands on crash course in skateboarding AND skateboarding video and photography" (https://youthinfocus.org/virtualclasses). The course combines teen interests of photography and skateboarding with the chance to be mentored and coached by experts in each of those fields. Pair that with the commitment to equity of Youth in Focus, seen in part through providing skateboards and cameras to participating teens, and you have all of the components required for a CL-based program.
- Schoolyard Roots, in Tuscaloosa, AL, works with schools in that city to bring environmental education opportunities to youth. The schools that the program works with see a majority of students qualifying for free and reduced lunch (Dugat, personal communication, October 2020). While available to all participating schools and students, Schoolyard Roots "Budding Entrepreneurs" program connects directly to the needs of lower socioeconomic students As described by Nicole Dugat, the interim Executive Director of Schoolyard Roots, students "learn how to harvest and sell their produce at a lower rate to their community" (Dugat, personal communica-

tion, October 2020). While not called CL, Schoolyard Roots embeds those principles into their work by giving youth the chance to engage in activities that connect to their real-life situations and learn from and with mentors with expertise in gardening, harvesting, and the business of selling produce.

• The Girl Scouts of America report Generation STEM: What Girls Say About Science Technology Engineering and Math found that "Girls are overwhelmingly interested in STEM. Our findings show that a total of 74% of teen girls are interested in STEM. Interest in STEM was defined as responding "somewhat" or "very" interested in the general field of STEM and in a STEM subject, such as science, math, engineering, or computer science/information technology." (Girl Scouts Research Institute, 2012). Within a CL context that interest is supported through the badges and activities sponsored by Girl Scout troops. These include badges in entrepreneurship, app development, and automotive engineering with activities such as building on ideas that will make life better, designing an app that solves a problem, and building and testing automotive prototypes (Girl Scouts of the USA, n.d.). Girls in troops have the opportunity to select badges to pursue based on their personal interest and are mentored by troop leaders and those with expertise in a related field. (www.girlscouts.org/en/our-program/badges/badge_explorer.html).

EMBEDDING CL ACROSS THE ECOSYSTEM

Putting the CL Framework into practice requires strategic thinking and planning. At the most granular level, it requires mentors who build relationships with the kids and teens they serve, that those mentors listen to the interests of the kids and teens and connect them with opportunities in and outside the organization to grow in their interests. Youth can engage in CL in libraries through large, grant-funded projects like YOUmedia Chicago, where teens connect with talented artists and mentors to do everything from designing clothing, to writing and producing their own music with professional recording equipment. Young people can also engage in CL activities throughout the allied youth fields ecosystem when staff know the interests of youth they work with, and then broker opportunities to connect with people in the community, or virtually anywhere around the world, who can help them to learn more about areas of interest. Applying the CL framework in the allied youth fields across the ecosystem means leveraging the resources at each organization and sharing knowledge and opportunities.

CL is scalable and continually reinforces itself through practice. As mentors and leaders in libraries and other allied youth fields continue to seek and find opportunities for the youth they serve, they will naturally develop relationships with other organizations and leaders, technically skilled community members, youth serving nonprofits, and formal and informal educational institutions across the community. In this way, the fundamental elements of the CL framework can be applied at a community level ensuring that youth serving organizations maintain strong relationships as a single ecosystem, and leveraging their collective power and resources to connect the interests and needs of the youth they serve with opportunities for learning and growth.

As allied youth fields struggle with budgets and staffing it's important to ask how members of the ecosystem can support each other in ways that help to create strong organizations and vibrant communities. An answer may be in the work of the Boone (KY) County Public Library. One of the library system's branches was housed in a housing complex in order to reach those who might not be able to travel to other branches across the system. Library staff realized that while their intentions for the branch were admirable, community members were not using the facility or its services. After analyzing usage data, staff recognized a key challenge with the branch was that by being located in the housing complex, library services were in competition with organizations nearby. These other services include a Boys and Girls Club, a learning center, and a community center. Library administration determined that it didn't make sense to continue to maintain the branch and instead opened up satellite locations and services in those other institutions housed nearby. As described by Veronica Rainwater, User Manager for the Library,

> We're developing a collection to distribute to each of those, we're working with the organization's needs to be able to promote it to the people who use the organization, and we're going to provide other services like computer services, a notary, all of that kind of thing, but in their building. So, we're just going to break down that level of competition and we're going to be right there where the people are already without making that extra step for them that obviously was not needed or working and we'll be able to support the organization's leaders as well (Rainwater, 2020).

By being "right where the people are already" the Boone County Public Library is able to engage with youth and adults to learn exactly what their needs and interests are. Then, when fully up and running, they will be able to provide CL based services that connect young people to resources, opportunities, and relationships that help these youth build the skills needed to succeed and thrive in the 21st century. Library staff will also connect more deeply with ecosystem staff and community to better understand youth assets and needs.

Opportunities to support each other across the ecosystem are not alien to organizations that embed connected learning into their practice. In 2011, the Mozilla Foundation took over hosting the Hive networks in NYC, Chicago, Toronto, Pittsburgh, Austin, and Chattanooga (previously Hive networks were facilitated by the MacArthur Foundation). During the time that Mozilla hosted the Hive work, organization staff from a variety of allied youth field organizations networked and worked together on grant projects, events and programs for youth, and on building overall capacity of youth serving organizations in each of the cities. Based on their work with Hive NYC, Santo et al. (2016), described the requirements for succeeding in allied youth fields collaborations. Their findings outlined five practices for success:

- Public storytelling and context setting—which includes having a shared mission across all those participating.
- Enabling community contribution—opportunities for all involved to "give back" proved essential and ranged from providing feedback on a project or resource to being integrally involved in project design and development.
- Rapid prototyping in the wild—centers on testing out smaller ideas in real life before they go to scale.
- Public reflection and documentation—demonstrates the value of letting others know about the work undertaken, reflecting on successes and challenges together, and giving others outside of the network with opportunities to get involved as they learn about activities, projects, and so on.
- Creation of remixable work projects—enables all involved to rework what was designed and developed for their own purposes and communities (Santo et al., 2016).

After a decade of support, the Mozilla Foundation moved on from working with Hive networks in each of the participating cities (Loup Editorial Team, 2019). The Chicago network demonstrated resilience in continuing the work started as a part of the Hive. The network, now called the Chicago Learning Exchange, continues to thrive as a community of organizations in the allied youth fields. Their work together includes the Connected Learning Guide, a useful tool to learn what CL is, and to gain insight into the practices that create for successful CL environments (chicagolx.org/resources/connected-learning-guide).

Remake Learning (remakelearning.org) in Pittsburgh is another example of a strong ecosystem of allied youth fields. The network of participating organizations work together to host meetups and events for those in the ecosystem to learn from and with each other. They also host community events so youth and families are able to engage in activities that promote CL-based learning. Remake Learning published a variety of resources for those interested in developing stronger ecosystems, including connected learning lesson plans (Sprout Fund, n.d.a) and the Remake Learning Playbook which helps organizations in an ecosystem plan for building strong innovative networks (Sprout Fund, n.d.b).

CL IS EVERYWHERE AND THE ECOSYSTEM MUST EMBRACE IT

Seeing opportunities for CL everywhere is not uncommon when just learning about the framework. As we've stated, even when not referred to as CL, it naturally is a part of the allied youth fields ecosystem. Embracing CL leads to opportunities to connect more deeply with others working to help youth succeed. This does not take completely re-thinking services. It may however require:

- Intentionally reviewing services provided at the local organization and highlighting those aspects that are CL aligned.
- Identifying the ways in which others in the local allied youth fields ecosystem support CL in their work.
- Leveraging intersections across the ecosystem where opportunities for deeper CL engagement exist.
- Connecting with public libraries in the area to investigate how, by using a CL lens, activities sponsored across the allied youth fields ecosystem can be leveraged throughout the community.
- Ensuring that as activities and services are refined and added, that connected learning is considered a central point for building engagement, equity, and meaningful learning opportunities for and with youth.

It's possible that, through bringing CL to the local ecosystem, pathways for youth to move across spaces in support of interests and learning will increase. Imagine a young person who is interested in social justice. They may start learning about activism at the local public library as a part of a connected learning project similar to the lawn sign project in Massachusetts mentioned earlier in the chapter. As they learn more about activism through that project, they may want to gain more experience in organizing meetings on social justice topics for and with adults and peers. The local public library staff, through relationships in the ecosystem of allied youth fields, is able to connect the interested teen to a local grassroots group that engages in the work that the teen is interested in. Once involved in the grassroots group, the teen meets other like-minded adults and peers and together they decide to build a coalition that will strive to make social change by engaging with the local city council. And, once connected to the city council, the teen that started on this path at the local public library meets decision makers, stakeholders, and politicians that continue to help build the teen's skills and interests.

If those working in allied youth fields commit to considering CL as a set of principles that can enhance their work with youth, youth opportunities across a community will align, allowing youth to move across their spaces of learning in ways that best support current needs, interests, and potential futures.

REFERENCES

About Connected Learning. (2018, October 12). *What is connected learning*. https://clalliance.org/about-connected-learning/.

ACT for Youth. (n.d.). *Principles of positive youth development*. http://actforyouth.net/youth_development/development/

Barron, B., Gomez, P. N., & Martin, C. K. (2014). *The digital youth network: Cultivating digital media citizenship in urban communities.* The MIT Press.

Benjamin L. Hooks Central Library. (2018). *Choose901.* Choose 901. https://youtu.be/uog1JHfNs5k.

Chicago Learning Exchange. (n.d.). *CLX Connected Learning Guide.* https://chicagolx.org/resources/connected-learning-guide.

Collaborative for Academic, Social, Emotional, Learning. (2020). *CASEL's SEL framework.* https://casel.org/wp-content/uploads/2020/10/CASEL-SEL-Framework-10.2020-1.pdf

Dewey, J. (1991). The child and the curriculum; The School and Society. In *The child and the curriculum; The school and society* (p. 107). University of Chicago Press.

Girl Scouts of the USA. (n.d.). *Award and Badge Explorer—Girl Scouts.* https://www.girlscouts.org/en/our-program/badges/badge_explorer.html.

Girl Scouts Research Institute. (2012). *Generation STEM: What girls say about science, technology, engineering, and math.* Girl Scouts. https://www.girlscouts.org/join/educators/generation_stem_full_report.pdf.

Hart, R. A. (1992). The meaning of children's participation. In *Children's participation: From tokenism to citizenship* (p. 8). Essay, UNICEF, International child development centre.

Institute of Museum and Library Services. (2014). (rep.). *Learning labs in libraries and museums.* https://www.imls.gov/sites/default/files/publications/documents/learninglabsreport_0.pdf

Ito, M. et al. (2020). (rep.). *The connected learning network: Reflections on a decade of engaged scholarship.* Connected Learning Alliance. https://clalliance.org/wp-content/uploads/2020/02/CLRN_Report.pdf

Kirkland, L. (2019, November 4). For freedoms: Empowering teens in election season. *School Library Journal.* https://www.slj.com/?detailStory=for-freedoms-empowering-teens-in-election-season-youth-active-citizenship.

Loup Editorial Team. (2019, May 31). *A Loup case study: PASE and Hive NYC.* Medium. https://medium.com/the-deep-listen/a-loup-case-study-pase-and-hive-nyc-87e3c6238954.

Papert, S. (1993). *The children's machine: Rethinking school in the age of the computer.* BasicBooks.

Providence Public Library. (2020, June 26). *Data for good summer employment.* https://www.provlib.org/education/teen-squad/summer-data/.

Reich, J., & Ito, M. (2017). (rep.). *From good intentions to real equity: Equity by design in learning technologies.* Connected Learning Alliance. https://clalliance.org/wp-content/uploads/2017/11/GIROreport_1031.pdf

Santo, R., Ching, D., Peppler, K., & Hoadley, C. (2016). Working in the open: Lessons from open source on building innovation networks in education. *On the Horizon, 24*(3), 280–295. https://doi.org/10.1108/oth-05-2016-0025

Search Institute. (2019, November 5). *The developmental assets framework.* https://www.search-institute.org/our-research/development-assets/developmental-assets-framework/.

Sprout Fund. (n.d.a). *Connected learning lesson plans.* Remake Learning. https://remakelearning.org/connectedlearning/

Sprout Fund. (n.d.b). *Remake learning playbook.* http://playbook.remakelearning. org/#license.

Widman, S., Chang-Order, J., Penuel, W. R., & Wortman, A. (2019). Using evaluation tools toward more equitable youth engagement in libraries: Measuring connected learning and beyond. *Young Adult Library Services, 17*(4), 36–45. http://yalsjournal.ala. org/publication/?m=53337&i=609310&p=3&pp=1.

Youth in Focus. (n.d.). *Mission and values.* https://youthinfocus.org/values.

CHAPTER 14

THE GROWING ROLE OF OUT-OF-SCHOOL TIME IN DRIVING EQUITABLE CAREER EXPLORATION AND PREPARATION

Candace Brazier Thurman and Saskia K. Traill

Do you remember your first job? Do you remember how you found it, what you learned from it, and where it took you next? For many, first jobs help us connect our school learning, our values, and social and emotional skills to a new setting. We are asked to solve problems, work in teams, and interact with strangers, perhaps at a cashier's desk, a summer camp, or in an office. These experiences help us to practice skills necessary for college and career success and broaden our perspectives of what we might want to be. Many first jobs tell us what we're sure we don't want to do as adults. Young people need a variety of early work experiences to try, to reflect on, and to weave into post-secondary planning. Increasingly, out-of-school time (OST) ecosystems are at the center of work-based learning and career development for young people. Over the next decade, the OST field should hone and expand its critical role in career exploration and preparation.

It Takes an Ecosystem: Understanding the People, Places, and
Possibilities of Learning and Development Across Settings, pages 263–277.

In this chapter, we will first take a step back to provide some background about early decisions that formed many of the characteristics of the current OST ecosystem in New York City, an ecosystem which has relatively strong links between youth-serving community organizations and partnering schools. We will then delve into an area of this evolving ecosystem that has continued to grow over the past decade, and for which attention has increased rapidly with the pandemic and renewed call for equity and social justice: school-connected OST ecosystems that intentionally offer career exploration and skill development for young people. In each section we will describe linkages among OST providers as a central function of OST ecosystems. We will also describe connections to individual schools. We have found time and again that school connections are a critical part of healthy OST ecosystems and worthy of focus, intentional cultivation, and support through system-level funding, research, practice, and policy.

DESIGNING SCHOOL-CONNECTED OST ECOSYSTEMS

ExpandED Schools was founded twenty-two years ago with the belief that partnership is necessary to transform learning and development for young people. As an emerging citywide intermediary in New York City, we were intentional in building structures that would facilitate partnerships among youth-serving organizations and schools. At the time, the organization's leaders made a few critical decisions that shaped a complex learning ecosystem, or, perhaps more accurately, a set of interconnected learning ecosystems, throughout the city.

First, ExpandED (then known as The After-School Corporation, or TASC) funded local youth-serving providers with roots in neighborhoods. Early leaders knew that these youth-serving organizations could place OST in the center of ecosystems that build strong local communities with deep cultural connections. Second, leaders decided that programs would be run in school buildings. Leaders at ExpandED anticipated that school-based OST would promote equity by making sure programming was where kids are and offer a more seamless learning day by bringing youth-serving nonprofits into contact with the school personnel serving the same young people during the school day. Leaders hoped these opportunities for physical contact would promote partnership between school faculty and after-school staff centered around young people and shared goals for young people's well-being and long-term success.

Finally, the model was grounded in positive youth development, requiring small group sizes with talented community educators who were expected to expose young people to new passions. ExpandED required a multifaceted set of offerings, including arts, physical movement, literacy, STEM, as well as homework help and supper. Insisting on a diverse array of activities required collaboration among youth providers with different kinds of expertise. Youth-serving organizations that were leading afterschool programs connected with nonprofit organizations that specialized in a particular curriculum or content area, such as music education or soccer.

Program providers developed relationships with their host, the school. School leaders and the OST provider would start by negotiating use of the space. As OST providers and school leaders got to know each other, they began to recognize their connectedness in a learning ecosystem. A study in ExpandED's first decade found that principal engagement in afterschool was key to afterschool attendance and academic outcomes, supporting the important role of school connectedness in OST ecosystems (Reisner et al., 2004).

ExpandED also created intentional collaboration to advance specific content-area alignment among educators. For example, with funding from the Noyce Foundation and STEM Next, we were pleased to convene STEM leaders within school, afterschool, and STEM-rich cultural institutions. We developed program models that brought together school-day teachers and afterschool staff. After-school staff leading STEM activities in OST learned more about what students were learning in school, and school-day teachers explored the hands-on engaging lessons in OST that help STEM learning come alive. This approach is now being investigated in a federally funded Investing in Innovation developmental research study. It also helped to spur a national movement to reconsider STEM learning ecosystems led by nimble, passionate lead organizations that build relationships with cultural institutions, family networks, youth-serving nonprofits, schools, and corporations (Traphagen & Traill, 2014).

It was clear early on that OST provision for high school needed to look and feel different for adults and young people. The connections among schools and the OST field in K–8 helped to advance stronger networks focused on career exploration for high school students.

LEARNING ECOSYSTEMS FOR HIGH SCHOOL STUDENTS

ExpandED built partnerships for high school students a bit differently than for students in grades K through 8. Recognizing the developmental and learning needs of high school students, rather than designing OST for broad exposure to small-group learning in school, we designed OST activities in high school to offer deeper, applied-learning opportunities, often individual and student-driven, drawing young people out of the school building and familiar neighborhoods into new places within the city.

These types of applied-learning activities are appropriate for teens. A comprehensive framework for young adult success, developed by the UChicago Consortium on School Research and funded by The Wallace Foundation, lays out the importance of rich and varied experiences that build knowledge and skills along with values, mindsets, and self-regulation (Nagaoka et al., 2015). The framework includes the importance of action and reflection in integrating these characteristics into a positive identity as young people emerge into adulthood. In the UChicago Consortium's developmental framework, middle adolescence is characterized as a time in which developmental focus is on building values and the emergence of competencies, agency, and an individuated identity. These are built through actions and reflections that enable young people to encounter new ideas, envision new values, and integrate these ideas and values within their identities.

The framework for young adult success reminds us that high school learning ecosystems should do far more to drive college and career readiness through support for high academic grades and a first job. Ecosystems must also ensure young people are able to act and reflect on their values and have experiences that enable the emergence of competencies, agency, and an individuated identity. These concepts are deeply rooted in race, gender, and equity. For young people of color navigating career interests in white-dominated industries, for example, identity may be tested in ways that their white peers do not experience. Teens speak of learning to code-switch in order to navigate multiple cultural contexts or feeling community abandonment traveling to an internship in another borough. Micro-aggressions and the lack of appropriate practices and activities among employers to foster inclusion and belonging may create conflict between interests and skills and realities of entering work contexts that are not welcoming.

What entities are critical in a high school OST ecosystem designed to support equity in career opportunities, and what role does each entity play? Partners in high school ecosystems include multiple government agencies, school systems, training institutions, for-profit and nonprofit employers, and nonprofit youth-development providers. Many of these categories are overlapping and use different terms and nomenclature to describe similar work. Many parts of this ecosystem are driven by complicated funding and policy structures that can make youth-centered partnerships difficult to design and implement. We will describe primary drivers of the New York City work-based learning ecosystem below, both to illustrate the complexity, and to help map what other communities may want to consider in building their own high school OST ecosystems focused on career exploration.

Government institutions and school systems compartmentalize work-based learning and career supports from other school activities. Most notably, federal, state, and local governments fund Career Technical Education (CTE) programming in designated CTE schools. CTE is a model of vocational education "that focuses on the skills and knowledge required for specific jobs or fields of work" (National Center for Education Statistics, n.d.). The desired outcomes for CTE schools are for students to enroll in post-secondary education, complete work-based learning experiences, complete industry-recognized credentialing, and have an understanding of career outcomes (New York State Education Department, 2020). The federal government sets the agenda for CTE education through funding requirements. For example, the latest authorization of Perkins, the Strengthening Career and Technical Education for the 21st Century Act, revised the definition of CTE programming to include a focus on in-demand sectors and alignment with state standards. The new act also gives states more authority to customize CTE activities to their students' needs (Advance CTE, 2018). Nationally, students in CTE high schools graduate at higher rates than students in traditional high schools

(U.S. Department of Education, Office of Career, Technical, and Adult Education, 2016). In New York City, this is especially true for Black and Latino high school students, who graduate from CTE schools at higher rates than traditional schools (Treschan & Mehrotra, 2014). Research also points to the importance of students who may not connect with traditional academic schools being able to self-select into CTE schools to increase graduation rates (Kreisman & Stange, 2017).

Outside of structured CTE activities, individual schools can support work-based learning through their own programming choices. In New York City, principals have autonomy to engage partners. School leaders can connect off-site activity to the school day via an academic credit or hours towards a career-development credential. The Career Development and Occupational Studies (CDOS) commencement credential, which can replace a required graduation examination (a fifth Regents Examination in New York), allows students to graduate with four passing Regents exams and one CDOS credential. One avenue to earn the credential is for students to complete 216 hours of career readiness preparation inclusive of courses, internships, and work experience. To earn these 216 hours, schools must track students' participation in career readiness activities. Students must also complete a career plan that includes their career interests, career strengths, and career goals (New York State Education Department, 2019). This is worthwhile to note because principals in non-CTE schools can still make work-based learning a priority and meaningful for their students through these mechanisms.

Government institutions can also shape work-based learning ecosystems outside the school system through funding internship wages. New York City has multiple city-funded employment programs for youth. A few prominent examples are the Summer Youth Employment Program (SYEP), managed by the Department of Youth and Community Development (DYCD); the Work Progress Program (WPP), managed by the Human Resources Administration; and Industry Scholars, managed by the Department of Education. Each of these opportunities have differing purposes and audiences, but each of their overall goals is shaped by a government agency. For example, SYEP is the largest summer youth employment program in the country. It provides both wages and job experience for youth. To run SYEP, DYCD relies on community-based providers to recruit and enroll selected teens and secure teens' job placements. Prior to 2018, youth selection into SYEP was primarily accomplished through a lottery with a small percentage of non-lottery slots available to academically on-track students and vulnerable youth. In 2018, DYCD introduced a school-based option, where a cohort of schools could select students who would be enrolled in SYEP without waiting for results of a lottery. The intent was to encourage schools and their partners to link SYEP to other career preparation activities in order to better achieve long-term career readiness goals. This idea is supported by a 2017 MDRC study that found that SYEP achieved short-term goals of wage increase, but that, after five years, students selected by the lottery were no more likely to be employed or earn more than their peers who were not selected (Valentine et al., 2017). This suggested a need to build stronger career preparation and exploration into the program while preserving paid work experience. The school-based model invited SYEP providers to apply to serve specific schools. Principals are involved in selecting their partner and are able to link coursework and other programming to the paid internship opportunities at their school. The growing school-based model of SYEP programming connects nonprofit providers more explicitly to applied and sequential experiences within school, strengthening school connections to work-based learning for traditional high school students. The ecosystem is therefore evolving to support the development of partnerships that enable internships to be used in a coherent school-connected system that includes career pathway exploration and sequential opportunities for youth.

Another key part of work-based learning ecosystems is the employers that create jobs and opportunities for students to learn from and through work. There are many avenues for employers to provide work-based learning experiences to young people, including career-awareness and -exploration activities such as career panels, job shadowing, training, career days, and paid work (NYC Center for Youth Employment, 2019). Ideally these work-based learning opportunities are connected to schools and additional programming so young people are provided with an understanding of a career pathway.

Employers typically include for-profit companies that participate in career awareness, exploration, preparation, and training programs. Successful partnerships are centered on both the needs of young people and of the employer (Renold et al., 2018). In Career and Technical Education, employers are industry partners who provide career exploration and work experiences for young people. This can range from informational interviews to apprenticeship programming where young people are training for industry credentials. Employers additionally can provide externships for teachers for skill development. Apart from CTE partnerships, for-profit employers also provide internships for young people as part of government-sponsored internship programs like New York City's Summer Youth Employment Program. For-profit employers may serve as guest speakers, review student portfolios, or provide internship and job opportunities after training is complete.

One major focus for ExpandED has been to expand the role of nonprofits as employers. Nonprofit jobs are often viewed by workforce professionals as less valuable than for-profit internship placements, whereas the grounding in youth development and equity make them terrific first experiences. Youth-serving organizations can serve as employers that offer groups of teens consultancies to take on projects together. These projects may be designed to solve a community problem, answer a question for an employer, or focus on a particular area of career exploration and development. These opportunities can introduce young people to a workplace and provide examples of what work is. While these project consultancies may be designed by nonprofit employers to encourage young people's development, they mirror how we work. As adults, our days are filled with workplace projects that require problem solving in teams. This type of programming can be training for a work experience or, depending on the outcome, an internship itself. The role of the ecosystem is to support the structure of these challenges to provide social capital and meaningful outcomes.

Nonprofit employers may also hire teens as youth counselors in programs for younger students. In New York City, thousands of teens are employed as summer camp youth counselors each year. These roles are often seen as being merely extra sets of hands; in fact, these programs may help develop presentation, preparation, and management skills. Ecosystem members can advocate for training and reflection that enable young people to develop communication, collaboration, and leadership skills through their roles as youth counselors.

Finally, nonprofits may lead content-specific work-based learning programs directly. For example, the Educational Video Center runs a New Media Arts internship program where students learn digital storytelling skills, how to use industry standard tools such as the Adobe suite, and how to research a community issue.

Ecosystem members can help ensure that all work-based learning opportunities, regardless of funding stream, nonprofit or for-profit employer, or type of high school, enable students to build networks, explore career options, and enhance their durable skills, such as collaboration, problem-solving and communication.

DRIVING EQUITY AND YOUTH-CENTERED WORK-BASED LEARNING

The variety and complexity of actors in high school ecosystems focused on career preparation can be overwhelming. And, because the system is not working toward coherent goals grounded in youth equity, empowerment, and choice, system misalignment can cause historical inequities grounded in race to persist or widen. OST leaders can address these challenges to drive equity and youth-centered redesign in three key ways.

One first step in strengthening an ecosystem is to bridge definitions and create intentional on-ramps for partnership focused on racial equity. ExpandED has hosted a work-based learning coalition focused on trust and exploration to examine common understanding of why parts of the system work the way they do, new policy changes that affect funding or implementation, and to develop common language to describe the importance of a comprehensive, equitable, universal work-based learning agenda for the city. Many people who join coalition meetings represent other coalitions or constituencies, so we are able to work in a distributed system. We have been careful in our communication and advocacy to build trust and cooperation among entities, public and private partners, school staff and nonprofit leaders. We have moved "at the speed of trust," taking time to make sure there is consensus and shared understanding before moving forward. This serves to create opportunities for people to name and confront inequities. For example, the group has noticed racial differences in internship programs for public school students and examined how to make sure high-profile internships don't only go to those who perform at a high academic level.

Second, an emerging role for OST ecosystem leaders is to drive explicit conversations with employers about creating opportunities for inclusion and belonging for young people of color, especially in white-dominated industries. Employers hosting interns are not always ready with the practices and policies needed to embrace a young, diverse workforce. OST leaders can help set expectations, train supervisors, and drive conversations about how corporate racial equity goals might manifest in internship programs. The New York City STEM Education Network, for example, which includes employers, city agencies, funders, STEM-rich institutions, and higher education institutions, has a social justice working group. The group has focused on the ways employers might review and assess hiring practices to create a more diverse STEM workforce.

Finally, one way to add youth-centered expertise is to invite partners into the work-based learning ecosystem that might not describe their work as work-based learning. Youth programming that focuses on building self-awareness and a sense of self help prepare students for success as young adults. Ecosystem leaders can help articulate the value of these organizations and make connections among other ecosystem members. In ecosystem discussions, the inclusion of those who understand their roles to be supporting leadership development and empowerment for young people of color helps ensure all ecosystem members are more aware of the importance of centering youth in work-based learning.

AN ECOSYSTEM AT WORK

How does this all come together? At ExpandED Schools, for example, we lead a nested work-based learning ecosystem through our ExpandED Options internship program. In Options, students participate in a creditworthy course created and facilitated by nonprofit organizations, academics, or cultural institutions. In these courses, teens are taught a skill and how to teach that skill to younger students. Upon successful completion, students are guaranteed a paid summer job where they teach their new skills to younger kids and peers in summer programming. To manage this initiative, ExpandED Schools works closely with city agencies, New York City high schools, community-based organizations, private funders, and cultural institutions.

ExpandED Options began with the belief that students could learn, and in fact were already learning rich academic content during out-of-school hours. Our hypothesis was that if out-of-school learning were connected to the school day, then students would be: 1) able to better connect school-day learnings to potential career pathways and post-secondary opportunities, and 2) more engaged in the school day due to opportunities for applied learning. To prove these theories and increase engagement in learning, we worked with a cohort of partners to create creditworthy courses for high school students that increase professional skills, youth agency, and understanding of post-secondary pathways. A second founding belief of our work is that teens can lead. Each summer, thousands of teens work in New York City summer camps but do not receive the adequate training that would make these meaningful career preparatory experiences. By providing school connected training in areas that were in demand for summer camp, we could increase work-based learning opportunities and have built-in employers. In our model, teens gain credit toward high school graduation, receive a paid job, and practice skills such as communication, collaboration, and problem-solving that are needed for any profession.

To implement this model, ExpandED worked to bridge the gap that exists between K–12 educators, afterschool educators, and workforce systems. As an intermediary, ExpandED worked to understand the needs of all partners to make implementation and collaborative learning possible. Our first step in forming this ecosystem was to understand New York City academic policy and discover how out-of-school programming could be connected to high school academic credit. New York State's academic policy is directed by the state's education department and overseen by New York City's local Department of Education. In NYC, students can receive academic credit for out-of-school time courses that are 54 hours in length, align to NYS educational standards, and are overseen by a subject-certified teacher. To figure out what this looked like in practice we partnered with two schools. Through program planning meetings, we worked to understand what schools needed to see from an offsite provider to be able to grant credit, what information teachers needed to oversee an off-site program, and what structures should be put in place to ensure open communication between partners. Based on these meetings we developed tools to help us scale: We developed a principal letter which explained how our program fits into academic policy, created a program overview template that easily showed a school information it needed to determine credit worthiness, and developed a shared attendance tracking system. We also communicated with the central DOE office of academic policy to ensure that the work we were doing met its policy requirements. Understanding academic policy on paper and in practice allowed us to create mechanisms that fit the needs of school partners and the requirements of the DOE.

To translate our understanding of school needs to the afterschool space, we worked with nonprofit partner organizations to create a syllabus and curriculum for each course that showed alignment with academic policy. We provided grants to create programming that was creditworthy in a subject area where their organization had expertise. ExpandED worked with partners to ensure that programming was connected to a career pathway, supported students' social and emotional needs, and featured youth-driven project-based learning. To ensure that the off-site courses were rigorous, programs had to be set up in a way that allowed teens to be prepared to facilitate instruction over the summer. Initially, we selected partners who specialized in visual and media arts, engineering, and cooking. The organizations that offer these credit-worthy courses are connected to schools that recruit students and oversee the awarding of credit. The providers are part of a formal learning community that encourages feedback among partners and gives partners support in creating activities that align to the needs of both schools and employers.

In ExpandED Options, our employers are youth-serving organizations who run summer programming. We worked with these organizations to understand how our program could meet their staffing needs. For example, our goal was to maximize the number of employment hours for teens. However, summer camps could not structure their programming so that teens could teach for the entirety of their 25 paid hours each week. Through initial conversations and an open feedback loop, we agreed that teens should be scheduled to teach for half of their time at a summer camp. With the remainder of their time, teens could participate in professional development, assist as general counselors, or support camp operations. The openness to joint program development allowed us to create a complex program model that serves multiple needs with quality programming for young people.

This model has proven successful due to our willingness to engage new partners and our openness to flexibility. For example, our understanding of the needs of school partners has evolved since we began to implement ExpandED Options. In its pilot year, we worked with a small cohort of three schools and discussed their needs in planning meetings. This informed how we structured school supports. While in early years we gave schools documents needed to create courses, we discovered that schools also needed support with translating the documents to their record keeping systems. This led to a reevaluation of school supports to include details for how schools should code courses in their record-keeping systems and how to enter student attendance. In our role as an intermediary, ExpandED Schools was able to take policy from the New York City Department of Education and give schools examples of how to make this policy a practice. Additionally, ExpandED Schools assisted schools by creating a guide and suggesting expectations for how teachers can oversee an out-of-school time course.

Our work with apprenticeship and internship providers has also evolved. Providers co-developed an assessment rubric that enables them to specify durable skills they expect participants to develop, such as collaboration, communication and problem-solving, along with content-specific skills. We have also added gardening, app development, culinary arts, and other activities of interest to teens. And for our internships, we broadened the idea of teaching experiences to include opportunities for our students to guide their peers through similar learning journeys.

The result is a program that connects applied learning to students' transcripts, ensuring credit and an explicit connection between practicing professional skills and high school. Teens test out an area of passion, have a guaranteed paid summer job, and build leadership skills. Many realize they would like to work with children; others realize they definitely do not. This exploration and discovery is at the heart of good work-based learning and youth-development programming.

While ExpandED Options is a model that can scale to serve thousands of teens a year, it cannot scale to the entire NYC school system. This model is rooted in the idea that teens can and are willing to teach; this does not fit the needs and wants of all teens. However, the lessons learned from ExpandED Options can be scaled to multiple work-based learning initiatives. We have intentionally shared our lessons with others in order to connect OST and other activities that build professional skills to credit accumulation and partnership with traditional high schools. For example, we are offering an open course for others to learn about awarding credit and have shared our guide with them and with leaders at the DOE who have found it a helpful summary of the DOE's policies. And, we are working with providers across the learning ecosystem calling for universal summer employment that offers a variety of work-based learning opportunities from which young people can choose.

ECOSYSTEMS MEETING EMERGENT NEEDS

Nurturing ExpandED Options has helped us to build trust with schools, city policymakers, multiservice youth-serving organizations, content-focused youth organizations, advocates, and others. When the City's summer internship program was canceled by the City in April of 2020, as the COVID-19 pandemic was raging through New York, we were able to convene organizations remotely to develop a new fully remote program design for summer 2020 and build a strong advocacy strategy in partnership with youth advocates and other policy intermediaries. We raised more than $2 million in private funds in a few months to support new work-based learning designs and fund new roles for nonprofits to lead content-focused project-based learning that would build career skills and engage teens socially and emotionally. New York City restored $52 million for the program at the end of June and the program launched on July 28th for 35,000 young people. This radical change and implementation would have been impossible without a strong and flexible ecosystem to adapt, work with one another, and retool opportunities for young people in just a few months. Additional evaluation documents are forthcoming at yes2020.nyc and www.expandedschools.org, and we invite those interested to explore those findings and deeper description.

LESSONS

We have nurtured our work-based learning ecosystem based on existing OST structures and relationships within New York City, and we recognize that ecosystems are sensitive to local context and relationships. Nonetheless, we believe there are common lessons, and offer the following with the hope that they might be useful for others and for our own future work.

1.   Clear understanding of individual and mutual goals helps build trust and clarity that boost quality.

We hold quarterly convenings of ExpandED Options partners with explicit discussion of our mutual goals, and how these goals can fit into the work of our partner organizations. Early on in our program development, this helped us each see the strains on various partners and find shared purpose despite these strains. Any changes we made to our expectations were framed in potential benefits to the field and shared purpose with understanding of individual pressures. In later years, this has helped us become a learning community where partners could learn practices to meet these shared goals.

Similarly, when we reached out to school leaders to participate, we spoke directly about our goals and offered what we hoped were mutual goals. We then asked for specific goals the leader had for his or her school. There was variation among school leaders in what they named as goals. Some prioritized meeting graduation requirements, some wanted to see career skill development in students at their school, while others wanted an internship program in order to make their school appealing to prospective students. Knowing these priorities helped us find common ground while still remaining mindful of what brought that school leader to participate in the ecosystem.

More recently, as schools and OST providers responded to abrupt school closures as the COVID-19 pandemic swept New York, we observed that schools and community partners with strong relationships leaned on each other to meet student and family needs more effectively. The stronger partnership enabled leaders to focus on shared goals and to act flexibly to meet them. School leaders and OST site directors reacted in a coordinated way to support the social, emotional, and academic needs of their students, such as calling families to check in on how remote learning was going, arranging technology distribution, setting up homework clinics, and offering remote enrichment clubs to reconnect young people to mentors and to one another. It is clear that these partnerships matter.

2.   Measurement should be done in ways that build trust.

One of the areas where trust and shared purpose can be eroded is in measurement of joint enterprise that may undermine the sense of shared goals. Evaluation methods that prioritize a shared goal may inadvertently seem to deprioritize individual goals. For example, a school leader that is held accountable to meeting graduation requirements and is therefore focused on ensuring that students accumulate credits may feel that an evaluation that focuses on student engagement undermines her concerns. We found that remaining loose on evaluation requirements and focusing on continuous improvement and partnership development created the most trust, which empowered partners to push each other to adapt to meet outcomes more effectively.

We created an assessment rubric that had five expectations for skill development for young people (Collaboration and Teamwork, Communication, Critical Thinking and Decision Making, Initiative and Self-Direction, and Workplace Readiness), followed by empty rows that partners could fill out together. They then worked together to write descriptions of what full or partial development looks like so that each organization could assess students based on their needs.

3.   Flexible funding gives ecosystem relationships time to grow.

Within a dynamic ecosystem, partnerships formed at their own speeds, and we were adaptable. Ecosystem members were fair with each other about where each other was. To create a space that shows how our hypothesis of ExpandED Options can be scaled up, we created funding mechanisms that were built on the importance of partnership. ExpandED built a network of work-based learning providers by providing flexible funding and a commitment to building buy-in from partners. Funding for apprenticeship partners in the ExpandED Options network is not tied to the number of students who complete the program or who are placed into internships; funding decisions are based on partners' participation in the learning community, capacity to create programming, willingness to adapt programming, and connection to each organization's mission. This nonpunitive approach to funding gave partners room to grow and buy into the program model. Our work is not possible without our partners, so the terms of our partnerships were developed with the needs of both ExpandED Schools and apprenticeship providers in mind.

At times, we have discontinued funding to a partner. In these cases, no one has been surprised or pushed back. We have reflected and realized that we might have stopped funding the partnership sooner, but we realize that the additional time is worth it to build change within practitioners over the long term. In one case, we had a member of our collective leave and return when their own work shifted and was more aligned to collective goals.

4.   Ecosystems loosely define entities working together and can be part of larger ecosystems.

Ecosystems are embedded in larger networks. Our work-based learning efforts have touched the STEM Education Network, networks of schools, employer associations, and content-focused networks. While this may be particularly true in large cities, given their size and complexity, we believe it's true everywhere. Taking time to define local connections may lead to positive outcomes, such as mutual support and collaboration. Multiple organizations may serve as nodes, connecting areas of the larger ecosystem; the more explicit this can be, the better.

5.   It is important to support intermediary functions for high school learning ecosystems.

Building quality standards, advocating for systemwide policy changes, and supporting collaboration and problem-solving across this dynamic and complex system takes investment and leadership. These functions may be carried out by multiple organizations. It is important to be clear about the roles an entity is taking on and to build buy-in and trust to avoid confusion or a sense of competition that can derail youth-centered design and collaboration.

CONCLUSION

The devastating economic effects of the COVID-19 pandemic for communities hardest hit by death and job loss—communities with predominantly people of color—should ignite our collective passion to lead ecosystems focused on high school students. OST can lead the way in developing the dynamic and effective ecosystems that develop young people's abilities. Those abilities will lead us in the decades to come. Young people will build our nation's resilience to withstand new crises, ensure our prosperity, and drive racial equity in our schools, workplaces, and communities. We hope that the description and lessons from our work to build OST ecosystems in New York City to further work-based learning inspires action. We invite you to reach out as you further develop local ecosystems and look forward to seeing growth in these important partnerships throughout the country.

REFERENCES

Advance CTE. (2018). *Perkins Side-by-Side.* Federal Policy Strengthening Career and Technical Education for the 21st Century Act. https://cte.careertech.org/sites/default/files/PerkinsV_Side-by-Side_Draft_Updated101618.pdf.

Kreisman, D., & Stange, K. (2017, September). *Vocational and career tech education in American high schools: The value of depth over breadth.* NBER Working Paper Series. https://www.nber.org/system/files/working_papers/w23851/w23851.pdf

Nagaoka, J., Farrington, C. A., Ehrlich, S., & Heath, R. D. (2015). *Foundations for young adult success: A developmental framework.* UChicago Consortium on School Research.

National Center for Education Statistics. (n.d.). *About CTE statistics.* https://nces.ed.gov/surveys/ctes/about.asp#:~:text=on%20trade%20schools%3F-,What%20is%20CTE%3F,jobs%20or%20fields%20of%20work.

New York State Education Department. (2019). *CDOS pathway to a Regents or local diploma. Curriculum instruction.* http://www.nysed.gov/curriculum-instruction/cdos-pathway-regents-or-local-diploma.

New York State Education Department. (2020). *CTE: Program approval process.* http://www.p12.nysed.gov/cte/ctepolicy/.

NYC Center for Youth Employment. (2019). *Employer engagement: Ways to help NYC build tomorrow's workplace.* https://cye.cityofnewyork.us/wp-content/uploads/2019/07/CareerReady-NYC-Employer-Engagement-Menu.pdf.

Reisner, E. R., White, R. N., Russell, C. A., & Birmingham, J. (2004). *Building quality, scale and effectiveness in after-school programs.* Policy Studies Associates.

Renold, U., Bolli, T., Caves, K., Bürgi, J., Egg, M. E., Kemper, J., & Rageth, L. (2018). *Comparing international vocational education and training programs: The KOF education-employment linkage index.* National Center on Education and the Economy.

Traphagen, K., & Traill, S. (2014). *Advancing STEM learning through collaboration: STEM learning ecosystems report.* The Noyce Foundation.

Treschan, L., & Mehrotra, A. (2014, February). *Challenging traditional expectations: How New York City's CTE high schools are helping students graduate.* Community Service Society. https://smhttp-ssl-58547.nexcesscdn.net/nycss/images/uploads/pubs/CSS_CTE_Print.pdf

U.S. Department of Education, Office of Career, Technical, and Adult Education. (2016). *Carl D. Perkins Career and Technical Education Act of 2006, Report to Congress*

on *State Performance, Program Year 2013–14.* https://s3.amazonaws.com/PCRN/
uploads/Perkins_RTC_2013-14.pdf
Valentine, E. J., Anderson, C., Hossain, F., & Unterman. R. (2017, April). *An Introduction
to the world of work a study of the implementation and impacts of New York City's
Summer Youth Employment Program.* MDRC. https://www.mdrc.org/sites/default/
files/SYEP_Embedded_Full_Report_508_rev2.pdf

CHAPTER 15

EXPANDED LEARNING AS A VEHICLE TO ADVANCE WHOLE-CHILD, WHOLE-FAMILY HEALTH AND WELLNESS

Jeff Davis

Out-of-school time (OST) learning and enrichment opportunities are guided by the principles of positive youth development, create positive developmental and health outcomes, and are a bridge between schools, families, and communities. A growing movement seeks to promote multi-sector and agency collaboration that aligns diverse resources to create ecosystems of support for whole children, whole families, and whole communities. California funds and maintains the largest publicly funded system of OST programs, referred to as Expanded Learning programs,[1] implemented by grantees of the state funded After School Educa-

---

[1] Expanded Learning refers to before and after school, summer, and intersession learning experiences that develop the academic, social, emotional, and physical needs and interests of students. Expanded Learning opportunities should be hands-on, engaging, student-centered, results-driven, involve community partners, and complement learning activities in the regular school day/year (California Department of Education, 2018a. p. 7, 2020a). Since the original submission of this chapter, California has significantly increased investments in Expanded Learning in addition to the ASES and 21st CCLC programs described. This includes a one-time investment of $4.6 billion into Expanded Learning Opportunity Grants and a budget allocation of $1.75 billion in the 21–22 school year which is expected to grow to $5 billion in the next 3–5 years.

---

tion and Safety (ASES) program and federally funded 21st Century Community Learning Centers (21st CCLC) program. This chapter utilizes the term Expanded Learning throughout, but the concepts discussed apply broadly to other OST programs not technically defined as Expanded Learning programs. In California, the Whole Child Health and Wellness Collaborative (WCHWC) including stakeholders from health, mental health, substance use intervention, nutrition, education, expanded learning, and child/family advocacy seeks to promote whole child, family, and community wellness through multi-sector partnerships with California's Expanded Learning programs. This chapter explains how California's WCHWC created multi-sector strategies outlined in a *Statement of Strategic Direction Toward Equity-Driven Whole Child Health and Wellness*[2] (WCHWC, 2021a). This statement offers guidelines for states and local communities to center the needs of youth and families, support and nurture an allied adult workforce, and leverage new and existing resources through collaboration across systems to promote whole child, whole family, and whole community wellness.

EXPANDED LEARNING IN CALIFORNIA

Economic, racial, and other forms of inequity have resulted in disparities in educational, health, and well-being outcomes and disparate challenges for low-income working families. This problem is exacerbated by lack of access to high-quality expanded learning and enrichment opportunities (Afterschool Alliance, 2020; Putnam et al., 2012). In 2002, California voter's approved Proposition 49 which created an annual ongoing appropriation for Expanded Learning programs once certain fiscal conditions were met in the state. Those conditions were met in the 2006-07 school year, resulting in a rapid expansion of Expanded Learning programs for the schools, families, and communities that need it most.

In California over 4,500 Expanded Learning program sites (see Figure 15.1) have the capacity to serve nearly 443,000 students each day and serve over 980,000 students annually (Williams, 2019, p. 5). On average, schools with Expanded Learning programs have over 75% of their students eligible for free or reduced-price meals and more than double the percentage of English Learners than schools without programs. Expanded Learning programs serve over 80% of California's low-income elementary and middle schools. In 2016–17 (the most recent data available), California's Expanded Learning programs served over 13,000 migrant students, over 89,000 special education students, and over 11,000 students in foster care. The nearly 38,000 students experiencing homelessness served by California's Expanded Learning programs represent 25% of the state's students experiencing homelessness. Additionally, the California Department of Education found (2018c), "as intended, schools that receive [Expanded Learning] funding predominantly serve economically disadvantaged students and students

---

[2] Sections of this chapter are adapted from the WCHWC (2021a,b) report in order to describe both the context and the result of this ongoing effort.

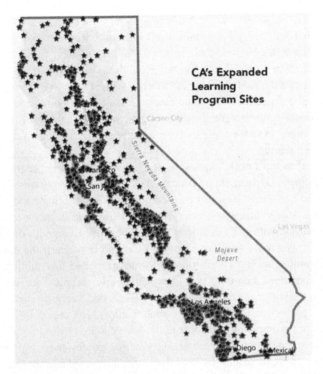

FIGURE 15.1.   ASES and 21st CCLC Expanded Learning Program Sites in California Originally published in Whole Children Health and Wellness Collaborative (2021b).

of color" (p. 2). California's Expanded Learning programs are well-positioned to foster positive youth development outcomes for the children, youth, families, schools, and communities that have been most impacted by inequity and systemic oppression.

EXPANDED LEARNING PROGRAMS GENERATE CONDITIONS THAT SUPPORT HEALTHY DEVELOPMENT

In 2004, Bonnie Benard authored *Resiliency: What We Have Learned,* a comprehensive review of research on human development which defines resilience as, "a capacity all youth have for healthy development and successful learning" (p. 4). Benard outlined that "certain characteristics of families, schools, and communities are associated with the development of personal strengths, and in turn, healthy development and successful learning" (p. 4). These characteristics, or "protective factors" (p. 43) include caring relationships, high expectations, and opportunities for participation and contribution. The presence of protective factors results in the development of personal strengths including social competence, problem solving, autonomy, and sense of purpose and result in long-term positive developmental outcomes. Benard highlighted that the benefits of protective factors outweigh specific risk factors or stressful life events for children who grow up under adverse conditions (Benard, 2004; Werner & Smith, 1992). Protective factors (or their absence) can be experienced in home/family, school, community, and peer group settings. Therefore, the people in these settings and the qualities of the relationships experienced in these contexts have a significant influence on the development of young people.

During California's rapid expansion of Expanded Learning programs (2006–07), the California Department of Education's After School Programs Office (now the Expanded Learning Division) partnered with Bonnie Benard and WestEd to launch a *You Matter* train-the-trainer series to build field capacity to create the kinds of environments and conditions that support positive youth development. Trainers were convened in every region of California to learn the content of a three-part training series. These trainers in-turn provided the training series to their local Expanded Learning providers. This early technical assistance effort would leave a lasting imprint on California's Expanded Learning system.

Benard's protective factors (caring relationships, high expectations, and opportunities for participation and contribution) were integrated into quality frameworks, assessment tools, and promising practice guides used by California's Expanded Learning programs. In 2014 they were integrated into the Quality Standards for Expanded Learning in California (California Department of Education and California Afterschool Network, 2014), which describe high-quality Expanded Learning programs as *safe and supportive environments* facilitating *active and engaged learning* and *skill building* supporting *youth voice and leadership* and *healthy choices and behaviors* in an environment that embraces *diversity, access, and equity* (p. 6). Positive youth development principles are baked into the DNA of Expanded Learning programs.

Data gathered in California by the California Healthy Kids Survey (WestEd, 2021) assesses the presence of protective factors for children and youth in fifth, seventh, ninth, and eleventh grades. One distinction is that the CHKS describes Benard's the protective factor *opportunities for participation and contribution* as, *opportunities for meaningful participation and decision-making* (WestEd, 2021). A recent analysis conducted by Austin et al. (2021) compared results for students who regularly attend afterschool programs in schools that operate Expanded Learning programs with those who did not regularly attend afterschool programs.[3] "Overall, the results support that California's afterschool programs that participated in this analysis are creating environments rich in all three developmental supports, which both contribute to preventing risk behaviors and lead to a wide range of positive outcomes" (p. 13). Students who regularly attended

[3] the survey used the term afterschool as opposed to Expanded Learning

afterschool programs experienced higher rates of all protective factors, with the most dramatic differences related to opportunities for meaningful participation. "This finding is not surprising given that major goals of many afterschool programs include providing engaging activities and giving student voice. This strong effect is also especially noteworthy, as low levels of meaningful participation has been a consistent finding in the California Healthy Kids Survey" (p. 13). Significant differences were also found in school connectedness for all age groups, particularly high school students. High school students participating in Expanded Learning programs also indicated higher levels of family involvement in school, and perceptions of the school as safe.

A growing body of research, referred to as the Science of Learning and Development (SoLD), continues to parallel Benard's analysis and have similar implications for educators and youth serving organizations (Science of Learning and Development [SoLD] Alliance, 2020). SoLD highlights the malleability and resilience of the human brain and emphasizes the importance of context and environment as *the* defining influence on development. A recent publication from the American Institutes for Research (2019) highlights that, "The SoLD work emphasizes many of the same elements that we know are central to high-quality after school" (p. 3).

Much of this research and its implications are summarized by a 2019 report from the National Commission on Social, Emotional, and Academic Development (SEAD Commission) titled, *From A Nation At-risk to A Nation at Hope* (Aspen Commission on Social, Emotional, and Academic Development, 2019). The SEAD Commission acknowledged the impact that context has on learning and development (including home, school, Expanded Learning programs, and community/peer environments, etc.). The commission outlined that safe, relationship-based, equitable settings, rich with a sense of belonging and engagement ownership and purpose create a foundation for cognitive, social, and emotional skill building resulting in positive long-term outcomes. The types of learning settings and experiences outlined by the SEAD commission to promote positive long-term developmental outcomes are consistent with Benard's protective factors and the features of high-quality Expanded Learning programs. Expanded Learning programs, by design, positively influence the healthy development of young people.

A HUB OF COMMUNITY RESILIENCE: EXPANDED LEARNING RESPONDS TO CRISIS

In "normal" times, Expanded Learning programs address opportunity gaps by providing a wide range of supports to under-served communities. They address food insecurity by providing meals and snacks (Williams, 2019); they increase positive social behaviors and self-perception (Durlak & Weissberg, 2010), school attendance (California Department of Education, 2018c), school bonding, and academic achievement (Pierce et al., 2013) by fostering a positive relationship-rich environment and meaningful learning and enrichment opportunities. California's Expanded Learning workforce of over 30,000 professionals (Opportunity Institute

& Partnership for Children and Youth, 2020) supports the broader workforce by helping working parents remain productive at work (Afterschool Alliance, 2020) while their children are safe and engaged during important hours to promote child and youth safety, 2pm—6pm (Council for a Strong America, 2019). Expanded Learning programs and opportunities are vital supports in good times. They are critical supports in crisis.

Expanded Learning programs have helped children, families, and communities navigate crises including wildfires and the COVID-19 pandemic. During the CO-VID-19 pandemic, Expanded Learning programs and staff located hard-to-find students and families; ensured students and families had access to food, technology, academic support, enrichment opportunities, and social and emotional supports (Williams, 2020). California's Expanded Learning programs increased administrative flexibility to broaden supports for high-need communities and critical infrastructure workers.

As we reconvene in schools and workplaces, Expanded Learning programs and opportunities will continue to be an essential asset. *Stronger Together: A Guidebook for the Safe Reopening of California's Public Schools* (California Department of Education, 2021) urges partnerships with Expanded Learning programs and describes them as a, "resource not only to complement academic skill-building, but more importantly, specialize in building positive relationships with young people and their families" (p. 27). This at a time when education, community, and state leaders are promoting coordinated efforts across sectors to support the whole child (American Institutes for Research, 2020; CASEL, 2020). The critical role Expanded Learning programs will play to support California's recovery is further illuminated through increased investment in Expanded Learning opportunities in California's budget (Fensterwald, 2021) and the Elementary and Secondary School Emergency Relief (ESSER) Fund included in the federal American Rescue Plan.

CALIFORNIA'S WHOLE CHILD HEALTH AND WELLNESS COLLABORATIVE: ADVANCING A MULTI-SECTOR VISION TOWARD EQUITY-DRIVEN WHOLE CHILD HEALTH AND WELLNESS

Recommendations to align school and community resources in support of the whole child are not only borne out of crisis. The Partnership for the Future of Learning (2019) highlighted the importance of Community School efforts that "take a 'whole-child' approach to supporting students' life success…(and) provide and coordinate a range of on-site services and supports" (p. 29) including expanded and enriched learning time. National Commission on Social, Emotional, and Academic Development (2019) recommends aligning resources and leveraging community partners in support of the whole child and ensuring each child has access to quality after school and summer learning opportunities. Additionally, the recent publication, *Thriving, Robust Equity, and Transformative Learning &*

Development: A More Powerful Conceptualization of the Contributors to Youth Success (Osher et al., 2020), describe learning and development ecosystems that promote transformational learning with intentional strategies to counter inequities (referred to as robust equity) across multiple domains.

In California, there is an opportunity to advance this powerful vision of learning and development ecosystems. Multiple state leaders, and state and local agencies, including the Governor's office (Amarji VRP, 2018; Fendsterwald, 2020), the State Superintendent of Public Instruction (California Department of Education, 2020b; Williams, 2019), California's Surgeon General (Zeitner, 2019), and the Mental Health Services Oversight and Accountability Commission (MH-SOAC, 2020) share a vision of school and community partnerships to support equitable whole child health and wellness. California's *Social and Emotional Learning Guiding Principles* (California Department of Education, 2018b) include, "adopt whole child development as the goal of education, commit to equity, build capacity, partner with families and communities, and learn and improve" (p. 1). The California Children's Trust (2020) has surfaced California's investment in Expanded Learning as a potential match to leverage Medicaid funding to sustain whole child health and wellness efforts. California's system of Expanded Learning programs is well-positioned as a critical partner to advance this shared national and statewide vision.

In December 2019, the California AfterSchool Network (CAN) convened over 120 multi-sector stakeholders to launch the WCHWC (n.d.) with support from a planning grant from the Youth Opioid Response California Program. The inaugural convening was informed by collaborative supporters from health, mental health, substance misuse intervention and treatment, social services, nutrition, education, Expanded Learning, community youth development, and child & family advocacy organizations (Collaborative Supporters, n.d.). Participants learned and reflected about the opportunity in California to leverage cross-sector partnerships with California's Expanded Learning programs to advance child, youth, family, and community wellness (see Figure 15.2).

During the launch, "the seeds were sown to create a movement to link policymakers, practitioners, funders, educators, families, and youth to create equitable and just whole child health and wellness systems in partnership with California's Expanded Learning programs" (CAN, 2019, p. 1). The convening informed diverse stakeholders of the whole child health and wellness opportunity and engaged them in processes to surface and inform priority focus areas for Whole Child Health and Wellness planning work.

Throughout the convening, participants informed and ultimately approved the following draft vision to guide the ongoing efforts of the Collaborative:

> The roots of whole child health and wellness are founded in equitable and just relationships between people and systems. We envision compassionate communities and networks where each and every child is well known, well cared for, and well prepared to thrive. California's Expanded Learning sites serve as vibrant nodes in

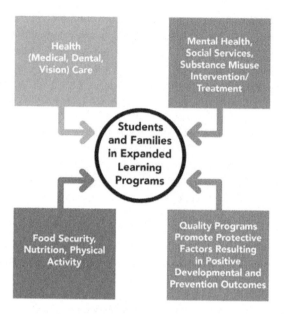

FIGURE 15.2. The Opportunity Presented to the Whole Child Health and Wellness Collaborative.
Originally published in Whole Children Health and Wellness Collaborative (2021b).

these networks ensuring quality care and support for the whole child, whole family, and whole community. As a result, California sees positive mental and physical health outcomes for youth and families and a reduction in substance/opioid misuse and addiction (CAN, 2019 p. 1).

Collaborative Supporters were invited to join a planning process that would culminate with the creation of a *Statement of Strategic Direction Toward Equity-Driven Whole Child Health and Wellness* released in March 2021 (WCHWC, 2021a).

Shortly after the initial convening, over 90 work group members and co-chairs collaborated to create strategies for priority areas surfaced during the original convening including focus on children and families; support and nurture the adult workforce; leverage new and existing resources; and collaborate across systems. Based on the guidance garnered during the launch, two cross-cutting work groups were created that included the advancing equity, healing, and mindset shift; and the strong narrative work groups. Members of these two groups would work across the four other work groups to ensure the collective work focused on equity and healing from prior injustice with a cohesive narrative and consistent voice across work groups.

The following months would test and sharpen the resolve of the Collaborative and its members. Shortly after work groups were solidified, the COVID-19 crisis magnified the social, health, economic, and racial inequities present in our society. These inequities were further magnified by acts of police and citizen violence against Black Americans, and the social unrest that followed. The WCHWC determined that their vision and purpose was more important than ever. It was also clear that this new context required additional reflection. The Collaborative was able to leverage an existing partnership between CAN and Equity Meets Design (https://equitymeetsdesign.com) to conduct an equity pause. Equity Meets design describes the rationale for an *equity pause* as follows:

> A sense of urgency can mask hegemonic strategy. Our common discourse of urgency and business-as-usual creates little time for reflection; our pace of life eclipses our awareness. Strategic equity pauses stop the clock to reflect on our language, ideas, and hunches in the context of a discourse of transformation. Without this moment to think, our brains default to the familiar and the known, making a repeat of past practice likely. Incorporating these discourse checks and pauses after each stage ensures that our ideas remain on the path of achieving equity. (equityXdesign, 2016, Equity Pauses section).

Over a two-day period, over 50 of the 90 work group members participated in an exploration of what it would mean to apply equity design principles (equityXdesign, 2016) into our processes and work products. This experience allowed the Collaborative to develop a common frame that, "advancing equity and racial justice are not something for us to do as part of our work... Equity is the work. To create equity and justice... we need to see equity and justice as verbs (WCHWC, 2021a, p. 10)." This critical step helped the Collaborative realize that it was not enough to create another plan to incrementally shift inequitable systems, the Collaborative needed to imagine something new. They describe the urgency to address pervasive inequities in the opening section of their *Statement of Strategic Direction Toward Whole Child Health and Wellness* titled *Whole Child Health and Wellness, Now is the Time.*

This is the Moment to Dream, Design, and Deliver Something Very New....

In spite of the growing recognition of the need for new ways to deliver whole child health and wellness, we recognized at the outset of our work that our society has long been plagued by policies rooted in white supremacy as well as environmental, economic, and racial injustice, and systemic oppression. As a result, too many children and families face inequitable access to opportunities, health care, mental health services, social services, healthy food, and safe, equitable places to learn and play...

...But California lacks a coherent and overarching statewide equity and racial justice strategy. So, we presented ourselves with this **challenge: Address the systemic conditions that create significant health and wellness disparities and prevent California's families and their children from reaching their full potential"** (WCHWC, 2021a p. 7).

With this new framing, the Collaborative continued to develop and refine its Vision, Mission, Call to Action, and Shared Equity Strategies that would inform the work going forward.

A CALL TO ACTION

Building from our work with Equity Meets Design, the *Statement of Strategic Direction Towards Equity-Driven Whole Child Health and Wellness* (WCHWC, 2021a) begins with a call for a statewide equity pause. Along with this call for an equity pause, the WCHWC created a framework for planning and implementation along with shared equity strategies that can be adapted for state agencies, and local communities (see Figure 15.3).

SHARED EQUITY STRATEGIES

The Collaborative referred to their co-created strategies as shared equity strategies to ensure equity was at the core of their recommendations. *Shared Equity Strategies* are defined as, "Actions or policies that acknowledge the multi-sector collaboration to ensure that every child, and particularly those from vulnerable student groups, is guaranteed the culturally appropriate and linguistically accessible supports and resources needed to succeed in school and thrive" (p. 29). The

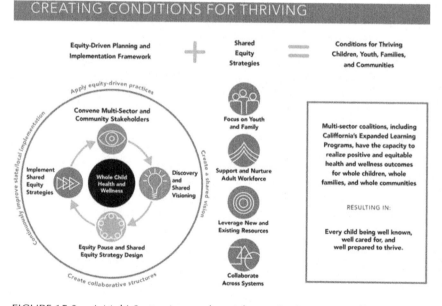

FIGURE 15.3. A Multi-Sector Approach to Advance Equity-Driven Whole Child Health and Wellness
Originally published in Whole Children Health and Wellness Collaborative (2021b).

TABLE 15.1. Examples of How the Shared Equity Strategies are Defined

What is the Strategy? (What Will Happen?)	How Might We Know That the Strategy Results in Equity-Driven Whole Child Health and Wellness?
Focus on Youth and Family	
Leverage community agencies such as Expanded Learning Programs to engage youth and families in processes to assess the assets, challenges, and needs of their communities and engage in the decision-making process on how such needs are addressed, including decisions related to their own case management.	Youth and families at the margins are engaged in collaborative efforts with host organizations. Processes, practices and procedures intentionally collect meaningful information from families.
Support and Nurture the Adult Workforce	
Invest in building allied youth workforce career pathways, education, and skills training, to strengthen the adults who provide services to promote whole child health and wellness, thereby recognizing the dignity of allied youth workers.	Allied youth workers receive higher wages, following a clear wage progression that is aligned with formal and informal education, skill development, and experience. Increased allied workforce engagement and continuity results in increased program quality and the associated positive developmental outcomes.
Leverage New and Existing Resources	
Support proven Community Schools models, including the identification and training of local coordinators, building their capacity to develop a "village" response, tapping into local resources and experts.	Mobilization of local resources in support of accessible and integrated service delivery, especially for those at the margins.
Collaborate Across Systems	
Network the System of Support for Expanded Learning, and the California System of Support with other County agencies as a nexus of collaboration because, "they (Counties) are well-positioned to form cross-sector partnerships that efficiently integrate a comprehensive suite of services in local schools... through Multi- Tiered System of Support (MTSS) and a Coordination of Services Team (COST)" (Learning Policy Institute, 2020)	Partnering County Collaboratives with Expanded Learning programs creates governmental and community-based partnerships to leverage the assets and address the needs of communities. The combined system of support leverages multiple systems and networks them with a variety of other human service agencies with aligned goals.

Excerpted from Whole Children Health and Wellness Collaborative (2021a)

recommended strategies apply for all sectors that make up the allied youth workforce defined as, "Adults who comprise the paid workforce and are employed to labor in contribution to whole child health and wellness across sectors" (p. 29). The strategies also apply to a broad range of stakeholders from the state, regional, and local levels and are outlined in detail in the *Statement of Strategic Direction*.

Overall, there were four shared equity strategies identified: 1) focus on youth and family, 2) support and nurture the adult workforce, 3) leverage new and existing resources, and 4) collaborate across systems (WCHWC, 2021a). Examples of how each of the four shared equity strategies are defined can be found in Table 15.1. The *Statement of Strategic Direction* (WCHWC, 2021a) and its associated appendices contain more detailed recommendations for stakeholders from the allied youth workforce to participate in each strategy.

A CALL FOR EVERYONE

The WCHWC recommends that, "Action should be taken immediately by all public and private sector organizations to advance the whole child health and wellness agenda outlined by this *Statement of Strategic Direction*" (2021a, p. 22). The Collaborative outlined actions that can be taken by a variety of stakeholders (see Table 15.2) to advance whole child health and wellness.

PROMISING PRACTICES AND LESSONS LEARNED

Convening the WCHWC yielded multiple lessons and promising practices. The Collaborative was established by a convening organization (CAN) who partnered with a neutral facilitator (The Glen Price Group) to promote authentic stakeholder engagement without attachment to particular outcomes or specific organizational agendas. The focus was on creating a vision that could be shared across sectors. CAN is a network with the motto, "of the field, for the field." As a network, CAN

TABLE 15.2. Recommended Actions for Key Actors and Sectors

Actor/Sector	Recommended Action
Convener	Using foundational equity practices (e.g., liberatory design), convene and facilitate design cycles that build capacity and community. Use data-driven practices as part of continuous improvement cycles to move, reflect upon, and advance the work.
Community	Activate, engage, inform, co-create and co-design strategies for change.
Intermediaries and Community Based Organizations	Lead equity processes and map systems, both internally within their organizations, and across multi-sector initiatives.
Local Government and Local Educational Agencies	Reorient local priorities to support effective supports for populations at the margins, as defined by those margins.
Philanthropy	Provide catalytic investments and other resources in support of statewide equity pausing, mapping, and further development of support systems for this work.
State Government	Incent equity pauses, collaboration, and the de-siloing of state investments and supports for California's children, families and communities.

Excerpted from Whole Children Health and Wellness Collaborative (2021a, p. 21)

applied the network principles documented by Wei-Skillern and Silver (2013) of *mission, not organization, trust, not control, humility, not brand,* and *constellation, not stars.* The Collaborative also embraced Wheatley and Frieze's (2011) notion of moving from "hero to host" which describes a shift from leading from a position of knowing toward trusting the community and creating effective processes for collaboration for them to develop and own their own shared strategies. Stakeholders of multiple fields were positioned to lead and participate in working groups and work group leaders and members were regularly convened to reflect on progress and offer insights to strengthen the process and products of the Collaborative.

The facilitation of the collaborative process was also structured to acknowledge each participant as a human being navigating a challenging context. One of the agreements established by the group in this context was, *Grace for how and when we commit. We are all doing the best we can with what we have.* Participants were honored for whatever contribution they could make to the evolving process. Meetings were designed to begin with mindfulness and self-care, individual reflection, and intentional community building. Because the work we were trying to promote was grounded in supportive and trusting relationships, it was important to reflect these principles in the convenings of the Collaborative.

Part of the Collaborative's efforts was to reflect and continuously improve. It was clear the evolving 2020 context called for an increased focus on equity. The equity pause that the Collaborative employed to strengthen this focus was important to the process and the product created. This allowed the group to see themselves as designers and apply equity design principles directly to facilitated processes and work products. This pause was not originally planned but proved to be a critical step.

WHERE DO WE GO FROM HERE?

The Whole Child Health and Wellness Collaborative has created a powerful vision, a call to action, and a collection of shared equity strategies, but our vision is far from being achieved. The next phase of this work will seek to increase knowledge and awareness; seed local implementation efforts; build capacity of the allied youth fields, and advocate for the policy conditions that will support and sustain the work.

A first step focuses on building the capacity of the Expanded Learning and allied youth workforce. The Expanded Learning 360-365 Alliance (http://www.expandedlearning360-365.com) is a coalition of five California-based intermediaries (including CAN) supporting the whole child, all year long. The Alliance is creating a technical assistance process and delivery system to enhance allied youth workforce capacity to promote positive youth development, social emotional learning, the science of learning and development, trauma-informed approaches, equity-driven practices and anti-racism, multi-sector partnerships, and safe practices to address the COVID-19 context. CAN continues to broadly promote the Collaborative's vision and support community implementation efforts.

Recommendations from researchers, leaders, and experts from around the country have called for new policies and funding structures that do not currently exist (Osher et al., 2020; SoLD Alliance, 2020; WCHWC, 2021a). The National Commission on Social, Emotional, and Academic Development (2019) highlighted the need for a shift in policies and practices to allow for the flexible allocation of staff time and the braiding of resources because, "too often, resources are not aligned and do not operate in coherent fashion because of multiple funding streams, conflicting rules and regulations, and lack of coordination" (p. 59). Allied youth fields are still challenged to navigate these policy and funding restrictions despite a growing consensus that collaborative, multi-sector strategies can achieve efficiencies in the use of limited resources to attain mutually beneficial goals. It is the hope of the WCHWC that we seize this moment to create sustainable partnerships that support whole child development and enhance those partnerships by addressing the policy barriers to effective collaboration.

CONCLUSION

Expanded learning programs are critical partners to create the conditions necessary for children, youth, and families to thrive. Years of research and thought leadership support a vision of ecosystems of support for whole children, youth, families, and communities. Expanded Learning programs and other community youth serving organizations are well-positioned to provide the kinds of supports that are foundational to healthy development and learning in good times, and they are even more critical in times of crisis.

California's Whole Child Health and Wellness Collaborative has created strategies that states, and local communities can use to create equitable whole child health and wellness outcomes in partnership with Expanded Learning programs. Informed by multiple sectors and the multiple challenges of our times, the work is deeply grounded in a vision of equitable and just communities and shared equity strategies. There has never been a better time to make this vision a reality, but this vision cannot be achieved by conducting business as usual. As our nation, our states, and our communities shift to this new way of being, there are many lessons that can be gleaned from the process, products, and progress of California's Whole Child Health and Wellness Collaborative.

REFERENCES

Afterschool Alliance. (2020). *America after 3pm: Today more families struggle to find and afford programs, and inequities are prominent.* http://afterschoolalliance.org/AA3PM/#challenges

Amarji VRP. (2018, September 20). *#Gavin Newsom—California Dream.* [video]. YouTube. https://www.youtube.com/watch?v=YCwgQixa7OU

American Institutes for Research. (2019, October 14). *The Science of Learning and Development in Afterschool Systems and Settings.* https://www.air.org/resource/science-learning-and-development-afterschool-systems-and-settings

American Institutes for Research. (2020). *COVID-19 and Whole Child Efforts: Reopening Update.* https://www.air.org/sites/default/files/COVID-Whole-Child-Efforts-Reopening-update-August-2020.pdf

Austin, G., Wendt, S., & Klinicka, L. (2021). *Promoting protective factors in California's afterschool programs.* WestEd. https://www.afterschoolnetwork.org/post/promoting-protective-factors-californias-afterschool-programs

Benard, B. (2004). *Resiliency: What We Have Learned.* WestEd.

California AfterSchool Network. (2019). *The Whole Child Health and Wellness: Strategic Planning Journey Launches!* https://www.afterschoolnetwork.org/sites/main/files/file-attachments/wchw_kickoff_convening_overview_-_two_pager.pdf?1583940729

California Children's Trust. (2020). *The Practical Guide for Financing Social, Emotional, and Mental Health in Schools.* https://cachildrenstrust.org/wp-content/uploads/2020/08/practicalguide.pdf

California Department of Education (2018a). *A Vision for Expanded Learning in California: Strategic Plan 2.0 2019–2023.* https://www.cde.ca.gov/ls/ex/documents/strategicplan2.pdf

California Department of Education. (2018b). *California's Social and Emotional Learning Guiding Principles.* https://www.cde.ca.gov/eo/in/documents/selguidingprincipleswb.pdf

California Department of Education. (2018c). *Report to the Legislature, Legislative Analyst's Office and the Governor: Characteristics of Schools and Students Participating in After School Programs 2017 Report.* https://www.cde.ca.gov/ls/ex/documents/lrafterschoolprograms17.pdf

California Department of Education. (2020a). *Expanded Learning.* https://www.cde.ca.gov/ls/ex/

California Department of Education. (2020b, October 30). *State Superintendent Tony Thurmond Announces $45 Million in Grant Funding to Support At-Risk Students and Their Families at Community Schools.* (October 2020c). https://www.cde.ca.gov/nr/ne/yr20/yr20rel88.asp

California Department of Education. (2021). *Stronger Together: A Guidebook for the Safe Reopening of California's Public Schools.* https://www.cde.ca.gov/ls/he/hn/documents/strongertogether.pdf

California Department of Education & California AfterSchool Network. (2014). *The Quality Standards for Expanded Learning in California.* https://www.afterschoolnetwork.org/post/quality-standards-expanded-learning-california

Collaborative for Academic, Social, and Emotional Learning. (2020). *Reunite, Renew, and Thrive: SEL Roadmap for Reopening Schools.* https://casel.org/wp-content/uploads/2020/07/SEL-ROADMAP.pdf

Collaborative Supporters. (n.d.). California AfterSchool Network. https://www.afterschoolnetwork.org/post/collaborative-supporters

Council for a Strong America. (2019). *From Risk to Opportunity: Afterschool Programs Keep Kids Safe.* https://www.strongnation.org/articles/930-from-risk-to-opportunity-afterschool-programs-keep-kids-safe

Durlak, J., & Weissberg, R. (2010). *Afterschool programs that follow evidence-base practices to promote social and emotional development are effective.* http://www.expandinglearning.org/docs/Durlak&Weissberg_Final.pdf

equityXdesign. (2016, November 15). *Racism and inequity are products of design. They can be redesigned.* Medium. https://medium.com/equity-design/racism-and-inequity-are-products-of-design-they-can-be-redesigned-12188363cc6a

Fendsterwald, J. (2020, February 18). *Gov. Newsom's big bets: Community schools, competitive grants, and new teacher incentives: Governor reveals plan to address teacher shortage, fix high-poverty schools.* EdSource. https://edsource.org/2020/gov-newsoms-big-bets-community-schools-competitive-grants-and-new-teacher-incentives/623699

Fensterwald, J. (2021, January 8). *Gov. Newsom proposes $4.6 billion for summer school, more learning time in 2021–22 budget.* EdSource. https://edsource.org/2021/gov-newsom-proposes-4-6-billion-for-summer-school-more-learning-time-in-2021-22-budget/646503

Learning Policy Institute. (2020). *Leveraging resources through community schools: The role of technical assistance.* https://learningpolicyinstitute.org/sites/default/files/product-files/Technical_Assistance_Community_Schools_BRIEF.pdf

Mental Health Services Oversight and Accountability Commission. (2020). *Every young heart and mind: Schools as centers of wellness.* https://www.mhsoac.ca.gov/sites/default/files/schools_as_centers_of_wellness_final.pdf

The National Commission on Social, Emotional & Academic Development. (2019). *From a nation at risk to a nation at hope.* Aspen Institute. http://nationathope.org/wp-content/uploads/2018_aspen_final-report_full_webversion.pdf

Osher, D., Pittman, K., Young, J., Smith, H., Moroney, D., & Irby, M. (2020). *Thriving, robust equity, and transformative learning & development: A more powerful conceptualization of the contributors to youth success.* Forum for Youth Investment. https://forumfyi.org/knowledge-center/thriving-robust-equity-and-transformative-learning-development/

Opportunity Institute and Partnership for Children and Youth. (2020). *No longer optional: Why and how expanded learning partnerships are essential to achieving equity in school reopening.* https://www.partnerforchildren.org/resources/2020/8/3/expanded-learning-in-school-reopening

Partnership for the Future of Learning. (2019). *Community schools playbook.* https://communityschools.futureforlearning.org/assets/downloads/community-schools-playbook.pdf

Pierce, K. M., Auger, A. & Vandell, D. L. (2013, April). *Narrowing the achievement gap: Consistency and intensity of structured activities during elementary school.* Unpublished paper presented at the Society for Research in Child Development Biennial Meeting, Seattle, WA. https://www.expandinglearning.org/docs/TheAchievement-GapisReal.pdf

Putnam, R. D., Fredrick, C. B., & Snellman, K. (2012). *Growing class gaps in social connectedness among American youth.* The Saguaro Seminar: Civic Engagement in America. Harvard Kennedy School of Government. https://hceconomics.uchicago.edu/sites/default/files/file_uploads/Putnam-etal_2012_Growing-Class-Gaps.pdf

Science of Learning and Development Alliance. (2020). *How the science of learning and development can transform education: Initial findings.* https://5bde8401-9b54-4c2c-8a0c-569fc1789664.filesusr.com/ugd/eb0b6a_24f761d8a4ec4d7db13084eb2290c588.pdf

Wei-Skillern, J., & Silver, N. (2013). Four network principles for collaboration success. *The Foundation Review, 5*(1), 121–129. https://doi.org/10.4087/FOUNDATION-REVIEW-D-12-00018.1

Werner, E. E., & Smith, R. S. (1992). *Overcoming the odds: High risk children from birth to adulthood.* Cornell University Press.

WestEd. (2021). *The surveys: California healthy kids survey.* https://calschls.org/about/the-surveys/#chks

Wheatley, M., & Frieze, D. (2011). Leadership in the age of complexity: From hero to host. *Resurgence Magazine.* https://www.margaretwheatley.com/articles/Leadership-in-Age-of-Complexity.pdf

Whole Child Health and Wellness Collaborative. (n.d.). *California AfterSchool Network.* https://www.afterschoolnetwork.org/whole-child-health-and-wellness-collaborative

Whole Child Health and Wellness Collaborative. (2021a). *Statement of Strategic Direction: Toward equity-driven whole child health and wellness.* California AfterSchool Network. https://www.afterschoolnetwork.org/sites/main/files/file-attachments/while_chld_health_statement_of_strategic_direction_march_2021_final.pdf?1618332120

Whole Child Health and Wellness Collaborative. (2021b). *Towards equity-driven whole child health and wellness.* California Afterschool Network. https://www.afterschoolnetwork.org/sites/main/files/file-attachments/whole_child_health_call_to_action_-_march_2021.pdf?1618332121

Williams, H. (2019). *The state of the state of expanded learning in California 2018–19.* California AfterSchool Network. https://www.afterschoolnetwork.org/post/state-state-expanded-learning-california-2018-19

Williams, H. (2020). *A hub of community resilience: Expanded learning responds to crisis.* The California Department of Education & the California AfterSchool Network. https://www.afterschoolnetwork.org/post/hub-community-resilience-californias-expanded-learning-programs-respond-crisis

Zeitner, B. (2019, March). *Change the environment, reduce kids' exposure to trauma says California Surgeon General at University Hospitals.* Cleveland.com. https://www.cleveland.com/metro/2019/03/change-the-environment-reduce-kids-exposure-to-trauma-says-california-surgeon-general-at-university-hospitals.html

SECTION V
LOOKING AHEAD

CHAPTER 16

BUILDING FORWARD TOGETHER

Toward Equitable Ecosystems for Young People

Merita Irby, Karen Pittman, Hal Smith, and Deb Moroney

Karen Pittman ended the Foreword with these words:

> We can, and must, as OST practitioners, administrators, researchers, funders, and advocates combine the power of the science with the disruptions of the times to not just build our OST systems back better, but to also be relentless in our commitment to do this in a way that propels us, schools and other community organizations and public systems committed to learning and development to build forward together ... to manage a fundamental shift from siloed systems-focused to dynamic ecosystem-focused thinking.

Multiple chapters in this volume—including but by no means limited to those contributed by us and our colleagues at the Forum for Youth Investment, the National Urban League, and the American Institutes for Research—come at this idea from various angles. While tempting, we will not take on the task of summarizing those angles in this concluding chapter. We will use our word allotment to explain why and how we plan to read, dissect, and repurpose the arguments, examples, and research summaries in this volume to contribute to a more urgent and cogent call to action that challenges school *and* OST leaders—practitioners, administra-

It Takes an Ecosystem: Understanding the People, Places, and Possibilities of Learning and Development Across Settings, pages 299–311.

tors, applied researchers, policy advocates—to fully leverage their instincts to collaborate and partner in ways that not only accelerate foundational *cross-system transactions* but also drive and support *ecosystem-focused transformations.*

The Readiness Projects were designed to accelerate progress towards this bigger, bolder goal. We, as the Readiness Projects coordinating partners, are optimistic that this country can dramatically change the odds for children and youth if we commit to upend inequities, embrace science-informed strategies, and accelerate progress by working together, across systems and sectors. This volume, and a related planning effort to mount a survey of the "keystone adults" in learning and development ecosystems (AIR, 2020a), were among the first project commitments we made in 2019 because they spoke to each of the Readiness Projects four priorities:

- Advance "stickier" narratives about how science and research on learning and development can be used to advance equity and thriving.
- Amplify the voices of youth and community leaders and ask how a more robust approach to equity and thriving can support and refine their agendas.
- Assert the essential role of all adults in all settings—when, where, and with whom learning happens—and prioritize efforts to recognize and act upon their perspectives.
- Articulate the need to advance the idea of a "thriving youth" field to align work within and across systems and solutions similar to the connections already in place to align goals and systems that support early childhood (Readiness Projects, 2020a).

These priorities, not surprisingly, dovetail well with the four themes explored in this volume: better use of the science of learning and development findings, equity and social justice, ecosystem frameworks, and advancing the allied youth fields. Our work with school, OST, social justice, and philanthropic leaders over the past year affirmed the importance of being explicit about the connections between these priorities.

Successful, sustainable efforts to align fields and systems usually have deeper roots than those that have been created through ad hoc, transactional, or project specific coordination and collaboration. The idea of learning hubs to provide in-person supports to young people who are engaged in virtual learning for example, became popular during the pandemic. Short term collaborations like this cropped up across the country. Sustaining these efforts, however, requires infrastructure. Building on a decade plus of intentional state and local partnership building, California was one of the first states to scale implementation of the hub model (for a description of California's expanded learning approach, see chapter 15 in this volume by Davis). Because of this history of partnership, they are already beginning to identify what it will take to leverage learning from hubs to continue to strengthen their overall partnership approach. A recent brief from Policy Analysis for California Education elevated emerging practices from field leaders, including prioritizing buy-in and alignment across partners; focusing on students most negatively impacted by COVID-19 disparities; investing in staff to ensure safety and effectiveness; and emphasizing integration and coordination in planning and implementation (Vance et al., 2021).

Laying the groundwork for long-term, cross-system efforts to create and sustain equitable, community-based, learner-centered ecosystems requires ongoing systematic work. Ecosystem leaders in all roles (front line to policy) will need support to consistently use an ecosystem framework to think and talk differently, see and hear differently, and act and react differently (The Readiness Projects, 2020d) within their own organizations and spheres of influence, as well as across sectors, all oriented towards better supporting children and youth.

THE CHARGE TO OST LEADERS

Leaders in youth development and community organizations, especially those who have worked with adolescents, often have a deep, intuitive understanding of what it takes to help young people beat the odds set for them by circumstances and contexts. Increasingly, they have become more vocal about what it takes to scale up practices, programs, and policies within their systems that go beyond helping individual young people *beat* the odds to actually *change* the odds (a phrase coined by Pittman, 1995). This requires ensuring that marginalized youth have the currencies they need to "make it"—to have a basic ability to acquire and expend competencies, connections, credentials, and cash needed to meet life's challenges (Krauss, 2021).

Anecdotal evidence suggests that OST and community organizations were, as a group, effective at building and maintaining relationships and creating meaningful learning experiences during the pandemic. But, narrow definitions of learning perpetuate inequity (See Chapter 3 by Pittman et al. in this volume). Without acceptance of the need to build forward together, there is no guarantee that the focus on relationships—and, concomitantly, the recognition of the value of the kind of flexible and free-choice learning experiences found in OST and other community programs—will be sustained and built upon once schools and communities fully reopen. The likelihood of abandoning such learning experiences is especially likely given the emphasis on addressing academic learning losses credited to the pandemic to the exclusion of the full range of supports, services, and opportunities that we know will benefit learners in the near and long term as they work to build not only academic proficiency and a broader range of competencies, but also build a strong sense of agency and strong, integrated identities (that are grounded in culture, spirituality, and collective belonging) (Osher et al., 2020). Without a strong, steady, strategic campaign, OST programs—however defined—could quickly be dropped back into the category of "nice but not necessary" once educators and policymakers conclude that a sufficient allocation of resources and enough energy has been devoted to re-establishing relationships, routines, and resilience (SoLD Alliance, 2020).

The next few years offer an incredible, unprecedented opportunity to position and strengthen the OST field. We believe, however, that system building work is best done within a broader focus on creating equitable, porous, learner-focused ecosystems. OST programs and systems are, because of their flexibility and youth-centered focus, best positioned to push for allied youth fields (or a reinvigorated thriving youth field) that positions and leverages:

a. The determination, resiliency, agency, and activism of youth and young adults;
b. The range of roles adults play to connect, support, and champion youth within learning and development ecosystems;
c. The array of settings where this work happens;
d. The roles frontline adults and youth play in critiquing and changing the systems where these settings are found; and
e. The varied types of coordinating infrastructure needed.

The chapters in this volume provide a solid base of evidence for these claims.

The best way to do this is to lead with language that centers the learners and, in doing so, showcases the nimbleness (albeit unevenness) of OST and community programs and organizations in *meeting learners where they are*. There is an opportunity to reprise and update the more inclusive ideas associated with the positive youth development movement (Benson & Pittman, 2001) to galvanize support for a learning ecosystem approach that operationalizes the definition of positive youth development adopted by the federal government via the Interagency Working Group on Youth Programs:

> [Positive Youth Development] is an intentional, prosocial approach that engages youth within their communities, schools, organizations, peer groups, and families in a manner that is productive and constructive; recognizes, utilizes, and enhances young people's strengths; and promotes positive outcomes for young people by providing opportunities, fostering positive relationships, and furnishing the support needed to build on their leadership strengths. (Interagency Working Group on Youth Programs, n. d., paragraph 1)

The Readiness Projects has had success calling out the extent to which program leaders, funders, and policymakers rarely specify who all is included in general calls (or claims) that endorse broader whole learner, whole community visions. There are real, concrete opportunities to get system leaders (including OST leaders) to be specific about:

All systems. To actively see themselves as a part of a broader community ecosystem that includes other public systems as well as the array of "invisible" community partners and to describe these partners by name.

All settings. To use the science findings to push beyond big descriptors that describe systems and organizations– school, youth program—to describe the settings within them (classrooms, gyms, playgrounds, cafeterias) where gathering happens with some regularity, some resources, and usually some adult supervision.

All learners. To not only disaggregate data, but document and discuss the learning gifts and needs of various groups of learners (including adults). To put more emphasis on developmental processes, including putting a spotlight on adolescents as a group that is much larger than "enrolled secondary students" and a group that is typically engaged with multiple systems.

All learning approaches. To emphasize the importance of nonformal and informal learning experiences (in addition to formal) for overall development of competencies, agency and identity and to emphasize that all learning approaches are used, to varying degrees, in all systems.

All adults. To call for sustained and more substantial investments in all of the adults (and young adults) who have assumed roles as contributors to youth success and who, therefore, need training, supports, and resources to optimize the relationships they have with youth and the experiences they co-create.

TURNING DISRUPTION INTO OPPORTUNITY

The opportunity to accelerate ecosystem thinking did not start with COVID-19. In fact, we think of this opportunity as one that has evolved over time in three distinct phases. The first phase started with the push for schools to make commitments to social and emotional learning (SEL) and to integrate SEL practices into academic instruction and, concomitantly, partner with afterschool and summer program partners. This phase was marked by an impressive array of foundation-sponsored studies, commissions, and demonstration projects (e.g., Susan Crown Exchange and the David P. Weikart Center for Youth Program Quality's guide *Preparing Youth to Thrive* (Smith et al., 2016); S. D. Bechtel, Jr. Foundation's National Character Initiative (AIR, 2020c); Aspen Institute National Commission on Social, Emotional, and Academic Development's investments to stand up Youth Development Working Group (NCSEAD, 2018); Wallace Foundation's Partnerships for Social and Emotional Learning Initiative (Schwartz et al., 2020); and many others).

But COVID-19 disruptions clearly created unexpected opportunities which we can consider the second phase. As school buildings closed, the second phase of acceleration in ecosystem thinking began. Out-of-school time (meaning time spent outside of the school building) became all the time and OST organizations, networks, and systems elevated their value and visibility as flexible learning and development delivery systems that were better equipped by design to be whole child/whole learner-centered: relationship-driven, family and community focused, problem-solvers (e.g., AIR, 2020b; Readiness Projects, 2020b).

The third phase started as school administrators, policy makers, and the country in general started to prepare for a post-vaccine landscape with ramped up school re-openings. This coincided with the design and release of American Rescue Plan funds to support schools' and community organizations' efforts to use summer to prepare staff, students, and buildings, while simultaneously shoring up a wider array of services, supports, and opportunities. There is no doubt, given the levels of disruption, that schools will build back differently, but how will communities reknit themselves and to what effect? As many have said, a functional return to what we once considered normal is not an option. Numerous inequities in access, quality, and resources that predated the pandemic are now regularly discussed in trade and public media outlets. Commitments to "build back better" are central to the Biden Administration's education agenda. There is good reason to believe that schools will build back better (Darling-Hammond, 2021; U. S. Department of Education, 2021), but we have an opportunity to build a more equitable, a more robust educational and developmental ecosystem, inclusive of schools, but not limited to them.

Addressing the most egregious of the stark pre-existing inequities exposed by the COVID-19 pandemic—from uneven broadband access to ever-increasing rates of food insecurity—will become a priority. So too, will engaging students and families whose disenchantment with public and private systems was exacerbated by responses and strategies not deemed safe, sufficient, or equitable. But there is no reason to believe that, without a strong and steady push, school leaders, education equity advocates will prioritize the need to build forward together with youth development, community, and social justice stakeholders to shore up multiple elements in the ecosystems that support youth thriving. Nor, frankly, is there a strong reason to suggest that these community stakeholders will find reason to work together more closely to support youth *and* families, address learning *and* basic needs (see Chapter 3 by Pittman et al. in this volume).

We want to be very clear why we think steady pushing is needed. There is no way that any single organizational system (e.g., local school systems, local OST networks) can fully address the whole child or fully involve the whole community. This is not because education leaders or educational equity advocates see children as less than whole people, or think academic success is the only goal. Nor is it because OST and community organizations believe that building relationships, experiences, and opportunities that support youth thriving is more important than academic competence and credentials. It is because these leaders—like the leaders of child welfare, family supports, juvenile justice, youth employment, and other systems—think, see, and act using the language, goals, and metrics of their individual systems, not those of broader learning and development ecosystems.

The National Research Council of the National Academies (2015) defines a learning ecosystem as "the dynamic interaction among individual learners, diverse settings where learning occurs, and the community and culture in which they are embedded" (p. 5). As noted in the title of this book and described throughout this volume, elements of this learning ecosystem include *people* (youth, family, teachers, community educators, administrators, funders); *places* (schools, libraries, youth organizations, community centers, arts, civic and cultural organizations, museums, recreation facilities); activities/resources associated with *possibilities* (internships, curricula, teams, interest clubs, on-line sites); and larger but no less important "intangibles" such as culture, politics, socio-economic conditions, racism (Hecht & Crowley, 2020).

In education, the term ecosystem tends to be used to describe the people, places, and possibilities associated with schools as a way of acknowledging the important relationships and resources the school relies on that are outside of the building and outside of its direct control (e.g., from families and community members). More formal acknowledgement of these connections is important. But as Akiva, Hecht, and Blyth note in Chapter 2 of this volume, dynamic ecosystems do not have centers, so schools are not at the center of learning and development ecosystems. Acknowledging the need to connect to other actors in the ecosystem to accomplish system-specific goals (e.g., improve reading proficiency) is not the same as acknowledging the contributions and constraints of the other elements in the ecosystem and taking these into account when making system-specific decisions. This distinction is especially important when there are power and resource imbalances within the learning and development ecosystem, such as between schools and community-based organizations.

Early, confidential COVID-19 anecdotes from local OST leaders underscored this distinction for us. In one community, excitement about the speed with which Chromebooks were distributed to students, which greatly helped OST providers stay connected with youth and families, dissipated quickly when schools announced that the equipment would be collected at the end of the school year. In another, a two-year investment in recruiting and training youth development staff to improve the quality of the city's recreation programs was lost because those staff were among the first let go to adjust to budget shortfalls. In several others, intentional work to set up afterschool and summer programs in school buildings was undone when buildings closed or when reopenings only allowed district personnel to return. Each of these decisions makes sense from a system perspective, since the goal was to temporarily curtail cross-system transactions. Each, however, has unintended and undocumented effects on the ecosystem.

Amidst the stress and strains of the COVID-19 pandemic, it was stories like these, coupled with "bright spot" stories (Readiness Projects, 2020b), where real ecosystem thinking was on display, that led the Readiness Projects to seize opportunity to leverage the disruptions of 2020 to sharpen and deepen discussions about what it will take to not only build schools and districts back better, but build forward together to create more balanced, equitable learning, and development ecosystems. In August 2020, the Readiness Projects entered a formal partnership with AASA, the School Administrators Association, to galvanize national and local support to specify what it takes to truly build forward together (Domenech, 2020; Readiness Projects, 2020c) and began to identify community partners (e.g., Pittman & Plog Martinez, 2021) who were equally excited about these opportunities.

Build Forward Together – Toward Equitable Learning and Development Ecosystems

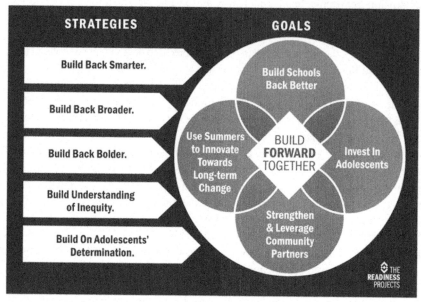

FIGURE 16.1.   Build Forward Together, Strategies and Goals.
Reprinted from Pittman (2021).

The Readiness Projects' coordinating partners summarized Build Forward Together goals and strategies (Pittman, 2021) based on what they were hearing from national and local leaders across the country (see Figure 16.1). Schools must build back better with more intentional learner-centered, ecosystem thinking. The full range of actors in community spaces and places must be strengthened and leveraged. Summers should be used for innovation and inspiration, encouraging the kinds of creative, de-siloed solutions that are too often restricted during the traditional school year and school day. And now is the time to increase our attention and investments in adolescents, particularly as their daily lives and demands for change require an ecosystem approach.

THE HARD CHALLENGES AHEAD

The scope and significance of the opportunities to disrupt the status quo have increased since March 2020. No one truly knows what it will take to get OST systems, the broader allied youth fields, and the champions who staff and lead them to come together at all levels—national, state, and community—to take collective and coherent action to seize the incredible "wall softening" opportunities that have become more visible in 2020 and that could be leveraged to accelerate prog-

BUILD BACK SMARTER
♦ Stop using the term learning loss.
♦ Stop making more instructional time the go-to remedy.
♦ Optimize learning experiences, even while prioritizing reconnection.
♦ Resist deficit thinking.

BUILD BACK BROADER
♦ See community organizations as complementary delivery systems, not just second shift responders.
♦ Embrace virtual environments as permanent assets.
♦ Create coordinating roles and structures that cut across delivery systems, elevate community, and connect to families.

BUILD BACK BOLDER
♦ Shift the focus from where and when learning happens to how and why.
♦ Diversify learners' experiences. Acknowledge adults' expertise and power.
♦ Respect and connect to young people's learning and development ecosystems.
♦ Double down on investments to embolden and connect adults in the "mesosystem."

BUILD UNDERSTANDING OF INEQUITY
♦ Get the right baselines. Cover all the bases.
♦ Acknowledge the skepticism.
♦ Work from the margins.

BUILD ON ADOLESCENTS' DETERMINATION
♦ Embrace adolescent risk taking, leverage the brain science.
♦ Commit to the age group, not just the enrolled student body.
♦ Address critical roadblocks and affirm multiple success pathways.

FIGURE 16.2.   Five Strategies to Build Forward Together.
Reprinted from Pittman (2021).

ress into 2022 and beyond. Many more of us now know what is at risk if we do not try. Young people and families must be at the center of the country's efforts to reopen, reengage, and build back better. OST leaders are often at the vanguard of these efforts—directly connecting to young people and their families and playing flexible, bridging roles between school systems and other community institutions. This has only increased as their staff, programs, organizations, and coalitions have become increasingly visible as key ecosystem elements. But this visibility brings a level of scrutiny the field needs to be ready for, especially if these all efforts are undergirded with a commitment to equity.

There are hard challenges ahead for every organization and system in the learning ecosystem as they reset post-COVID no matter what their starting focus (e.g., leveraging summer, reopening schools, reconnecting with and supporting adolescents, strengthening program capacity). The Readiness Projects organized the recurring themes heard from national and local ecosystem thinkers under five "build" strategies that, if considered, can help all system leaders not just build back better but build forward together (Pittman, 2021). These are summarized in Figure 16.2. We speak to each of these below, noting where OST and community leaders, in particular, could step forward to take the lead and where, in some cases, they need to lean in to address shortfalls.

BUILD BACK SMARTER—Make All Learning and Development Experiences "Learner-Centered." OST and community programs pride themselves on being learner-centered and relationship driven. But to claim space as critical ecosystem contributors, leaders must be comfortable developing, refining, and utilizing indicators that demonstrate the impact of the work of the OST community on cognitive, social and emotional growth, on content mastery in various areas including but not limited to academics, and on the larger success metrics such as agency and individual and collective identity. Demonstrating value in the learning ecosystem does not mean bringing school-based accountability and frames into community spaces (e.g., an emphasis on academic learning loss) but rather identifying and demonstrating the intended impact of developmental supports and opportunities on children and youth—both near-term and long-term.

BUILD BACK BROADER—Be Prepared to Come to the Table Not Just to Support, But to Lead. Stronger alliances must be built across the full range of community organization and institutions that comprise the community-based learning and development space (see Chapter 3 by Pittman et al. in this volume). The walls between OST programs, recreation departments, arts and culture organizations, family resource centers, faith-based learning settings, youth employment, and youth and community organizing programs are not as high as those between schools and OST. But they exist. OST intermediaries are a critical and undeveloped part of the coordinating infrastructure (see Chapter 10 by Donner and Little in this volume). Going forward, however, receptivity to investments in these entities may depend on how effective they are at reaching, connecting, and aligning the work of the broader set of community providers. Rather than shying away from broader strategic partnerships within the community sector and with school systems and other public systems (public health, workforce development, social services, etc.), now is the time to lean in to them.

BUILD BACK BOLDER—Respect How, Why, and With Whom Learning Happens. The sheer diversity of OST and community programs and organizations, and their commitment and need to work cooperatively with families, means that OST staff and administrators are more attuned to the variation in how, why, and with whom learning happens. This makes OST and community leaders well positioned to help larger, more bureaucratic systems value the time needed to understand what happens outside of their walls, recognize that these experiences are not happenstance, and invest not only in partnerships, but in the connecting and coordinating roles at all levels (from success coaches who help connect individual youth to opportunities to local intermediaries). Brands (e.g., Boys and Girls Clubs, YMCA) can get in the way of seeing ecosystem elements. Advancing "cross-brand" ideas about the importance of empowering youth and young adults will help demonstrate the power they carry as savvy, ecosystem "keystones" (See Chapter 2 by Akiva et al. and Chapter 7 by Colvin and White in this volume).

BUILD UNDERSTANDING OF INEQUITY—Advance Ideas About What Robust Equity Means and How It Is Achieved. Equity is the goal, but inequity is the reality. Most OST and community programs have a commitment to serve low-income communities, BIPOC (Black, Indigenous, and people of color) communities, and marginalized populations. Most, in this era of heightened attention to equity, acknowledge that much more is needed. Acknowledgement that supporting positive youth development and social and emotional skill building approaches are necessary but not sufficient to support belonging and ensure equity is growing, but concrete actions are needed. Program access is geographically uneven, as are broader commitments to equity and social justice. Commitments to cultural responsiveness and robust equity (looking beyond equity within the program) are uneven. As new funding becomes available (e.g., via the American Rescue Plan), acknowledging these patterns of underinvestment in certain communities and populations will be critical to address skepticism among youth, families, and smaller neighborhood-based organizations that have not been the focus of attention.

BUILD ON ADOLESCENTS' DETERMINATION—Focus More on Adolescents. OST programs are ideal environments for adolescents because of their relative flexibility, community grounding and commitment to youth, family, and community development. These assets make them ideal environments for helping young people make meaning out of real, complex challenges (personal, local, and global). Meaning making, research shows, is critical to adolescent brain development (Immordino-Yang & Knecht, 2020). Retention rates drop off quickly in many programs, however. And even fewer are equipped to connect to young people who are struggling in other systems.

Many of these ideas may not seem new. They build on the focus of OST and community programs for the last two decades. We urge you to speak to those that resonate and make visible the work already underway. Simultaneously, we urge you to acknowledge and address shortcomings, recognizing that like other sectors OST programs have often worked within our own comfortable boundaries, accepting basic coordination in lieu of deep collaboration and partnership. Schools are not the learning and development ecosystem. Nor are OST and community programs. It is only in efforts to build forward together that the potential of an equitable learning and development ecosystem can truly be realized.

REFERENCES

American Institutes for Research. (2020a). *Youth fields workforce survey.* https://www.air.org/sites/default/files/Youth-Fields-Workforce-Survey-August-2020-rev.pdf

American Institutes for Research. (2020b). *Recognizing the role of afterschool and summer programs and systems in rebuilding and reopening.* https://www.air.org/sites/default/files/downloads/report/Recognizing-the-Role-of-Afterschool-Summer-Programs-Reopening-COVID-May-2020rev2.pdf

American Institutes for Research. (2020c). *S. D. Bechtel, Jr. Foundation national charter initiative retrospective.* https://www.air.org/sites/default/files/National-Character-Initiative-Final-Retrospective-Bechtel-Dec-2020.pdf

Benson, P., & Pittman, K. (2001). *Trends in youth development: Visions, realities and challenges.* Kluwer Academic Publishers. doi: 10.1007/978-1-4615-1459-6.

Darling-Hammond, L. (2021, April 5). Accelerating learning as we build back better. *Forbes.* https://www.forbes.com/sites/lindadarlinghammond/2021/04/05/accelerating-learning-as-we-build-back-better/?sh=33c50e436722

Domenech, D. (2020). Coming back better. *School Administrator, 77*(8), 44. https://www.pageturnpro.com/AASA/96367-September-2020/sdefault.html#page/1

Hecht, M., & Crowley, K. (2020). Unpacking the learning ecosystems framework: Lessons from the adaptive management of biological ecosystems. *Journal of the Learning Sciences, 29*(2), 264–284. https://doi.org/10.1080/10508406.2019.1693381

Immordino-Yang, M. H., & Knecht, D. R. (2020). Building meaning builds teens' brains. *Educational Leadership, 77*(8), 36–43.

Interagency Working Group on Youth Programs. (n.d.). *Positive youth development.* https://youth.gov/youth-topics/positive-youth-development

Krauss, S. (2021). *Making it: What today's kids need for tomorrow's world.* John Wiley & Sons.

National Commission on Social, Emotional, and Academic Development. (2018). *Building partnerships in support of where, when & how learning happens.* The Aspen Institute. https://www.aspeninstitute.org/wp-content/uploads/2018/10/Aspen_YD_FINAL_2_web-11.18.pdf

National Research Council of the National Academies. (2015). *Identifying and supporting productive STEM programs in out-of-school settings.* The National Academies Press. doi:10.17226/21740

Osher, D., Pittman, K., Young, J., Smith, H., Moroney, D., & Irby, M. (2020). *Thriving, robust equity, and transformative learning & development: A more powerful conceptualization of the contributors to youth success.* Forum for Youth Investment.

Pittman, K. (1995). Changing the odds. *Youth Today, 4*(2), 46.

Pittman, K. (2021). *Normal is not an option. [Summer is an opportunity]. Five ways to leverage summers to upend inequity and accelerate progress over the next few years.* Forum for Youth Investment.

Pittman, K., & Plog Martinez, K. (2021, March 18). *Normal is not an option: One community's journey to build forward together.* Medium. https://medium.com/changing-the-odds/normal-is-not-an-option-aa47d4985bf0

Readiness Projects. (2020a). *The readiness projects.* Forum for Youth Investment. https://forumfyi.org/the-readiness-projects/

Readiness Projects. (2020b). *Bright spots.* Forum for Youth Investment. http://brightspots.forumfyi.org/

Readiness Projects. (2020c). *Build forward together.* Forum for Youth Investment. https://forumfyi.org/the-readiness-projects/build-forward-together/

Readiness Projects. (2020d, September 8). *When everything is different: Act different.* Medium. https://medium.com/changing-the-odds/when-everything-is-different-act-different-1c1400198944

Schwartz, H. L., Hamilton, L. S., Faxon-Mills, S., Gomez, C. J., Hueuet, A., Jaycox, L. H., Leschitz, J. T., Prado Tuma, A., Tosh, K., & Whitaker, A. A. (2020). *Early lessons from schools and out-of-school time programs implementing social and emotional learning.* RAND Corporation. https://doi.org/10.7249/RRA379-1

Smith, C., McGovern, G., Peck, S. C., Larson, R., Hillaker, B., & Roy, L. (2016). *Preparing youth to thrive: Methodology and findings from the social and emotional learning challenge.* Forum for Youth Investment.

SoLD Alliance. (2020). *The 3R's—Relationships, routines, resilience: A conversation with Pamela Cantor, M.D.* https://www.soldalliance.org/post/the-3r-s-relationships-routines-resilience-a-conversation-with-pam-cantor

U. S. Department of Education. (2021, April 26). *U.S. Department of Education launches National Summer Learning & Enrichment Collaborative to help students most impacted by the pandemic.* https://www.ed.gov/news/press-releases/us-department-education-launches-national-summer-learning-enrichment-collaborative-help-students-most-impacted-pandemic

Vance, F., Wolforth, S., & Gunderson, J. (2021). *Learning hubs in-person learning for the whole child.* PACE: Policy Analysis for California Education. https://edpolicyinca.org/sites/default/files/2021-01/pb_vance_2_feb21.pdf

BIOGRAPHIES

ABOUT THE EDITORS

Thomas Akiva, Ph.D., is an associate professor at the University of Pittsburgh School of Education and director of the Schoolwide EdD program. Prior to his doctoral studies at the University of Michigan, Akiva spent nearly two decades working as a practitioner and consultant in the youth development field, with most of that time at the Weikart Center for Youth Program Quality. He is the winner of the Out-of-School Time Emerging Scholar Award (2011) and Scholar Award (2016) from the American Educational Research Association. His research areas include continuous improvement and professional learning, youth program features, social emotional learning, equity in out-of-school learning, and citywide ecosystem approaches to learning and development.

Kimberly H. Robinson, Ph.D., is a social scientist and nonprofit leader passionate about effectively using data and research evidence to improve the ways that organizations and systems support children and families. Her career has spanned academia, public education, philanthropy, and nonprofit sectors. Over the last decade, she has led applied research and related improvement efforts at

It Takes an Ecosystem: Understanding the People, Places, and
Possibilities of Learning and Development Across Settings, pages 313–324.

the W.K. Kellogg Foundation, Baltimore City Public Schools, and the New York City Department of Education. She is currently an executive vice president at the Forum for Youth Investment and managing director of the Forum's David P. Weikart Center for Youth Program Quality where she leads the Forum's efforts to strengthen youth program quality through the development and support of continuous improvement systems that focus on organizational and staff practices that support positive youth development. Dr. Robinson earned her bachelor's degree in psychology and sociology from Bethel College in Mishawaka, Indiana, and a master's degree and a Ph.D., both in developmental psychology, from the University of Notre Dame.

ABOUT THE CONTRIBUTORS

Horatio Blackman, Ph.D., is the Vice President of Education Policy, Advocacy, & Engagement at the National Urban League. He was previously a Research Associate at the Center for Research in Education and Social Policy (CRESP) and an Assistant Professor in the College of Education and Human Development at the University of Delaware. Dr. Blackman completed his doctoral degree at the University of Pennsylvania's Graduate School of Education. Dr. Blackman's research explores challenges and strategies moving evidence into practice in k–12 settings, and examines the experiences of black youth in schools and society. At the National Urban League, his work centers on educational equity, directing evidence-informed educational programs for black youth and communities. He also serves as the advocacy voice on educational policy and engagement.

Dale Blyth, Ph.D., is a senior consultant and Professor Emeritus at the University of Minnesota where he served as the Howland Endowed Chair in Youth Development Leadership. For over 15 years he served as Associate Dean directing the Center for Youth Development home to the Minnesota 4-H Program; the Youth Work Institute (focused on professional development); the former Minnesota statewide afterschool network; and applied research and evaluation studies on nonformal learning opportunities. He has served as a consultant to CASEL, the University of Illinois Chicago and the Forum for Youth Investment, and serves on several community, state and national. Boards

Poonam Borah is an educator and researcher and works at the Forum for Youth Investments' Weikart Center as a Senior Research & Practice Specialist. She works closely with education stakeholders to negotiate relevant research questions that are useful in policy and practice and leads applied research studies to enhance professional development for youth workers. She also has many years of teaching experience in both school and out-of-school settings in India, Bhutan, and the US. Along with her professional experience, Poonam holds a Masters in

English from the University of Delhi and a Masters in Educational Leadership and Policy from the University of Michigan.

Michelle Boyd-Brown, Ph.D., is a researcher at American Institutes for Research (AIR). She engages in projects on youth development with a focus on science of learning and development, positive youth development (PYD), and safe and supportive learning environments. Dr. Boyd-Brown served as a policy fellow for the U.S. House of Representatives' Ways and Means Committee supporting policies and legislation for underrepresented young people and families. She was also an analyst in the Office of the Assistant Secretary for Planning and Evaluation at the U.S. Department of Health and Human Services focusing on policies and programs for youth in areas including bullying, parental incarceration, opportunity youth, PYD, violence prevention, and youth engagement. Dr. Boyd-Brown earned a master's degree and a doctorate in child development from Tufts University.

Linda W. Braun is a Learning Consultant with LEO, and works with educational institutions across the U.S. to design and deliver quality learning experiences for youth, families, communities, and staff. Linda has a Masters of Science in Library Science from Simmons College and a Masters of Education from Lesley University. Linda co-authored the reports, Ready to Code: Connecting Youth to CS Opportunities Through Libraries, The Future of Library Services for and with Teens: A Call to Action, and Transforming Library Services for and with Teens Through CE, Library Staff as Public Servants: A Field Guide for Preparing to Support Communities in Crisis, and has authored numerous books and articles.

Candace Brazier-Thurman is the founding Director of ExpandED Options at ExpandED Schools. She is motivated by how out of school learning can broaden youth's sense of possibility. She has coordinated multiple high school, intergenerational and professional development programs. Her work has included coordination of ExpandED Options, After-School Apprenticeship Program (ASAP), New York Times Summer Jobs and RampUp, a site-based mentoring program that connected professionals to students. Candace has a BA from Columbia University and an MPA from Baruch College. During off hours, Candace enjoys creating, sewing, and crafting.

Fatima Brunson, Ph.D., is post-doctoral researcher in the School of Education at the University of Pittsburgh. Dr. Brunson earned her doctorate degree in Policy Studies in Urban Education from the University of Illinois at Chicago (UIC). Her research is used to connect literature on teachers' collaborative practice and culturally relevant pedagogies. Currently, she works with schools and districts to better understand how youth practitioners can work together to enact responsive pedagogies in racially isolated schools and culturally mixed middle schools, high schools, and higher educational institutions. She provides consultation services while engaging in online trainings and dissemination of strategies specific to enhancing student engagement in science and math classrooms, through supporting teachers' adoption of culturally sustaining innovations.

Tanja Burkhard, Ph.D., is an Assistant Professor of Human Development at Washington State University, Vancouver. Aiming to work toward equity and justice for culturally and linguistically diverse learners, Tanja's research agenda examines the intersections of language/literacy, racialization and immigration through a transnational Black feminist lens. In particular, she focuses on critical feminist qualitative methodologies as pathways for meaning making and knowledge production.

Roderick L. Carey, Ph.D., is an Assistant Professor in the Department of Human Development and Family Sciences at the University of Delaware's College of Education and Human Development. Roderick is also director of The Black Boy Mattering Project, a school-university research partnership. In addition to researching school-based mattering with Black boys and young men, Roderick also research focuses on family and school influences on how Black and Latino adolescent boys imagine and actualize their postsecondary future selves. His research appears in such outlets like the *Harvard Educational Review, American Journal of Education,* and the *Journal of Applied Developmental Psychology.* Roderick taught high school English in Washington, DC schools prior to earning his PhD in the College of Education at the University of Maryland College Park.

Edward Cleofe served as Youth Development Executives of King County (YDEKC)'s Communications & Database Coordinator from 2016 to 2019. During his time at YDEKC, he helped lead racial equity work with an interest in the development of informal and formal cross-organization support systems for people of color. Edward is now a PhD student at UCLA, conducting archaeological research in the Philippines. His archaeological work is deeply invested in public engagement, particularly projects that introduce archaeology to young people in ways that open conversations about the contemporary relevance and power dynamics of how narratives of the past are produced.

Sharon Colvin recently completed her Ph.D. in Learning Sciences and Policy at the University of Pittsburgh. She is interested in identity development and how non-familial adults can support that development, especially in informal learning contexts. She (with Dr. Annie White and others) has been developing a qualitative research tool to help explore the complexities of identity in context. Before returning to academia, Sharon worked as a youth services public librarian for 10 years.

Jeff Davis is the Executive Director for the California AfterSchool Network (CAN). Jeff was fortunate to begin his expanded learning career in AmeriCorps. He has strong knowledge of expanded learning as author and editor of the State of the State of Expanded Learning. Jeff has played an integral role in creating quality frameworks and standards. He has also provided leadership to efforts to advance positive youth development, social emotional learning, STEM, nutrition and physical activity, older youth, English Learners, and rural programs. Most recently, Mr. Davis has been working to advance whole child health and wellness through convening the Whole Child Health and Wellness Collaborative that recently released their *Statement of Strategic Direction Toward Equity-Driven Whole Child Health and Wellness.*

Lori Delale-O'Connor, Ph.D., is an Assistant Professor in the Center for Urban Education and the Department of Education Foundations, Organizations, and Policy at the University of Pittsburgh's School of Education. Her research focuses on examining the connections between families, communities, and education across spaces with a particular focus on fostering equity and justice for children and youth in urbanized educational systems. Dr. Delale-O'Connor earned her Ph.D. in Sociology from Northwestern University and an M.Ed. in secondary education from Boston College. Dr. Delale-O'Connor's research has been published in the American Educational Research Journal, Teachers College Record, and Urban Education, among other outlets. She is also co-author of the book, "These Kids Are Out of Control": Why We Must Reimagine "Classroom Management" for Equity (Sage Publications).

Jessica Donner is the Executive Director of Every Hour Counts (EHC), a coalition of citywide organizations that increases access to quality learning opportunities, particularly for underserved students. The organization is a leading voice promoting expanded-learning systems, which provide learning and enrichment through after-school, summer, and other initiatives. Jessica manages EHC's efforts to develop policy recommendations and solutions, test the feasibility of policy and practice recommendations and disseminate findings, and deliver technical assistance to communities to build expanded learning systems. Prior to joining EHC, Jessica directed statewide and national service-learning initiatives at the National Service-Learning Partnership at the Academy for Educational Development and the Massachusetts Department of Education. She holds a master's degree in urban policy and management from The New School, and a bachelor's degree in English from the University of Pennsylvania.

DaVonna Graham is a doctoral student in the Department of Instruction and Learning at the University of Pittsburgh. She serves as a Graduate Research and Teaching Associate in the Center for Urban Education. DaVonna's research interests include learning from Black educators the ways in which they engage in race talk with their students centered on equity, justice and scholar activism. She most recently co-authored an article in the International Journal of Qualitative Studies in Education titled, Storying Youth Lives: Centering in Teaching and Teacher Education (2020).

Marijke Hecht, Ph.D., is Assistant Professor of Recreation, Park, and Tourism Management at Penn State Greater Allegheny. Her research and teaching weave together environmental education, community-based ecological design, learning sciences, and naturalist practices. Before entering academia, she led non-profit urban environmental education and stewardship projects, including work on the Nine Mile Run aquatic ecosystem project, one of the largest urban stream restorations in the U.S., and managing the design and construction of the Frick Environmental Center, a certified LEED Platinum and Living Building Challenge public education facility. She received her PhD in Learning Sciences and Policy from the University of Pittsburgh, her MS in Botany from the Field Naturalist program at the University of Vermont and her BA from Hampshire College.

LaRon Henderson is the Director of Program Quality for Collective for Youth. He is a former Certified Teacher with more than 20 years' experience working with students from Elementary to College. His career path has allowed him to work with individuals in prisons, schools, athletic programs, and churches. He is the author of "You Are Somebody," a leadership development curriculum for young men, and Co-Founder of Prepared Performance, a fitness and leadership development center for athletes, coaches and professionals. His passion to helping leaders maximize their full potential and accomplish their purpose in life. LaRon received his bachelor's degree at the University of Nebraska at Omaha in psychology. He also holds Master's Degree in Organizational Leadership and Teaching. LaRon is married to his wife Heather and the proud father of Noni (24) and Justus (21).

Mac Howison is the Program Officer for Creative Learning at The Heinz Endowments, where his work focuses primarily on initiatives that intersect with the Endowments' Creativity and Learning goal areas. Mac is responsible for advancing the foundation's work through the Creative Learning initiative—A creative youth development funding strategy to cultivate an equitable creative arts and cultural learning network, improve access to transformative learning experiences for young people, and support meaningful professional opportunities for teaching artists. For more than 15 years Mac has designed and implemented trust-based funding approaches for nonprofits, foundations, and intermediaries that deepen relationships in community and provide resources in consultation with neighborhood partners. Mac is a 2016 PLACES Fellow with The Funders Network and prior to The Heinz Endowments he was Senior Program Officer at The Sprout Fund. A former museum educator, rock musician, and someone who loves to run, hike, and play outside, Mac holds a BFA in Fine Art from Carnegie Mellon University.

Merita Irby is a chief architect of both the Forum for Youth Investment and its signature initiative, Ready by 21®. Having founded the Forum with Karen Pittman in 1998, she is managing partner of Big Picture Approach Training & Consulting and a coach to state and local partnerships. Merita works with leaders in school districts, governmental departments, community collaboratives and non-governmental organizations nationwide. Merita began her career as a classroom teacher in Central America and inner-city schools in the United States. As a senior research associate at Stanford University, she worked on a five-year study of community-based urban youth organizations and co-authored Urban Sanctuaries: Neighborhood Organizations in the Lives and Futures of Inner-City Youth. Merita earned a master's degree in Public Policy from the John F. Kennedy School of Government at Harvard University.

Robert J. Jagers, Ph.D., is CASEL's vice president of research. Prior to joining CASEL, he was a faculty member in the Combined Program in Education and Psychology at the University of Michigan, a Co-PI of the Center for the Study of Black Youth in Context (CSBYC), and the founding director of Wolverine Pathways, a university-sponsored diversity pipeline program for qualified secondary school students. Among his various CASEL duties, Dr. Jagers is leading work with partner districts to explore how social and emotional learning can be leveraged to promote equitable learning environments and equitable developmental outcomes for students from historically underserved groups. He has a particular interest in participatory approaches to SEL research and practice and their implications for the civic development of children and youth.

Valerie Kinloch, Ph.D., is the Renée and Richard Goldman Dean of the School of Education at the University of Pittsburgh. Her scholarship examines literacy engagements in schools and communities. Author of publications on race, place, literacy, and equity, she has written on poet June Jordan, critical perspectives on language, and community engagement. Her book, *Harlem On Our Minds: Place, Race, and the Literacies of Urban Youth,* received the 2010 Outstanding Book of the Year Award from the American Educational Research Association. *Crossing Boundaries: Teaching and Learning with Urban Youth,* was a staff pick for *Teaching Tolerance Education Magazine.* Her most recent co-edited book is titled, *Race, Justice, and Activism in Literacy Instruction.* Currently, she is completing a project on engaged pedagogies and justice.

Junlei Li, Ph.D., is Co-Chair of the Human Development and Education Program and the Saul Zaentz Senior Lecturer in Early Childhood Education at the Harvard Graduate School of Education. His research and practice focus on understanding and supporting the work of helpers—those who serve children and families on the frontlines of education and social services. Working in orphanages, schools, youth programs from North America to China, he develops the "Simple Interactions" approach, a public domain resource (*www.simpleinteractions.org*) to help identify what ordinary people do extraordinarily well with children in everyday moments. Dr. Li teaches about improving human interactions and supporting helpers, and delivers keynote addresses and workshops for child-serving professionals nationally and internationally.

Priscilla M. Little is a Senior Consultant with the Forum for Youth Investment. A core component of her work is to help leaders understand and apply the science of learning and development to how they promote equitable learning environments across the day and year, with a particular focus on supporting OST intermediaries. Prior to being with the Forum, she oversaw The Wallace Foundation's $15 million effort to assist nine cities in providing more high-quality afterschool programs through a coordinated systems approach. The former Associate Director of the Harvard Family Research Project, Priscilla has been working in education and conducting educational research for more than 20 years, with a particular emphasis on research and evaluation to support and improve afterschool experiences. She received her undergraduate degree in music history and theory from Smith College, and her master's degree from the Eliot-Pearson Department of Child Study at Tufts University.

David Martineau is the Director of Design and Innovation at the Forum for Youth Investment's David P. Weikart Center for Youth Program Quality. He leads efforts to design and deliver powerful learning experiences and scalable quality improvement systems that strengthen practice and programs for young people. Dave has more than 25 years of experience in youth development, social justice education, group facilitation, and social services. He earned his MSW from the University of Michigan, Ann Arbor. After finishing his MSW, he worked with High/Scope Educational Research Foundation. Dave was the Executive Director of NCCJ St. Louis, where he worked for ten years to provide powerful, in-depth learning and coaching experiences to those committed to making systemic change for diversity, inclusion, and equity. In addition to NCCJ, Dave's served as Diversity Director at HelpSource, then Michigan's largest non-governmental social service agency; facilitated for the Anti-Defamation League of Eastern Missouri's A World of Difference Institute; and studied the impact of intergroup dialogues on MSW students. He lives in Michigan with his partner and their son.

Deborah Moroney, Ph.D., is Vice President for Youth, Family and Community Development at the American Institutes for Research. She serves on multiple peer-reviewed journals, and she co-authored the *Beyond the Bell* toolkit. She has edited two book volumes: *Creating Safe, Equitable, Engaging Schools* and *Social and Emotional Learning in Out-of-School Time*. She serves on boards and committees, including the National Academies of Sciences and YMCA of the USA. She is a member of the C.S. Mott Foundation Afterschool Technical Assistance Collaborative and a lead partner on the Readiness Projects. She has led large studies of youth development initiatives, such as School's Out New York City, Girls Inc. and NatureBridge. Previously, she was a clinical faculty member in educational psychology at the University of Illinois at Chicago.

Esohe Osai, Ph.D., is a community engaged scholar who has served in urban communities for 20 years. Currently, she serves as an Assistant Professor in the

School of Education at the University of Pittsburgh. A graduate of the Detroit public school system, Dr. Osai was a high school teacher in Detroit before earning a Ph.D. in education and psychology from the University of Michigan. Her interests include youth development, youth-engaged scholarship, and post-secondary pathways for youth from educationally marginalized schools and communities. Dr. Osai employs a social justice-centered, positive strengths approach in her community engaged praxis.

David Osher, Ph.D., is Vice President and Institute Fellow at the American Institutes for Research. Osher leads and advises on research and practice support work on violence prevention, school safety, supportive school discipline, conditions for learning and school climate, social and emotional learning, youth development, cultural competence, family engagement, collaboration, mental health services and implementation science. He led the research time that synthesized what is known about the science of learning and development. His recent books include Creating Safe, Equitable, Engaging Schools: A Comprehensive, Evidence-Based Approach to Supporting Students (Harvard Education Press); Keeping Students Safe and Helping Them Thrive: A Collaborative Handbook on School Safety, Mental Health, and Wellness (Praeger); and the forthcoming The Science of Learning and Development (Taylor Francis).

Karen J. Pittman has made a career of starting organizations and initiatives that promote youth development—including the Forum for Youth Investment, which she co-founded with Merita Irby in 1998. Karen started her career at the Urban Institute, conducting studies on social services for children and families, and has also worked at the Children's Defense Fund, the Academy for Educational Development, the President's Crime Prevention Council, and the International Youth Foundation. She is a respected writer and public speaker and serves on numerous boards and commissions; she currently sits on the Turnaround for Children board and is a governing partner of the Science of Learning and Development Alliance.

Camila Polanco is a doctoral student and National Science Foundation Graduate Research fellow in the Department of Human Development and Family Sciences at the University of Delaware. With expertise in both qualitative and quantitative school-based research methods, her interests broadly entail understanding the educational experiences of Black and Latinx school-aged youth through investigating their perceptions of teachers' instructional practices, school climate, and teacher-student relationships.

Lance M. Simpson is a Research and Instructional Services Librarian at The University of Alabama, where he teaches STEM-focused information literacy. He holds a Masters of Library and Information Studies from The University of Alabama. Lance currently represents Alabama as a facilitator for the IMLS-funded project, Transforming Teen Services: A Train the Trainer Approach. In addition, his previous experience working with teens in public libraries includes managing two labs in the YOUmedia Learning Lab network. He has also worked with youth and families as a facilitator in the Alabama cohort of the Prime Time Family Reading program.

Hal Smith is the Senior Vice President for Education, Youth Development and Health at the National Urban League. He leads the organization's programmatic, advocacy, policy and research work in those areas. Across his career in the higher education, community and nonprofit sectors, Hal has focused on the intersections of opportunity, equity, access and excellence for historically and systemically underserved communities. Prior to joining the National Urban League in 2008, Hal held teaching, research, administrative, policy, engagement and advocacy positions focused on P–16 education with the New York City Department of Youth and Community Development (DYCD), the Annenberg Institute for School Reform @ Brown University, the City College of New York, the College of the Holy Cross, Northern Illinois University, Lesley University and Harvard University.

Mike Snell is the Chief Executive Officer of the California Teaching Fellows Foundation, whose mission is to inspire next-generation leaders with a passion for teaching and learning while impacting the lives of youth. Mike's mission is to increase the access and alignment of the diverse expanded learning staff to credential programs and to careers in education. Mike received his Bachelor's degree and MBA from Fresno State and is currently pursuing a doctorate in Education Leadership. Mike invests a significant portion of his off-work hours volunteering for organizations aligned with his mission and vision for positive impact in California's Central Valley

Saskia Traill, Ph.D., is the President & CEO at ExpandED Schools, dedicated to leveraging afterschool to advance educational equity. She has studied and written articles and papers about ecosystems to support early care & education, STEM, summer learning, and other areas where people and institutions can come together to ensure all children thrive. With a background in research and policy, Saskia has been named to the City and State Education Power 100 in New York in both 2020 and 2021. She earned her Ph.D. in Psychology from Stanford University. She lives in Harlem with her family.

Wokie Weah, as President of Youthprise provides executive leadership and vision, works in partnership with the board of directors and brokers relationships to reduce disparities with and for Minnesota youth. In 2020, Wokie was recognized as one of Pollen Midwest's "50 Over 50" and has been awarded the Annual Community Leadership Award from the Charities Review Council. Wokie is a champion for young people and under her guidance Youthprise has become recognized nationally for its leadership in youth engagement and youth philanthropy.

Throughout her career, Wokie has upheld and promoted values around youth leadership, racial equity and reducing disparities.

Jessica Paul Werner has led Youth Development Executives of King County (YDEKC) since its inception in 2011, building the coalition of more than 100 youth serving organizations and establishing YDEKC as a thought leader in the fields of youth development, social emotional learning and collective impact. Jessica has over two decades of experience advancing the youth development field, with a focus on creating more equitable environments for our kids and the adults that support them. Jessica holds an MPA from the University of Washington and Bachelors from Occidental College. Jessica is a member of the Tlingit-Haida Nation, and lives with her family in Shoreline, Washington.

Annie White, Ph.D., is the Senior Research Associate at the Fred Rogers Center where she learns from and works with educators to support their everyday interactions with children, families, and communities across contexts. Annie holds a PhD in Applied Developmental Psychology from the University of Pittsburgh. Previously, Annie ran an extended day program for children ages 3–9 and was a research fellow at the Children's Museum of Pittsburgh.

Alicia Wilson-Ahlstrom is a nationally-recognized expert in youth development, youth organizing, and human-centered systems design that reflects the needs of children, youth and families. Over the last 20 years, Alicia has worked with youth, families, and organizations in strengthening community partnerships and advancing efforts that ensure that the social and community ecosystem supports all youth. Over the course of this work, Alicia has authored numerous journal articles and professional reports. Alicia has earned a BSW from Calvin University and dual Masters' degrees in Social Work and Public Policy from the University of Michigan. Alicia has completed fellowships with the Moody Exchange Professional Fellowship in South Africa, the New Leaders Academy of the National Youth Employment Coalition, and the Coro Foundation Fellowship for Leadership in Public Affairs.

Dana Winters, Ph.D., is the Rita McGinley Professor of Early Learning and Children's Media and the Executive Director of the Fred Rogers Center at Saint Vincent College. She is also the co-creator of the Simple Interactions approach to support children, families, and their helpers. She frequently delivers keynote presentations and workshops across states and countries to describe and affirm the essential, relational practices of professionals who serve children, youth, and their families. She has led numerous federal, state, and foundation grants in early childhood education, family engagement, and statewide training and technical assistance. In addition, she studies and advances the legacy of Fred Rogers by directing the Center's partnerships with educators and communities. Dr. Winters received her Ph.D. in administrative and policy studies from the University of Pittsburgh.

Jill Young, Ph.D., is a senior researcher at the American Institutes for Research. She leads and supports multiple research, evaluation, and capacity-building initiatives focused on youth development and out-of-school time programming at the national, state, and local levels. Previously, she served as the senior director of research and evaluation at After School Matters. She also worked as a statistical analyst at University of Chicago and as a research manager at Northwestern University. She graduated from Drake University with honors, earning her BA in journalism and mass communication. She earned her MA and PhD in research methodology from Loyola University Chicago. She also serves as the research and evaluation section editor for the *Journal of Youth Development*.

Made in the USA
Columbia, SC
18 November 2022

71688332R00187